AN ECHO
IN MY BLOOD

AN ECHO
IN MY BLOOD

The Search for a Family's Hidden Past

❦

ALAN WEISMAN

HARCOURT BRACE & COMPANY
New York   San Diego   London

Requests for permission to make copies of any part of the work should be
mailed to the following address:
Permissions Department, Harcourt, Inc., 6277 Sea Harbor Drive,
Orlando, Florida 32887–6777.

Library of Congress Cataloging-in-Publication Data
Weisman, Alan.
An echo in my blood: the search for a family's hidden past/Alan Weisman.
p.   cm.
Includes bibliographical references.
ISBN 0-15-100291-6
1. Weisman, Alan.   2. Weisman, Simon, 1912–1992.   3. Jews—Minnesota—
Minneapolis Biography.   4. Journalists Biography.   5. Minneapolis (Minn.)—
Biography.   I. Title.
F614.M6W398   1999
977.6'004924'0092—dc21
[B]   99-25485

Portions of this book have appeared in different form in *Harper's* and the
Los Angeles Times Magazine.

Designed by Ivan Holmes
Printed in the United States of America
First edition
A C E D B

For Brian and Peter

This winding, gyring, spiring treadmill of a stair is
my ancestral stair...

—W. B. YEATS
Blood and the Moon

PART ONE

CHAPTER 1

꧁ꙮ꧂

June 1993

It had taken less than an hour to make the trip from Kiev to Chernobyl, driving north past crisp fields of wheat, flax, and potatoes under a bleached June sky. After forty-five minutes, the collective farms abruptly gave way to a tangle of scrub, thistles, and pale sunflowers. Soon, we pulled up to a glossy white booth with a pneumatic bar gate. This was the security check at the thirty-kilometer perimeter that enclosed the area known as the Zone of Alienation. Twenty kilometers farther, at a second checkpoint, we were required to park our van and enter a squat concrete building sheathed in blue aluminum siding.

My companions were all scientists: three Americans, and two Ukrainians who knew Chernobyl better than they wished. They led the rest of us inside, where a terse, tight-faced woman in loose navy work pants and a black sweater instructed us to leave our clothes and jewelry in a row of lockers. In paper slippers and undershorts, we shuffled down a long white cinder-block corridor to a sealed steel doorway. A uniformed guard, also female, unclanked the bolts and passed us through.

On the other side awaited an identical bank of lockers, containing long-sleeved plaid shirts of coarse cotton, hooded stiff polyester coveralls, heavy leather ankle boots, breathing filters, and surgical caps to mask our hair from specks of wind-borne plutonium. Moments before, I had also slipped on an extra pair of jockey shorts—a pretty pathetic buffer, I supposed, between plutonium dust and whatever offspring I might somehow yet conceive. Over the previous few months I had been shaken by a series of personal losses, among them a soured two-year courtship. I now found myself in my mid-forties, single and alone. With my hopes for fatherhood dwindling, an extra layer of gonad protection at this point seemed hardly worth the effort.

But coming into direct contact with plutonium particles was no small concern, and reassurances from Chernobyl officials that the heavy clothing they'd issued us was an adequate shield somehow did not convince. Once we reached the ruined reactor, background radiation would be several hundred times normal. As I adjusted the elastic strap on my white air filter, it occurred to me to wonder why I was doing this—a question that had become rather familiar in recent years. My stock answer was that if no one bore witness to the consequences of the greedy, heedless, stupid, often downright heinous risks people take with the world we live in, they would blithely continue taking them. The article I'd come to write would conclude that not only could the earth not afford another Chernobyl, but we couldn't afford the first one, either: Mere money could not contain what had been unleashed here. But as I boarded a bus so contaminated it could never leave this restricted zone and rode to the huge steel and concrete sarcophagus that encased the hot remains of Chernobyl's Number 4 reactor, I again recalled the other reason I had come.

This was Ukraine, where my father was born. This was the land where he had watched his own father die, victim to yet another atrocity on this soil. Ukraine, the place where my father vowed he'd never again set foot. And now he, too, was dead. The previous fall, we'd laid him to rest wearing his *tallis* and World War II dog tags, in an Orthodox Jewish ceremony at a military cemetery, to the accompaniment of taps and rifle salutes and *Kaddish*.

Then, unexpectedly, just seven weeks later my sister and I

4

buried our mother beside him. Half a year had now passed, but I was still stunned by this double bereavement. Over the intervening months, kind editors had sent me to write about benign places like Spain and Trinidad instead of the somber stories I usually covered. Then, this assignment was proposed to me—a report about how, in the aftermath of Chernobyl's terrible explosion, thousands were trying to cope with survival in an indefinitely poisoned landscape. Grim a prospect as this was, its setting was in Ukraine, and I leapt at this chance to return to my family's source.

And maybe, time permitting, to solve a mystery.

Chernobyl's blocky gray sarcophagus, nearly five stories high and sixty feet thick in places, had been patched so often that its sides resembled the tarred, caulked hull of a derelict ship. Coils of concertina wire, cyclone fencing, and floodlights surrounded the area—as if anyone would try to break in. In the seven years since the accident, hundreds of men who built this vault had died from radiation poisoning. Despite their labor and sacrifice, it kept corroding: One reason why our Geiger counters were screaming was that more than a thousand square meters' worth of leaks had sprung in the sarcophagus's roof and walls.

A French firm contracted to erect another tomb around the first one warned that it could not be completely sealed while the melted core was still hot, which essentially meant never, since plutonium has a half-life of 24,000 years. Nor could radioactive runoff from Chernobyl's cooling ponds, impounded by dikes hastily constructed along the nearby Pripyat River, be kept from seeping into the watershed. Once there, it flowed directly to the Dnieper River, Ukraine's Mississippi, the source of drinking and irrigation water to thirty-five million people. Chernobyl had blown a hole in reality that no human effort could ever close.

Our Ukrainian hosts were two nuclear physicists: Andriy Demydenko, who was now Ukraine's deputy minister of the environment, and Volodya Tikhïi, who had helped track Chernobyl's spreading radioactive stain in the immediate aftermath of the disaster. The three American scientists were from the University of Oregon. In collaboration with colleagues at Moscow State University, the Oregonians had designed a computerized tool to help thousands of former Soviet citizens living in contaminated areas minimize their daily exposure to radiation from eating locally grown foods. Their program, which ran on portable computers, combined topographic details with field-by-field fallout measurements and data on how different crops absorb radionuclides from the soil. A farmer who knew, for instance, that wheat and barley tend to concentrate radioactive isotopes in non-edible parts like their stalks, could reduce his family's lethal intake by sowing grains to suck radiation from the surface before planting lettuce or cabbage, which store radioactivity in their leaves.

This still left the problem of what to do with the tainted chaff after the wheat was harvested, since burning or burying toxic organic wastes would return the radioactivity to the ecosystem. But this was the best anybody could do, the scientists told me. There was simply no way to stuff the damage back in the vessel it came from. Their efforts represented science's best attempt in the face of a bleak, inescapable fact: Much of the best farmland in the former Soviet Union would be hot for nearly two centuries to come, until the cesium-137 and strontium-90 deposited by Chernobyl sufficiently decayed.

During the previous week, I had visited Russian villages hundreds of kilometers from Chernobyl, so radioactive that they had to be evacuated. But no one realized that until three years after the accident, when researchers like my hosts had discovered a dreadful secret: For days following the explosion, the Soviet government seeded clouds headed east so that contaminated rain would not fall on Moscow. Instead, it had drenched the country's richest breadbasket.

With a trembling, nail-bitten forefinger, Andriy Demydenko indicated a peeling sign above a clump of rusting, radioactive machinery that exalted the V. I. Lenin Chernobyl Nuclear Power Station as a "Victory for Communism." Like many former Soviet scientists, the tall, bearded Demydenko had been catapulted from the uproar born of that cataclysm into the unexpected role of bureaucrat. At forty, under the strain of trying to help organize a shaky new country following the U.S.S.R.'s collapse, his sandy hair was already graying to match the sallow void of his skin.

"Those Party bastards," he spat into my tape recorder, "knew all along that citizens were plowing radioactive dirt, eating radioactive vegetables, and feeding radioactive hay to their cows. Cesium-137 is a chemical analog to calcium. It concentrates in cows' milk, the source of eighty percent of a rural Soviet child's protein."

Just after the accident, as radioactive ash settled over Kiev while the reactor still burned seventy miles to the north, Andriy Demydenko learned that his wife was carrying their first child. He immediately raced her away from the capital. Happily, their daughter showed no signs of thyroid disease or lymphoblastic leukosis, the form of leukemia filling children's cancer wards in Kiev that had also surged after Hiroshima. They were all holding their breath, Demydenko told me—literally: "The first thing we had to teach her," he said, "was to close her eyes and not breathe whenever she sees blowing dust. And to never, ever smell flowers."

Chernobyl had vented a hundred times more radiation than the A-bombs that fell on Japan. In Ukraine and Belarus, some human immune systems were so depressed that forgotten diseases like diphtheria were reappearing. Forests of red pines near the reactor died within weeks of the explosion, while surviving trees sprouted distorted branches and needles of different lengths and colors. But before we left the accident site, Kit Larsen, a systems analyst on the Oregon team, handed me his binoculars. I looked where he was pointing. Several families of barn swallows were nesting in debris surrounding the sarcophagus that was still flecked with plutonium and bits of uranium fuel. "Strange," he said. "This would be their sixth generation since the explosion."

Apart from occasional white flecks in their blue and orange coats, they seemed normal. Later, at a bridge railing over the now-deadly Pripyat River two miles downstream from the devastated reactor, we watched marsh hawks cruise over the willows lining banks that flattened into a floodplain covered with meadow grass, daisies, and purple lupine. To his bird list Larsen added three species of raptors, a black tern, wagtails, stilts, mallards, hooded crows, magpies, and a European goldfinch we heard singing in a stand of maples.

"It's the best birding I've done in the ex-Soviet Union," he said, baffled.

Driving through Chernobyl's silent streets, branches of un-pruned chestnut trees grazed the radioactive sides of our bus. It seemed that both Chernobyl and neighboring Pripyat, from which fifty thousand stricken workers and their families had to flee, were being reclaimed by nature. Once-trimmed hedges now ran wild, their foliage so dense that many houses were nearly covered. As we arrived at St. Ilya's, the old Ukrainian Orthodox church in the town of Chernobyl, I asked Volodya Tikhii, who now worked for Greenpeace, how to explain this apparent proliferation of life in a sickened land.

Tikhii, a gaunt man in his early forties with sparse blond hair and thick, owlish glasses, spoke deliberate, thoughtful English, gleaned from scientific texts at Moscow State, then humanized through increasing contact with international environmentalists. Chernobyl's birds, he replied, absent when he was hoisting lethal water samples from the Pripyat River in 1986, began returning a year later. With few humans or predators to bother them and with no more agricultural pesticides, they seemed to be flourishing. For that matter, a growing population of radioactive roe deer and wild boar now thrived in the surrounding forests, proliferating so rapidly that there was now talk of allowing hunting, lest they spread across northern Ukraine, bringing their radionuclides with them. "Plant growth is sometimes stimulated by radiation," Tikhii said with shrug. "Some researchers think that other organisms may also be."

"Maybe nature appears healthy here," Andriy Demydenko interjected. He stood in the thick churchyard grass, long gone to

8

seed, his head tilted toward a pair of skylarks perched on St. Ilya's eaves. "But who knows what the life expectancy of these birds will be? Or what chromosomal deviations will erupt in future generations? Animals can't understand the risk they take here." The skylarks took flight; he paused to listen to their pleasing warble. "Humans understand risks. But even we often fail to calculate those we can't see. Appearances deceive."

Demydenko ascended St. Ilya's short flight of front steps, which in sunnier times had been alternately painted red and green. The wooden door was padlocked. He leaned against it and sighed. "I wanted to show you something. But I'll tell you about it instead. A little coincidence from the Bible."

He described a passage from the Book of Revelations, verses 8:2-11, which recounts breaking the seventh and final seal on the book at God's right hand, to release the angels who herald the beginning of the Apocalypse. The first angel's trumpet summons a hailstorm, followed by a mixture of blood and fire that scorches the earth, incinerating trees and grass. The second causes a fiery mountain to slide into the sea.

> *And the third angel sounded, and there fell a great star*
> *from heaven, burning as it were a lamp, and it*
> *fell upon the third part of the rivers and upon the*
> *fountains of waters;*

> *And the name of the star is called Wormwood; and the*
> *third part of the waters became wormwood, and many*
> *men died of the waters, because they were made bitter.*

"Do you know the Ukrainian word for wormwood?" Demydenko asked me.

I didn't know any Ukrainian, but I knew that wormwood, an extremely bitter herb, was used to purge intestinal worms and parasites.

"It's *chornobyl*." That was also the correct name of this abandoned town, whose spelling had been corrupted in Russian. "But

9

the village wasn't named for the plant," Demydenko added. "It's actually named for the falling star." He indicated a sagging sign commemorating Chornobyl's 800th anniversary, which showed a meteor dropping behind the spire of the church where we stood.

In my notebook, I jotted: "Revelations, again."

As we filed back to our bus, Demydenko asked if I would like to visit a Jewish cemetery before we left Chernobyl. "There are two. One for the old believers, and a newer one. There were Jews here for at least four centuries, you know."

By "old believers," I understood him to mean Hasidim: Chernobyl had once been a vigorous center of the fundamentalist Hasidic movement, born during the eighteenth century in Podolia, the neighboring region to the west. Toward the end of the Czarist regime, that center began to crack under pressure from anti-Semitic massacres that swept Ukraine, home at that time to the world's greatest concentration of Jews. During four years of anarchy following the Bolsheviks' 1917 October Revolution, Jews became the helpless prey of free-booting bands of plunderers who roamed the Ukrainian countryside, igniting pogroms of astonishing depravity.

One of the most infamous had occurred not far from where the wreckage of Reactor Number 4 now stood. For a week during April 1919, a gang of renegade peasants led by a twenty-three-year-old warlord brigand, the Ataman Struk, commandeered steamships coming up the Dnieper from Kiev, throwing overboard every Jew they found. Then they marched a thousand Chernobyl Jews at gunpoint into the Pripyat River—the Dnieper tributary where an hour earlier we'd been birdwatching. Anyone who swam ashore was shot. The rest drowned.

The newer Jewish cemetery, I suspected correctly, held the few hundred who survived until occupying Nazis finished them off in 1944, just as they wiped out two thousand other Ukrainian Jewish communities. Well before Chernobyl blew, its Jews were already dead. "Thanks. We don't have to," I told Demydenko. I had

10

seen enough of cemeteries lately. The worst nuclear tragedy in history was enough sorrow for one day.

In the van back to Kiev, Volodya Tikhïi sat beside me. "I'm sorry about your parents."

"Thanks."

My father had died on his eightieth birthday. Though his end was an excruciating, slow-motion ordeal, it was expected—even a relief, especially for my mother, who had nursed him through a long decline. The big shock, I told Volodya, came when she suddenly followed him.

"Very terrible," Tikhïi murmured. Yet the anguish in which I'd wallowed during the previous months felt self-indulgent compared to what he had endured. Seven years earlier, Tikhïi's father had perished in the Gulag (his crime, for which he was jailed repeatedly, was teaching the Ukrainian language). Volodya hadn't seen his father for the last six years of his life. Just recently, Oleksa Tikhïi's remains had been exhumed in Russia and carried back to Kiev, where he was re-interred in a massive public funeral as a martyred hero.

"Losing my parents one right after the other was a double blow," I said. "But they were elderly. Your father was still vital. It's so unjust." He nodded, staring outside as the van slowed to thread through a herd of dairy cows. "You know," I added, "my father was also from Ukraine."

Surprised, Tikhïi turned to me.

"He had to flee when he was a little boy," I explained, "after his own father was assassinated. He came with his mother and brothers to the United States when he was eleven."

"Do you know what town they were from?"

I did. I had heard the name many times, along with the story of my grandfather's murder, which my father repeated so often when I was growing up that I recalled it in his voice and could still picture him telling it, his big silhouetted frame weighing down the foot of my bed.

"A village called Mala Viska," I said.

Tikhïi didn't know of it.

"It's supposedly about halfway between Kiev and Odessa," I said. "The nearest city, I think, was called Elizabethgrad. That was where my grandmother took him and his brothers after my grandfather was killed. They lived there three years before they could get to America."

Elizabethgrad also drew a blank. "Its name may have been changed to something else," Tikhïi said. "The Soviets did a lot of that. I'll look it up when we get back."

That night in a Kiev restaurant we ate gefilte fish, sliced cucumbers, tomatoes, red cabbage, roasted chicken, rye bread with duck pâté and horseradish, red caviar, and prune compote, washed down with Crimean and Carpathian wines. My great-grandmother—my mother's grandmother, from Podolia, who left Ukraine in 1890—often made gefilte fish from the northern pike and carp we caught in lakes in Minnesota, where I was raised. That week, I had seen Dnieper River fishermen in shallow skiffs catching pike and carp to sell in the streets, a practice theoretically prohibited because the fish were now radioactive. "Where does the restaurant get this fish?" I asked Andriy Demydenko.

"Don't ask," he said, filling my tumbler with purple Crimean port.

Tikhïi, seated next to me, drained his own glass. "By the way," he said. "It's Kirovograd."

"Sorry?"

"Yelisavetgrad. The city where your father lived. The Communists changed it to Kirovograd. I found Mala Viska, too."

I paused, a forkful of irradiated gefilte fish hovering between plate and mouth.

"Would you like to go there?"

"Is it far? How could I get there?" I had a solid week of interviews ahead, and my visa locked me into a departure the following Monday. "I just have Sunday free. Are there buses?"

"No. But I have a car. We can get there and back in a day. If you want."

I wanted. In that instant, I was sure that I was fated to go there, destiny having appeared in the form of Volodya Tikhïi's car and his offer to be my guide and translator. Bringing the remains of his own father home had at last accorded his family some peace and closure—a consolation that, I gathered, he now kindly wished to extend in some way to me.

The following Sunday, we filled his aging blue VAZ sedan with black market gasoline and drove into the steppes of central Ukraine to find my father's village. What I hadn't told Volodya Tikhïi was that this journey involved more than honoring my late father's memory. All my life my father had told me what had happened to him and to my grandfather back in Ukraine ("which," he always added, "was part of Russia"). I'd heard the story so often it had assumed mythological dimensions. I read it again in newspaper columns that eulogized him. But not long before his death— yet after strokes had so ravaged his memory that I could no longer challenge him—I'd heard a sharply different account of the same events. Now I was driving through a rolling landscape of collective farms, whose vast, pale fields of wheat and hops disappeared over the horizon toward Mala Viska, where I hoped someone could tell me the truth.

This is the story my father told me all my life:

My grandfather, Avraham Weisman, was born in a village between Kiev and Odessa. Because his father—my great-grandfather—administered a powerful man's lands, he survived the pogroms that either killed or banished many of his own relatives around the turn of the century. Although the law limited the right of Jews to own property, over the years my great-grandfather nevertheless managed to acquire substantial acreage in reward for his services.

In his early twenties, my grandfather Avraham traveled to Hungary, where for two years he worked in a mill, studying its function and memorizing its construction. When he returned to his Ukrainian village, he built one on his family's land. By the time his first child—my father—was born in 1912, my grandfather had more than one hundred employees and lived in a large house overlooking a river. Milling wheat and pressing sunflower-seed oil had made him rich enough to marry a rabbi's daughter.

There is a sepia photograph taken in their yard, probably in 1918 or early 1919. My father, Simon Weisman—*Shimon Vaisman* in Yiddish; Simon Weisman after Ellis Island—is in knickers, mounted on a tricycle with large iron wheels. A younger brother sits on the lawn nearby. My father and uncles were attended by a governess. My grandmother, Rebecca Weisman, née Gellerman, did not have to work, although she often sewed clothes from fine fabric with my great-grandmother Frieda, the rabbi's widow, who lived with them.

My father clearly remembered the day the soldiers came, he would tell me. They were not Czarist troops, but Bolsheviks. He recalled how they tramped into the house with muddy boots. When his grandmother barred their passage across the imported carpet, the revolutionary who led the ragged column drew a sword and slew her. Six-year-old Simon ran at her attacker and pounded him with his little fists. The soldier hit him with the butt of the sword that killed my great-grandmother. At this point in the story, my father would show me the scar on his forehead, next to his dark widow's peak.

They marched the family outside. My grandfather was summarily tried and convicted of being a capitalist collaborator for selling wheat to the imperial Czar's army. His mill and adjoining fields and forests were confiscated for the revolution. With his wife and children helplessly watching, Avraham Weisman's Communist captors stood him against the house and shot him.

My broad-shouldered grandfather had measured well over six feet. My father recalled struggling to help drag his body, enshrouded in one of my grandmother's sheets, to the grave they dug before they fled. Rebecca Weisman took her sons and what little

14

she could carry to the nearest city, Yelisavetgrad, sixty kilometers to the east. Her only skill was sewing; by night she made clothes to sell each day in the market.

"You kids don't know how lucky you've got it," my father told my sister and me. "When your grandmother sold something, we ate. It wasn't too damn often."

She wrote to relatives who had left years earlier for the United States. After months, a reply arrived from a sister, whose husband had found work in Minnesota as a kosher slaughterer. They knew someone lending money to help Jews escape the chaos and menace of the fledgling Soviet Union. Much of the cash they sent went to coax officials. Three years after my grandfather's execution, my grandmother Rebecca and her sons traveled to Moscow, for paperwork and more bribes that dragged on for months. My father's principal memory of those times was bald Vladimir Lenin parading like God through the streets. Then a train to Riga, on the Latvian coast. Then a boat to America.

They arrived in late autumn 1923. My father, eleven years old, sold newspapers in a language he couldn't read on freezing Minneapolis street corners. To her death, my grandmother remained what Yelisavetgrad had transformed her into: a dressmaker. Years later, along with my father's exploits in World War II, the legends of their poverty became my bedtime tales: Simon and his brother Harold rising for their predawn bakery route each day before high school; baby brother Herman, sent one morning to buy cracked eggs—all they could afford—and, upon finding none, asking if the grocer could crack him a dozen.

It was this brother, my Uncle Herman, who first cast doubt on my father's story. That happened on January 16, 1991, the night that war began in the Persian Gulf.

❧❦☙

"We'd better wrap up if we don't want to be late for your uncle's," Cecilia informed me. "It's nearly six."

15

We were in a cubbyhole at National Public Radio in Washington, D.C., in the fourth-floor Special Projects division. I was sitting on the floor, surrounded by legal pads bearing notes and lists. My partner, Cecilia Vaisman, swiveled in front of a computer terminal, scanning news wires for mention of Colombia, Argentina, Paraguay, or Nicaragua—the four countries where we'd worked together during the preceding six months. Following a morning of interviews across town, that afternoon we had been using NPR's phones to schedule appointments in the places we were headed next: the Dominican Republic, Brazil, and Chile.

We had been in Washington for two days, questioning officers at the World Bank for a documentary about the longest dam in the world, which was then under construction along the Argentine-Paraguay border. During the 1980s, the Bank had loaned Argentina more than a billion dollars to build it, which the military government instead used to finance a war with Great Britain over the Falklands Islands. Upon learning that not a single bag of cement had been poured with all that money, the World Bank's response simply had been to loan the Argentine generals more.

With two other freelance journalists, Cecilia and I were under contract to produce a special series for National Public Radio. Set in a dozen Latin American countries, *Vanishing Homelands* would show how so-called progress and development were often literally ripping the ground from beneath traditional cultures—or, as in the case of this hydroelectric dam, drowning it. Upon completion, the homes of 50,000 people would be submerged by a stagnant, parasite-breeding tropical lake. It was the largest urban displacement in history by a development project, but somehow the funds designated for resettlement had also mysteriously evaporated.

"Everything's about Iraq," Cecilia said, shutting down the terminal. "C'mon."

"I need to call my parents first."

"*Bueno, pero rápido, ¿ok? Voy al baño.*"

When she left I called Scottsdale, Arizona. The phone answered on the third ring.

"Mom."

A pause, then, "Oh, honey, hi." I'd awakened her from a nap, I guessed. "Gee, we were hoping you'd call. Are you at Herman's?"

"Not yet. I'm at NPR. How did you know I was going there?"

"He called us this morning. He and Margaret are so excited to meet Cecilia. Wait a minute, let me put Dad on. Wait a minute, Alan."

"I'll wait. Don't worry."

She would be in a lightweight housecoat, uncurling creakily from the cushioned rattan recliner in the living room that nearly swallowed her, removing from her knees a green afghan she'd knitted and marking her place in the paperback that would have fallen in her lap. Setting aside her reading glasses, she would rise with a grunt to her slippered feet and shuffle down the short hall toward the den, until she could see my father's bulk filling his own black leather recliner, surrounded by walls encrusted with his diplomas and plaques and war medals. He, too, would appear to be reading, either the newspaper he'd fetched from the driveway that morning, or one of the golf magazines he still received. But this was only habit. For a while now, we'd realized that he scanned the same page for hours.

"Bobe." I could hear her voice trickling back, calling him by the pet name whose derivation not even she could recall. "Bobie, it's Alan."

"*Who?*" His bellow remained unchanged.

"Alan. Your son."

As he fumbled with the receiver of the desk phone she brought to him, I heard the background babble of an afternoon television host. The TV was permanently switched on; we suspected he only dimly registered what appeared on the screen. At some point, my mother had noticed that he never changed the channel.

"Hi, Dad. It's Alan."

After a beat, he remembered. "Oh, hi, son," he replied, his voice modulating from confusion to pleasure. "Are you coming over?"

17

"I'm out of town, Dad." It had been six months since I'd seen them.

"Oh, Si," my mother interjected, back on her own extension. "You know that Alan's been gone since July."

"He has?"

"Certainly! We just talked to him two days ago."

"For the life of me, Charlotte, I can't remember—"

"He can't remember *kasha* anymore, Alan. You wouldn't believe—"

"It's all right," I interrupted, before she had a chance to warm up. "I'm in Washington, Dad. I've been out of the country this year, working in South and Central America, and just came up here for some interviews. I have to go back down there in a couple of days."

"Well, that sounds real nice, Alan."

Interesting, perhaps. But not nice. "It is, Dad," I agreed. No use getting into that.

"Well, you be sure to come see us when you get back. You know your mother and I love to see you."

"Thanks, Dad. Me, too."

"Don't hang up, Alan," my mother said, as he clicked off. "Oh, Alan. I don't know how I'm going to take it. All day long he asks the same things, over and over."

"I know, Ma. I'm sorry I'm not there."

Seven years earlier, in 1984, a series of strokes had forced my father, then seventy-two, to retire from the distinguished law firm he'd founded in Minneapolis, something he swore he'd never do. When my mother announced that they were moving to Scottsdale on the eastern edge of suburban Phoenix, I was alarmed. Early on, I'd learned that my relationship with my parents improved in direct proportion to the distance between us. Nearly all my adult life, except when I was periodically based out of the country, my home had been a renovated cabin in the central Arizona mountains, just two hours northwest of where they would now reside. But two hours had turned out to be a manageable buffer, and we had actually grown closer. "Mom, you shouldn't say things like that in front of him, like how he can't remember."

18

She uttered a Yiddish obscenity. "Dad doesn't know from one minute to the next. Believe me, it goes in one ear and out the other."

"But he still has feelings." It fascinated my sister and me how, once he became the weaker one, our mother didn't miss a chance to finally get in her own licks.

"Where's Cecilia? We can't wait to meet her."

"She's in the bathroom."

"Didn't she want to talk to us?"

"I'm pretty sure she really needed to go to the bathroom. This was the only chance I had to call all day. We have to get going to Uncle Herman and Aunt Margaret's. They're expecting us for dinner."

"Well, you give Cecilia our love. Dad and I are real happy for you."

"I thought Dad doesn't know from one minute to the next."

"He knows what makes you happy."

Now that would be a first, I mused, as I said good-bye.

"Let's go," Cecilia said, returning. She had wrapped a knee-length navy blue coat over her bulky turtleneck and gray wool skirt, and added gold button earrings. Her brown hair with its natural flashes of gold had been trimmed in New York, where she'd spent Christmas with her mother, and hung prettily at her collar. Cecilia and I had met on this project six months earlier in the desert and immediately set out for the tropics. Until she picked me up me on New Year's Eve in the Newark airport, I had never seen her dressed for winter. Her cheeks were two rosy blooms that made her wide-set hazel eyes even greener. She looked alive, wonderful, and something else I'd never previously beheld: relaxed.

I stood, reached for my jacket, then stopped. "Don't we have to call Costa Rica?"

"*Ay, Dios.* I almost forgot."

"The subway only takes twenty-five minutes. There's enough time."

We dialed our coproducers, Sandy Tolan and Nancy Postero, who lived in a cottage up the hill from us at our field base in La Piedad, Costa Rica, a coffee plantation twenty miles west of San

José. Nancy answered first, and a second later Sandy picked up the extension in the recording studio that we'd rigged in their extra bedroom. Over the previous months, while Cecilia and I were on our various travels, Sandy and Nancy had worked in Bolivia, Ecuador, and Panama. Between research jaunts that averaged three weeks, the four of us would reconvene in Costa Rica, compare notes, transcribe the forty-or-so hours of tape each team had gathered, and then head off again. "What's it like back in the States?" they asked simultaneously.

"Hard to tell. Everything's wrapped in yellow ribbons." War with Iraq was expected to break out any minute now, we added—unaware how literally accurate this was.

"You get right back down here where it's *safe*," ordered Nancy. This was our little joke: We had chosen Costa Rica for our base because it was central to the rest of Latin America. Until we lived there, however, we'd never fully grasped how the United States had turned this small Third World country into a billboard touting the rewards of democracy, counterposed against the grand display for Communism that the Soviets had erected in Cuba. Both sides had poured billions into these tropical alter egos. Upon arriving in San José, the capital, we had the sensation of having driven three thousand miles from Tucson, Arizona, only to reach a city that resembled suburban Phoenix. The cloying split-level architecture and Bermuda grass lawns, the large placid middle class, and the fleets of excursion buses ferrying binocular-packing Auduboners to well-marked rainforest trails suggested not so much Latin America as a Latin American theme park.

"The U.S. must be pretty scary," said Sandy. "We worry about you two up there."

He was kidding, too, but I sensed how isolated he felt from the sudden rush of world events. Only in his early thirties, Sandy Tolan's superb radio documentaries had already earned him some of journalism's highest honors. While crafting an award-winning series for NPR on the 1985 Sanctuary trials, in which the U.S. government prosecuted religious workers for running an underground railroad to smuggle Central American refugees into the

United States, he'd met Nancy, then one of the defense attorneys. He maintained his ethical distance while covering the trials, before asking her to dance at a post-verdict party. Within a year, they were married.

On our way to catch the subway for Silver Springs, where my Aunt Margaret and Uncle Herman lived in a retirement complex, we stopped by the second-floor set of NPR's nightly news program, *All Things Considered,* which was among the shows where Cecilia had been a producer before becoming a freelancer. The regular evening newscast had just ended; reporters were leaning against their gray cubicle partitions, sipping coffee, slipping into overcoats. Suddenly, every TV monitor in the room flared with the same live images from CNN.

Staffers on their way out poured back in, including a few senior producers who had just changed into shorts and sneakers for their Tuesday night basketball league. One of them, Michael Sullivan, leaped onto a table, barking directives, mobilizing the newsroom into a war room. Although war had been imminent for days, no one had expected it at quite this moment. Earlier that afternoon, Scott Simon, the host of NPR's Saturday morning *Weekend Edition,* whose programs Cecilia had often produced, had confided that as one of the journalists selected to accompany U.S. troops to battle, he'd be given twelve hours' secret advance warning of the hostilities to catch the official press plane. "If you're around and notice that I'm not," Simon had joshed, "you'll figure it out."

Unsmiling now, he was pushing through the clogged newsroom toward the door, wearing a leather flight jacket. Part of his dismay was realizing that he and several other correspondents had been duped, a military deception that set the pattern for press manipulation throughout the conflict. But mainly, Scott Simon's trademark sparkle had been doused by an age-old shock: He was really going to war. That knowledge now infused his handsome, fallen face, even though the TV monitors thus far showed nothing more than what resembled a bad display of fireworks occasionally sputtering over a darkened city.

I knew this feeling, how a journalist's reflexive thrill at the

21

prospect of witnessing the ancient rite of combat is quickly dissolved by the sickening reality of men willfully firing at each other. In the past year, I had accompanied Guatemalan insurgents clashing with army troops and found myself—and Cecilia—on a forced march with Colombian guerrillas in the Andes, a situation that nervously recalled an assignment two years earlier in that same country. That previous occasion had ended badly—a firefight in which most of my companions were killed, although it provided vivid reading in the *New York Times Magazine.* This time we had been luckier, but now she and I lingered in the NPR newsroom's doorway, wondering how our current material could ever compete for attention with Operation Desert Storm, with its instant replay and colorful ribbons for the home team. By contrast, our present commission to chronicle how entire cultures were becoming endangered species was exceptionally resistant to diversionary gloss.

During the previous six months, my partners and I had seen Ecuadoran Indians driven nearly to extinction by an oil rush in their Amazonian homeland; Colombia's richest farms turned to chemical sumps to raise flawless flowers for export; the forests of Guaraní hunter-gatherers in Argentina replaced by uniform rows of California pines for cardboard production; the last wild tribe in Bolivia tamed by missionaries; Nicaragua's Miskito Indians abandoned by their former CIA-backed contra allies to an invasion of foreigners snatching their lumber and lobsters; and peoples of the Panamanian jungles watching their culture disappear along a new highway. It was engrossing stuff, but no match for a patriotic American resource war against a swarthy villain in the Middle East, now unfolding on prime-time TV. For several minutes we blended into the great American audience, mesmerized by the newsroom's monitors. Finally, Cecilia drew on her gloves and pulled me away. "Now we're really late for your uncle's. *Vámonos.*"

☙❀❧

Before meeting her, I'd occasionally noted the similarity of our surnames when I would hear on NPR that ". . . we had production help this week from Cecilia Vaisman." This was shorthand for Cecilia locating exactly the right musician in Cuba or the perfect mountain hamlet in El Salvador, or Cecilia staying up all night in the editing booth with a steaming gourd of *yerba maté* to confect seamless interviews from hours of inchoate tape, like a surgeon splicing precisely the right capillaries amid a glob of vascular spaghetti.

Weisman, Vaisman, Weissman, Weitzmann: The variant spellings, I assumed, depended on whichever shores successive waves of diaspora had deposited my ancestral clan, or whichever steamship clerk or immigration officer had transliterated the name from Yiddish (ווײסמאַן) or Cyrillic (Вайсман) to the Roman alphabet. In Latin America, where the letter *w* is rarely used, I became *Alán Vaisman* myself. But as far as Cecilia and I were concerned, another issue had become increasingly pertinent: How closely might we actually be related?

The previous summer, driving the length of Mexico and Central America, we'd had sufficient time to explore the business of our similar surnames, and beyond. The story she'd always heard was that her Jewish paternal grandfather, like my own, was born in rural Ukraine between Kiev and Odessa. Just after the turn of the century, *Moishe* Vaisman had escaped the pogroms by migrating to Brazil, where he married a woman he met on the boat from Europe. Within two years, they moved to Uruguay and then to Argentina, where he became Mauricio. Two generations later, Cecilia was born in Buenos Aires, the youngest of four children.

That was 1961, the same year that her father tired of the ruinous Argentine economy, whose currency various Perónists and generals had stretched one way and then the other, until it was the softest in the Americas. Mayer Vaisman had tried several businesses that he believed would have succeeded anywhere else. When his Catholic wife, Carmen, a gifted seamstress who partly supported them, became pregnant again, he finally decided to do something drastic.

"I think it was pretty amazing," Cecilia told me, her eyes widening. "At forty-three, he borrowed from his brothers to get to

New York. Then for a year he sold pots and pans door-to-door to earn enough to bring us to the States. My mother still tells about flying twenty-eight hours with airsick kids, changing planes in every airport in Latin America, all the while dragging everything we owned and taking care of a four-month-old—me."

My mother's grandfather, who came to America from the Russian Ukraine in 1891, had also begun as an itinerant peddler. It seemed odd that this still happened—yet, as the familiar Mexican landscape reminded me, why shouldn't it? During the early 1980s I'd lived in Mexico, and later wrote a book describing how millions of *latinos* cross the border into the United States and do anything to earn passage for the families left behind. So why should the story of Cecilia's father strike me as strange?

Because, I realized a bit uncomfortably, he wasn't just a *latino*. He was also a Jew, like me. But why should that matter?

"Tell me about your family, Alan."

When she made this request we were climbing into the Sierra Madre Occidental, almost exactly where another young woman had asked the same question a decade earlier. On that occasion, I had reached back to the story of our family's flight from Ukraine that my father had told me all my life. In doing so, it had struck me then how much my identity was still wrapped in his, despite years of struggle to disengage and forge my own way. Nevertheless, that woman, a biologist, was deeply moved, and the following year became my wife.

Five years later, she wasn't my wife anymore—a sorrow I attributed, among other things, to the fact that we were nearly ten years apart. Now, half a decade again later, at forty-three myself, I surely knew better than to get involved with, say, Cecilia Vaisman, fourteen years my junior. Nevertheless, I was about to her tell the same story, knowing—and, despite my better judgment, hoping—how powerful its impact could be.

A few years before the night I took Cecilia to meet my Uncle Herman, he had retired from a second career as a bureaucrat for various federal agencies in Washington, which paid better than being an English professor. It was work he regretted, but ever since my Aunt Margaret, the brilliant classmate he'd married, was stricken with multiple sclerosis, he couldn't easily decline more money.

As an undergraduate, Herman had written plays that were staged at the University of Minnesota. His dreams of becoming a dramatist, however, succumbed to the Depression: "a starving writer," I was frequently reminded by my parents. Since, as a boy, I displayed few active symptoms of becoming any kind of writer—I kept no diary and never wrote stories, although I did read a book a day—I was always mystified by these warnings. I was puzzled by something else, too: Around the time I was four years old, my father and Uncle Herman had stopped speaking. The pall that darkened my father's features whenever his brother's name was mentioned warned me not to inquire why. Once, I dimly recalled, my sister asked my mother. "You kids wouldn't understand," she snapped.

"You mean he and your father don't talk?" Cecilia exclaimed. "You didn't tell me."

"They do now. They didn't the whole time I was growing up."

"Why not?"

"I have no idea."

"*Qué pena*, Alan." Then: "*Ay*, we should have brought wine."

"Too late." We were at the last stop in Silver Springs, hailing a cab. My watch said it was past seven-thirty, and I knew that because of Margaret's health, this evening couldn't go much beyond nine. Sensing my anxiety, Cecilia squeezed my hand. With her woolen glove she brushed her light brown hair out of her eyes, revealing a broad, smooth forehead. From her temples, the lines of Cecilia's face descended straight to her jaw before converging toward her chin. Although we had known each other only six months, I had seen these distinctive, square features all my life.

25

"Let's see the pictures again," I said inside the taxi.

She kept them under the clear plastic flap of her address book. The top one was a wallet-sized photographer's portrait of my family, taken in 1949. In it, I am two years old. We are in the house in north Minneapolis my parents moved to just before I was born, the one they built when my father returned from World War II. I'm on his lap, dressed in shorts and suspenders; my hair, like my older sister's, is light and curly. My dark-eyed mother stands behind us, in puff sleeves and pearls, leaning toward the camera. My sister, Cooky, then seven, has her arm around Dad's shoulders. We look happy.

During the first part of my life, everyone remarked on my resemblance to my mother—obvious in this photograph—until years later, when my father's expressions surprisingly began to appear in the mirror. But even more intriguing is this smiling, youthful Si Weisman in an open-necked shirt, the shape of his face identical to Cecilia's.

The first time she saw this picture, she made me give it to her. The one she kept just below it persuaded me that the likeness was beyond coincidence. It showed a thin, distinguished, graying man in a dark suit and tie, next to a buxom woman wearing a V-neck blouse and black skirt. They were seated in lawn chairs; around the edges of the picture were hints of broad-leafed foliage. These were her grandparents in Argentina, now deceased. Mauricio Vaisman's head was cocked slightly toward his wife, Leah. His forehead was high, his nose straight, his ears slightly protruding, his expression erudite. He looked uncannily like my Uncle Herman, whose driveway we were just about to enter.

The garage door opened, and Herman himself greeted us, wearing an apron. Since Margaret was confined to her wheelchair, he had taken over the cooking. I introduced him to Cecilia. They smiled with recognition.

Herman had prepared seafood salad. My Aunt Margaret, wheeled to the table, wore a turquoise robe. Her red hair was styled and she was still slender, but the multiple sclerosis had advanced since I'd last seen her. Margaret's wit and insight, accrued from a lifetime of reading, were still apparent, but she had to ask Cecilia several times where she was from and what she did. "Sorry, dear," she apologized. "I ask myself the same things just as often," she added, winking. Cecilia winked back. They both laughed.

Their home reminded me of the one in Arizona where my parents had retired: even the Israeli prints on the walls were similar. A bookcase held copies of *Basic Technical Writing*, the textbook Herman had authored, which had been reissued in six editions. Herman and Margaret's youngest daughter, Abbi, had joined us with her new baby. I had seen Abbi only once before, when she was nine, the same day I first met her older brother and sister. By then, I was already twenty-five. "Tell Abbi what you're doing in Washington," my uncle requested, turning off the television that still showed the Baghdad rooftops. "We'd all like to hear."

Around the dinner table, Cecilia and I described how we'd grilled a World Bank vice-president that morning about the dam in Argentina, whose litany of disasters included a $30 million elevator built by the dam's Canadian contractors to lift fish over the dam to their upstream spawning grounds. "There was only one hitch. It works fine for northern hemisphere species like salmon and trout, which go upstream, spawn, then die. But the tropical species down there go upstream, spawn, and return. And there's no down elevator."

"So they can't get downstream?" asked my uncle.

"Only through the turbines—which, unfortunately, turns them into fish meal." The worst part was that the Bank's own biologists had warned that the elevator wouldn't work, but it was built anyway, because it was in the contract. "That's why we're doing this series. The contractors had run out of northern rivers to dam. So they get some international lending agency to finance some expensive project in the developing world, which local politicians love because they skim millions from the deal. Ultimately a few privileged industrialists benefit, but it's a tragedy for everyone else."

"Never underestimate the incompetence of government," my Uncle Herman declared. Late in his Washington career, he'd been assigned to the Federal Emergency Management Agency. At FEMA, he was once assigned to design a form that refugees from cities destroyed by nuclear attack could submit to their former post offices to have their mail forwarded—notwithstanding the fact that such post offices by then would be glowing rubble. "Let's talk about more pleasant things," he said, filling our wineglasses. "What about you two?"

He smiled invitingly at Cecilia, who managed to diplomatically reply, "We're in the process of finding that out. It's been wonderful getting to know Alan. It's wonderful to finally meet some of his family."

Coming to her rescue, I described what we called our first date: a night march in the Andes of southwestern Colombia, with a guerrilla group comprised of Páez Indians who specialized in terrorizing haciendas stolen from their ancestors four hundred-fifty years earlier. We'd shared a tent with two *guerrilleros* named Francisco and Claudia, whose loaded AK-47s clanked sweetly together as they made love in full gear.

Aunt Margaret, who appeared to have nodded off, woke up with that story. "My heavens! Be careful, you two."

That night, Herman cleared up speculation over a question that interested us: whether Avraham Weisman and Mauricio Vaisman possibly had been brothers. Cecilia knew that her grandfather had two male siblings, but Herman was certain that his father had only a sister, named Rivkeh. Maybe, Herman surmised, our great-grandfathers were related. "It's possible," he said. "My grandfather may have had brothers. I know only that his name was *Shuel*—Saul."

If Saul Weisman and Cecilia's great-grandfather were brothers, that would make us fifth cousins, a sufficient dilution of the bloodline regarding any future concerns that might arise between us. "I wouldn't be surprised if they were," said my cousin Abbi, fingering the pictures. "He really looks like you, Dad."

Herman gave Cecilia a hug. "Welcome back, relative."

He went to a closet and returned with an oval-framed portrait of my grandfather Avraham. The severe man in this antiquated photograph was balding and bearded; nevertheless, he resembled several people in the room. I could also see my father.

"What happened between the two of you?" I asked my uncle.

He knew who I meant. "That was a long time ago, Alan."

"I know. I remember the last time I saw you. At Grandma's." His picture of my grandfather, which had formerly hung on my grandmother's wall, stirred dusty recollections of her dark, cramped house in Minneapolis. It was a gloomy little gallery of the deceased, featuring framed tintypes of her rabbi father and his wife; of her husband, Avraham; a photo of Milstein, the hypochondriac she married in the States, who surprised everyone by actually dying from one of his multiple complaints; their daughter Frieda, taken at thirteen by pneumonia; and a graduation picture of Herman and Si's brother, my Uncle Harold, dead at twenty-seven from infected kidneys.

The same year that Harold died, my grandmother had remarried again, this time to the widower of my grandfather Avraham's sister, Rivkeh. This third husband, her former brother-in-law, had contributed his own photographic cache of deceased relatives to my grandmother's dreary display, including an enlargement framed in white gold of his first wife, invalided in a pogrom, which hung from a tasseled cord. As a child, it was not a joy to go there. Among my few pleasant memories was playing with Uncle Herman on my grandmother's thin floral carpet. Then, at one point, whenever we made our usual Sunday visit, he was absent. "Why?" I repeated.

Herman and Margaret exchanged glances. "All right," he said. "It was around the time when Si started his law firm."

By then, Herman was teaching at Brooklyn Polytechnic Institute. One evening my father found himself dining with one of his brother's colleagues, a physics professor. He was visiting Minneapolis, and Herman had given him his brother Si's phone number. Sometime after his third whiskey, my father turned to him and inquired, "Tell me: Is my brother still a goddam Communist?"

This was 1951, the McCarthy era. When this comment filtered back to my uncle, he confronted his brother and raised hell. After forty years, Herman's mild face still colored as he remembered. He had demanded an apology and had insisted that my father call their mutual acquaintance and retract the remark. "Of course, he refused. Si can be pretty stubborn."

I could picture my father's response to such a request. Herman saw my eyes roll. "But," he hastened to add, "so can I. I'm ashamed to admit that I didn't forgive him for quite a while. We lost seventeen years."

During a trip in 1968 to see his mother, Herman contacted my parents. The feud had lasted long enough, he said. My mother phoned me that night at college to describe the lovely dinner they'd had. Now I realized why she had called: Her relief at seeing her husband reunited with his left-wing intellectual brother was partly because history was echoing itself with his son.

"I understand completely," I told Herman. "You can imagine what we went through during Vietnam." Actually, he probably couldn't, because our rupture was pretty spectacular. At the 1968 Democratic National Convention in Chicago, my immigrant father, now a prominent attorney, was serving as a strategist for Vice President Hubert Humphrey's presidential bid.

"Yes," my uncle said, nodding. "Your father, I gathered, became an important man in the Democratic Party."

I, meanwhile, was encamped with thousands of anti-war protestors across from the Conrad Hilton Hotel, where he and all the delegates were staying. The evening before the riots started, we met in front of his hotel. Following that encounter, our own silence began.

Cecilia hadn't heard this story. "My God. What did he say when he saw you?"

"Among other things, that I was supporting the sons-of-bitches who killed his father."

"What do you mean 'killed his father'?" asked Herman.

"Communists. All my life I've heard how they assassinated my grandfather—your father—in Russia. And now I wanted to hand them Southeast Asia on a silver platter. Et cetera."

Herman looked at me quizzically. "Communists didn't kill my father."

Now it was my turn to ask what he meant. "I've heard that story all my life," I repeated.

He shook his head. I stared at him. "Then who?"

"It was the Cossacks."

For three years following the 1917 October Revolution, civil war convulsed the Russian federation. The Ukraine especially was bedlam. When occupying German forces left after World War I, parts of the region were seized at various times by Ukrainian nationalists, Bolsheviks, the counterrevolutionary Volunteer and Cossack armies, and even the Poles. At one point, according to Herman, the Cossack Army led by General Anton Denikin launched a massive plunder of Ukrainian Jews. One evening, Denikin's marauders rode their horses into Mala Viska.

They set fire to the village, burning my great-grandparents alive, seizing jewels and property, raping and disemboweling my grandmother's sister. When my grandfather Avraham saw them coming, he ran with my grandmother and their sons through the fields. The Cossacks fired after them. My grandfather, a big, easy target, was hit. He told Rebecca to take the boys and flee. Late that night, after the pogrom had waned, she returned to find he had bled to death. A neighbor helped bury him, then hid them overnight in his haystack. The following day, they left on foot for Yelisavetgrad, where they had a cousin. My grandmother carried a suitcase filled with Czarist rubles. She kept them until they left for America, but they remained worthless.

Herman removed his glasses and massaged his eyes. "Once," he said, "when we were still in Yelisavetgrad, but after Denikin had left the Ukraine, she went back to see what she could rescue.

31

Everything had been confiscated. All she got were some sacks of flour. She shared them with the neighbors to make *matzohs* for Passover."

"Wait a minute, Uncle Herman," I interrupted. "You were only a couple of years old when this happened. My father was nearly seven. How could you possibly remember all this?"

"What I remember is my mother telling it, all the time I was growing up. I can still hear her, cursing the name of General Denikin."

CHAPTER 2

July 1960

A ripple of interest followed the bulky, white-haired man in the shiny blue suit as he passed through the hotel dining room, moving from table to table. He headed to ours.

"Good to see you, Si. Nice work. This your boy?" he said, shaking my father's hand.

"My son, Alan."

He shifted to my hand and pumped. "Well, Alan, you can tell your friends you met Melvin Belli."

He faded toward the door. "Who's Melvin Belli, Dad?" I asked my father.

"A lawyer. A jerk."

"Is he important?"

"He thinks so, doesn't he? Eat. We have to go soon."

I returned my attention to my prime rib with creamed horseradish, which I'd never tasted before. I wasn't quite finished when my father wiped his mouth with his napkin and rose. "Let's go." I hesitated. "On the double, mister!"

"Yes, sir."

I dropped my fork and leapt up, glancing wistfully at the remaining gob of horseradish, which I'd just discovered how much I liked and had been saving for last. It wasn't, however, worth the consequences of failing to carry out his orders immediately.

But my father was in a good mood today, as he had been all week. It was probably one of the best weeks of his life. As we boarded the chartered bus ferrying the Minnesota delegation from the hotel over to the Los Angeles Coliseum to hear John F. Kennedy accept the Democratic Party's presidential nomination, people were treating Si Weisman as if he, like the narcissistic Mr. Belli, were important. Another of the attorneys present clapped him on the shoulder and, removing his cigar, informed me that my father had written much of the address with which Minnesota Governor Orville L. Freeman had placed Kennedy's name in nomination.

"You're confusing me with Arthur Schlesinger, Mac," my father said.

"No," Mac insisted, "your dad was responsible for major chunks of that speech."

It was possible. The day before the balloting, Kennedy had surprised Minnesota's governor with a phone call, explaining that he had asked Adlai Stevenson to nominate him, but was still waiting on an answer. If Adlai Stevenson decided not to, would Freeman be willing?

The Minnesota delegation apparently knew more than John Kennedy at that moment, because its caucus was loudly divided over contending candidates, and one of them was Stevenson himself. The governor had sequestered himself with a small group of advisers that included my father, to plan what to say if he were called upon. No one got to bed until 4:00 A.M., and two hours later Freeman's phone rang. It was Bobby Kennedy, asking if he were ready to nominate Jack.

The Kennedys sent Arthur Schlesinger to help Governor Freeman draft the speech, but that afternoon, just as he began to deliver it to the full convention, the TelePrompter went dead. Having barely practiced the Schlesinger version, Freeman improvised.

"Si's just being modest," Mac the lawyer assured me.

"Knock it off already," my father told him, but I could tell he was pleased.

34

This trip was my parents' present for my bar mitzvah, the Jewish initiation into manhood, which I'd celebrated three weeks earlier. According to ancient practice, that event should have occurred in late March, on the Saturday immediately following my thirteenth birthday, but my mother's veto overrode even Talmudic tradition. "The snow is melting at the end of March. I don't want people tracking slush onto my beige carpet," she announced to our rabbi.

"But Mrs. Weisman, bar mitzvahs take place on the Sabbath right after—"

"*Kishmeer en tuchis,*" she interrupted, a reference to which part of her anatomy the rabbi could kiss if he didn't like it. She wagged a menacing finger at him as he backed away in shock. "Either you bar mitzvah him in June or we'll take our money to a synagogue that will."

At that, he relented. My own protests had also been useless. The wall-to-wall carpeted living room, where the reception would be, was sacrosanct: My sister and I could only venture in there to practice piano and were forbidden to sit on the furniture unless company was present. "Don't bother me" was all my father contributed when, venturing into his den, I dared broach the subject. "You'll do what your mother says."

But when they told me I would attend the Democratic National Convention, all was forgiven. In our house, the significance of politics had long since transcended that of religion. In 1956, when I was nine, my father had paid the remarkable sum of fifty dollars apiece so we could eat hot dogs and baked beans in the Minneapolis Armory and hear a speech by Adlai Stevenson, the Democrats' presidential candidate. Stevenson was then running for a second time against Dwight Eisenhower. Driving there in our blue Pontiac, which sported a new Stevenson-Kefauver sticker, I asked my father why he wanted Stevenson, since he had voted for Ike four years earlier.

"He did not!" my mother said, turning around and glaring at this blasphemy. "You were too young then to—"

"Quiet, Charlotte," my father interrupted. "He's right." His eyes found mine in the rear view mirror. "What a memory you have, son. I voted for General Eisenhower in 1952 because I fought under him in the war. But the Democrats know what's best for the country. They don't just care about big shots. Ike's had his chance to be president. He'd rather play golf anyway."

That night, I shook hands with and secured autographs from Minnesota Governor Orville Freeman, Senator Hubert H. Humphrey, and Congressman Eugene McCarthy. Over the next few years, my mother would often phone her cousins to describe a previous evening's dinner with one of these luminaries. During the spring of 1958, our phone was especially busy, because my father was named chairman of Minnesota's most important annual Democratic fund-raiser, the Jefferson-Jackson Day dinner, from which he brought home a red-white-and-blue menu signed to me by the main speaker, Senator John F. Kennedy of Massachusetts.

The following year, my parents gave a party in our downstairs rec room. By then, we no longer lived in the little north Minneapolis bungalow where I was born. Before I turned seven, we had moved to a three-bedroom rambler my parents built on two acres in St. Louis Park, the first Minneapolis suburb that permitted Jews. That evening, my father gave Senator Humphrey, Governor Freeman, and a young lawyer he introduced as the next attorney general of Minnesota, Walter Mondale, a tour of his war trophies that hung on the knotty pine walls: a German arsenal of tasseled officers' swords, bayonets, swastika-emblazoned helmets, sheathed stilettos, canteens, .32-bore field rifles, and a Spandau machine gun he had snatched from a fallen enemy on a battlefield in southern France and used himself, fighting all the way to the Rhine. At one point that night I was chauffeured in the governor's limousine to buy more ice. I returned to find my father and mother standing behind their well-stocked linoleum-covered bar with their arms around each other's waist, smiling proudly as the governor of Minnesota and a U.S. senator danced cheek-to-cheek with their wives in our finished basement.

A year later my father and I flew to Los Angeles on a special Western Airlines charter for the Minnesota convention delegation. At our hotel, I learned that my mother's oldest sister, my Aunt Sylvia, would be picking me up the next morning and taking me to the house she and my Uncle Mike owned in Bel Air.

"The first few days of the convention are boring platform stuff," my father said. "I'll come get you when things get interesting."

"Can't I stay?"

"I'll be too busy to keep an eye on you. Now that's enough."

Enough meant enough. My cousins were away at camp, so I spent three days in Aunt Sylvia's swimming pool, until my fair skin was so blistered that she dared to call my father to come get me before I either got bored out of my mind or developed sunstroke. I could clearly hear him through the receiver inform her that he'd planned to have her send me back in a cab that very evening, so she should mind her own goddam business.

"I'll do no such thing. I'll drive him myself." Which she did, right after he hung up on her.

The next day, from the balcony of the Los Angeles Sports Arena, I watched my father and other delegates generate American history. At his suggestion, I wrote down everything in a pocket notebook he made me buy for the trip. I was unprepared for the half-hour of pandemonium after Lyndon Johnson was nominated. "Does it mean he's going to win?" I asked my father when he returned to fetch me.

"Not at all. You'll see. Now it's our turn."

He clipped a green tag to my shirt and led me down to the convention floor, just as Orville Freeman was ascending to the podium. Minnesota's delegation, I learned, was torn. Governor Freeman was up there nominating Kennedy; that morning, Senator Eugene McCarthy had shocked everyone by announcing that he was nominating Adlai Stevenson; and Hubert Humphrey, still sulking because Kennedy had beaten him in the primaries, refused to support anyone. We stood with the Kennedy contingent, and at one point a perspiring man in a white shirt with rolled-up sleeves came by to offer us placards that read, "KENNEDY—LEADERSHIP FOR THE 60'S," for the imminent demonstration.

"Thanks for your support," he said. "My name's Sargent Shriver."

"Si Weisman," my father said, shaking his hand.

"Si. Of course," he replied, just as Freeman finished and the screaming for JFK began. It lasted nearly an hour. I jumped on a folding chair next to Sargent Shriver and stayed there for the duration, shaking my placard, hoping that the cameras would seek out this Kennedy brother-in-law who was still conversing in shouts with my father, so that everyone I knew would see me on TV.

After breakfast the next day, the phone rang in our hotel room. "I have to go see the governor," my father said, after he hung up. "You wait here. I won't be long."

I spent the morning reading through my notes, recalling the previous day's highlights: the convention floor battle; the nominator for Mississippi Governor Ross Barnett, who boasted that his candidate remained a loyal segregationist; Eugene McCarthy's extraordinary stem-winder for Adlai, so different from all the other speeches that for a moment it seemed like the old two-time loser might rise again; Minnesota's sentimental, diplomatic decision to give all its votes to its un-nominated favorite son, Hubert Humphrey; and my father lifting me in the air when Wyoming put JFK over the top on the first ballot.

I ended up waiting all day, feeling increasingly abandoned and cheated because I couldn't even go to the swimming pool for fear of missing his call. By four o'clock, the vice presidential nominating session had already begun, and I was missing it. When I finally heard his key in the lock an hour later, I was so indignant I actually gave him a dirty look. On any other occasion, he would have slapped me silly, but all he said was "Listen to what I have to say, and then you can decide whether to be mad at me. And you can also decide whether you even want to go to the convention tonight, or do something else."

He explained that a few days earlier, in answer to a press conference question about who might be his running mate if he were nominated, Jack Kennedy had put his arm around Governor Freeman's shoulder and replied that he hadn't decided, but this was the kind of man who'd make a good vice president. Then, this morning, a call had come to the governor's suite from Kennedy himself. Could Freeman come over right away?

He brought a few trusted advisers, my father included. Once there, Kennedy took Freeman aside. For political reasons, he explained, he'd had to offer the vice presidential nomination to Lyndon Johnson. He hadn't really expected LBJ to take it, and had actually hinted that Freeman was his real choice. But Johnson had surprised him by accepting. "And that was that. But after he broke the news to Orville, he invited the rest of us inside. That's where I've been all day, with Kennedy and his brother Bobby and the governor, talking about the election and the future of our country. I'm sorry I couldn't call you, but I knew you'd understand."

Years later, when I asked Orville Freeman about that meeting, he agreed with my father's recollection, except for the part about them spending the entire day with Kennedy. By then, I knew enough about my father to guess where else he might have gone that afternoon. At the time, however, the excuse that he had been chatting with John F. Kennedy earned him total absolution.

On the final evening, after watching JFK exhort us to ask not what our country could do for us but what we could do for it, we ended up in a white limousine with Governor Freeman and his family. At dinner we were joined by Arthur Naftalin, the Jewish mayor of Minneapolis—which only fourteen years earlier, just after my father had returned from World War II, had been described in the national press as the most anti-Semitic city in the United States. Yet here were Mayor Naftalin and my Jewish father, drinking Irish coffee with the Lutheran governor of Minnesota, toasting the victory of their candidate, the Catholic Kennedy. I sat among the Freeman and Naftalin children, proudly sensing that my father's arrival in this land was complete.

What had been impressed upon me repeatedly as a small child was doubtlessly true: Due to his prodigious efforts, we truly belonged in this great country.

※⌘※

In September 1972 we gave my father a surprise sixtieth birthday party at my Aunt Sylvia and Uncle Mike's summer home at Lake Minnetonka, a half-hour from Minneapolis. At the time, my relations with him felt like being enmeshed in cobwebs: sticky, uncomfortable, and tenuous. In the space of a few years, I had brought him repeated shame. I had resisted donning a uniform and fighting a war, as he had done—a war against Communists, no less. I had done so deceitfully, keeping my draft board at bay by getting a peacemongering Minneapolis Jewish doctor whom my father detested to whip me up a heart condition. To his charge that I probably used drugs, delivered full-decibel in a Chicago restaurant following the antiwar protest some of us staged at my college graduation, I'd defiantly pleaded guilty. To whatever extent I had earlier muffled his wrath by acquiescing to apply to law school, I'd rekindled it by choosing Berkeley over more prestigious and far less inflammatory options where I'd been accepted. When, two months into the first semester, I announced that I was quitting, I accomplished what no one in our family ever had done: I stunned him into silence.

Now I was back in Minnesota, renting a drafty old clapboard house for seventy-five dollars a month on a lake west of the city where I was born, attempting to be a freelance photographer. Whenever I couldn't afford groceries, I put the fishing tricks he taught me as a child to good use, and lived on sunfish, crappies, small-mouth bass, and northern pike. During the winter, my house, whose insulation had fed generations of squirrels, was so cold that mornings found me chopping through the skin of ice that formed on my developing trays, my opaque breath fogging the enlarging lens. Because of the limited capacity of the ancient cesspool, I'd had to choose between having a darkroom or a bathroom. There was an outhouse thirty yards away, through snow that was often knee-deep. My daily challenge was to read the entire front section of the morning paper seated there, while the thermometer outside averaged fifteen below.

My father was less than impressed by my survival skills. He refused to visit me there, although we lived just twenty minutes apart. My mother came once, shuddered, and never returned. Whenever I visited them, my father's habitual reaction was "*Ach,* look at him!"

"Alan, please let me at least buy you some pants," begged my mother.

"I'm wearing pants."

"Not jeans. Pants. Oh, Alan, is this the way we brought you up? Can't you be a *mensch?*"

For his sixtieth birthday, I tried hard to please him. I proposed to my mother a slide presentation of his life: I would make transparency copies of the photographic record that existed, beginning with the few surviving pictures from Russia. I would photograph every place he'd ever lived in Minnesota and fashion a photo montage of his war years, his career, his family, and his two grandsons that my sister had thoughtfully begotten.

My mother said it was a wonderful idea. "Just try to look nice at the party. Please don't embarrass him."

I promised, drawing the line at cutting my hair. "Where do I start? Do you know where he lived when he first came from Russia?"

"With his cousin Harry Friedman."

"You mean the ophthalmologist?" I had never even known that my father had a cousin Harry until a night when I was ten years old and rubbed sawdust into my eye while earning my Cub Scout woodworking arrowhead. At 2:00 A.M. my father rushed me and my inflamed cornea to Dr. Friedman's house. I had never seen the man since, and to my knowledge, neither had my father. I didn't even know how he and my father were related.

"Where did they live? How is he Dad's cousin?"

The house still stood, conspicuously older than the post-war bungalows across the street, and far older than the post-Jewish-era brick housing project on the corner. It was white stucco, with a second-story dormer that faced the oak-lined street below a steeply gabled roof of red shingles. In the triangular pediment above the dormer windows was a small ornamental touch: an incised scallop shell. A cement stoop ascended to a screened front porch.

My father had never mentioned this place, 1204 Knox Avenue North, Minneapolis, Minnesota, U.S.A. Yet that was the destination given for him, my uncles Harold and Herman, and my grandmother Rebecca on the ship's manifest I found years later for alien passengers occupying the steerage compartment of the British steamship SS *Canopic,* which docked at New York Harbor's Pier Seven on October 5, 1923. It was the home of my father's Uncle Samuel Friedman, a *shochet*—a rabbi trained in the kosher slaughter of animals. He was husband to one of my grandmother Rebecca's sisters: Their father, a noted Talmudic scholar, had wanted all his daughters to marry rabbis. Only my grandmother, the baby of the family, had refused.

I'd never even heard of these great-aunts and rabbi uncles. "How come I never met them when we were growing up?" I asked my sister. "Did you?"

"I saw them once or twice at Grandma's. But I gather that Dad didn't talk to them much. Which isn't too big a surprise. Who did he talk to in his family, unless to holler at them?"

These relatives had arrived nearly a decade before my father, during a lull between storms in the Russian empire. The barbaric anti-Semitic pogroms at the turn of the century had calmed; the current czar, a cruel but weak man, was too preoccupied with his strange wife and their even stranger courtier, the monk Rasputin, to enforce aggravations such as the obligatory conscription of Jewish men to serve twenty-five-year army terms. Lax press restrictions had spawned hundreds of Yiddish literary, political, and religious publications. Jews were finagling ways around official quotas to attend universities, and a few—like my grandfather Avraham—had even contrived to own land. No one yet saw World War I, the Russian Revolution, and the worst pogroms in Jewish history seething just below the horizon.

Yet even without pogroms, a great transmigration of Eastern European Jews to America that had begun in the 1880s continued unabated. In a single century, the population of Europe had doubled, and jobs in European countries, with their traditional landed aristocracies, couldn't be created fast enough to absorb everyone. Unemployment was rife in the Pale of Settlement, the part of the Russian Empire where Jews were forced to live, which encompassed most of today's Ukraine, Belarus, eastern Poland, Latvia, and Lithuania. Since nearly all Jews were landless, most were either artisans—shoemakers, tailors, smiths, or carpenters—or engaged in urban occupations such as shopkeeping, trading commodities like grain and sugar, or serving as agents for absentee landlords of the nobility. Forbidden to live in cities like Kiev or Moscow, Jews had to crowd into poor villages known as *shtetls,* where there were few opportunities to prosper.

They heard mythic tales of America: the surging industries of its eastern cities, the steady westward roll of population across rich, open land—all provoking a ravenous thirst for labor. Some had even heard of *Minyapolis,* via sacks of flour that appeared in *shtetl* shops marked "Pillsbury Company, Minneapolis, Minnesota." But to most Jews, the United States was the place where they landed: New York. By 1920 fully a third of that city—more than 1.5 million people—was Jewish. Prior to 1900, New York's small Jewish population traced mainly to entrepreneurs who had arrived during America's early years from Germany, following the defeat of Napoleon. By the 1880s, several—Levi Strauss, the Lehmann brothers, the Kuhns, Loebs, Gimbels, and Sulzbergers—were prominent in merchandising, banking, and manufacturing. Many had become so-called Reformed Jews, assimilated enough to wear top hats to worship instead of yarmulkes, if they still covered their heads at all.

The sudden new torrent in the late nineteenth century of pious, bearded, Yiddish-speaking, Eastern European Orthodox Jews threatened to upend the established New York and Philadelphia Jewish society. A similar crisis faced old Jewish families in London, who shared Anglican fears that Jewish refugees from Russia might overrun the British Isles. A committee there was organized to divert the flow of immigrants to America. In New York, counterparts of the London Jews quickly formed a Hebrew Emigrant Aid Society to keep these Eastern European *landsmen* moving west.

One Friday afternoon in 1880, a messenger appeared at the Mt. Zion synagogue in St. Paul, Minnesota, a small Reformed congregation of the German Jewish mercantile class that helped found Minnesota's capital. The governor needed to speak to the rabbi at once. Unannounced, a trainload of two hundred Yiddish-speaking Russian Jews had steamed into St. Paul's Union Depot. Unbathed, bewildered, and hungry, they had been shunted ever westward, first by the London committee and then the New Yorkers. This was the end of the line.

It was only a few hours before the Sabbath. St. Paul's Jewish community mobilized in time, settling the refugees in tents on the west side of the Mississippi River. Just downstream, a new town, Minneapolis, had been congealing during the previous decade around mills that Scandinavian immigrants were building near a waterfall. There were no Jews there yet, but with this first trainload of Eastern Europeans, there were about to be.

The flour mills attracted railroads from Chicago, Canada, and both coasts, and the population of Minneapolis soon eclipsed St. Paul's. By 1914, nearly eight thousand Jews lived there, in two enclaves on the north and south sides of the city, surrounded by Swedes and Norwegians. Most Scandinavians had never seen Jews, and many didn't like competing for jobs and housing with the strange newcomers, whom they understood to be descended from the devils who killed Christ. Yet there was no stopping their arrival. The first of my father's relatives to appear there was the eldest son of his rabbi Uncle Samuel Friedman. He had emigrated early, studied engineering in New York, and then written home that he had found work building a Catholic cathedral in this northern city on a beautiful river called the Mississippi, which was longer than the Dnieper, in a region where the deep black topsoil and grain fields reminded him of the Ukrainian steppes.

He urged his father to bring the family to Minneapolis, whose North Side was filling with shops and *shuls* that seemed right out of Russia. All these Jewish immigrants, he reasoned, needed rabbis and *shochets*. They arrived in April 1914, just before World War I halted nearly all immigration from eastern Europe. After 1918 it resumed, but by early 1924, with so many refugees fleeing the ominous new Soviet Union that the Jewish population of Minneapolis alone had tripled, the exclusionary Johnson Act finally stanched the flood of Eastern Europeans to the United States.

My grandmother Rebecca, arriving on the Friedmans' doorstep mere months before with my father and uncles, got out just in time.

✣✣✣

We had moved away from the North Side of Minneapolis nearly twenty years before I went to photograph my father's houses. Occasionally, I still ventured up there. My best friend from high school, now a dentist, worked in a welfare clinic housed in what had once been the synagogue where we were both bar mitzvahed. Besides filling poor people's teeth, he would inlay diamonds—or, on one occasion, an enameled heart, club, diamond, and spade—into the incisors of North Side pimps. Sometimes his satisfied clients invited us to a club on Plymouth Avenue, not far from all the former Jewish shops, most of which were torched one night in 1967. The only white guests, we'd be honored for my

45

friend's deft handiwork with a complimentary silver bucket of iced champagne and a trip to the closet behind the hat check, where cashmere suits and silk dresses were fenced at tantalizing prices.

Except for gaping empty lots where kosher delicatessens and fish markets once stood and the dark skin tones of its current residents, the North Side I photographed for my father's birthday party looked remarkably much as the Jews had left it. The solid frame, stone, and stucco houses, built to endure Minnesota winters, still had neat lawns separated by lilac hedges. The quiet streets were lined with century oaks whose boughs met to form shady arches. Behind the white three-story house that once belonged to my maternal great-grandparents, Jacob and Bessie Meshbesher, the tree was still heavy with my *baubeh* Bessie's enormous green cooking apples. The Friedman house where my father arrived as a fatherless refugee still even had the vegetable patch that one of his cousins, an agriculture student, had begun sixty years earlier.

That garden would have been ripe for harvest by the time they arrived in October 1923. After three years of near-starvation in Yelisavetgrad, its carrots, lettuce, rhubarb, acorn squash, and cabbages must have seemed to them a veritable cornucopia. By night in Yelisavetgrad, my grandmother Rebecca had crafted the garments she bartered by day for the flour they lived on. Each morning, her youngest, Chaim—later Herman—would ask if there would be bread for supper. "Maybe," she would say, and burst into tears. There was no planting vegetables in the courtyard of their huge dank apartment complex, because a Bolshevik battalion was always bivouacked there. Her only relative in Yelisavetgrad, a cousin named Shika, had joined the Red Army, currently scouring the remnants of the White and Cossack armies from Ukraine.

The Communist revolution was now an accomplished fact. The new leader, Vladimir Lenin, had promised freedom and equality for all, Jews included. My grandmother was pleased that her two oldest sons, Shimon and Aharon, were able to take Hebrew studies. But when she went back to Mala Viska to reclaim their home, she returned with only three bags of flour. The new government now owned everything.

The people's revolution was stronger on rhetoric than structure. There was hunger everywhere. In Mala Viska, she saw people bloated from eating *makuach,* pressings from her husband's sunflower-oil factory normally used as cattle feed. As unrest mounted, at night from their iron balcony she and her sons watched the Communists stage executions in the courtyard. She wrote to America. Rabbi Samuel Friedman read her letter aloud as his wife, Sheva, sat by the window and sobbed to him that they had to save her youngest sister. That afternoon, Sam went to see Mr. Latz, the secretary at a Jewish loan company that had already reaped a fortune from lending money to Jews for just such purposes.

My father's journey out of Russia took three weeks. From Riga on the Latvian coast, they shipped for Danzig, where a load of Polish Jews joined them, swelling the ranks in steerage to 430. By the time they reached Bremen, the fourth-class hold was so slippery with vomit it was hard to stand. At Cherbourg, they took on a flock of U.S. citizens, heading home after summering in Europe. Little Chaim, the only Weisman who wasn't perpetually seasick, would sneak up to third and second class to beg food from these cheerful passengers. They sailed to Southampton, then two more stomach-turning weeks to Halifax. Finally, New York.

Two days later, their train arrived in Minneapolis in time for Sukkoth, the harvest festival. Sam Friedman had removed the sheet metal roof from the back porch and hung garlands of fruits and vegetables from the beams. There was actually meat: Working in the slaughterhouses, even a poor *shochet* could always find nourishing scraps to bring home that no one wanted: throats, organs, hearts, the ends of livers.

Sam Junior, the engineer son, came, smoking a huge cigar, and gave the new boys each a nickel. The refugees had nothing to match the abundance heaped upon them; before boarding ship in

Latvia, Rebecca had finally left behind her suitcase full of useless Czarist rubles. She brought out the last of her jewels, strings of pearls she had saved, and gave one to Sheva. Together, the sisters cried over their unfathomable losses and miraculous reunion.

My father, Shimon, and his younger brothers, Aharon and Chaim, became Simon, Harold, and Herman. My grandmother sewed with her older sister, Sheva, but after a while tension arose between them. Rebecca had always been their rabbi father's darling—alone among her sisters, she had been permitted to learn to read and write, which she did in Russian, Yiddish, and Hebrew. She was closer to Sheva's daughter Bertha, who was attending the University of Minnesota. Bertha was being courted by several eligible young men, and Rebecca Weisman, in her early thirties, was still young enough to attract several suitors herself.

The Friedmans wanted her to marry one and find her own place to live—for a year, they'd all been sleeping two and three to a bed. The thirty-five cents young Simon earned hawking the *Minneapolis Journal* on street corners each day didn't nearly fill the four extra Weisman mouths. Every month, when the debt incurred on their behalf came due and the youngest Friedman son, Harry, had to take an envelope stuffed with cash to Mr. Latz at the loan company, the pressure grew. Then, when the remaining sister in the old country, Chana, also arrived with her own family of five, the Friedman house was seriously bursting.

Something had to be done. The local matchmakers had proposed several *schiddechs* for my grandmother. She narrowed her string of suitors down to two candidates. One was short, bald, and not particularly appealing physically, but everyone agreed that he was a good man—and, he was a jeweler who could afford to both maintain Rebecca's three sons and help retire the debt at the loan company for their passage.

The other, named Milstein, was a junk peddler. Not even a good junk peddler, the Friedmans noted contemptuously, because he never seemed to work.

"A lazy hypochondriac," snorted my father, years later.

"Ish," added my mother. "That good-for-nothing *schtunk*."

"An ugly, selfish little man with a big Roman nose. The toilet stank for at least an hour after he was in there," said my Uncle Herman.

At this point, my photographic essay had to skip the next two places where my father lived, because they had been torn down to make way for housing projects. One was a second-floor walk-up where my grandmother took her sons after they'd outstayed their welcome at the Friedmans'—and where, as she admitted in tears to her boys after a year, her dressmaking sign in the window failed to lure enough business to feed them, let alone pay the rent.

The second, just down the street, was where they moved when she married that *schtunk* Milstein.

CHAPTER 3

❧

"What did your parents teach you?" Sandy Tolan demanded suddenly, as we drove along the southern coast of the Dominican Republic. Before us, the horizon was flat and changeless as a dead brain wave: a mat of clouds suspended above green sugar cane that spread thickly in all directions from a gray slab of torpid Caribbean.

"What did they teach me? You mean like I should only date Jewish girls? How to execute a downfield block?"

"Seriously. My parents taught us that if we all lived responsibly and did our part for social justice, it would eventually come about. Were you raised thinking that you were supposed to do something to make the world a better place?"

I knew what he was getting at—or what was getting at him. As in other places we'd gone for our NPR series, a week here had revealed that our own prosperous country—founded and peopled by refugees and their descendants—seemed less likely to spread liberty, justice, and equality than to make refugees out of everybody else. U.S.-owned businesses that paid female Dominican factory drones thirty-nine cents an hour to stone-wash designer blue jeans or Haitian cane-cutters a dollar per twelve-hour shift to keep the cost of our sugar cheap had squeezed wages so tightly that they were squeezing the people right off their island. Each month, thousands risked a journey across an eighty-mile, shark-filled stretch of water in wooden boats called *yolas,* in hopes of reaching the U.S. possession of Puerto Rico. Often more than a hundred desperate people crammed into a single homemade boat, and many had drowned en route.

We had just emerged depressed from an interview with the U.S. ambassador, who seemed more concerned about aliens invading U.S. territory than about medieval labor practices inherent to our country's Caribbean Basin Initiative—hence, Sandy's frustrated query regarding whether my parents had bred me to social activism. "Not overtly," I replied. "My father was a labor lawyer. He could have made a lot more money practicing other kinds of law, but he always said that the working class deserved the same kind of justice as the rich. He was fanatical about truth; I guess he taught me to be truthful."

Even as I said that, I realized that I now knew better, having learned things since childhood that belied my father's zealous devotion to honesty. But as a kid I was instructed that lying was a sin—one that, if I were caught, would earn me a whipping of Biblical proportions, a threat that resonated into my adulthood. "I don't remember being taught, though, that it was my duty to help the world. Unless you count serving in the military."

That was definitely not what Sandy had in mind—in his family, they'd also marched against the Vietnam War. "My dad was a veteran," I said, shrugging. "In fact, the war made his career. Before that he was a starving young Jewish lawyer in the Depression. Then he came home with a chestful of medals and everybody wanted to hire him."

"Oh. World War II." Something in Sandy's reply suggested a wishful illusion that the days when a Hitler justified the use of arms were somehow over. "We just were raised to believe we could make a difference," he repeated. A grandson of the publisher of the *Milwaukee Journal,* Sandy Tolan regarded his journalistic birthright as a moral imperative to defend the weak and fight injustice. He was proud that he had once overheard an editor at NPR describe him as being too sympathetic to the little guy. The chasm into which his path had plunged on our *Vanishing Homelands* project was the understanding that there were probably too many little guys in the world to save. Nothing we wrote would change much, because there was too much to change.

Sandy stared through the windshield, his lean Irish face clenched. His high forehead was always creased now, and his lank brown hair was lately racing conspicuously away from his temples, as if singed by molten thoughts. As well as sharing his mounting outrage over a world in which everything had become fodder for the great global marketplace, I also had more immediate concerns. Cecilia hadn't accompanied me to the Dominican Republic, as we'd originally planned.

"I need space, Alan. I have needs, too," she had announced. "You got to go work alone in Bridgeport," she reminded me. She was referring to the week I had stolen from our schedule while in the States, when the *New York Times Magazine* sent me to Connecticut to update an article that had languished too long before publication.

"Lucky me. Standing on street corners in January all night with crack dealers."

"I didn't ask you to write about them. It's what you wanted. And now I want to work on my own for a while."

"Okay, Cec. Fine." At the time, we'd been standing on the balcony of our house in Costa Rica, overlooking a hillside of coffee bushes. As we talked I'd kept my binoculars raised, watching a pair of blue-crowned motmots flitting among the dark green foliage.

"*¡Pucha!* You don't get it, do you? We've been together practically twenty-four hours a day since July!"

"I get it, Cec. I said okay, didn't I?" I lowered my binoculars and looked at her, to show how sincerely I meant it. Treading carefully, I didn't plead that my week spent freezing in Connecticut had felt like separation enough for me. Instead, I promised that I understood and supported her. On some level, I did understand. Like sniffing rain before storm clouds appear, I was receiving all the signals and portents. But I wouldn't acknowledge, either to her or to myself, the tempest heading our way. Cecilia and I unquestionably cared for each other, in spite of frequent squalls that struck without warning. We marveled over our good fortune that the work we currently shared had allowed us, in just six months, to travel to ten different countries together. The problem was that in each of those countries we had also fought.

So Cecilia had gone to Brazil to work by herself for a while. I went to the Caribbean with Sandy Tolan, while his wife, Nancy, remained in Costa Rica to catch up on our paperwork. "That's a shame," my mother said over the phone when I explained this during a stopover in the Miami airport en route to Santo Domingo. "You and Cecilia could have taken a nice little break together at Casa de Campo."

"Oh sure, Mom. Casa de Campo."

"What's wrong with that? It'd do you good to go to someplace civilized for a change, instead of the kind of places where you kids run around."

Casa de Campo, draped like jeweled silk over seven thousand acres along the Dominican Republic's southeastern coast, was the Caribbean's lushest resort. Exactly one decade earlier, in February 1981, my parents had spent their annual winter vacation there. When I later asked them what the Dominican Republic was like, the impression they gave was of a continuous chain of golf links: Casa de Campo alone had three eighteen-hole courses.

"Your parents could afford to stay here?" Sandy whispered.

"Probably not exactly in this room."

A public relations officer had just informed us that this seaside villa rented for $2,300 a night. Its soft white rugs lay over imported terra-cotta tiles; its parqueted ceiling, I guessed, was teak; and its amenities included a private pool, a gardener, a cook, and a chambermaid whose uniform—plaid skirt, white apron, ruffled blouse, and colorful kerchief—was an original by Dominican designer Oscar de la Renta.

My parents had probably stayed in one of the more

conventional *casitas,* costing around a tenth the price. But even that amount was impressive, especially a decade back, and I was reminded that at one time they could indeed afford Casa de Campo. Every year, besides my father's midwinter Caribbean or Hawaiian golf fix, they'd traveled to places like Europe, Brazil, Hong Kong, Iran, Israel, or Morocco. Perhaps that's where so much of the money went. Upon his forced retirement from his law practice in 1984, it turned out that there was surprisingly little saved.

To my mother's shame and unconcealed resentment, my father's retirement was far more humble than expected. Unlike his law partners, who had invested their earnings and now owned winter retreats in Florida, beyond their home and the pension fund from his office, my parents' wealth was contained in a single passbook savings account. To purchase their modest tract house in Scottsdale, they needed help from my sister and her husband, co-proprietors of a baby furniture business, and my Aunt Sylvia and Uncle Mike, who owned television and radio stations in Las Vegas. They now lived on Social Security and proceeds from his pension—a little over $2,000 a month.

When my mother realized that my father's greens fees at a Scottsdale public golf course could easily run $400 a week, she panicked. "I don't know what to do, Alan. I tell him that we can't afford for him to play every day, but he just doesn't listen. Can you try to talk to him?"

"You're not serious, Mom."

"I know, honey. He'll just holler. But what am I going to do if we run out?"

She borrowed against their life insurance policies. But before the situation grew critical, it was resolved during their second year in Arizona when he tipped over a golf cart, an accident he couldn't explain or even recall. Suddenly, it was lying on top of him.

I was on assignment in Mexico at the time, and learned of this a few days later when I checked my answering machine for messages. "My God, Mom, is he all right?"

"Oh, Alan, I'm so glad you called. Where are you, honey?"

"Guadalajara. Is Dad—"

"We love Guadalajara. You know Dad and I have been there lots of times."

"I know. Mom, please. Tell me how he is."

"It landed on his leg but nothing's broken. But he's so banged up, Alan, you should see. He had to have stitches. And it's the leg that still has shrapnel, so it really hurts him."

"I thought the shrapnel was in his back."

"His lower back. He feels it in the nerve that runs down his leg. Believe me, he lets me know about it. But that's not what worries me. Alan, he just doesn't remember what happened. He's so confused. The doctor says not to let him drive anymore. But how can I stop him?"

"Hide the keys."

"He'll kill me."

"I'm serious, Mom. Remember the last time?"

My father was still practicing law then. One morning, the police had appeared at their home. The two officers knew my father, of course: He was the attorney for the Minneapolis Brotherhood of the Police, pal to every cop in town. Apologizing for disturbing his breakfast, they asked permission to inspect his car. On his bumper, they found paint matching a maroon convertible whose door had been crunched the evening before in a supermarket parking lot. "Supermarket?" my mother had sputtered. "Since when does he go grocery shopping?"

My father claimed no recollection of being there, let alone of an accident. But a witness had noted the license number of his Bonneville when he screeched away. The officers accommodatingly wrote up an accident report that overlooked my father's premature departure from the scene. But the incident scared him enough to stop drinking.

"He's not an alcoholic," my mother assured everyone. His new blood-thinning medication mixed badly with booze, the doctor had told her, and likely had caused the mysterious supermarket blackout. Together they went to a meeting—"It was *not* an AA meeting," my mother emphasized, when she called with the news that he was permanently on the wagon. "Your father's not a drunk."

Then, ten months later, she called again, hysterical because she'd discovered he'd been sneaking drinks. Her first clue was a half-empty case of Canadian Club she found stashed under his old army duffel in their basement cedar closet. After making the men who trimmed her hedges take it away, she padlocked the cabinet where they still kept liquor for guests. That night, she awoke to the sound of him ripping the cabinet door from its hinges.

"Please come talk to him," she'd wailed. "He won't listen to me. All he does is scream. He'll listen to you, Alan."

That statement surely topped every fantasy she'd ever harbored about me. "What exactly makes you think so, after thirty-five years of him not listening to me yet?"

"Oh, Alan, don't exaggerate."

"Mom—"

"Just come. Please."

So, for her sake, I flew up from Arizona. He was in his den when I arrived, reading the paper in his black leather recliner. Above a fireplace hung his war medals; another wall was filled with portraits of my sister's sons, who had been at exceptionally cute ages during my short-lived career as a Minneapolis photographer. There was even one I'd taken of him, which, after failing to get him to relax, I'd snapped after having him close his eyes. My mother claimed I'd made my father appear dead, but his own response was so uncharacteristically gentle—"It looks like I'm praying"—that she hung it with the rest.

"What are you doing here, son?" he asked, surprised and sounding genuinely pleased. He folded his newspaper and we shook hands. Just shy of seventy-one, he still looked damn good. Too heavy, but he carried his weight well on a big, powerful frame. His sideburns and eyebrows were now quite gray, but the hair he combed back from his widow's peak was thick and dark.

I sat down and answered his question. The roaring commenced. I glimpsed my mother hovering in the hallway, both hands stopping her ears. He actually ordered me out of his house, something unprecedented.

"Fine, Dad. But I'm taking Mom with me. To an Al-Anon meeting."

"I don't give a good goddam where you go. You can both go straight to hell, for all I care. Now, GET OUT! OUT! MARCH!"

He was at gale-force wrath, but I gripped the couch and made one last try: "Well, we care. We'd prefer it if you didn't kill yourself. You know as well as I do what Dr. Wexler said."

"Just mind your own business. You're just a no-good little shit, is what you are."

"Oh, Si," said my mother, now entering.

"Both of you!"

"I don't want to go to another of these," my mother said on the way home from the Al-Anon meeting.

"I don't blame you." I ached for her. At sixty-eight, she was still so beautiful, so proud that she weighed the same 118 pounds as the day she graduated high school. But that night, I'd watched the years seep into her eyes as she listened to one sad woman after another describe life with a husband who refused to admit he was lost.

The next day, I got rid of every last bottle I found in the house. Then I made the rounds of the restaurants he frequented and went to his country club, begging bartenders and waitresses I'd known all my life not to serve him liquor anymore, knowing it probably wouldn't do much good. An alcoholic always finds a way, and later I learned how and where my father did so. But following his golf cart spill three years later, something went out of him. He put up a brief battle when he couldn't find where she'd secreted the car keys, throwing a typically thunderous fit that spilled from the garage out onto the driveway, mortifying my mother in front of the curious neighbors. But after that, it was as if he had forgotten that he had ever driven at all.

It became her duty to take him for a ride every afternoon. Like a child, his gaze followed her as she moved through the house with vacuum or dust mop, anxiously waiting until she told him it was time to get his jacket and shoes on. No more driving also meant no more booze, of course, because he couldn't get to where they sold it without her, but he seemed to have forgotten his thirst as well. Even his obsession for golf ebbed. At first, she arranged foursomes for him with other Jewish retirees, until she noticed he stopped asking. Within a year, his passion was reduced to a set of clubs gathering desert dust in the garage, and Sunday tournaments on the television that he may not even have noticed.

꧑꧑

In the summer of 1988, three years before Sandy Tolan and I went to the Dominican Republic together, I'd been invited there as a writer-in-residence at an artists' colony called Altos de Chavón, near La Romana, a small city two hours east of Santo Domingo. Before leaving, I spent a few days with my parents, who by then had been retired in Arizona for four years. There was an unfortunate moment when Federal Express delivered a new word processing program I needed while I was out jogging and my mother was in the bathroom. My father answered the door, accepted the package, opened it, and kept opening. I returned minutes later to find the destroyed plastic casing of the floppy disk, from which protruded the exposed, now useless filmy circle inside that must have puzzled him so when he'd shredded his way as far as he could go and found nothing recognizable.

At that moment, however, sympathy was the furthest emotion from my heart. I exploded. My mother backed against the stove as, apoplectic, I screamed, "He's fucking ruined everything! EVERY GODDAM FUCKING THING!" I ranted on, my rage compounded by the futility of impressing upon elderly parents the intricacies of the computer age that made it impossible for me to buy a replacement disk at an office supply store. "I'm sure I've seen ones that look just like it at Walgreen's," my mother tried, but gave up when she saw this probably wasn't true, and just held her head in fear and grief at how her husband's appalling temper could burst forth in full, terrible bloom in their son.

My paroxysm ended only when my father, dimly realizing himself to be the cause of all the commotion, screamed, "I wish I were dead!" and rushed from the room.

My mother and I looked at each other, shaken by his terrible acknowledgment that he was aware how diminished and inept his life had become. "Alan, go tell him you're sorry. You know Dad didn't mean to ruin your whatever-you-call-it. Poor guy. He feels terrible."

I knew that, but for a moment I flared anew to hear her defend him the way she'd done all my life: "You know Dad loves you. You know he didn't mean it." Ironically, after all those years of him steamrolling over us, finally she was right. He was no longer responsible for the pain he wreaked. "All right," I said at last. "Give me a minute."

I took two minutes, then walked down the hall to the television room my mother called his den. He was in his recliner, glancing around as if he wasn't sure what he was supposed to be doing. Behind him, the wall was filled to the ceiling with plaques that had once lined his law office. In that room, a choice corner office high above downtown Minneapolis, the diplomas connoting his many legal academy memberships and the parchment certifying his admission to practice before the U.S. Supreme Court had looked grand and impressive on the walnut paneling. Here, against the black-and-white patterned wallpaper my mother had chosen, they practically screamed of exile from their former, rightful setting. As, so often, did he.

"Dad, I'm really sorry," I said. I was. He looked so pitiful in his robe, completely gray and big as ever, but all the power in that big body now useless to him.

He looked at me, perplexed. "What for?"

"For getting upset and yelling."

"When?"

When I arrived at the artists' colony in the Dominican Republic, I was a little shocked to learn that my home for the next two months was part of Casa de Campo, the posh resort where my parents had once golfed in opulent tropical splendor. Altos de Chavón, it turned out, was a village replicated from sixteenth-century Tuscany, built from imported Italian limestone on a bluff overlooking a river that flowed through lush stands of coconut palms to the Caribbean. Dazed by this incongruity, I wandered over its stone bridges, through massive doorway arches, and down its cobbled passages connecting ornate piazzas flanked by restaurants and boutiques. I inspected Altos de Chavón's Roman amphitheater, the scene of weekend rock concerts attended by the next generation of Santo Domingo's sugar elite, during which it became a giant stone woofer that shivered my apartment's windows through the night.

Feeling somewhat like a specimen in a gilded cage, I spent as little time there as possible. With binoculars and a bird guide to the West Indies in hand, I tramped through the surrounding coastal woods. Or, I hitchhiked into La Romana, a company town built around La Central, its sugar refinery—which, along with several hundred square miles of surrounding cane fields, an adjacent industrial park, and Casa de Campo, belonged to a family of Florida sugar barons.

La Romana was composed chiefly of little wooden row houses, many painted the same pale green, strung along narrow streets through which flocks of motor scooters swarmed like hornets. I met a group of young women, daughters of maids and sugar mill workers, who had formed a feminist solidarity group, put themselves through night school, and become professionals. They called themselves Las Esclavas del Fogón—The Slaves of the Cook Stove—and their mission was to convince the coming generation of La Romana girls to seek something better for themselves than a life of wearing Oscar de la Renta aprons.

"*Cuéntame de tu familia*," L. said to me one evening.

I exhaled a brief, mirthless laugh. What, she asked, was so funny about wanting to know about my family?

I pulled away the tangled sheet and raised myself to my knees to open the shutter, hoping to lure a breeze to cool us down now that we were lying quietly and talking. Since Casa de Campo was off-limits to locals—unless they were employed there as gardeners or housekeepers—L. didn't often visit me at Altos de Chavón. But I would be leaving soon, so she was being bolder about evading the security patrols on her white Suzuki scooter in the evenings.

"Well," I said, "until he retired, my father was an attorney."

"Like me!" The lights were out and there was no moon, but her teeth were so white against her mahogany skin that even by starlight from the window I could see her pleased smile.

"Exactly like you," I agreed, fingering the wiry curls at the base of her neck.

She never mentioned her own father. I had met her mother in their wooden row house that shared a wall with a tiny neighborhood grocery. Plastic curtains partitioned their bedroom from the rest of the house, which held a stuffed brown couch and a table lamp alongside a straight-backed wooden chair, a kitchen sink with a single tap, and a refrigerator that, due to the incessant blackouts, served mainly as a cupboard. Her mother, whom L. called Mami, a large jolly woman in a flowered dress, sat in the doorway mashing a *mafongo* of garlic and fried plantains in a mortar and pestle. We spent an hour one twilight drinking warm beer during a driving rainstorm, while the lights flared twice and then died. On such evenings, a distant glow still always emanated from La Central: The refinery burned sugar cane wastes around the clock to generate its own electricity, and also to assure that the guests at Casa de Campo were never without power.

L.'s mother howled when I protested this injustice. "Getting mad at La Central is like getting mad at God," she told me, sampling a lick from the pestle, then reaching for the salt. "What good did it ever do anybody?"

"Mami," said L., "if people believe that, that's why nothing ever changes."

I was in awe of their poverty, of L.'s struggle to put herself through law school at night while working days in a factory, of the consciousness-raising she and her *compañeras* did with the women of their community, of the free legal advocacy she provided the poor. In my darkened, spacious apartment at Altos de Chavón, I told her a story about how my father had seen his own father assassinated, how they'd emigrated penniless to America, where he'd worked to support his family and to eventually to pay his way through law school, only to go off to World War II. It was a sad story, and after a while L. turned on her side to face me and pulled me to her again.

CHAPTER 4

"As much as the thought nauseates me, he must have been good in bed. Why the hell else would she have married him?" my Uncle Herman wondered.

I had no idea. By the time I was born, that *schtunk* Milstein was long gone, and my grandmother was on her third husband, the widower of my grandfather Avraham's sister Rivkeh, who had died from rheumatic fever contracted while fleeing Russia. But marry Rafful (Ralph) Milstein my grandmother Rebecca did, to everyone's shock. Perhaps it was an act of contrition for being the only daughter of her family not to marry a rabbi like her father. From girlhood, she had sworn that she wanted a businessman, and she had found one: my agro-industrialist grandfather Avraham. But what had it gotten her? A dead husband, killed by savages after his wealth. Milstein, although not a rabbi, was deeply pious, a lover of Talmudic law and a righteous critic of Jews who failed to heed it; perhaps in his stentorian voice she heard echoes of her dead father's. And certainly, this time she wasn't repeating the risk of marrying a rich man.

Two years after my grandmother, her sons, and Milstein moved into a north Minneapolis second-floor walk-up, they purchased a little square house a mile away on Russell Avenue. She had gone to the bank with no money for a down payment and scant knowledge of English, but she had calculated an amortization schedule, and her arithmetic skills apparently convinced the bankers that this was a shrewd dressmaker, because she got the loan.

Milstein, as usual, had stayed home. Soon after they married, he'd relinquished his peddler's cart and now seldom ventured forth, except to synagogue. Despite his religious zeal, apparently even God had failed him, having bestowed upon him a mellifluous voice which, he was convinced, had destined him to be a cantor. But no one else took notice. At home, he sang along to Victrola recordings of famous cantors, but if he ever actually auditioned to get work in a *shul*, he kept it a secret from the family. Mostly, Milstein remained in his slippers, blowing his hyper-allergic beak that protruded through his long reddish beard and demanding to be served only white chicken meat and other specific foods required to maintain his delicate health. One autumn the two older boys, Simon and Harold, taught their stepfather to operate a Model A Ford panel truck, so he could drive a bakery route that became available. That lasted only until winter, however, because he refused to drive in snow, and they ended up taking it over from him.

The three Weisman brothers became famous on Minneapolis's Jewish North Side for the way they struggled to support their family. They delivered bread and newspapers, and worked in a box factory. They appended a little dressmaking studio to their tiny house, where my grandmother took in sewing. She had two daughters by Milstein, Frieda and Florence. Everyone agreed that Frieda, until encephalitis took her at age thirteen, was a strawberry-blonde angel. Years later, my sister, Rochelle, better known as Cooky, would grow into nearly an exact likeness of the Aunt Frieda she never knew—proof to my father that Frieda's saintliness came from his mother's genes, and not the despised Milstein's.

Frieda's younger sister, Florence, resembled their father more, but her female version of his aquiline features, her half-brothers kindly assured her, was far more attractive. She knew how they mocked Milstein. "People didn't understand my father," Florence lectured me over dinner one evening. Until the afternoon when I called her, I hadn't seen her for thirty years—it had been that long since my parents stopped speaking to her.

We were in a steakhouse near her apartment complex on the western margin of greater Minneapolis, land that was maple and birch forest when I was growing up, now displaced by a tangle of highway interchanges studded with chain restaurants. Aunt Florence, still pretty and looking much younger than sixty-nine, wore a pale blue pantsuit; her hair was tinted more toward blonde than the reddish auburn I recalled. She clinked her scotch against my glass of chablis.

"He was a very sick man. Nobody ever acknowledged that," she said. "But no matter what they say, I never saw him abuse my brothers."

She waited for me to challenge this, so I acknowledged hearing allusions to the contrary. "Uncle Herman says that at least twice Milstein took a poker to him."

"I never saw it. I never saw him not be nice to them."

"My father once said that Milstein didn't dare lay a finger on him."

Florence shuddered at the thought. "Your father would have killed him. Look," she said, pointing a scarlet nail at me across the table. "All I know is that to me he was gentle and kind. He'd put me on a toy horse, sit on the back steps, and talk with me while I played. When Mom divorced him, I realized that he was irresponsible, but also that he was sick. He'd get these panic attacks and make my mother call an ambulance. They all thought he was crazy. Today they'd have given him Prozac. Back then, nothing like that existed."

She finished her drink. "But you know how your father was. When I started coming down with hay fever, Si would say, 'Ach— that's ridiculous.' Your mother and father pooh-poohed everything, as I'm sure you know. They were so judgmental. They didn't understand my father." Her empty glass clattered against the butter dish as she put it down. "Your parents didn't understand anybody."

My father was eleven when he arrived in the United States and thirteen when his mother married Milstein. That year there was no money for his bar mitzvah. He was initiated into Jewish manhood with minimal ceremony, ascending to the *bimah* on the

Sabbath morning to recite a single blessing over the Torah during another thirteen year-old's celebration, whose parents could afford the full passage rites of *maftir, haftorah,* and *kiddish.*

His half-sister Frieda was born when he turned fourteen, and he was sixteen when she was followed by Florence. That year, 1928, he'd arise before dawn to deliver fresh loaves of *challah* and pumpernickel before his classes at Minneapolis's North High. Afternoons, he lifeguarded at a junior high school pool. Then, until well past dark, he delivered the *Minneapolis Journal,* having acquired his own route after years of defending the choice downtown corner he'd won with his fists against Jew-baiting Scandinavian newsboys. Yet no one recalls him as a hotheaded adolescent. Back then, Herman, the future soft-spoken professor, was the defiant son. Instead of raging against Milstein, my father simply spent as much time away as possible.

In between Herman and Simon came sweet-faced Harold, who got along with everyone. Harold managed their finances, assuring that bills were paid. Like his beatified dead sister Frieda, he later became Saint Harold in everyone's memory when he, too, suddenly died far too young.

Harold and Herman were both fine-boned, slight editions of their older brother. By high school, Simon stood five-foot ten inches: a half-foot shorter than my dead grandfather Avraham, but just as broad. One afternoon during the fall of 1929, he went to his first American football game. His initial impression was that the object was for the opponents to kill each other. He may not have been too far off: By the third quarter, North High was out of substitutes. "Hey, you," the coach called to the husky, lean-waisted, dark-haired boy he spied in the lower bleachers.

"Me?" my father replied, though he could see where the coach was pointing. Classmates were turning to look at him.

"You. Get down here and put on these pads."

ꙮ

That same autumn, Louis B. Meshbesher's world crumbled. Millions of Americans could say the same: The implosion of the stock market sucked much of the country down the huge hole that investors had dug themselves. But Louis had already been in free fall for two years, and in 1929 he hit the bottom hard.

Not long before he died in 1969, he gave me a gold-filled pocket watch that he'd carried back then and had managed to keep during the five years that followed, a shadowy time when his children rarely knew where he'd gone or how he'd survived. "Now read to me what that says," he said, indicating with a stubby finger the watchmaker's imprint in the gold filigreed face.

"It says 'Illinois,' Grandpa Lou."

"Right. Wonderful watches. Not cheap *chazzerei*. I bought it because Illinois is where I was born." Which was because his parents, Jacob and Bessie Meshbesher, had run out of money again. That had happened first in London, where they had arrived in 1890 with two sacks containing their clothing, a few pieces of Russian gold jewelry, and a brass samovar. They had left their Ukrainian village of Medzhibozh—renowned as the home of the Baal Shem Tov, the founder of Hasidism—because Jacob, an asthmatic who weighed barely one hundred pounds, had been conscripted into the military, a twenty-five-year sentence for Jews.

England's foggy damp nearly crippled him. With London's Hebrew Emigrant Aid Society coaxing poor Eastern European Jews to try America, Jacob and Bessie went willingly. Believing that an Ellis Island immigration agent had asked his birthplace, Jacob replied, "Medzhibozher," and their name became Meshbesher. ("But there was a name before Meshbesher. What was it?" I asked. No one knew. Seven surviving children, sixteen grandchildren, dozens of great-grandchildren—and none, apparently, had ever dared to ask my great-grandparents. "They wouldn't talk about it," everyone told me. "It was too painful.")

Their destination was Minneapolis, the name on those Pillsbury flour sacks, but their cash lasted only as far as Jacksonville, Illinois. By the time they earned some more, Bessie was in labor.

She bore Louis, and the following year, finally in Minnesota, came another son. Then a pair of twins. Then another, and another: four sets of twins in all, of which two survived, and later a final daughter, who wasn't born until Louis was nearly married.

They lived on Sixth Avenue, a road that began somewhere out by the Dakota border and ended at the Minneapolis farmers' market. By the turn of the century, the final three blocks leading to the produce stalls were all Jewish businesses, among them Jacob Meshbesher's soda pop factory and his kosher wine and *matzoh* distributorship. Their house was next to a synagogue he'd helped to found; each Saturday, he'd invite a crowd of men over to drink schnapps and eat Bessie's gefilte fish and *challah*.

The seven Meshbesher children assumed that maps to their house were for sale in the *shtetls* back in Russia, because new arrivals were always camping with them. Jacob Meshbesher was the man who could find jobs in the farmers' market or get an immigrant set up with his own horse and wagon. Jews wary of a court system run by *goyim* would come to Jake, renowned for his *sechel*, to settle disputes. When a case involving Jews did go to formal trial, he was often called to the municipal judge's chambers to arbitrate in Yiddish.

He was good friends with the alderman, a *shaygetz* whose son they employed as their *shabbos goy*—the Gentile who would light their stove on Fridays after sundown and on Saturdays, when devout Jews were forbidden even to pick up a stick of kindling. Jacob Meshbesher could get his friend the alderman to waive the five-dollar peddler's license fee for any poor immigrant to whom he took a liking. Later, when the *shabbos goy* grew up and became the governor of Minnesota, he could do even more.

At eighteen, Jake and Bessie's oldest son, Louis, had a silky brown pompadour that swooped to the back of his stiff collars, and was known among Jewish girls as a hot dancer. His favorite partner lived on the south side of town, where Romanian Jewish immigrants had their own enclave, apart from the Yiddish swathe of

Russians, Ukrainians, Latvians, Lithuanians, and Poles spreading across Minneapolis's North Side. The two contingents didn't often mix, but the barrier dissolved for Louis Meshbesher the first time he saw Rose Cohen dance the black bottom.

Rose, he learned, had never known her father, a Romanian sailor so handsome he was called *Moishe der shayner.* Her mother, a seamstress to Romanian royalty, was pregnant with her the winter she received a letter saying that her husband had succumbed to pneumonia aboard ship on the Black Sea. Shortly after giving birth, she herself died of a broken heart. Baby Rose was taken in by her mother's sister, who was childless, the family believed, because she'd married her first cousin. He was a cattle rancher in the Transylvanian Alps until the Russian Revolution spilled across the border, in the form of Tatar hordes looking for rich Jews. They escaped through Turkey where—collective memory weakens a bit here, as fragments retained by Rose's various descendants fail to fit perfectly when reassembled—Rose was stolen by gypsies.

"Arabs," said my Aunt Sylvia.

"Gypsies," insisted Aunt Eleanor.

"Oh, Ellie, what do you know about it? You were only a baby."

"What do you mean, a baby? This all happened before either of us were born."

Any second now, my sister and I were certain, our mother, Charlotte, the middle sister who lay between them as they clashed over her deathbed, would chime in. Staggered by our imminent loss, sick with laughter as our aunts' divergent memories once again had them shrieking at each other, our tear-blurred eyes never left her face. I knew that despite her coma our mother wasn't missing a word, and was probably livid over how her sisters were garbling the correct version—hers, of course.

Whoever it was—likely neither Arabs nor gypsies but Turks—they were bewitched by Rose's dark nine-year-old beauty and her ability to sing in several languages, and hid her in a mosque.

Somehow, her uncle discovered where, and paid a substantial chunk of the money they had grabbed before escaping to buy her back. Months later in Minneapolis, where other Romanian Jews had settled, he used his remaining cattle profits to begin a business from cattle scraps: a shoemaker's shop. His adopted daughter Rose grew into a ravishing charmer who danced as fetchingly as she imitated popular singers or conversed with her immigrant neighbors in Romanian, Hungarian, Russian, French, and unaccented English. The night in 1910 that she met my grandfather Lou and they won the first of many dance contests together, she was sixteen and he was eighteen. Before either celebrated another birthday, they were married.

Jacob and Bessie Meshbesher had decreed that their firstborn, Lou, attend the University of Minnesota, an expense to which the younger sons had been expected to contribute. But with a wife, that was now out of the question. The privilege of higher education descended to brother Si, the male half of the eldest surviving pair of twins, and Lou apprenticed to an electrician. Beginning with daughter Sylvia in 1913, every other year he had another mouth to feed: In 1915, Charlotte was born; son Marvin arrived in 1917, and baby Eleanor in 1919.

During Lou's apprentice and journeyman years they lived in a duplex down the street from the family soda pop factory, crowded into a single bedroom so they could rent the other to a boarder. But by the 1920s, in a city grown prosperous from flour mills and intersecting rail lines, there was plenty of work for a master electrician. By early in the decade, Lou Meshbesher had installed his growing family in their own two-story, white stucco two-bedroom house, on an oak-lined street a few blocks north.

꙳⦙⦙꙳

"Look how old he's gotten," my mother whispered to me, forgetting that I had no prior image for comparison. I immediately picked the Meshbesher face out of the line of arriving passengers. The pompadour had collapsed and whitened; at sixty-two he was stooped and thick, like all his brothers except skinny Max, shell-shocked during World War I and left with a twitch that consumed hundreds of calories daily. Instantly, I adored him. I spent the two weeks of my grandfather's stay clinging to his side, making up for years we'd missed. Every day, we went fishing. I overheard my mother tell a cousin on the phone that she didn't know what to make of this. She had barely seen her father over the previous quarter-century. Her eight year-old son's automatic devotion to him both disarmed and disturbed her. When finally he returned home to New Orleans, I sobbed piteously all the way to the airport.

"Now do you see what happens?" my mother said to him accusingly.

Certainly he couldn't have seen it coming, back when she was a child herself. In those years, Lou and Rose were still just a pair of married kids. Some nights he'd run with his bachelor friends, and when he came home past midnight a battle would await over the dinner she saved for him. "Look how your mother spoiled you, you overgrown baby!" their children heard her yell. But during the sanguine postwar 1920s, life mainly seemed a bubble of loveliness that only grew bigger and shinier. Rose was just twenty-four by the time all her children were born. She wore short skirts like the flappers and did the Charleston. She sang Caruso arias along with the Victrola. She spoke every language on the block, and could mimic their neighbors so well that the kids would close their eyes and swear they were in the room.

She filled the yard with flower beds, and grew dahlias big as saucers. She planted sweet corn, dill for the pickles she put up every fall, and all their summer vegetables. She brought home a black-and-white dog named Sparkie, a mixture of many breeds with the intelligence, she assured her children, of all of them. Because she had the same knack with pets as she did with plants, she was the neighborhood veterinarian, splinting the broken legs of dogs and cats when they'd have encounters with the ever-proliferating automobiles. They were sure she could fix or cure anything—until Marvin, her red-headed, freckle-faced nine-year-old son, got leukemia.

Daily, she bathed and sponged him with herbal teas and wrapped him in poultices, but he declined swiftly as diphtheria set in. Marvin used to earn nickels delivering bag lunches from his *Zaydeh* Jacob's store to the old men praying in the synagogue, and would share the proceeds with his sisters. Now, not only was that income gone, but their father got fired from his job. It was winter, a bad time in Minnesota to have money woes. Lou was still unemployed on the first day of spring of 1927, when the girls crept up the stairs with the news that the grocer wouldn't give them any more credit for milk and eggs—only to hear their mother scream as she entered their brother's sickroom and discovered his lifeless body.

"I'm sure my mother wouldn't have gotten sick if Marvin hadn't."

The pain in Rose's abdomen, which had begun just before his death, had intensified like the howl of an approaching freight train. "She grieved so. He was her only son. Sons were much more important in those days. I read somewhere that cancers come from viruses."

"But then why didn't we get sick, Sylvie?" Ellie asked.

"Maybe we are. Look at Char."

We looked. For a month she had shriveled like a raisin, as lymphoma, smouldering slowly in her for years, was suddenly ignited by the infection she caught at my father's funeral. Now, barely seven weeks later, the edema was creeping up from her feet, filling her with the fluid that, in a matter of hours, would rise through her lungs until there was no place left for her breath. Already it was flowing under her skin, filling and smoothing her cheeks as she lay there, slightly propped on an extra pillow, her gray hair soft and silvery on either side of this resurrected face.

A nurse entered. "Is this your mother?" My sister and I nodded. "She's so beautiful."

To Sylvia, the oldest, fell the chore of cooking. She would bring the ingredients and the pots and pans upstairs, where Rose, lying in bed, would tell her what to do. Then she'd go down and try to make the chicken soup, the *matzoh* balls, and *kugel*.

"Sylvia cooks, you clean," Rose gasped to my mother, and Charlotte cleaned. And never stopped.

Ellie, holding my mother's limp right hand and rhythmically stroking her forearm, looked up at my sister and me. "That's when your mother became so obsessive about cleaning," she said. It was true. Our mother never had to wipe dust from the furniture, we would joke, because she would catch it in midair. "Do you remember," Eleanor asked us, "how Char would clean the house every Monday, so the cleaning lady who came on Tuesday didn't think you lived like pigs? That's where it all started. When our mother was dying."

"Oh, Ellie, what do you remember? You were barely five years old."

"Would you stop it, Sylvia? How could I not remember? She was my mother."

Still watching my own mother's breathing, now faint as a snowfall, I asked, "Had Grandpa Lou gone back to work by then?"

Ellie looked up from caressing my mother's arm, puzzled. "Was he even there?"

"Oh," Aunt Sylvia sighed, "who knows where Lou was? Was he ever there when we needed him?"

They had little recollection of their father during this time. Was he paralyzed with denial? Half-crazed with depression? Did he stay away from home, unable to watch his gorgeous wife dying at barely thirty-three? The legacy of what is forgotten, I have learned, is as powerful as what is remembered. In my mother's family, there were so many gaps, starting with our real surname. Of our ancestral Medzhibozh, only a shred of memory survived along with Bessie Meshbesher's brass samovar and a few necklaces of spun Russian gold. At my mother's deathbed, however, we heard a story about my great-grandmother Bessie's grandfather's great-grandfather. Supposedly, this ancestor was a Kabbalistic rabbi with

73

disciples all over Russia and Poland, because he could heal and foretell the future. He would have visions of events in distant *shtetls,* and Medzhibozhers would rush off in oxcarts to corroborate what he had seen.

My Aunt Eleanor stroked my mother's acupuncture points, crooning in her ear about a bright light down a long tunnel she'd be seeing soon. Eleanor of yoga and mysticism classes, whose husband was in the tenth year of his second cancer remission, still playing his daily eighteen holes of golf a decade after his doctors wrote him off for dead: Every day, Eleanor had made him listen to meditation tapes. Together, they'd visualize the cancer melting away like a summer ice cube, and his tumors miraculously shrank. Was the Kabbalist trickling through her genes?

She looked up at me and answered what I was thinking. "You should have called me sooner," she said.

After Rose was moved to a sanatorium just beyond the southern outskirts of Minneapolis, Lou reappeared. He was working again: The synagogue that his father, Jacob Meshbesher, had cofounded, was building a fine new brick *shul,* and Lou got the lighting contract. It involved thousands of dollars' worth of crystal chandeliers to be imported from Vienna and Prague. It was lucrative work, but he didn't know what to do with three daughters.

The girls were distributed among various aunts and uncles. They would save streetcar fare to ride as far south as streets went, then walk into what seemed a wilderness to see their mother. They rarely saw each other, and it was rarer still that they saw their father. "You're the oldest: Take care of your sisters," Rose said to Sylvia just before she died, doubtless knowing that her husband couldn't be trusted to raise them himself.

But even she couldn't have foreseen the knockout punch aiming for my grandfather Lou, already reeling from the consecutive losses of his son and his wife. The synagogue's building fund was invested in the stock market. Two months after the market crashed, that fund wasn't worth the dust settling over America, and Lou was left holding the tab for all the European crystal lighting fixtures he'd ordered. He went bankrupt, and then he went, period. It was five years before they saw him again.

"Do you know what it means to a girl to be orphaned by her mother and abandoned by her father when she's entering puberty?" asked Aunt Sylvia. "You have no idea what that's like."

"Of course not," I said. But later, it occurred to me that I did. Early in my own wanderings, I'd spent a year at a Mexican orphanage, where I'd learned Spanish interviewing scores of teenaged girls who fit exactly that description: Their mothers had died; their fathers had then vanished. I'd heard how confidence was yanked from under them, how unfinished parenting left a void that, even in the brightest and prettiest among them, remained as an abiding sense of inadequacy, and a wary suspicion that somehow they were to blame.

By going to that orphanage, was I unconsciously responding to my own mother's trauma over being reduced at age thirteen to foster status and shuttled among a succession of aunts? Was an inferiority complex born of her bereavement what impelled her to become my father's lifelong accomplice in the care and nurturing of his reputation (which, by association, also became hers)? Was that why she would clutch any opportunity to show her cousin-stepsisters that her husband was better than any of theirs?

For the latter, there was no other explanation. When her mother died, auburn-haired Charlotte Meshbesher was already blossoming. Never without a date, her beauty became the envy of those cousins. But in turn, she envied their intact homes. She made the rounds of the Meshbeshers, first living with her Aunt Jennie, the twin sister to Si Meshbesher, who had four daughters of her own. When that arrangement began to sag under the added weight of the Depression, she moved in with Uncle Ben Meshbesher, his wife, Helen, and their two kids. But she and Uncle Ben fought; perhaps to spite him she joined her sister Sylvia, who was staying with Ben's twin brother, Uncle Nate, and Nate's wife, Esther.

Ellie, the baby sister, by then was eight blocks away with their grandparents, Jacob and Bessie. Their fine corner three-story home had a sunporch and a staircase nook that housed the samovar they'd lugged halfway around the world. In the backyard were a pear and an apple tree, and a white trellised arch heavy with climbing roses. Between them and the neighbors grew a wall of lilacs. On Saturdays, all the grandchildren lined up to kiss *Baubeh* and then eat a *shabbos* meal climaxed by her apple strudel dessert, at a table set with linens she'd carried from Russia. For years, those Saturdays were the only times that Charlotte, Sylvia, and Ellie saw each other.

"God, I met the handsomest boy last night," Charlotte confided to Sylvia one day, as they lolled in the grass under *Baubeh's* garden trellis. It was the summer that my mother was eighteen. The night before had been Fourth of July. On a pine-covered knoll in North Commons Park, friends had introduced her to a husky, black-haired, twenty-year-old North High grad, and for the rest of the evening they had walked arm-in-arm under the fireworks.

Sylvia's eyes widened. "Si Weisman? You mean the football hero?"

CHAPTER 5

In August 1988, a week after I returned to the States from my writer's residency at the Dominican Republic's Altos de Chavón, my sister and I gave our parents a fiftieth wedding anniversary party in Minnesota. They had not been back to Minneapolis for four years. It was a subdued affair, because my father was mostly disoriented by an onslaught of old friends, relatives, and colleagues whose names he couldn't recall.

Following the party, I drove them to Aunt Sylvia and Uncle Mike's summer home on Lake Minnetonka, where they were staying. My father fell asleep in the car. After my mother and I put him to bed, we went out to the screened porch. An evening breeze that smelled like the fishing boats of my youth blew off the lake. My mother talked about relatives who had attended that afternoon. "Do you realize," she inquired, "that of all your cousins you're practically the only one who isn't married with kids?"

No, I lied, I hadn't realized that. "Nor do I particularly care." I wasn't close to any of them; aside from a few, such as Aunt Sylvia, who shared my mania for reading, most of my relatives and I shared little in common. At the same time, I absurdly felt intimidated in their presence. After I'd abandoned law school and, after various false starts, decided to become a writer, I'd run a gauntlet of their skepticism: How, several Meshbeshers had smugly demanded, did I expect to make a living? For years afterward, until the balance of acceptances to rejections began to tip in my favor, visits home meant enduring the accusing example of their suburban success, their latest newborns, their salaried security.

"Well, you're going to have to settle down someday," my mother reminded me. "Don't you ever get tired of being lonesome, gallivanting to all those places?"

"They have women in those places. I generally meet some."

"I can just imagine what kind of women."

"Pretty interesting ones, usually." Almost everywhere, I'd meet someone—sometimes a journalist, sometimes a protagonist in whatever situation I'd be covering—who became a window into my understanding of the story. Someone female.

"Who did you meet in the Dominican Republic? No one you'd want to date."

"Why not?" I told her about L.

"You mean from that town?" my mother asked. "At Casa de Campo they told us it was dangerous to go there. Was she colored?"

"Colored? Nope."

"What was she then?"

"Black."

"Oh, Alan. That's disgusting."

I sat upright in my Aunt Sylvia's porch lounger. "*What* did you say? Do you find Aaron and Reatha Brown disgusting?"

"Don't be ridiculous. You know Dad and I adore them." Aaron and Reatha, my sister and brother-in-law's closest friends and sometime business partners, had attended my parents' anniversary gathering. My father had once sponsored Aaron's admission as the first black member of the country club where he played golf—a generation after one of his Gentile law partners had persuaded a club board to admit him as their first Jew. During the party, my mother had gushed over the Browns' two children, now handsome young adults.

"So what's the difference? Because Aaron was a football star?" Aaron Brown had been an All-American defensive end at Minnesota and a pro standout with the Kansas City Chiefs.

"Of course that's not it. You know Dad and I aren't prejudiced."

"Then what is it, pray tell?"

"I just don't know how you can do that with those people."

"She happens to be a lawyer. You've been doing it with a lawyer all your life."

"Oh, Alan, don't be so smart. You know what I mean."

"I don't." Of course, I did: A mother who waged holy war to keep her children from dating across religious lines could hardly be expected to digest such interracial fraternizing. But I wouldn't let her off easily. She actually squirmed, trapped in a classic Jewish contradiction between compassion for other persecuted minorities and xenophobic fear of them.

"I don't know what I mean either," she finally muttered.

L. arrived at the restaurant on her motor scooter, managing to keep her pale green full skirt spotless—a feat that always struck me as graceful and dignified. Three years had passed since I'd seen her. She had shorn her festive mass of black curls, her hair now hugging her face like a helmet of shining black leather. It was still attractive, but more severe: This was a more somber L. than the one I'd kissed good-bye at length on our final night together.

Over dinner, Sandy and I told her of our interviews in the assembly factories and the cane fields. Afterward, we walked outside. "If you two will excuse me," Sandy said politely, and headed back to the little hotel where we were ensconced.

L. and I walked through La Romana's puddled streets, where women sat in rockers on cement stoops in front of their cottages. The damp evening exhaled the sweet ferment of the sugar refinery. Along the Río Salado, a short brackish inlet, we could see cook fires at the water's edge and smell mullet frying. We passed the three-room, slump-block cube that housed L.'s women's street theater group, Las Esclavas del Fogón. Late one night three years before, we had sneaked in and grappled each other to its unpainted cement floor. It was our first time, and we'd giggled afterward over this desecration of a feminist organization's headquarters. Now we exchanged glancing smiles at the memory.

"*Estás enamorado,*" she guessed. I nodded. "Tell me."

I told her how Cecilia and I had met on this project. I explained our common backgrounds as journalists, our shared passions for the subjects we chose to cover, and our strange ancestral connection. "It's hard to find someone compatible," L. said. "You're lucky."

If so, then why was Cecilia in Brazil by herself?

No reference was made to our own previous liaison. But as we meandered aimlessly through the humid Dominican night, I wondered why I hadn't tried to hold on to this disconcertingly alluring, intelligent female—whose company at the moment felt like such a relief, compared to the muddle Cecilia and I were lately making.

Once I had fantasized taking L. away from a life of doomed struggles in La Romana, and bestowing upon her the sumptuous bounty of the United States. Again, as then, I tried to picture this dark *caribeña* who spoke no English, bundled against the winter snows of my Arizona mountain home. Again, I found the image inconceivable, despite the thousands of Dominicans that arrive in New York every year. The difference, I reminded myself, was that in the United States, L.'s Dominican law degree would be worthless. Lifting someone out of her professional context—especially someone so deeply committed to her community—was surely out of the question, I had unilaterally concluded.

But what stopped me, a roving journalist who could work wherever there was a phone and an airport, from making L.'s country my base of operations? Language would present no problem—but an image came to mind of the La Romana club where we used to drink Quisqueya beer and watch beautiful young couples dance the liquid merengue. Try as she might to teach me to move my hips that way, it felt pretty obvious that I belonged somewhere else.

"Why so silent?"

I glanced at her. Was the real question not whether L. would wither if plucked from her element, but rather if I would still desire her outside of it? Did I embrace the woman herself, or was she just part of my experience of a place—the sensuous embodiment of a country whose plight had moved me to passion? "How do you define yourself?" I suddenly asked.

The question puzzled her. "How do you mean? As a woman?"

"I mean as a person. *Tu identidad.*"

For a few moments she pondered. It was past midnight, and we were the only ones on the streets, save for a La Romana policeman who leaned against a utility pole necking with a barefoot girl in a clinging red dress, her dark head tilted up to him. A rat scuttled past them. "Just one more *caribeña,*" she finally answered. "Just another faceless person, cluttering up this island."

"You're hardly one of the faceless masses. You have a profession, you are part of a sisterhood that raises your community's awareness, you—"

"That is exactly what I am. One of the masses. Whose protestations don't make one bit of difference."

I started to disagree, but she took my arm and gently turned me to face her.

"Listen, Alan. The only awareness this community has is that we have no rights. To anything. Foreigners come here and get whatever they want. Everything is given to them. Dominicans don't get that kind of treatment in other countries, and we don't get it in our own. *Somos nada.* We're nothing. No one hears us." She gestured at the company town around her, and beyond. "So much land here now belongs to foreigners, that the only reason we still have room to stand is because so many people are fleeing in *yolas.*"

Two nights later, Sandy and I stood in Miches, a village at the sandy eastern edge of the Dominican Republic, watching three sisters—workers who sewed baby wear all day in a factory owned by Gerber's—gaze across the Mona Passage toward Puerto Rico, assessing their chances. An east wind had kicked up a light chop on the surface of the water, and carried bits of foam onto the beach.

The little Miches anchorage was empty, but the steady thonk of a hammer we could hear coming from just beyond a nearby rise was someone building another *yola*.

Out on the high seas, these women knew, smugglers would threaten to throw them to the sharks unless they paid more money, and bandits on the Puerto Rican side likely awaited to mug and rape them. Many crude wooden *yolas* never made it across the treacherous currents, and simply disappeared. The government admitted that each month up to ten thousand Dominicans risked fleeing to Puerto Rico in rowboats, while behind them desperate Haitians appeared in their place. The Puerto Ricans, of course, headed for New York: These islands were like slippery stones upon which people leapt about, frantically seeking firm ground.

Yet they were also so unbearably beautiful. The scalloped shorelines, the transparent sea, the groves of perfect coconut palms, the hibiscus and flaming poincianas, the sparkling, fine-grained sand: How could humans grow so desperate in such a setting? Nevertheless, everyone was going—factory workers, even accountants and lawyers. An eight-year-old girl told us that she was no longer in school, because after waiting months for paychecks that never arrived, her teacher had gone to Puerto Rico in a *yola*. In all, five teachers had departed in wooden boats, and now none were left.

The pity I felt for these people couldn't touch the root of their problem. Very simply, my world had undermined theirs. Yet months later, when my own firmament began to quake and crumble, I would realize how quickly we forget—or deny—that we need look no further than our own families' chronicles to remind us how things can go so wrong, and so quickly. Merely a single generation before me, attorneys, professors, scientists, teachers, artisans, and businessmen who were my own blood kin had risked their lives and lost their languages doing what these three Dominican sisters, huddled together in the sand, were screwing up their courage to attempt.

One day, each of them might be somebody's grandmother in the United States, as Rebecca Weisman had been mine.

❦

She had been dead nearly a decade, and he rarely talked about her, so I was surprised one day, a few years before my father retired, when he unexpectedly detoured during a conversation about his own grandchildren—my sister's two sons—to say: "I have a hell of a lot to thank your grandmother for." I waited for the expected story about how she got them out of Russia, but something entirely different followed. "If it weren't for my mother, I would never have become what I did. When I wanted to quit law school, she refused to let me. She hollered until I got that silly idea right out of my head and knuckled down—"

"Why on earth did you want to quit law school?" This was the first I knew of such a thing. This story had certainly never emerged during those dark days when, to his disappointment, I had done exactly that. Until now, prevailing mythology had always portrayed Si Weisman's unflagging will as a template of grit and courage.

Realizing that I'd noticed this discrepancy, he actually reddened, then stammered something about wanting to be a football coach. "But my mother wouldn't hear of it. She insisted that we become professionals. And, by God, we did. Where the hell would I be today if I hadn't stuck to that?"

The conversation was now moving in a safe direction that he could control, reminding me that I would likely pay for my own foolish choice for the rest of my life. Even today, the memory of his disapproval stings; at that moment this diversionary thrust quashed my interest in further discussion. Later, I remembered his slip and wondered what it had meant. When I asked my mother, she also seemed oddly flustered, but she confirmed his brief coaching aspirations, attributing them to the struggle of having to work his way through law school.

Years passed before I discovered what all that was really about.

His explanation seemed plausible enough, because in our home, football was exalted as the first of two providential pivots in my father's destiny, the second being World War II. In his senior year, he was named an All-City tackle and captain of the North High Polars. He never forgot how the coach had changed his life by plucking him, a big Jewish kid with an accent, off the bleachers and sticking a leather football helmet on his head. The first toy my father would place in my crib was a rubber football. Football had begun his metamorphosis from immigrant to American. Girls began to notice him. He began drawing a weekly allowance of fifty cents from the bakery income for his social life.

My grandmother agreed to this indulgence, even though Harold and Herman had assumed the afternoon newspaper sales because Si had football practice, and even though the Depression was deepening. His brothers, a little resentful, went along because they were all proud of him. Somehow, my grandmother perceived that in America, success at a sport that the *goyim* played was a quicker route to esteem than knowledge of Talmud. This was a breathtaking departure from centuries of changeless *shtetl* life, but what had their Jewish faith brought them over those centuries besides persecution?

At the University of Minnesota he starred at freshman football, switching from the line to quarterback. During his sophomore year, however, he entered an accelerated program in order to begin law school a year early. The increased load ended his football career—until, that is, he resumed it with me. But that same year brought compensation for this sacrifice, in the form of Charlotte Meshbesher.

His brothers and half-sisters couldn't get over how beautiful she was. Her mother Rose's only flaw had been a straight but large nose: My mother's was perfectly proportioned to her fine cheekbones. She was five-two and had bow-shaped lips, dark eyebrows, and even darker eyes. During their five years of courtship, my dressmaker grandmother happily rose to the challenge of outfitting this *shayna punim* in their midst, arraying my mother like a living doll in wool suits, frilled skirts, long taffeta dresses—whatever she found in fashion magazines, Rebecca made for her.

Charlotte auditioned well for the role of daughter-in-law. Several nights a week she cooked meals and washed dishes at the Weisman house. She learned to sew from her *mechutenasteh* and became an adopted older sister to Frieda and Florence, who idolized her. My grandmother set out to teach this motherless girl how to properly attend to her future husband's needs. She could hardly instruct her by example: Long before, she had ceased treating her own husband with any respect whatsoever. *"Ach,"* she would dismiss him, extolling my dead grandfather Avraham's virtues right in front of Milstein, who simply hung his head and waited to be fed.

Impatient with my mother's limited third-generation Yiddish, Rebecca would frequently yell and sometimes even shake her in order to be understood. But Charlotte tolerated it. After being shunted from aunt to aunt since her mother's death and her father's withdrawal, she suddenly felt on the verge of truly belonging somewhere. She performed as she was taught, down to ironing her boyfriend's underwear. A notorious coquette at North High, once Charlotte Meshbesher met my father she focused her loyalty and affection on becoming Charlotte Weisman.

※◉◉※

"Ugh," my mother said one day, serving me tuna fish on her patio in Scottsdale, Arizona, where I sat rereading *Heart of Darkness*. "Your father used to make me read things by him."

"My father? Joseph Conrad?"

"Conrad, Thackeray, Hawthorne, Emerson—the whole kit-and-kaboodle. He used to always make me go to the theater with him, too, to see things like Shakespeare and Chekhov."

Si Weisman was possibly the only adult I knew in Minneapolis who had never attended Sir Tyrone Guthrie's world-renowned repertory theater, which opened there in 1963. "Surely this is some father to whom I've never been introduced."

"You know who I mean. Your dad used to love that kind of

thing. It was very important to him that I learned about it. Whenever he gave me a book to read or when we'd go to a play, he'd quiz me afterward to see if I understood it."

"So what in God's name happened to him? Some lobotomy nobody ever mentioned?"

"He changed. In a lot of ways."

According to my Uncle Herman, this love of literature, of which I'd never seen a glimmer, was owed to my grandmother. "While we were growing up, we were so poor that we could never afford more than one chicken for all of us to break the fast after Yom Kippur."

"So I've heard. What does that have to do with Hawthorne and Melville?"

"We couldn't afford any kind of entertainment, either. But library cards were free, and the library branch on Emerson and Sixth maintained a collection of works in Yiddish. Every week we'd be sent there for a new armful. Every night, we'd sit around the big table in my mother's sewing room and she would read to us."

I remembered that wooden table, its white glossy paint visible around the base of her black Singer sewing machine, but mostly buried under bolts of fabric and the Yiddish newspapers she subscribed to. It stood on a yellowing linoleum floor, surrounded by turquoise walls. Opposite a red plastic clock hung a large framed photograph of naked baby Frieda on a bearskin rug. Nothing in that room ever hinted to me of the Tolstoy, Walter Scott, and Ibsen she once read out loud to her children, complete with dramatic renderings of all the parts and voices. Her theatrics, Herman said, could bring even bad romance novels and potboilers to life. When Si's high school class was studying Shakespeare, she read each play in Yiddish and Russian, and then drilled him on Lear's fatal flaws and whether or not Hamlet was mad. The way his sad mother was so transformed by words later inspired Herman to seek a theatrical career.

If these sessions occurred when my own mother was present,

I never heard about it. Her main function, I gathered, and one which she was apparently happy to fulfill, was to be dutiful and beautiful. Six-year-old Florence and eight-year-old Frieda watched adoringly as she stood before the mirror applying her deep red lipstick. She painted their nails and modeled the clothes their mother made her, and everyone agreed she had a better figure than a department store mannikin—surely fulfilling the dreams of any American boy, like the one my father had become. The girls would cry at 10:00 P.M. when it was time for Si to walk her the two blocks to her current home: the wood-trimmed bungalow belonging to her Uncle Nate and Aunt Esther Meshbesher.

In January 1973, growing disillusioned and somewhat broke in my photography career, I hitchhiked from Minnesota to the Bahama Islands, to study yoga at an ashram. En route, I stayed two days in Nate and Esther Meshbesher's Miami condominium. They had begun spending each winter in Florida after Nate discovered he could get a WATS line, which meant he could still pester everyone in Minneapolis all day long. "Whaddya think, punk?" Nate said, thumping his small paunch. He stood about five-five, and still had his hair, gray since the 1940s, which he always slicked straight back. Nate Meshbesher had a way of leaning close when he talked, forcing listeners to lean away to avoid contact with his bulbous nose. Even as a child, it was this mannerism that distinguished him for me from his brother Ben, who always kept a cigar between himself and everyone else but otherwise looked exactly the same. "Pretty damn good shape for seventy-two, right?" demanded Nate. "Goddam right I am."

"You're seventy-three, Uncle Nate. You were born in 1899."

"What do you know, punk? Were you there?"

"Uncle Benny told me."

"Benny? That *meshugener*? How the hell would he know?"

I pointed out that since Benny was his identical twin, he was probably present. Nate was unimpressed. For reasons neither could recall when pressed on the subject, Nate and Benny held each other in such contempt that not only didn't they speak, but they celebrated separate birthdays: one in December, one in April. "Tell him to *gai kacken*, punk," Nate advised.

During that visit, while Aunt Esther played solitaire and munched on tranquilizers in the kitchen, Nate had me as captive audience. "Hey punk, did I ever tell you what I got your folks for a wedding present?"

No, but I'd heard what he and Benny had given my grandparents when they got married: a set of the *Encyclopaedia Brittanica*. A month later Lou and Rose discovered that the twins, twelve years old at the time, had only made the first payment, and that subsequent installments were up to them. "Uhn-uhn," I grunted. I was on the living room carpet practicing the scorpion, a tricky yoga *asana* that involved lifting my head off the ground during a headstand, so that I was balanced solely on my forearms.

Nate didn't seem to notice. He proceeded to explain that my parents got married just after my father passed the Minnesota bar examination. "Si was trying his first case, a drunk driving charge." Nate decided he knew just the way to get the young couple off to an auspicious start. "Know what I did, punk?"

"Uhn-uhn."

"Fixed the jury."

I hit the carpet with a thump, narrowly missing the corner of a glass coffee table. I rolled onto my side and gaped at him. "My father knew?"

"Sure he knew: I told him. Otherwise, how the hell would he have known he was getting a present?"

"He went along with it?"

"Oh, he got all *fahrshimelt* and started screaming that we'd get caught and his career would be ruined before it started. 'Don't be a punk,' I told him. 'Who's gonna catch us—the cops? I got them all covered too.'" He grinned his goofy Nate grin, revealing little gaps between his incisors. "And I did, too. Goddam right."

At the time I heard this story, my father was president of his county bar association and on the board of both the American Trial

Lawyers Association and the International Academy of Trial Attorneys. I knew better than to ask him about this: He'd murder Nate, or worse. But preposterous as Nate Meshbesher might be, his boasting usually didn't require him to lie, because so many outrageous stories about him were known to be true. If this one also were, what struck me most was that the father who raised me to hallow law and integrity above all else allegedly hadn't objected because jury tampering was wrong, but that they might not get away with it.

Long after both Nate and my father were dead, I asked one of Nate's sons what he thought. Ronald Meshbesher by then was Minneapolis's best-known criminal attorney. Once, when I was three, he'd taken me to North High where, holding pieces of a U.S. map puzzle upside down and backwards, he challenged his classmates and teacher to beat me at identifying the states of the union solely by their shape. No one could. Fifty years later, his whitening hair and V-shaped beard now made him uncannily resemble my great-grandfather Jake Meshbesher. When I related the tale his father had told me, he clutched his forehead and groaned.

"Even if he'd wanted to, your father couldn't have stopped him. I couldn't keep Nate out of court myself," Ronnie said. "Once I was trying a case, and I looked over and saw my father leaning on the jury box, whispering to the foreman. During the recess, I nearly strangled him. For God's sake, Dad," I told him. "The judge is going to declare a mistrial."

" 'The judge ain't calling no mistrial,' he said, swinging his key chain in my face. 'Who do you think's giving him a ride home this afternoon?' "

If my mother found a place where she could belong with my father's family, what did he find with the Meshbeshers? The family patriarch, my great-grandfather Jacob, was well-known and well-connected, venerated in the Jewish community both as a pioneer merchant and a founder of the Mikro Kodesh synagogue. Yet for an Orthodox Jew, he was a far cry from my father's sanctimonious stepfather Milstein. Jake Meshbesher chain-smoked, played poker, took two shots of whiskey before lunch and dinner, and was known to pass a bottle in *shul*. During Prohibition, he wangled a dispensation for his soft drink bottling plant to make forty-gallon lots of sacramental wine to sell to the Catholics, a thin veil for what was really going on there. The afternoon my mother returned from school to find the paddy wagon hauling off *Zaydeh* and her Uncle Nate for bootlegging wasn't the only time he got caught.

In his seventies, my great-grandfather turned over the bottling company to Uncle Nate. Soon the business went under. Soda pop, Nate claimed, had become a luxury during the Depression. They'd been offered an exclusive bottling and five-state distribution contract for a new beverage called Bib-Label Lithiated Lemon-Lime Soda, but Nate claimed that this new product, which had recently changed its name to Seven-Up, tasted too much like their own three-cent drink, which *Zaydeh* had invented from lemon juice and sugar. Nate did a sort of test-marketing, rechristening their own brand Buddy-Up after his oldest son. But business didn't improve, so he turned the Seven-Up folks down. "Whadda they know?" he reportedly said.

Nate's job also was collecting rent from the *schwartzes* who now lived in the old brick apartments and duplexes *Zaydeh* had bought when the original Jewish immigrant tenants moved into houses of their own. Sometimes Nate was gone all night on those rounds, and Aunt Esther learned not to ask what he was up to, or with whom. During Prohibition, Minneapolis, a major transshipment hub for Canadian liquor, was controlled by two bootleggers. One was a North Side Jewish cohort of Bugsy Siegel and Meyer Lansky named Isadore Blumenfeld, better known as Kid Cann. Jacob Meshbesher had known Blumenfeld since he was a kid coming around for soda pop, but he was even closer to the other local mobster, a big, barrel-chested Scotsman named Tommy Banks. Upon Jake's retirement, his son Nate inherited that friendship. He cozied up to Kid Cann as well, and often served as the liaison between the two thugs as Prohibition ended and they began dividing up the territory for various other rackets. Soon, Uncle Nate was doing well enough to purchase a two-story home on the corner diagonally across from Jacob and Bessie.

My mother went with them. But she didn't stay long, because that same year my parents were married.

⁓👀⁓

"Char wanted lots of guests and a real bridal gown," said Sylvia. "She made them bring Aunt Jennie's organ into the Mikro Kodesh. *Baubeh* and *Zaydeh* didn't like that, and neither did the rabbi—not just one rabbi, mind you: They had two. But Charlotte got her way. She wanted the wedding to be perfect. And it was."

My mother's picture from that day—it hangs on my wall now—attests to how perfect. She wears the pearls her mother-in-law, Rebecca, brought from Russia. My grandmother made her dress as well: pure white silk, more pearls embroidered at her bosom, and a long gossamer train. In her hands she holds a white, leather-bound Old Testament with their names and the date, August 14, 1938, embossed in gold. She looks not merely gorgeous, but triumphant.

My father's smile is tighter, almost embarrassed. He wears a faultlessly tailored white double-breasted linen suit and white shoes. Had not my grandmother been a master seamstress, I can't imagine how they would have afforded such clothes; even then, the fabric must have cost plenty. But my mother had worked for five years as a salesclerk in a department store, and later at a typing job Nate got her in the mayor's office, to help put my father through law school and to pay for this wedding. She was not to be denied.

Just as when, a quarter-century later, she refinanced our home to buy the wedding she dreamed up for my sister, nothing would undermine her vision. There was the matter of a cousin of my grandfather Avraham, who'd emigrated to Philadelphia and grown rich making men's underwear, which he sent by the crate-load to the three Weisman boys every Chanukah. When this boxer-shorts magnate arrived for the wedding with his family, he let it be known that he expected his daughter to be a bridesmaid. My mother took one look at this chunky cousin and declared that no fat cow was going to ruin her perfect wedding. Even my grandmother couldn't budge her. True to Rebecca's dire predictions, the magnate's antic-ipated expensive present devolved into a single pair of bath towels. *"Hob im in bod,"* my mother snorted.

Perfect was what she needed, I understand now, because all her cousins in whose homes she'd felt like a poor relation were pres-ent, and my mother intended to show them that she'd landed the handsomest husband of all—and a lawyer, to boot. Besides, she had two charming, eligible brothers-in-law to dangle before their eyes. Harold, considered even better-looking than Si, was about to graduate as a pharmacist. And there was Herman, majoring in theater at the University of Minnesota, a choice that my parents considered somewhat nuts, but it added a romantic touch for my mother to introduce him as a playwright. She was in extravagant spirits: Ronnie Meshbesher, the ring bearer that day, remembers her giggling through the ceremony.

Ronnie's older sister, Shirlee, remembers something else. As they dressed for the wedding, my mother confided to her that the night before, she and Si had spent the evening readying their apartment. "And on that night, they did it for the first time."

This was startling news, but not exactly for the reason that Shirlee thought. "She told you that?"

"She did. Can you believe it? Your mother?"

Throughout our upbringing, my mother had regularly vowed to disown my sister, or worse, if she weren't a virgin on her wed-ding night. The threat of excommunication upon premarital con-summation must have been especially excruciating, because Cooky met my brother-in-law Gary when she was only fifteen. As he was just starting college and later went on to law school, they waited a total of seven years before marrying—and, my sister claims, they actually did wait. So she should have been stunned by Shirlee Meshbesher's story of how my mother squandered her maidenhood with a mere twenty-four hours to go.

But by the time I told her, we knew it was a lie, calculated to divert Shirlee from guessing the truth.

CHAPTER 6

"Happy birthday, Mom. It's me."

"Same to you, my little birthday *boychik*. But our birthday's not until tomorrow." I was born the day she turned thirty-two, eighteen months after my father returned from World War II.

"There aren't any telephones where I'm going to be tomorrow. So I'm calling tonight."

"I'm so glad you did. Where are you now, honey?"

From the door of the phone booth I saw the dark waters lapping against the river quay. "At the mouth of the Amazon, Mom. In Brazil."

"Dad and I were there. I hope you're having fun."

"Not exactly. But work is going well."

"We went to Rio, and to Brasilia."

"I was there two days ago."

"We liked Brasilia, all those new buildings. It wasn't dirty like the rest of it down there. Is it still nice and clean?"

"Not exactly."

She asked about Cecilia. I assured her that we were working together again. "I'm glad, honey. Oh, Alan, I hope you're coming home soon."

"We have to finish up here, then go to Chile. Then our field research will be done. Maybe then."

"I just don't know what I'm going to do here anymore."

"Why? Is something the matter? How's Dad?"

"Oh, Dad. You know how he is. Except now he's worse. Whenever I take him with me to a store or restaurant, he yells at me and it embarrasses me so. You wouldn't believe how he yells. The only reason he's not yelling now is because he's sleeping."

"Ma, he's always yelled. When didn't he yell?"

"When we were dating he never yelled at me."

"So what changed?"

"Alan, how should I know? I've been asking myself that for years."

"How's your mom?" Cecilia asked, when I returned to our table.

"She sounds ten years older."

"Why?"

"After five-and-a-half decades, suddenly she can't take my dad's yelling anymore." For Passover, I explained, she had taken him to *seder* at a synagogue, and he'd immediately plunged into the food. When my mother whispered that he had to wait until they finished the service and said the blessing, he'd hollered that he'd eat when he goddam pleased, and that she and everyone else could just go to hell if they didn't like it.

"God, has he always been like that?"

"Normally, he wouldn't embarrass her in public—I take that back," I said, recalling several times when he'd shrieked at me in front of my friends for some infraction, and I knew he'd done the same to her. "What I meant was: Before he started slipping, he would never have embarrassed *himself* in public. But yell, yes. That he always did."

"I suppose that's where you get it."

"Ceci, *por favor*. This is my birthday dinner. Can we just move on, for a change? Haven't I been good lately?"

"I don't know. I haven't seen you for weeks."

Good point. I decided not to mention a night in the Dominican Republic when a disagreement with Sandy had somehow

95

escalated into a screaming fit. She reached for my hand. "Yes, you've been good. Sorry."

We were in a waterfront restaurant in Belém, eating thick fillets of an oily river fish called *tucunaré*, smothered in onions and some herb that momentarily numbed the palate before allowing the flavors to rush back in. It was an oddly pleasant sensation, and not unlike my reunion with Cecilia. Being apart for nearly three weeks had not diminished my feelings, but somehow I'd managed to temporarily store them in my emotional freezer. In the plane, I kept trying to generate more warmth than foreboding over seeing her. When I finally did, the ice cracked quickly, and affection trickled forth, then fairly gushed.

I had flown to Rio from the Caribbean, then shuttled to Brasilia to interview a U.S. development expert Cecilia had found, who, after two decades of bringing progress to the Amazon, had concluded that his efforts had only primed its destruction, and was ready to confess. Cecilia, meanwhile, was finishing what was supposedly the hopeful story of our series, about a cooperative founded to harvest a renewable resource, Brazil nuts, for a forest-friendly, sweetened mixture called Rainforest Crunch. But during a quick phone call between flights, I'd gathered from her that the project had already soured. Apparently, the product had proved so popular that the co-op couldn't keep up with demand. So their U.S. client, whose ads touted its cultural and environmental sensitivity, had started buying nuts from a commercial supplier widely accused of exploiting workers.* "Gotta run," she'd said. "Tell you the rest when I see you."

Which she had done, immediately upon banging through the doorway of the hotel room where we rendezvoused. "So as I started to explain," she said, untangling from her backpack and recording gear, "the co-op gatherers worked incredible hours, increased their production, but they also voted to pay themselves a living wage, which meant raising the price of their Brazil nuts—above, it turns

*Rainforest Crunch is now produced by a different company.

96

out, the going rate on the world market. So now the Rainforest Crunch people are telling them they have to learn to operate in a competitive world economy, and the co-op is demanding to know why they have to live with no electricity or running water, while their partners in the United States have modern offices and fly around in jets and wear shoes. They claim these U.S. do-gooders are just profiting in the name of the forest peoples, and—"

"Hi, Cec," I interrupted. "You look great." She did: rosy and healthy in jeans and an untucked white cotton blouse, her sleeves rolled up.

She stopped and looked at me. Quite visibly, it dawned on her that it was nice to see me. She smiled. I smiled back.

"It's just that I get so frustrated, seeing all that we've seen," she suddenly blurted over my birthday dessert: passion fruit ice cream. "Why can't our stories do something besides just depress people? Don't you worry that we're getting too depressed from all this?"

I considered the difference between being depressed and being genuinely sad. Depressed didn't seem like the right term for what we were feeling—it reduced the tragedies we had witnessed to the dreary level of somebody's neurosis. By comparison, neurosis felt like a luxury of the privileged, an emotional inconvenience in otherwise comfortable lives. Dispossessed people, like those we were meeting, weren't merely inconvenienced. They'd been deprived of their birthright. They'd been amputated from their own source. They'd been profaned.

Cecilia misread my silence. "Sorry, Alan. We were talking about your parents. I got off the subject. Your mother's really having a hard time, ¿sí?"

"That's okay. We can talk about something else. No, wait. I do want to say something about my parents."

"Fine. Tell me."

"I feel so helpless, Ceci," I said, "knowing my dad's on the way down, and knowing that my mother won't accept that. She won't stop treating him like a sick child she can cure with enough food and unconditional love. I get encouraged, because for the first time in her life she's admitting how angry she is at him. But then she drags him to some specialist for more tests and different pills. She keeps denying that he has Alzheimer's, and insists that it's 'just strokes' and that he can be rehabilitated. She keeps trying new diets on him. And I just want to tell her—oh, hell: It wouldn't make a difference, anyway. What I'm really feeling is that this is our joint birthday, and I ought to be there. I miss them. I really do."

She took my hand. "I've never heard you say that. Tell me what you miss about them."

"Just them."

"No. Tell me a story of something really beautiful or really important about them."

Something beautiful. I tried to think. I had a sudden recollection of my mother sitting me on her knee and singing to me in the sweet voice she inherited from my grandmother Rose, then embracing me. She always hugged us—as did my father. Despite his harrowing tirades, we were a physically affectionate family. No matter how anxious Cooky and I got whenever the sound of the garage door opening signaled his arrival, we never questioned that we were loved. I recalled how, when I was small, he would take me in his arms and, drowsy with drink, fall asleep with me on his lap. Then there was the jewelry he bought my mother each Valentine's Day, because it was their six-month anniversary. And the roses—"Okay," I said. "Every Fourth of July, the anniversary of the day they met in 1933, my dad sent my mother long-stemmed red roses. Each year he added another rose for every year they had been together. I remember when I was twenty-one, realizing they'd known each other thirty-five years. That was a lot of roses."

"You're using past tense. Doesn't he do it anymore?"

"Somewhere around fifty-three or fifty-four roses—1986, I think—he stopped. We realized that he had just forgotten: By then he was forgetting everything else, too. But my mom still took it pretty hard. So the next year, my sister and I sent them in his name. Same for her birthday presents and valentines, ever since. The cute part is she knows we're doing it, but she still calls to tell us what he got her and reads us the soupy cards we buy for him to sign."

"What loyalty."

"You don't know the half of it."

"Didn't she ever disagree with him?"

"Disagreeing with him and being loyal are two different things. I only know of one time she defied him in public. And when he ended up vindicated and a hero, I'm quite sure that she never wavered again."

***

My mother's sole public rebellion against my father had occurred one evening in October 1942, in my Uncle Mike and Aunt Sylvia Gold's secondhand Buick. They were headed to dinner. The Golds had brought along Mike's best friend, a young pharmacist named Arnold Grais, who was on his first date with Ethel Stein, the daughter of a prominent Jewish pharmacist from northern Minnesota. When they picked up my parents, Ethel was struck by what a beautiful pair Charlotte and Si Weisman made as they came down the path through the fallen leaves. "Where are we going?" Charlotte asked, looking around the car happily as they piled inside.

"Ethel's sister Tessie is at the Nicollet Hotel, meeting her fiancé," said Sylvia. "He's on leave before he ships overseas."

The car grew strangely quiet. Soon, Ethel noticed that Si and Char, pressed into the corner of the backseat, were whispering heatedly. Halfway to downtown Minneapolis, Charlotte expelled a loud gasp. "How can you do this?" she suddenly shrieked. "You have a child!"

"Goddammit, Charlotte," Si hissed, "I said to keep your big mouth shut!"

Immediately, Sylvia was leaning over the seat. "What's wrong, Char? What'd he do to you? You tell me!"

"Sylvia, mind your own business!" my father roared.

"Let's quiet down, everybody," my Uncle Mike begged.

Nobody paid attention to him. Si, it appeared, had enlisted. "How can you do this to me?" my mother sobbed again.

"Nobody's doing anything to you. I have to do this for my country."

"And who's going to take care of Char and the baby while you're off getting killed?" Sylvia demanded.

"Sylvia, please. Sylvia!" pleaded Mike. "Let's all try to calm down now. Simon? Can we all quiet down?"

"You keep out of this, Mike," growled my father, and at the menace in his voice, Ethel Stein clung tighter to the arm of her date, Arnold, the only other person not screeching. It was a first date she never forgot, partly because she and Arnold Grais held on to each other for the next fifty years, partly because Mike and Sylvia became her best lifelong friends—and partly because, for reasons she never completely comprehended, by the end of that night she also grew to love each of my parents. Unlike Mike and Sylvia—who, by sticking up for Charlotte, became objects of my father's wrath until the war was over—the future Ethel Grais sensed that somehow they were both right.

᠅᠅᠅

It wasn't until the day in 1972 when we spread the pictures I'd taken for my father's sixtieth birthday party on my mother's living room floor that it occurred to me that in 1942, when he joined the army, he was already thirty years old. That was half his life ago—a half that, beginning with the Russian Revolution, was more upheaval than anything else. But the most tumultuous years were yet to come.

From a cabinet my mother hauled out three bulky photo albums she'd begun when she met him. With my sister, we began choosing pictures to pair chronologically with my shots of his dwellings. Many of her photos were from high school—she with her girlfriends, he in his football uniform. There were a few of the family in the Ukraine that my grandmother had contributed, although none showed the house my grandfather Avraham had built. Their courtship was well-documented, with many shots of my mother posing in smart outfits my grandmother had sewn for her, and several of my father with his brothers, Harold and Herman. My grandmother was represented, somehow growing both smaller and thicker through the years, but there was only one of my Aunt Florence and none of her dead sister, Frieda.

"You're not using that one," my mother said, removing a rather pretty picture of Florence, posed in the arms of the clarinet player who later became her first husband. "Your father would have a fit, he's so mad at her."

My parents hadn't talked to Florence in years. I didn't ask why. I was used to them being mad and not speaking to people. "Why aren't there pictures of Frieda? Shouldn't we have one?"

"Probably because she died so young," my mother said. "It's just as well—we don't want to make your father sad on his birthday. We should look for happy pictures."

My sister and I exchanged glances. This would require inspired editing. "Happy pictures," echoed Cooky. "Got that, little brother?"

"I can hardly wait until we get to the part about World War II."

"Your father," my mother reminded us, "was a wonderful soldier. Don't you ever forget that. He risked his life for you kids."

Apparently full-strength revisionism was in force, so we nodded in agreement and returned to the task at hand. We chose a wedding picture. I matched it to a slide of their first apartment, the lower half of a brick North Side duplex. "Do we have any from when you were newlyweds?"

She found just one, showing my father in a black vest and white shirt, clowning with three male friends on the floor. I recognized one of them; his wife and my mother were practically an

Olympic shopping team. "Hey," I said. "Did we remember to invite them?"

"*Hob im in bod*. Who wants those two?"

"Isn't she one of your best friends?"

She gave a little shudder, suggestive of trying to rid herself of an insect crawling on her. Another one she wasn't talking to. One challenge we hadn't even dealt with yet were pictures showing any of the Meshbeshers. Except for her sisters, my mother was no longer on speaking terms with most of her relatives, either. "What'd she do to you?" I asked.

"That *schtunk*. She's been running around on her husband for years. She still is."

"So?"

"So I don't want to have anything to do with her. I don't think that's the way married people should behave. Don't let me ever catch you doing that."

"I'm not married," I reminded her.

She turned to Cooky. "That goes for you, too."

"Mother, please." My sister, who refused to date anyone else for three years while the boyfriend she had chosen for her future husband was away at college, could pass any loyalty test that my mother could.

"Back to the pictures," I suggested brightly. "I don't see anything until Dad's gone into the army and you and Cooky are living at Uncle Nate's. There's a four-year gap from when you got married in 1938 until when she was born in 1942. What happened?"

Several things had happened, all supposedly secret. Within months of their wedding, my parents' conjugal bliss was foundering. The stress had commenced even before their nuptials, when my father's half-sister Frieda sickened. A phys ed teacher wouldn't excuse her from swim class, and a bad cold advanced to pneumonia, then flared into encephalitis. Frieda was barely thirteen when my grandmother rolled back the living room carpet and laid her out on the bare floor, then summoned her children to gaze upon their beautiful dead little sister. It was during this vigil that her husband, Milstein, committed his fatal error.

Perhaps he was groping for an Old Testament explanation for the death of his daughter. The one that occurred to him, an object lesson he shared with everyone as they mourned over her body, was that God had punished her because she failed to properly honor her father. Him.

Harold had to restrain Herman from leaping at him. "You bastard," he sputtered, "she waited on you hand and foot!" Fortunately, my father wasn't present, because no one could easily restrain him. Nearly sixty years later, Herman was still livid over his stepfather Milstein, whom my grandmother Rebecca divorced shortly thereafter. The one thing everyone agreed was that nobody could fault sweet Frieda, ever. Frieda cooked and cleaned, doted on her father and brothers, coddled her little sister Florence, and always helped her mother.

"That's exactly what she was doing when she got sick," Herman told me. "My mother was in the hospital, and though Frieda was sick herself, she kept doing everything—cooking, cleaning house, washing clothes. She worked herself to death."

I'd never heard that part of the Frieda story. "Why was Grandma in the hospital?"

We were at his dining room table in Silver Springs, where, a few years earlier, I had brought Cecilia to meet him. This time, I'd come alone. "We weren't supposed to know why my mother was in the hospital," Herman said slowly. "But afterwards I found out. It wasn't actually a hospital. She'd gone to have an abortion."

"Come again?"

He cleared his throat. "An abortion. My mother had an abortion."

I glanced at Aunt Margaret, weeping silently in her wheelchair. Herman sat with his elbows on the table, his temples propped against his fists, eyes cast downward. In a monotone, he told me how my grandmother Rebecca had taken a bus by herself to a small town north of Minneapolis, where a doctor took care of her.

"It was the Depression. We couldn't afford more mouths to feed. And I don't think she wanted to bear any more children by Milstein. Not that she didn't love her daughters. But she'd had enough of him." He named a doctor, well-known in the Jewish community, who had come to their house, whom he overheard discussing it with his mother. "I gathered that he arranged it for her with the doctor up north."

My poor grandmother must have blamed herself for Frieda's death until her own. In the space of a few days, not only had she undergone the tragedy of giving up an unborn child, but, possibly as a consequence, endured the unspeakable pain of losing another. Talk about God's punishment: Small wonder that Frieda's death meant the end for Milstein and her. "It's so sad," I said. "And so strange to think of an Orthodox Jewish woman having an abortion."

"It happened. Jews are no different from everyone else. She wasn't the only one, you know."

"What do you mean?"

He averted his eyes. "What?" I repeated.

"Your mother did."

"My mother?" *My mother?* I felt the world spinning backward.

Herman stared at my microphone. I was accustomed to how people often utter things to journalists they hadn't planned to say—or, to their own surprise, blurt memories unrecalled for years. Interviews can become unexpectedly confessional, but there's a key distinction between them and the Catholic rite of confession, which is a way to voice a secret without violating secrecy. Only a priest and God will hear—or, in the secular form of confession, only a therapist. But what people do in interviews is the opposite: They know they're making a public declaration. Perhaps later they regret it, but at this literal moment of truth, so much catharsis is straining just beneath the surface that revelation simply explodes. I had seen it often, but never before had I been among the targets for the shrapnel fragments of truth that, once expelled, can lodge and wound deeply. *My mother? My unborn . . . did I almost have an older—what? A brother?*

"Why?" I asked my uncle.

My father was halfway through law school when he learned that she was pregnant. He announced that he was quitting to get married, but my grandmother Rebecca would hear none of it. "You'll end up a *zhlub*, a nothing," she screamed, and proceeded to do what no one else ever did: outshout him.

"I'll coach football," he kept arguing, but she prevailed, and took my mother up north to the same doctor where she'd gone herself.

Later, two others corroborated this story. One had overheard them arguing; the other learned it straight from my mother. It explained a lot of things. "It doesn't explain a damn thing to me," said my aghast sister. "My God, do you realize . . ." Her throat, already choked from weeping, was clogged by a swarm of responses trying to emerge simultaneously.

"I do, Cooky," I said, holding her. I realized all the different things she must be feeling. Rage, for instance, over having been duped by our mother's fanatical cult of virginity.

"The utter hypocrisy! All those years she rammed that crap down my throat about how no man would stay with me if I let him do *that* before we were married. And, all that time, she herself. . . ." She stopped. "Oh, poor Mother," she moaned. "My God, it must have killed her. All those years, acting like—"

"She did it to protect you, Cook. She didn't want you to go through what she did."

She dabbed at her eyes. "God. Can you imagine the shame she felt? She must have been ashamed all her life. And so needlessly; it's nothing any woman should ever have to be ashamed of. Dammit, it should be her choice."

I agreed, on all counts. How wretched I felt for her. How unjust her shame. But I also knew something else that my sister couldn't, because she'd been spared such trauma herself. And that was: how fathomless the loss. Because I'd been there.

They'd waited until my father graduated law school to get married. Two years later, my mother began suffering from mysterious stomach pains. At the time, she was working fifty hours a week at a magazine clearing-house and keeping their apartment utterly immaculate. Once, when my Aunt Ellie visited her, my mother led her to the couch, then vacuumed the rug from the door where she'd entered, right up to her feet.

If she wasn't cleaning, she was doing laundry. "I want Si's shirts to be perfect," she told Ellie. "And underwear—do you know he only used to get clean underwear on Saturdays, when we'd go out? I give him freshly washed, ironed, and folded undershorts every day. He can't believe it. He's so grateful." Since they couldn't afford a washer, she did everything by hand, even ironing the sheets. "Your dad and I were so poor," she would tell us, "that half the time we lived on ketchup and crackers." She left out the part about how often she ate them alone.

By their second anniversary my father rarely came home evenings. By day, he shared an office downtown with another fledgling lawyer. By night, as he explained to my mother repeatedly, he was out trying to drum up cases. I have a memory of their fights during that time, a recollection confirmed later by my Aunt Sylvia, but mystifying because I wasn't born until seven years later. Perhaps, back when I was so small that they thought I couldn't understand, I overheard them flinging old sins at each other. Or perhaps some memories, coded in chemistry, slip in among the chromosomes that get passed along:

CHARLOTTE: "Exactly what kinds of cases do you expect to find hanging out in bars with a bunch of hoodlums and prostitutes?"

SIMON: "Who the hell do you think's hiring brand-new attorneys? Mr. Pillsbury? I don't know why you're always nagging me. Look who your Uncle Nate does business with."
CHARLOTTE: "You didn't go to law school to become like my Uncle Nate."

Yes, but at times during the Depression he probably wondered why he'd even bothered. And Nate Meshbesher, meanwhile, was doing just fine. True, the liquor store he'd opened after the soda pop factory went under suffered from neglect, but that was because Nate was having fun playing bagman for Tommy Banks, the former bootlegger who had branched into other activities after booze was legalized. Banks, resplendent in tailored silk suits, with every shining hair in place under his fedora, held court in his mistress's suite in the Dyckman, the newest hotel in downtown Minneapolis. Mainly, he surrounded himself with a coterie of big Irishmen, but whenever his Cadillac was double-parked in front of the hotel, Nate Meshbesher's green Buick was often right there behind it.

No one ever knew exactly what Nate did for Tommy Banks, but it involved a great deal of cash, much of which was hidden in ammunition boxes in Nate's basement. At Christmas, Nate and his eldest son Buddy made the rounds in the gangster's Cadillac, delivering presents to the police and judges and city councilmen. "Please remember to thank Tom for us," the police chief and his wife would remind Buddy, standing in the doorway under the wreath.

And Buddy would, earning himself a crackling new hundred-dollar bill. Nate would get—well, nobody knew for sure. It must have been worth it, because he was always eager to play go-between for Banks and Kid Cann, whose rackets ranged from police protection to granting liquor licenses. Strange men showed up at Nate and Esther's house at strange hours, some of whom my father followed into Minneapolis's nether straits as he scrambled after work.

The thick clipping file at the *Minneapolis Star and Tribune* on my father's legal career doesn't document any cases he tried during the late 1930s when he was just beginning. In applications to Officer Candidate School and the army's Judge Advocate Corps, he described himself as specializing in "trade regulation and trade practices." This puzzled me, because business was always his blind spot. Poring through a yellowing stack of papers my mother saved, I determined that the extent of this trade expertise was his appointment as counsel to the Minnesota Package Liquor Dealers' Association, a position that sniffed strongly of Uncle Nate.

Doubtless, it paid just a token retainer. Whatever other clients he was defending probably didn't tip hundred-dollar bills like Tommy Banks. For the five years between his marriage and his departure for the European front, my father reported average annual earnings of $1,800.

Press attention or not, my mother knew about some of my father's unsavory associates, because rumors began drifting around the North Side about Char and Si Weisman. She was often overheard yelling at him for running around until all hours with lowlifes. He hollered back and stayed away more. Early in 1941, their third year, her intestinal anguish became too acute to ignore. Her sister Sylvia made her see a doctor, then grew frightened when the doctor forwarded her to a specialist. Stomach trouble was the first signal of their own mother's fatal decline.

At a time when she was probably earning more than my father, my mother had to quit her job. For months she was bedridden, and, I was later told in whispers, highly medicated. Only dark glimpses of this story ever reached my sister and me—fragmentary remarks that gradually accumulated until they coalesced and formed a critical mass. There were the hints about my father's drinking during those post-honeymoon Depression years, when he discovered that even though a law degree might mean he was no longer an ignorant immigrant, he was still a Yid in a city where Jews mostly hovered at the fringes or wormed their way into cracks. We heard that his womanizing was frequently the topic of their loudest fights. Eventually, the euphemism used to describe my mother's condition—"gastric ailment"—sharpened into "nervous breakdown." Was this abdominal manifestation an echo of her mother's death, or of the child wrenched from her womb so that my father could stay on the path of his career? Or both?

There is no clear recollection of what kept them together, though I suspect her illness made the difference. My father was capable of cruelty, but also of remorse. By late summer of that year, when she learned that she was pregnant again, her dark spell lifted.

The respite was brief, however, because between that discovery and the birth of my sister, Pearl Harbor intervened.

"Your father," my mother would say, shaking her head at me. "You're stubborn just like your father. He didn't have to go into World War II. He had a baby. He was a lawyer. When he decided he wanted to do something, heaven forbid anybody try to stop him. And then it wasn't enough for him just to enlist. You know him. He always had to be the best. In basic training, he had to be the top soldier in his camp. They weren't going to let him just be a lawyer. Oh, no. They needed soldiers like him."

"Your father," my Aunt Sylvia said, "drove your mother crazy with that damn war. For months after he enlisted Char wouldn't sign the papers, and he'd threaten her, telling her she had to, and she would come crying to me. He didn't have to go. But something was boiling inside of him. He wanted to fight. He wanted to get into the thick of it. He wouldn't take a commission, like every other college student or lawyer did. He wouldn't even take a battlefield commission when they offered it to him." She paused, considering something she'd just said. "Maybe that was the only thing he could do about that anger inside him that came out against everybody. I think he carried it since he was a little boy and saw his father murdered. It was subconscious. He didn't know what he was angry at."

"Why the hell do you *think* I went into the army?" my father snarled. "For your information, there was a war going on. Hitler wanted to rule the world. Japan attacked us. I worked damn hard to make the grade in this country, and those bastards wanted to take it away from us. Let me tell you something, mister. You don't turn your back on the place that's given you everything. I just hope you're prepared to defend it someday when the next bastard tries to take it away. You damn well better be, if you know what's good for you. You kids don't know how good you've got it."

"Look," said Buddy Meshbesher. "Don't be naive. Your father went in because he was broke. He had a wife and a kid, and he was trying to make a living, and was getting nowhere. Now what would solve that? You go into the army, they give you a salary, and an allowance for your wife and kid. Your father saw World War II as a financial solution."

There was something to all these versions. Indisputably, he was a patriot, and now that he had a baby to feed, he was certainly under more pressure than ever to make a living: Among those yellowed papers, I discovered that in those desperate days my father had even applied to the FBI, emphasizing his abilities both in the Russian he learned as a child and the German in which he excelled in high school, it being a small linguistic step from Yiddish. He never received a reply. As for his anger, rather than resolving it, he soon had yet one more reason to be furious.

My sister, named Rochelle for my grandmother Rose, was born on May 3, 1942, the same day as Dagwood and Blondie Bumstead's comic-strip daughter, hence her nickname Cooky. Ten days later, my parents were awakened after midnight by the telephone. It was my grandmother. Harold hadn't come home.

"Did you call the drugstore?" my father asked. At the time, Harold was working at a pharmacy in St. Paul. She had tried there: No answer. My grandmother was convinced that something had happened to him. Harold was now the main support of their mother and her surviving daughter, Florence, because their other brother, Herman, had a commission in the army transportation corps and was in Camp Upton, Long Island, awaiting orders to ship out. Harold had a girlfriend, but it was unthinkable for him to stay out late without calling.

My father dressed and drove across the river to St. Paul, a half hour away, to the Walgreen's where Harold worked. The lights were still on and the door was unlocked. Behind the counter, he found his brother lying facedown, unconscious.

Harold awoke the next afternoon in the hospital, diagnosed with pneumonia. He'd been ill for days, but had said nothing because they needed money and there would be none if he stopped working. The doctors guessed that he'd collapsed from exhaustion, and after three days of hospital bed rest he seemed better. But then they noticed something else: His kidneys were inflamed and wouldn't respond to treatment. Within a week, uremic poisoning set in.

"Did you know about your Uncle Harold committing suicide?" my father's cousin Harry Friedman asked me fifty years later. We were in Minneapolis, eating lunch in a Greek restaurant.

"Saint Harold? That's impossible."

"It doesn't seem likely," Harry agreed. "But that's what people said. You never heard anything about that?"

All I'd ever heard was that Uncle Harold, whom I never knew, had been canonized for his perfection, like his dead sister Frieda and my grandfather Avraham. I was named for him—my middle name, Harley—as was Uncle Herman's son, Harlan. Harry Friedman, who knew his cousin Harold from the day he arrived from Russia, concurred with everyone's opinion of him. But Harry was also a doctor on the University of Minnesota medical school faculty, and I knew he wouldn't refer to a death casually. "The story," he told me, "was that Harold was depressed and was taking drugs. As a pharmacist, he had access to them. They say he overdosed."

"That's rubbish," said Aunt Sylvia. "Harold was sick as a dog. Sure, he may have overdosed, but because he was trying to cure himself, not kill himself. He was self-medicating the way all those pharmacists do, except he took too much. And it infected his kidneys."

"Si found him in the drugstore the day they brought Cooky home from hospital," Aunt Florence, my father's half-sister, told me. "They say he committed suicide: that he took an overdose of pills and was climbing up a ladder and he fell. Maybe he was manic-depressive. I remember his behavior was erratic at times. He would spend a lot of money, and he wasn't really like that. I think that's what was wrong with him, though they said it was because he took on so much responsibility. Just like when Frieda died, no one ever talked to me about it, ever. But I would overhear things. Things your father said."

"Bull," Uncle Herman said. "Harold wouldn't do something like that to our mother. He was the epitome of goodness. I heard he was putting in seventy to eighty hours a week at Walgreen's. He died of overwork."

Herman had been summoned from his barracks at Camp Upton by his captain, who told him there was an emergency at home. The Red Cross loaned him plane fare to Minneapolis, then garnisheed his wages for a year until it was repaid. My parents met him at the airport.

Harold was laid out in a coffin in the family living room. "My mother had them open it. 'Here is your brother,' she said. I was home less than twenty-four hours."

"You heard nothing of suicide?"

"Years later. I don't believe it."

"Did you ever ask my father about it?"

"I never discussed Harold's death with Si or your mother. We always thought that the good die for no reason and bastards like my stepfather go on living."

Because they were Orthodox Jews, there was no autopsy. The hospital records I located seemed to support the theory of an accidental overdose. Harold had been admitted with bronchial pneumonia. Three days later, he developed acute inflammation of the kidneys, and terminal uremia three days after that. It was likely that he had been trying sulfa drugs, newly available in the early 1940s. An incorrect dosage, or failure to drink large amounts of fluid, would cause the sulfa to crystallize in the kidneys, causing irreparable damage. Such a scenario would fit Harold's last few days, when he seemed to improve as the pneumonia subsided, even though his ruined kidneys were about to shut down.

My parents had just moved to a new four-plex with their baby. My mother and my Aunt Sylvia took turns watching Cooky and going to the hospital to see Harold. One morning he was sitting up in bed, joking with my mother. That afternoon, he died.

"We were all sobbing. Your grandmother was literally tearing her hair out. But your father sat there reading the newspaper. How could he be so cold?" Sylvia asked.

There is much I will never understand about my father, but I knew the answer to this one: ineffable fury. Normally, he would shout; in fact, to him, shouting meant that things were normal. As much as I feared his bellowing rages, especially when he embarrassed us publicly, I dreaded his silences even more. They meant that someone had erred unpardonably.

Who was he so angry with? For one, himself: He was maddened by his own helplessness, unable to stop his father, then his sister Frieda, and now this brother from dying.

Then, Harold: The suicide rumor, I knew well, would have triggered my father's greatest antipathy: a loathing for mental weakness. Once, when I was eight, we visited Aunt Sylvia and Uncle Mike, then living in California. Their oldest child, my cousin Dick, a shy, curly-headed boy bright enough to repair televisions when he was fourteen, was already under assault from inexplicable fears that would soon burst into lifelong schizophrenia. My father watched my mother and aunt try to soothe him, then took over. Grabbing Dick's trembling shoulders, he shouted pointblank, "There's not a damn thing wrong with you. Now shape up!"

Shape up: Early on, I'd learned that fear and pain were never to be acknowledged. The first time I ran home, seven years old, bloodied and tearful after three older boys jumped me for being Jewish, my father ordered me to stop crying, wash my face, and report back to him. A few minutes later, biting my lower lip, I stood at attention before him. He handed me paper and pencil. "Write this down," he dictated: "Laugh and the world laughs with you, cry and you cry alone." He made me tack it to my bulletin board where I'd see it every day.

Later, I never uttered a peep when I repeatedly dislocated my shoulder on high school athletic fields. But like weighted corpses in a river, things inexorably work their way to the surface. One afternoon during my sophomore year in college, I suddenly found myself transfixed by the pebbled concrete pavement three stories below my dorm window and the knowledge that would be concentrated in the microsecond before impact, after which I would never again know anything. When I finally pulled myself away from the window nearly an hour later, my heart was pummeling my breastbone, trying to bolt. A frightened trip to the infirmary led from an internist's office to a psychologist down the hall, who looked up my symptoms in a book and read me the definitions.

The following week I went home for spring break. I called my own physician. "Routine nervous anxiety," he assured me. "Nothing to worry about." He handed me a bottle of pink-and-white capsules. "Three times a day. When the bottle's empty, you won't need them anymore."

Somehow vastly relieved, I drove home. At dinner, my mother asked me how my appointment went at the doctor's.

"Are you sick?" my father asked.

"Just a little nervous anxiety—" I began, but he was already off.

"WHAT THE HELL DO YOU HAVE TO BE NERVOUS ABOUT? WHO DO YOU THINK PAYS THE BILLS AROUND HERE? YOU? YOU'RE GODDAM RIGHT YOU DON'T!"

It was the loudest sound I had ever heard. It never entered my mind to protest that since age fourteen, I had worked full-time each summer—as a stock-boy, then at McDonald's, then for years in a millwork factory, and then as a lifeguard—and banked all my paychecks toward my college tuition. At that moment, ashamed of my fragility, I could only miserably agree with him.

He jerked my chair around to face his. "Do you see me go whining to the doctor every time I've got some care in the world?" I shook my head. "Well, let me tell you something, mister. It doesn't work like that. Someday you're going to be on your own, and you'd better start stiffening that backbone of yours. And I mean now. Understand?"

"Yes."

"Yes what?"

"Yes, sir. I understand."

"That's better."

Milstein's hypochondria, I imagine, was much at the root of my father's intolerance. To that would soon be added the abominations he was about to know, which would place him in the company of brave soldiers and even actual heroes, but also of men whose emotions would disintegrate under fire. These battlefield impressions would lodge in his psyche, somewhere among the agony of his father and the resilience of his mother, and add up to a fear of being too weak to survive. The mystery of Harold's death, yet one more tragedy in my father's family, was buried with his brother, although he doubtless often wondered about it. An adjusted memory, very pure, was prepared for us, the children of Harold's brothers, about the uncle we never knew.

Grief-stricken, guilt-ridden, appalled by his brother's mortality, incensed with his own impotence and terrified of failure, my father had to lash back. He enlisted.

PART TWO

CHAPTER 7

"Alan, look at these," my mother said one day in 1988 at their home in Scottsdale. We were in the kitchen; she was holding a box made of stiff black tagboard stuffed with envelopes, each edged in red, white, and blue. I guessed immediately what they were.

"I think you should read them," she said.

"Ma, I really don't have time—"

"Take them," she ordered. She was standing in her nightgown and terry-cloth bedroom slippers, looking tiny and vulnerable. I took them. "Your father wrote these to me from the war," she said. "You know what I think you should do with them?"

"No, Mom," I replied, though I did.

"I think you should write a book about Dad."

The box of letters landed on a shelf in my storeroom. Four years passed. He died, and, acquiescent as ever, she followed a few weeks later. Shortly thereafter I locked the storeroom, rented my house, and didn't return for two years. When I finally did, it was to empty the place and put it on the market. I carted several cubic yards of my past to the dump, but when I came across the box of letters, I stuck it in a crate of framed photographs I'd inherited that had once hung in my grandmother's house in north Minneapolis. Then I went to my father's village in Ukraine and returned with much to think about. One night, while moving into a new home, I encountered the black box. I sat down, took a swig of beer, and opened it. The first letter was dated the very day he went off to war: January 28, 1943.

"My dear Meshie, I thought it well to start writing right off the bat . . ."

This missive, a postcard of St. Paul, Minnesota, was written even before his train to Camp Croft, South Carolina, pulled out of the station. Over the next twenty-four hours, he sent two more, one from Chicago and one from Cincinnati, plus a two-page letter. He was proud of her, he wrote, "for not going to pieces the night before I left. I know why I've been in love with you so much. The thought that I won't see you or Cooky today weighs heavily. This is your enlistment as much as mine, and I know you'll make good."

He wrote every day, even if it meant sneaking into the latrine at night after lights out. Within a week, it was obvious that at least *he* was making good; already he'd been named acting corporal, a squad leader with fifteen men under him. But it was also plain that he was miserably lonely. A week went by with no letters from my mother. His own now averaged six pages. When her first finally arrived, accompanied by a box of fudge, his gratitude gushed on for paragraphs. He described the rigors of boot camp—"my pants get bigger on me every day"—and kept reassuring her that taking basic training didn't mean he was preparing for infantry duty: "Everyone has to do this." His plan was to qualify for Officer Candidate School, and then military intelligence. He was sure that the fact that he spoke and wrote both Russian and German would enhance his chances.

Only a week into his war, and I was already finding surprises. All my life, the gospel according to my mother (never contradicted by her husband) was "Your father didn't even have to join the army, a man with a baby daughter. But no, he had to go. So let him go into the Judge Advocate Corps and be a lawyer for the army. Or at least go in as an officer, like all the other Jewish boys did. No. Your father wanted to fight. He wanted to beat Hitler himself. So, *chotz clotz*! He goes and becomes the best enlisted man in his entire boot camp, to make sure that they don't stick him behind a desk somewhere."

But the letters revealed that he was trying like crazy to get into Officer Candidate School.

After my first commission as a second lieutenant, I'll get to specialize in military intelligence. This means more school and additional rank when I get through. So we can be together again. You may only see me two or three nights a week, since the work is tougher the higher you go. But at least weekends I'd be home for sure.

He warned her about the competition he faced, but he was determined to be the best. He was learning to both follow and give orders, wearing the shortest haircut of his life, cutting out potatoes to trim himself into great shape, impressing his superiors by organizing a company track team. He scored a hundred in marksmanship and led his squad to the best rating in camp. All this, he wrote in letter after letter, was so they could soon be together again.

Meshie, you could nag me all day if I could have you in my arms for but a minute. It's been more than a month since I've seen you. One night on guard duty I went over our entire life together—it was thrilling to relive it all over again. Do you remember that first evening? Remember how I took your hand and how we ran off, up the knoll at North Commons? How we sat and talked and told each other our likes and dislikes in the opposite sex? Of course, my sweetheart, you remember the ecstasy of our first kiss that wonderful night! And all the ones that followed, each more thrilling than the previous—until someone caught us and yelled, "I wouldn't do that if I were you!" Remember? I am trying to explain my thoughts and getting nowhere. You just can't substitute words for kisses. I never expect to undergo greater misery than this separation.

Reading these pages, I wondered if rumors about their early marriage troubles and how he joined the army to get away from her were exaggerations. These were letters from a man to a woman he's crazy about. But then I found:

February 24, 1943
My dearest Meshie,

I received your letter in which you tell of current Northside gossip about us considering a divorce. Nothing I've heard in a long time made me so <u>disgusted.</u> Of all the mean, rotten, low-down, insidious blasphemy I've ever heard of, this wins hands down.

So something *was* going on before he left for the army. I read on:

The low, vile, rotten skunks who cooked this up are not only malicious but stupid. Any damn fool should know that if you wanted to divorce me, you would not allow me into the army, because you <u>can't divorce a soldier while he is in the army during wartime.</u> Also, if I wanted to split from you, being a lawyer I wouldn't be sap enough to get into the army and lose my residence in Minnesota—the only place I could legally file divorce proceedings against you.

For several more paragraphs, he fumed about the gossips. Then:

They have no business picking on us. God knows we've had our arguments—but only because we are honest with each other and tell each other off when we get steamed up. But darling, I've never once had any doubt about wanting you always. God only knows how much I miss you and need you now—and I'm sure you feel the same about me, or you wouldn't have stood for my temper.

I couldn't stop reading. I was privy to something extraordinary: eavesdropping on my own parents conversing before I was born.

I was meeting them, not as the fully formed benchmarks against which children measure themselves until time proves parents to be otherwise, but as youngsters just figuring out their lives. It stunned me to see my big, scary father, the hero who brought back so many German enemy scalps, petrified that his wife might leave him. It felt disorienting to be older than him, hearing this frightened kid in boot camp who happened to be my father try to convince his wife that even if she wanted to leave him, she couldn't. That, of course, was hogwash. Divorce or not, she could leave whenever she wanted, and he knew it. From then on, his letters grew more passionate and painful. Either separation had made him realize how much he loved his wife, or it had occurred to him that from a distance, he no longer wielded the considerable leverage of his formidable presence over her.

He missed his brother Herman too, who, after graduating from the University of Minnesota, had been living in New York. In between stints as a stage manager in summer stock theaters, Herman had survived by writing geographical abstracts for the WPA. Drafted in April 1942, he was accepted to officer training, and upon earning his second lieutenant bars was assigned to the army's transportation corps.

From his port of embarkation in Brooklyn, Herman wrote my father that his first assignment would be as assistant transport commander on the SS *Mariposa*, a requisitioned luxury liner ferrying troops to Casablanca in north Africa. It was normally convoy work, but because the *Mariposa* was capable of doing twenty-two knots, it would be traveling alone.

"I am very proud of him," my father wrote home. "But I am worried: His work will be very dangerous, crossing back and forth through waters patrolled by German submarines. I'm both happy and feel like crying. Don't say anything to my mom about the danger."

With her husband gone, my mother and sister moved in with Nate and Esther Meshbesher. On a trip back to Minneapolis before shipping out, Herman visited them. Apparently, Nate and Esther's sixteen-year-old daughter, Shirlee, developed a crush on the handsome young lieutenant, which my father tried to encourage.

"Though he is my brother," my father wrote Shirlee in a letter enclosed to my mother, "I haven't had a chance to get to know him as well as I'd like to. If he runs true to the breed, he may not make an ideal husband, because he'll have a temper like mine and no money to match its size. But he would certainly love some girl a lot if she married him and gave him a little girl like my Cooky."

This may have been enough to persuade Shirlee—who once saw my father pick up houseplants and throw them at his wife—to have second thoughts, as references to her prospects with my father's brother soon faded from his letters. But he wrote often about Herman, who generously shared his officers' perks by sending my father a book of army post theater passes and, on one occasion, ten dollars, because he knew what an enlisted man earned. If my father envied his little brother's swifter progression through the ranks, it wasn't apparent: He spent the money Herman sent trying to call him in New York before he shipped out.

Boot camp slogged on; his letters told of night hikes, exhaustion, of men who couldn't take the strain and ended up hospitalized, of other acting corporals who got busted back down to private. Not him. He was named top man in his platoon. He aimed to be a stern, exacting squad leader, but also fair. On Easter, he volunteered to take KP duty for one of his privates whose wife and daughter were visiting; the private had only three dollars to his name, and while others insisted on the going rate of ten dollars for KP relief, my father did it for free so the guy could afford to buy his wife dinner.

This, he told my mother, won him respect. "It got around pretty fast. All the *goyim* were saying, 'pretty white of Weisman to do it.' Funny, isn't it, how the *goyim* say that Jews are money crazy—yet it's a Jew boy who does it for nothing while the others hold out for blood money."

He was commended by his captain for arranging a volleyball tournament. He won the shot put competition in his own track meet. Encouraged by officers for his coming OCS exams, he felt confident enough to write my mother: "Are you taking care of yourself, my sweetheart? Are you keeping up your looks? Remember, honey, I want to be proud of you—don't let yourself go!"

In April she wrote that a couple they knew was breaking up. He replied, "I am disgusted with people who don't give their marriage a chance. Such people are dangerous. If their parents were smart, they would spank both of them and make them go back to each other. Believe me, if our Cooky ever comes crying to us about the way her husband treats her, I'll kick her right out and make her go back and work out her own adjustment to married life—just like her Mammy and Pappy did!"

Could my mother sense how insecure he was? Only one of her own letters survived; once overseas and on constant march, he had to burn all the pages she wrote to him. Her voice and her own concerns, though, were reflected in his replies. No, he wasn't running up to Spartanburg to hang around with southern dames, no matter what she'd heard about what went on down here. No, the USO stationery didn't mean he was going to lots of dances; it was what they gave them to write on. No, when he got commissioned, he couldn't request to be stationed stateside: "Whatever duty your name comes up for, you have to go. Otherwise, they wouldn't have any officers overseas, would they? But I am dying to be with you and Cooky again, and I'd be very happy to be sent to some post in the U.S.A. Keep your fingers crossed."

My mother, meanwhile, had been dropping hints about going to work. Her brother-in-law Mike Gold, ineligible for service because of childhood scoliosis, had begun an advertising agency. She could assist with layouts and accounts. This prospect upset my father. His shame at being unable to support them as a lawyer was clear; things had gotten so desperate that they'd had to move in with his mother and Milstein. And he wasn't crazy about Mike Gold, either, something not entirely explained by the shouting match in the car when Mike and Sylvia defended my mother the night he enlisted. In his letters, he quibbled about legal work he'd done on the Golds' recent house purchase: On the one hand, he did it for free; on the other, they never offered to pay him. There was a disagreement over furniture from my father's office that Mike was now using. When Mike apparently mentioned this to my mother, my father called him a draft-dodger.

Behind this, I suspected, lurked jealousy that had begun earlier, during the Depression when everyone was scrambling to make money. Among my father's attempts was a design for a self-lighting cigarette—remarkable, as he was both a nonsmoker and notoriously nonmechanical. Removing a pinch of tobacco from one end of a cigarette, he dipped it into powdered phosphorus and twisted the paper. Onto this, he clamped a small cap lined with sandpaper. When the cap was pulled off, the abrasive sparked the phosphorus, igniting the cigarette.

My Aunt Eleanor, who smoked during high school, was his tester, and verified that it worked, even headlong in a Minnesota blizzard. My father was so encouraged that he paid for a patent. But according to my mother, during the Depression cigarette companies wouldn't invest to retool their factories for an innovation that required not only new cigarettes but longer packs.

"No, that wasn't it," Aunt Ellie insisted. "It was because matchbook companies fought it. It would have put them out of business."

Aha—matchbooks. That, I realized, would explain a great deal, because my Uncle Mike had come up with his own invention: a matchbook that, when opened, caused a small advertisement to pop up. Not only did he sell this idea to the Universal Match Corporation, but besides paying royalties they hired him as a designer, at an excellent salary. Until he left years later to form his own ad agency, he did so well there that when his father-in-law, my grandfather Lou, resurfaced, Mike got him a job selling matchbook advertising in New Orleans that he kept for thirty-five years. Might not my proud, destitute attorney father have been seething over his brother-in-law's success in the very industry that had dashed his own chances?

"Pretty likely," said Aunt Eleanor. "You know how your father felt about disloyalty."

In his letters, he blamed the rumors about their marital distress on Uncle Mike and Aunt Sylvia, suspecting they tried to deflect attention from Mike's alleged unwillingness to serve his country by telling people that Charlotte's husband was irresponsible for leaving his family to join the army.

"I wish he could get a two-day taste of the hardships each soldier bears by being in the army while our country is at war, and while <u>the future of all Jews is at stake</u>."

His ranting about my uncle being unpatriotic—despite my mother's insistence that Mike was designing military posters and war bond ads for free—must have pained her deeply: She loved her sister and brother-in-law, and, when she began working, was grateful to them for her job. Did she understand that my father felt threatened because he'd joined the army for a steady paycheck, but with a full-time job, she would again bring in more than he did? And because he feared her independence?

He didn't admit such anxieties, of course, but instead grew self-righteous. "Not for a moment do I regret being here. Our Cooky Belle would despise us forever if we shirked from fulfilling the obligation of our generation. We both knew what we were doing when <u>we</u> enlisted. Just because it is turning out as rugged as we first suspected gives us no license to complain."

"What do you mean, 'we'?" she must have howled when she read that one.

༝꙰༝

Perhaps beginning with the house they could afford because of all the money my mother saved from her wartime employment, over the years his feud with my aunt and uncle ebbed. At the end, other than his wife, Aunt Sylvia was the only person my father still recognized. By the time I was born, they were all speaking again, and the families visited back and forth when the Golds moved out west. But what never flagged was his contempt for suspected malingers who evaded what my father considered to be a man's rightful duty. After he was shipped overseas, this litmus test of masculinity expanded to include a willingness to face actual combat. Twenty-five years later, it was a test he still held sacred, and I would fail him.

So it was a surprise in these letters from Camp Croft to see him so fearful of exactly what he would one day excoriate me for shirking. Months went by, and while he excelled at marksmanship, jiu jitsu, and bayonet exercises, his OCS application remained in incomprehensible limbo. His commanding officer assured him that he received the top recommendation in camp. He was told to prepare for a transfer after boot camp to Ft. Benning, Georgia, for officer training, and he made plans for my mother and sister to join him there. By applying for military intelligence, he wrote, he could prolong stateside training indefinitely. He encouraged my mother to splurge on a fur neckpiece: "After all, honey, officers' wives must dress nice."

But basic training ended, summer came, and still nothing. His entire class was shipped to Pennsylvania en route overseas, while he alone remained behind, awaiting assignment. The fact that he'd been singled out heartened him, but time passed and he was still taking twenty-five-mile training hikes in 115° heat. The company clerk informed him that not only did he get the highest Officer Candidate School recommendation in the entire battalion, but his rating was the highest in camp history. Nevertheless, the clerk said, some mysterious freeze was under way in OCS processing. Not even the colonel understood it.

At my mother's suggestion, he petitioned Washington for a transfer directly into military intelligence, then learned to his regret that this request now officially took precedence over his OCS ruling, meaning he would have to wait until it was resolved before he got back in the OCS queue. It was rumored that commissions were on hold because there were too many officers in the army. He sent my mother his intelligence application photo, joking that it was "to help ward off the 4-F wolves lurking in Minneapolis." But it clearly was not a joke to him.

Suddenly, in early July 1943, he learned that he was being transferred to Fort Rucker, Alabama, the following day. There was no officers' school there, but his chances of being quickly reassigned to OCS from Fort Rucker were much better. He hoped so; after months of refusing my mother's offer to see if her Uncle Nate Meshbesher could shake something loose for him, he'd finally agreed, and Nate had been squeezing Minnesota's congressmen. Correspondence had been flying between them and my father. Maybe this was finally the break he wanted desperately.

In a letter fraught with apprehension, he wrote that just before the private whose Easter KP duty he'd taken was shipped overseas, his wife came to see him off. "Then his goddam wife hung around for a month and carried on something awful with a sergeant in Company B of the twenty-ninth Regiment, until a chaplain broke it up." Arriving in Camp Rucker, he learned of a suicide the week before: A young soldier's wife had written that she'd run off with an Air Force lieutenant, and hoped her husband would get sent overseas and killed soon so she would be free. The following night the lad was issued a weapon for guard duty, which he promptly turned on himself.

> All the *shaygetzes* worry when their wives write that they are
> buying a new dress—they wonder who they are getting
> prettied up for. When I show them your snapshots, they tell
> me I'd better watch you—you're too pretty and too dolled up.
> It makes me laugh to hear them talk that way—you know
> how *goyim* are. Because, my darling, I have always believed
> in you, so much that doubt has never entered my mind. As
> for myself: Honor bright. What I tell you is the absolute
> truth. That is my full confession.

Of course, he'd told her nothing—but this was celestial music to my mother's ears. His declaration of faith was exactly what she had wanted all along. "Every night in my bunk I pray for peace and our early reunion. There is nothing else I want: Esteem and position don't mean anything to me anymore. I don't care what I do when the war is over as long as you and Cooky and I are together."

In Minneapolis, she read this letter out loud to Nate's family, then went to bed secure in her man's love and hopeful that they'd soon be reunited. Her cousin Shirlee fell asleep with the sound of my mother's voice repeating her husband's sweet words, already memorized.

The next morning Shirlee awoke to the sound of the telephone, and then my mother's voice again. But this time she was sobbing.

CHAPTER 8

❧👀☙

February 6, 1944
Pvt. Simon A. Weisman
Co. H 30th Infantry
A.P.O. 3. ℅ P.M., N.Y., N.Y.

My dearest darling sweetheart "Meshie" and "Cookybelle,"

I know you must be more than uneasy at my failure to write you in more than a month. I have been on a very active front in Italy. If you have been reading the papers, you probably may correctly infer the location. Among other things, writing was impossible.

From my end, however, I am pleased to report that the bureaucratic dam which kept your mail from reaching me has at last finally burst, and a virtual flood of long-delayed letters has inundated my foxhole. My darling, nothing except the end of the war is more welcome than your mail. It reached me at a time when I needed it the most. I must have received two hundred of your precious and inspiring communications. I would have kept all of them, but I have to burn them after reading them—all except the pictures, of course. Thanks ever so much for the package. Please send more candy, chocolate, cakes, cookies, handkerchiefs, salami—but above all, send more snapshots.

I can't tell you much about life at the front except that I have adapted to its hardships and with the Lord's help can now take good care of myself. I intend to come back the way you want me to. Someday I may be in a position to tell you more and then I will write as much as I think you can bear to know about the horrors of this curse called war.

Until next time, my loves, I am forever your loving Si and Da-da.

He'd gone nearly three months without hearing from her. Other boys who shipped across with him received mail regularly during the months he waited in Algeria with a replacement battalion in Patton's army, wondering what would happen next—and frantically wondering what was happening at home. In a V-mail on December 12, he wrote,

It has been so long since I have had a letter from you that each blank mail call is a transition from eager anticipation to pathetic disappointment. I miss you so much that a thousand of these sheets would be insufficient to describe my love and longing. Yet I must confine myself to the boundaries of this page. Therefore, consider each stroke of my pen, each punctuation mark, yes, even each blot of ink as a beat of my heart and yearning for you.

Nothing in return. At night, he stood guard in the desert, talking, he admitted, to the very stars. In her last letter, which he read just before embarking from New York in a troop transport, she had written of a friend who had just been accepted to Officer Candidate School. This, after my father had told her that all OCS quotas were closed because the army was now on a state of alert. Her tone seemed almost accusing, and he pleaded that he had no control over what the army did. If even Nate Meshbesher and his bevy of congressmen couldn't sway anyone, how could he?

Well before he arrived in Algiers, the British and Americans had finally turned the tide on Rommel's forces and liberated North Africa from the Germans. Then, with Italian Axis troops also thoroughly routed in Tunisia, by mid-1943 Italy's southern flank was now practically undefended, and the Allies could, for the first time, take the war into western Europe. On July 10, American and British forces jumped across the water to Sicily, overwhelming fierce but outnumbered resistance, and in five weeks cleared the island of Germans. By early September, the British had a foothold on the mainland, and five days later seven hundred U.S. ships bearing 55,000 men disembarked at the Gulf of Salerno, near the main road to Naples.

Over the next two months they were followed by 115,000 more, my father among them. He had been assigned to the Thirtieth Infantry Regiment of the Third Division, now fighting in the Allied Fifth Army under General Mark Clark. My mother's worst nightmare had come true.

"The army knows my qualifications, they know my education, they know my language skills. They'll put me where they feel they need me the most," he had assured her. Instead, her educated, quadrilingual husband was now a front-line foot soldier, a practically anonymous private in the division that would see more sustained battle than any other in the European Theater.

✸❀✸

As the British swarmed up the toe and boot-heel, the Americans advanced on Naples, taking it within three weeks. All this occurred nine months before the D-Day invasion at Normandy, which originally was to have been the first Allied thrust into the continent. But the summer before, Mussolini had been deposed in a coup by an anti-war faction that immediately began negotiating with the Allies. With the Italian peninsula seemingly ready to topple, it was too irresistible for Eisenhower and his staff to pass up. Italian Armistice was declared hours before American forces reached Salerno, and from then on Italy's troops were fighting on their side.

Italy may have capitulated, but the Germans had not. A barrier of southern Italian mountains separated the Allies from Rome, where the Nazis were fortified to hold them through the winter. They fought the Americans and British to a standstill into January, when Fifth Army troops finally broke through this winter line. From atop Monte La Difensa, my father looked down across the Garigliano, Rapido, and Liri valleys, only to see that the Germans had merely retreated to their main line of defense, the Gustav line, which lay deeply entrenched across the bottleneck corridors leading to Rome. In winning the mountains, the Fifth Army had paid terribly, with nearly 40,000 dead and wounded. Even more had fallen sick from fighting through the winter. German losses were far fewer, and penetrating the Gustav line would be far more lethal. If Italy were in fact going to fall into Allied hands, something else had to be done.

That, the Allied Command decided, must be an amphibious landing to establish a beachhead behind enemy lines. The site chosen for this invasion was a gullied yellow plain along the western Italian coast, near the twin seaside resort spas of Nettuno and Anzio, about forty miles from Rome. The Anzio Beachhead, as it became known worldwide over the next four months, ran for fifteen miles along the shore with the town of Anzio at the center, and was ten miles deep. The surrounding twenty-six-mile perimeter was comprised of low mountains and hills, surrounding a marshy bowl etched by steeply banked streams and bisected by a reclamation project, the Mussolini Canal.

"Listen closely, son," my father said, sitting at my bedside. "Are you listening?" I nodded, trying to stay awake enough to understand.

General Eisenhower, he proceeded to explain, had planned a double-pronged strike to leave the Germans with two fronts to defend simultaneously. First would come a diversion: The Allies would attempt to break through the Liri Valley pass that led to

Rome. Once German forces amassed at the Gustav line to hold them, the surprise landing at Anzio would follow. The Germans would have to pull their forces northward to meet this new threat to their rear, allowing the Allies to pour up the valley behind them.

In the beginning, the plan ran so smoothly it seemed too good to be true. That, in fact, turned out to be the case. On January 12, 1944, French and British Allied troops attacked the right and left mountain flanks of the Gustav line. A week later, they were joined by American forces at the center. The Nazis were immovable, but the heavy thrust served to divert German reinforcements down from Rome, away from Anzio.

The amphibious invasion came from Naples on January 22, in the form of an assault convoy of more than two hundred landing craft accompanied by a host of cruisers and destroyers. For three weeks before, 36,000 soldiers had trained on the beaches south of Salerno for a nighttime landing under simulated fire, learning to clear the wire and minefields they expected to find and to take out machine-gun pillboxes. At the same time, Allied planes bombed German supply routes and railroad lines in northern Italy to cut off support and isolate the Nazi forces in the south. Knowing that the Germans had fortified the coast, dummy U.S. naval convoys roamed the Tyrrhenian Sea just offshore to trick the enemy into anticipating a landing further north. The landing site itself was divided into two beaches, code-named Peter and X-Ray. The British would take Peter, the beachhead's northern extreme, while the Americans would split into two forces landing on either side of Anzio Harbor.

The southern flank of the American force was its entire Third Division, which had entered the war in Casablanca, marched across the top of Africa, jumped to Sicily, taken Salerno, and now was waiting to splash ashore just after 2:00 A.M. on January 22. The Minneapolis newspapers that my mother saved later reported that among the first doughboys to hit the beach—if not the very first, as one claimed—was the North Side's own Private Simon A. Weisman.

Press accounts would later call him a hero for his actions in the Anzio landing, but his heroics actually came later. The landing itself was an anticlimax. The harsh winter seas they had expected were calm, the surf gently lapping the offshore sandbars. The beach that the Germans had heavily mined was several miles to the north, along the mouth of the Tiber River. The British, who landed nearest to that coastal defense, quickly dispatched the only significant resistance: a single Panzer engineer company guarding nine miles of shoreline. The Third Division poured in over beaches empty of all except three German patrols in armored cars, which they took out with bazookas. They knocked over pillboxes, which turned out to be unmanned, then set about dragging fully loaded supply trucks and gasoline dumps inland and taking their positions.

By midnight, twenty-two hours later, all 36,000 men, plus 3,200 vehicles, were ashore. They had seized Anzio Beach practically unopposed. In the starlight, they could see silhouetted pastel villas on bluffs overlooking a tranquil Anzio harbor. What followed, however, was best depicted by cartoonist-correspondent Bill Mauldin in a clip my mother saved in scrapbooks that traced my father's sojourn for the next two years through Europe: a sketch of two GIs on a hilltop, looking back down at a flat plain that extended to the sea, surrounded by mountains. "My God!" says one, gaping into this fishbowl. "Here they wuz, an' there we wuz."

Hitler promptly vowed to drive the Allies back into the Tyrrhenian. Soon, thirteen German divisions were nested in the hills ringing Anzio, their view of the entire beachhead virtually unimpeded. Except for a few scattered farmhouses and natural trenches formed by the gullies, there was no place to hide. By February, after a week of shelling by Nazi artillery and mortars, British and American military tacticians worried that they might be looking at the most costly debacle since the World War I massacre at Gallipolli.

❧⟨ʘʘ⟩❧

March 2, 1944

My dearest "Meshie" and Cookybelle,

Perhaps you had already received official G.I. notice that
I have been wounded. I am one of the lucky ones. I got away
with slight wounds on each hand; until my bandages are
removed, writing will be a laborious process. You remember
in my last letter I was happy to inform you how light our
platoon's casualties were—well, darling, our luck ran out two
days ago. Two of them aren't with us anymore. May the Lord
have mercy on their souls. Six others are wounded and will
be out for a long time. Please, darling, don't worry about my
injuries. I was able to continue duty for a whole day after I
was hit. In fact, I am scribbling this letter with my so-called
wounded hands. Lying here on this hospital cot, Meshie
darling, and reflecting on the number of close shaves I have
had, I am convinced that but for the grace of God and my
strict adherence to soldierly conduct I should no longer be
here. It is for you and Cooky that the merciful God must
have seen fit to spare me.

I am also convinced that every time I act in the line of
duty, dangerous as my undertaking may be, it will be the
most prudent course under the circumstances. Going to do
something vital for my unit during an enemy artillery barrage
may seem dangerous, but every time I have done so I have
escaped certain death or injury that would have been my lot
had I stayed in my foxhole for protection. Even this last close
call; if I had neglected my duty before seeking shelter from
enemy fire, I would have shared the fate of my two comrades
who are no longer with us.

I reassure you again, my darling, that my wounds are
really trivial. Nevertheless, I have been awarded the Order of
the Purple Heart, an award for meritorious service given to
men wounded in combat with an armed enemy. I don't know
if I deserve it, yet I want you to have it.

He did not tell her how he was wounded, but she read about it later in the newspapers. Within a week of their surprise landing, it was evident that the Allies had missed a chance. Their object was to divert German troops from the main action along the mountainous Gustav line, specifically at a pass called Cassino, where the Allies hoped to break through and drive toward Rome. Had they immediately forged inland from Anzio to cut off a pair of major routes supplying German troops to the south, the tactic might have worked. Instead, digging in at the beachhead gave the Nazis time to assess the situation. Realizing that their armies at Cassino weren't at risk of losing their lifeline of food, gasoline, or ammunition, they kept them in place and brought reinforcements down from the north to contain the Anzio invaders right where they were.

Which they did for the next four months, despite repeated Allied attempts to dislodge the Germans from their surrounding hilltop fortifications. When my father's Thirtieth Infantry Regiment took the bridges over the Mussolini Canal that first night at Anzio, the Germans had 20,000 men in the vicinity. Within a week, they added 50,000 more, including two Panzer tank divisions. For the next ten days, successive waves of American and British troops drove toward a strategic hamlet called Cisterna, on the main road out of Anzio. They got nowhere. To the south, the Allied troops storming Cassino fared no better. In early February, Germany attempted to break the stalemate by hurling its entire Fourteenth Army—some 120,000 troops—against the 100,000 men the Allies now had at Anzio. Instead of advancing, the Allied invaders now had to defend their marshy foothold in the narrow beachhead. Within two weeks, losses on both sides were huge.

In addition to his daily patrols, once his superiors learned of his German fluency, my father was called upon to interrogate Nazi prisoners. One of these now revealed to him that another counter-offensive was forthcoming. It would be a tank drive to split the beachhead in two, then destroy its isolated halves. At the same time, Anzio Harbor would be mined, leaving survivors no way out except to swim back to Naples.

Aerial reconnaissance confirmed this. The roads leading south from Rome were filling with artillery units and German troops. Like a poker table on which the ante mounts ever higher before someone finally strikes, the Allies rushed in another British division and several support brigades. The German counterattack came on February 16. It was met by an onslaught of fighter-bombers unprecedented in the history of warfare: More than six hundred sorties were flown, of aircraft ranging from light bombers to B-17 Flying Fortresses, in support of the practically exposed Allied personnel fighting on the ground below.

"How loud was it, Dad?"

"You couldn't hear yourself pray."

For the next two weeks, nobody on either side advanced, and nearly nobody slept under continual artillery barrages that turned the howling night skies perpetually orange. On February 29 the Nazis launched a third counteroffensive, this time throwing five divisions against the U.S. Third Division. My father's regiment was sent to plug the weak breach between the American and British forces. His Company H and two other units, companies I and F, were assigned an objective: a multimachine-gun stronghold in a stone farmhouse, two hundred yards from their command post.

My father's platoon was manning that post, covering a reconnaissance squad that was creeping on the machine-gun nest, when suddenly they were engulfed by a firestorm. With his rifle protruding just over the lip of the foxhole he shared with two other men, my father took a burst that melted the skin from the tops of both his hands. He held his position, then dared to look. Through the smoke and flare he saw that at least twenty men of the reconnaissance team had been hit. Over his two companions' protests, despite his searing wounds he crawled forward under the incessant artillery and dragged as many as he could to safety. Returning finally to his foxhole, he found his two mates dead from a direct hit.

Along with the Purple Heart, he was awarded the Army's third highest decoration, the Silver Star for gallantry for attending to others before seeing to his own injuries. He didn't feel deserving, he wrote my mother, because he was just performing his duty as he'd been trained: Had he remained instead in his foxhole, he would be as dead as his comrades.

But the action of his regiment had successfully repulsed yet another assault. By the beginning of March 1944, German losses at Anzio totaled more than 20,000 men. Although the numbers of combined Allied dead, injured, and captured were about the same, the Nazis were too depleted to attempt a fourth blitz to push the Allies into the sea. Nevertheless, the stalemates at Anzio and at Cassino to the south wore on, and over the next two months each side would lose 10,000 more before something broke.

❀

"Here at the Anzio Nettuno Beachhead," my father wrote home, "there are no ▮▮▮▮ and no ▮▮▮▮ . The whole ▮▮▮▮ of Allied occupied ground feels the impact of the enemy's barrages and bombardment." I hold the aged V-mail up to the light, and discern that the words the censors have blacked out are "front lines," "rear lines," and "perimeter." To get a sense of what the war in Italy was like, he directed her to specific issues of *Life* and *Time* magazines. "I was in the places that the articles portray, and experienced what is described in them."

The *Time* magazine piece, dated January 3, 1944, which showed pictures of men bivouacked on jagged Cassino hillsides overlooking a smoke-filled plain, was my mother's first indication of where he had fought before landing at Anzio. The article insinuated that the Allies' Italian campaign was a deeply flawed undertaking that could deteriorate into a military disaster, an opinion that sharpened over the coming months as they became mired at the beachhead. The *Life* article was a four-page Robert Capa photo essay, mainly showing dead American soldiers strewn among rocks and stubble above the Liri Valley.

He would see these issues five or six weeks after they were published; the earliest he'd get her letters was two weeks after she wrote them, but usually more. His took far longer to arrive: One air letter he mailed in April 1944 wasn't delivered for eleven months. Amid the maddening gaps and delays in their communication, they tried to respond to each other's urgent questions.

> As to your suggestion that I "need not try to be such a good soldier so that perhaps the Infantry might fire me"— Darling, even if I could get into that frame of mind, it would be suicidal. We don't dig a good foxhole to please our sergeant, we dig it as well as possible to protect our precious fannies and family jewels.
>
> As for the attractive Italian signorinas, believe me there isn't a soul here who could touch any of the girls back home, much less come close to you, the queen of them all. The only female in Italy I have found nice enough to get close to and hug is good old Mother Earth. I have often nestled at her ample bosom, and she has lavished her affection by protecting me. She is one female, my darling, for whom I will always have a tender spot in my heart—I hope you won't mind.

Mother Earth, however, grew fickle. The weather turned to steady sleet, and her embrace meant lying for days in a hole full of water. The marshy Anzio soil was relatively easy to dig, but treacherous. On one occasion my father—at thirty-one, the oldest enlisted man in his company—was lured from his foxhole by a wise guy of eighteen who kept taunting him for being too creaky to climb out even for a cup of hot coffee.

"All right, you little s.o.b., I'm coming out, but you'd better not be around when I get there," he warned. He returned to find that his sodden foxhole had collapsed, burying his gear under two tons of mud; had he remained inside, he would have been buried with it.

His wife also wasn't behaving exactly to his liking. "I am per-plexed by your letter in which you state that when you come home from work Cooky greets you with a special speech. By that do you mean your Red Cross work, darling. Or did you get a job? I hope it's the former; I don't see why you should have to work, nor how Cooky can get along without your constant attention. Please clear this up in your next letter."

By the time she did, he had already gotten the idea: She was definitely working for my Uncle Mike's advertising agency. She was exhausted by the hours, she admitted, because she still rolled ban-dages at the Red Cross and donated blood as often as they let her. Yet as she told me later, it wasn't just to earn money for the house they dreamed of owning. It was because she'd need it if he never came home.

She never wrote my father that, however, and she knew better than to dwell on the other reason she'd taken a job. She loved it. She not only assisted in the page layouts, but sometimes got to sketch illustrations, and she began to dream of becoming a com-mercial artist. She sprinkled her letters with marvelous little ink drawings—of the mailman delivering Si's letters, of my parents dancing together, of baby Cooky spilling her cereal, of exercising with a tummy massager to stay svelte for him, of the house they would build, and of the stork visiting them again.

I show my mother's sole surviving wartime letter to my sculp-tor wife. Startled, she sits down to savor these line drawings, con-firming my impression that, both technically and emotionally, they are gems. I picture my mother waiting for my father to respond to them with something like, "My God, Meshie, you should be an artist." He never did, of course. At best in later years it was: "My Meshie could have been a talented artist. But she just wanted to be home with her husband and children. Right, honey?"

His fear and loneliness were so acute that he didn't dare anger her by insisting she quit. Instead, he rationalized this small rebel-lion as a wartime exception. But his disapproval was clear in his spiteful refusal to forgive my Uncle Mike and Aunt Sylvia for the vague offenses of which he still accused them. For months, his letters rarely spared them, and my mother's pleas only made things worse: "I refuse to forgive and forget their vicious tongue-wagging, not because 'I don't love you' but because they don't deserve it! Do you expect me to make overtures to them when it should be the other way around?" Yet he inquired constantly after Mike and Sylvia's children, sending profuse thanks for the candy, cheese, and salamis he received in their name—even though, since they were toddlers, it was obvious who really sent them.

He especially lavished affection, however, on his brother. Within six months, Herman was promoted to first lieutenant. In less than a year, after making ten crossings to Africa, he made captain and was given his own troopship. Whenever his boat reached home port, he grabbed an overnight train from New York to Minneapolis. On March 24, 1944, my mother wrote that Herman made it home in time to treat her to a birthday dinner. Next, he'd told her, he was headed to Naples, and he would do his damnedest to get to Anzio to see his brother.

"I am so glad that you and Herman went out," my father wrote back. "Isn't it funny how it took a war and a separation of thousands of miles to bridge the gap that the differences in our ages imposed? He is certainly getting to be a man. I am proud to have him for a brother."

His letter went on for many onionskin pages:

I can't tell you exactly where on this beachhead I was in body on your birthday, but in thought, hope, and wish I was with you, sweetheart. My imagination, fired by my love for you, was prolific. I saw you so plainly that night, a vision of tender loveliness. Your arms were around me tight. The wonderful warmth of your love vanquished the chill in my bones as well as the moment's cares. Though we were thousands of miles apart, I felt you so near that the sweet fragrance which is yours alone rendered me impervious to my odoriferous surroundings. This was not the first time you were with me, darling. I have found secure shelter in your love from many dangers. In moments of weakness you were my strength, in my despair you were my courage. Without the vision of your blessed loveliness to guide me, I would have never been able to traverse this valley of darkness.

In Naples, Herman impulsively bought a pair of genuine eighteenth-century French vases in an antique shop and mailed them to my mother. They arrived five weeks later, smashed to bits, but they forever endeared him to her. "I am only a hundred miles from Si," he wrote in the accompanying card. "I'm not in port for long, but I'm really hoping I can go see him." From the ship's steward, he procured candy bars, salami, cigarettes, and cans of Spam, which he sent to my father with a note saying that he was trying to find a way to get there.

More than weary of Spam, my father gave it away to the few Italian sheepherder families that remained in Anzio. A nonsmoker, he traded the cigarettes for handkerchiefs and khaki thread. He wrote to thank him, but although he was a private and Herman a captain, he ordered his baby brother not to even consider coming to Anzio. "It's too dangerous," he told him.

That same day, he wrote my mother that he was no longer interested in OCS.

If I had obtained a commission in the States we could have lived together. But out here, a commission wouldn't mean a reunion with you. I know you are concerned that I'm still a private. But I feel more of a success than some of the commissioned men who are still in the States and untried in battle. The fate that keeps me in the army as a private may be a guiding angel in disguise. I sincerely believe I was too self-centered and too overcome with my own self-esteem. For that reason, I am fortunate to get a lesson in humility.

My father did not remain a humble private for long. In late March 1944, after sixty-seven consecutive days at the front, his division received a two-week break at a provisional field rest camp outside Nettuno. He took his first hot shower since January. The rest camp was concealed among a grove of pines and further hidden by smoke screens, but the Germans knew where they were. Periodically the Luftwaffe appeared overhead, bombing and strafing, sending everyone diving for foxholes. The men swam in the sea, watched movies provided by the USO, played baseball, and trained for forthcoming deep reconnaissance and combat raids. On April 5 my father attended Passover services, and on April 8, at an Easter honors ceremony he was made an acting communications sergeant. On April 12, they returned to the front. The fighting at Anzio had never ceased, but now the Allies were pushing for an advantage against a weakened enemy.

For weeks, they had been trying to seize a strategic hilltop that jutted from the plain along the Cisterna road, a vantage point from which the Nazis harassed them at will. Now the Thirtieth Infantry tried again. The very day they returned to action, Company H was called to move on the objective. My father's platoon was assigned to a so-called defensive position by a major who had just joined the regiment, holding the forward slope of an exposed knoll between two deep ravines that drained the Cisterna hill, through which the Germans frequently were known to strike.

Late that afternoon, they found themselves stranded, cut off from their ammunition supply routes by two enemy machine-gun posts. Thirteen years later, in 1957, we would read in the Minneapolis newspaper what happened next; for some unexplained reason, it took the army that long to act on the major's recommendation that my father receive yet another medal, the Bronze Star, after he volunteered to eliminate the enemy machine-gun positions. This he accomplished by slithering twenty-five yards on his belly in plain sight through low grass and scrub, until he was close enough to lob a hand grenade at each.

A month later, the Third Division would still be in the same place. But to the south, a major spring offensive of two Allied armies finally took Cassino and broke through the Gustav line.

Now Nazi forces had to shuffle to meet the Allies coming from several directions. On May 25, the Allies at Anzio launched an enormous artillery barrage at Cisterna. After two days and more than four thousand casualties, they took the rocky little hill they were fighting for, from which the Germans had rained so much hell upon their heads.

My father, now officially a sergeant, again took part in that offensive. There were no letters from him for two weeks. But by the time his next missive, dated June 8, reached my mother, she already had pasted the news in her scrapbook. They had broken out of the beachhead, and were safe in Rome.

CHAPTER 9

On Thanksgiving Day, 1988, I spent nine hours in a boatman's cottage in a jungle clearing on a river in central Colombia, peering through slits between drawn plastic curtains as mayhem erupted just over a nearby hill. Each time circling aircraft dropped a bomb or bursts of automatic weaponry tore through the humid air, a raucous cloud of terrified scarlet macaws rose from the trees like a puff of tinted debris, then settled back into the forest canopy.

Whenever the helicopters came, hovering over the boatman's house for fifteen minutes at a time, the macaws and even the babbling cacique birds grew quiet. Inside, we humans remained motionless as possible and kept away from the open doorway, lest we be spotted when the choppers dropped low, the backwash from their rotors blowing away the chickens and ubiquitous purple butterflies, and ripping laundry off the line.

The night before, when my party had appeared on the opposite shore, the boatman, whose name was José Antonio, had puttered across in a dugout canoe carved with a flattened stern to accept a small outboard motor. He wore a fraying straw hat atop his silver hair, a sleeveless undershirt tucked into khakis belted with a rope, and a perpetually tragic expression. Clutching a riverbank root, he'd steadied his boat as we clambered aboard. Besides myself, there was Jorge, a tall young agronomist I had met a week earlier in Bogotá, and our two escorts: guerrilla soldiers named

Anselmo and Lucho, members of the FARC: las Fuerzas Armadas Revolucionarias Colombianas. José Antonio knew them both, and didn't look especially pleased to see them.

We had been marching for the previous six hours, hoping to reach an airstrip where forty members of the FARC's Forty-fifth Front were encamped, a half hour's boat ride downstream. But by the time we arrived at the river, the sun was already setting behind the Andes, and both the guerrillas and José Antonio agreed that it was impossible to traverse the rapids ahead without daylight. So we spent the night with him and his wife and daughters, who served us fish with rice and plantains by kerosene lamplight. After dinner, we listened over a battery-powered wide-band radio as Colombia's president, Virgilio Barco, declared he'd had enough of guerrilla ambushes that had humiliated the country's armed forces over previous months.

"Big talk," hooted Anselmo. "Let him come after us already, instead of us poking sticks in their eyes all the time."

There was truth to this. Except in the banana-growing region near the Panamanian border, which was currently under martial law, Colombia's army had remained mostly hunkered in its barracks during the three months I'd been in the country, rarely taking the offensive. Newspaper maps indicated that nearly three-fifths of this nation, twice the size of France, was under guerrilla control. The statistic was somewhat misleading, because during twenty-five years of internecine warfare, the Marxist guerrillas had never taken a major city. Nevertheless, control of Colombia's vast, resource-rich hinterland was no small matter, and some audacious guerrilla urban assaults, which included kidnapping nearly half the foreign diplomatic corps and seizing the Supreme Court building (until army tanks leveled it), had undermined any sense of civil security in the land.

"We're ready," Anselmo proclaimed as the presidential saber rattling ended. In his early twenties, Anselmo was short, sandy-haired, olive-skinned, and cocky. The settlers and coca growers we had encountered in this forest visibly had mixed feelings about him: He was good-humored, but always managed to remind them that his green FARC fatigues and semiautomatic Israeli Galil demanded respect. This came in the form of free meals that everyone served us without asking, although not necessarily out of the solidarity Anselmo claimed. *"Traen armas"*—they have guns—a woman muttered when I expressed appreciation for the generous plates of eggs and steaming cassava she provided when we'd appeared unannounced.

Anselmo's taciturn companion, Lucho, a light-skinned whippet just eighteen, had been a guerrilla soldier for five years—ever since his peasant father was shot, he told me, by right-wing paramilitaries. *"Perdón,"* he'd said politely that evening, relieving me of my snarled hammock and mosquito netting and installing them between two ceiba trees in less than a minute. After dinner, he laid his weapon aside and insisted on bathing my blistered feet in salt water, comprehending little of my explanation that in temperate climates we used leather hiking boots, not the rubber irrigation boots that were the only footwear these rainforest guerrillas knew. At times that day, I'd notice Lucho staring at me, amazed: His only knowledge of *norteamericanos* and the United States came from FARC Marxist-Leninist indoctrination, the only school he had ever attended.

The following morning we were awakened by a brief, warm sprinkle from clouds that instantly boiled away before the rising sun. Still in my hammock, I trained my binoculars on a dangling oropendola nest, from which emerged a series of magnificent musical gargles, and reached for my copy of Dunning's *South American Land Birds*. As a child, lugging heavy German field glasses that my father had captured in the war and the first book I ever owned, *The Audubon Guide to Eastern Birds*, I'd regularly escape into a wetland next to our suburban home to commune with ring-necked pheasants, blue-wing teals, pileated woodpeckers, and saffron-hued goldfinches. It was the one place where my family would never pursue me. Surrounded by feathered guardian angels, that marsh became my refuge.

Now, I was supposedly in another, a seventy-five-mile-long uplift known as the Serranía de la Macarena—Colombia's oldest wildlife preserve, but lately safe haven to no creature. "Listen!" hissed Anselmo, suddenly materializing beside me.

All I could hear were the oropendolas, but his ear was trained to darker registers. Anselmo was like ornithologists I'd known who can identify distant passing birds from their silhouettes or the faintest fragment of their call. "There's a Blackhawk and at least one other helicopter. Plus two or three fixed-wing twin-engines," he said, while I was still straining to distinguish aircraft sounds from the wind ruffling José Antonio's roof. Sure enough, presently two open-sided Blackhawk troop transporters with turret-mounted M60s came in over the trees, followed by a pair of small Vietnam surplus Huey choppers. A minute later, two World War II–era T33 bombers dashed overhead. And then the sky was filled with smoke and gorgeous scarlet macaws.

Weeks earlier, near the Panamanian border, I'd heard striking banana pickers testify how the army, suspecting them of being guerilla sympathizers, had bombed their houses from helicopters, manually dropping explosives out the open sides of a big green dragonfly buzzing above them. I recalled this more than once during that long day while my guerrilla companions trained their Galils through the thin galvanized roofing, waiting for the hovering choppers to make a move. Any moment, I guessed, it could happen here, since there was no question where the allegiance of the colonists in this forest lay. Anyone who lived in Colombia's Reserva Nacional Serranía de la Macarena either was friendly with the guerrillas or about to be dead.

❧❧❧

Predating even the Andes, the densely forested Serranía de la Macarena is among the most ancient land forms in South America. It was the first nature reserve designated in a country that leads the world in bird species, ranks second in flora and amphibians, and third in reptiles—the result of terrain ranging from torrid tropics to Andean tundra, which provided an ideal niche for practically any species that arrived when North and South America linked there about three million years ago. As the director of Colombia's national parks had explained to me, during interglacial epochs when much of the continent lay inundated, the Serranía de la Macarena became a natural Noah's ark for plants and animals. In the 1930s, scientists realized that the lush Macarena was not only the most biologically complex spot in the country, but quite likely in the entire world. Yet the park director himself had never seen it.

"You can't go there," he said. "It's too dangerous." The command base for the FARC guerrillas' entire eastern forces was concealed beneath its forest canopy. But despite his warning, and an even sterner directive from the U.S. embassy, I knew that I had to. The Serranía de la Macarena was exactly what I was looking for.

I'd arrived in Colombia in September 1988, a month after my writing residency in the Dominican Republic, with a Fulbright grant to study how local and U.S. news media cover topics of mutual interest. I soon realized that my project was doomed. A single topic—drugs—had overwhelmed the rest, and so many Colombian journalists were now either dead or in exile that the ones who still covered *narcotráfico* were forced to write anonymously. Few wanted to discuss their reporting techniques with a North American who, for all they knew, might be a CIA agent. After discovering that such suspicions were in fact trailing me around Bogotá, I abandoned my proposal altogether and began looking for something else to do.

"¿Te van a quitar la beca?" D. asked me.

No, I explained, my Fulbright grant was an all-expenses-paid vacation, courtesy of U.S. tax dollars. They couldn't take my funding away from me, because I wasn't required to produce anything. All I was supposed to do was research, a term open to broad interpretation. *"Ah, bien,"* she said, snuggling next to me under the wool blanket. At nearly 9,000 feet, Bogotá was a chilly city, and aside from side trips to hot spots like Colombia's banana country, until I met her I had shivered nightly in my unheated apartment.

In solving that problem, however, she had created another. One reason that rumors were circulating about me was because D., a green-eyed Colombian journalist in her early thirties, worked for a Soviet news agency. Her father was a high official in Colombia's Communist Party. Our tryst, which began soon after we met at a gathering of the Foreign Press Association, had not only alarmed her party friends, but directly violated my instructions from the U.S. embassy, where I'd been required to appear for a security briefing when I first arrived.

It took place in the office of a no-nonsense black U.S. Marine who had "just evacuated" a listening post in the Colombian city of Medellín, currently assailed by drug-related bombings and assassinations. "The first thing you need to know about this place is that it's hell. Don't forget it. If you want to stay alive, memorize these instructions." He ticked off a list of things I couldn't do: ride buses, live in ground-floor dwellings, maintain a predictable schedule, stand near windows, visit small towns, travel to rural areas, or even dream of going to Medellín.

"I have to visit regional newspapers," I protested. "Our government is paying me tax dollars to do the study I proposed."

"Forget it. Those jerks in Washington don't know shit about what it's like here on the ground." He delivered his final admonition: "Report any contact with Communists in writing to this office." He paused. "That means anybody who doesn't like Reagan." I looked up from the notes I was jotting, ready to smile at this little joke. Apparently, he wasn't joking.

His list became my reverse guide to the country. Within a month I'd ridden buses to several small towns, visited Medellín twice, and joined a hiking club that trekked through the countryside each weekend. And then I'd met D., a Communist with whom I was most decidedly having contact. She wasn't surprised about the briefing, having spent much of her adolescence protesting in front of the building where it took place. As both a Latin American and a Communist educated partly in East Germany, my country loomed as the pall that darkened much of her world view. Although I found reasons to agree, I soon tired enough of her sweeping anti-American diatribes to finally inject some balance into our little dé-tente: I told her the story about how Communists butchered my grandfather right before my father's six year-old eyes.

"Ay, Alán," she cried, touching my face. "¡Qué tragedia tan cruel—tan brutos, los bolcheviques!"

"Exactly," I said. "Nothing's black-and-white. Life's compli-cated."

"Sí, mi amor," she agreed, hugging me. "Como nosotros." Like us: Gringo meets latina, American meets Communist, at times we speculated on our motivations in this affair: Fascination with for-bidden fruit? A purer desire to transcend mistrust by literally em-bracing the Other? Mostly, we didn't stop to analyze. We were both lonely, both still unsteady after barely cooled divorces, and we grasped at each other for reasons that needed only satiating, not explaining.

With nothing else to do, I took a New York Times Magazine as-signment. I was to portray Colombia as an extravagantly endowed land—more rivers than Africa, two coastlines, bountiful coal and oil, ambrosial coffee and other agricultural exports, diverse indus-tries, arguably Latin America's healthiest economy, stunning art and literature that filled thirty-three museums and twenty-seven universities in Bogotá alone—yet a land that was killing itself. That was what drew me to the Serranía de la Macarena: the crowning jewel among Colombia's—and the world's—natural treasures, cur-rently being smashed by all the forces tearing apart this country. Forced off their land by violence or development, thousands of squatters were now toppling the Macarena's incomparable forests to plant coca under the protection of guerrillas who claimed to be defending the dispossessed poor.

I asked D. how to get there. She contacted somebody, who arranged a meeting with somebody else. I sat around a table with several men who wanted to know exactly why the New York Times might be interested in an obscure mountain range in central Colombia. I explained that the Macarena was the perfect symbol of their country—a place blessed with everything, but under siege—and that Colombia, in turn, was a symbol of our world: a beautiful planet, likewise being ruined instead of revered.

A message was conveyed to the FARC. A few days later, I was informed that my request had been approved. I would be accompanied by Jorge, an agronomist who had worked in the region. For a day, we rode a bus through towns where recent civilian massacres were alternately attributed to guerrillas or to right-wing paramilitaries—mercenaries frequently in the employ of drug lords, who ingratiated the army by hiring goons to do useful dirty work against alleged Communist sympathizers. At periodic military checkpoints, we had to spread-eagle alongside the bus and submit to body searches. In the main square of one sullen town called Granada, we did this standing atop dark stains on the pavement, remnants of a bloodbath two nights before.

The last American to enter the Macarena had been a Peace Corps botanist whom the FARC captured in 1979, held hostage for three years under a black plastic tent, and released only when he went mad. Soon after, he committed suicide. Only a week before, I'd just learned, another guerrilla group had captured the staff of a neighboring national park and summarily convicted them of using the elitist contrivance of a nature reserve to deny people their rightful access to land. Forcing the park superintendent to kneel, they executed him with a bullet to the back of his neck.

In Colombia, the so-called Cold War was red hot, with innocent Mother Nature caught squarely in the crossfire. And now I was heading directly for her heart, right where the crosshairs were trained. Five hours after the pavement ran out, the bus reached a frontier town of unpainted dwellings built of hand-hewn lumber. "From here we walk," said Jorge.

Back in Bogotá, Jorge had told me that he had studied in the Soviet Union. "What do you know about this guy?" I had asked D., as we lay on her floor mattress two nights before I left.

"Nada." She lit a cigarette. *"Un amigo de las FARC, me presumo. Espero."*

"What do you mean, 'you hope'?"

Well, she didn't wanted to worry me, but there hadn't yet been actual confirmation from the FARC that I would be welcome in the Macarena.

"I thought I'd been approved."

I had—by the ones in Bogotá. Radio communications to the Macarena were spotty. They were still trying to get through, she said. It was probably all right. "Unless you'd rather wait," she added, turning to look at me. "But if you postpone now, there's no guarantee. . . ."

"I'm going."

She put out her cigarette and kissed my check. "I figured you would."

Long after she fell asleep that night, I lay propped on an elbow, looking at the curve of her body under the sheet and wondering whether I should have listened to the Marine at the embassy. Was I waltzing directly into a genuine Communist plot—a big fat gringo trap?

❧🌀❧

As Jorge and I trudged into the Macarena, I was astonished at how quickly I tired. Years of jogging and backpacking in North America hadn't prepared me for this. The heat was liquid, and my lungs felt sopping wet. I began to suspect that schemes to save rainforests through ecotourism were based more on wishful thinking than experience. In this most fabulous of all natural tableaus, the air was leaden, the sky perpetually gray, and the calls of parrots and tanagers like sinister omens.

We followed a *trocha*, a footpath, along a river that formed the Macarena's western boundary, where land had been burned and cleared, passing though scattered settlements of families who'd arrived with crates of live chickens and treadle sewing machines on

155

their backs. Occasionally we encountered mule trains hauling processed coca flour. On the second day, we turned away from the river and entered the forest canopy. Titi monkeys shrilled above us. Yellow-tailed crested oropendolas whizzed among the liana vines. The ground was swampy, and I understood why Jorge made me leave behind my hiking boots and purchase calf-high rubber irrigation boots: protection against snakes. They were hot and uncushioned, though, and the soles of my feet were soon afire from huge blisters.

We crossed many small canyons, inching over logs suspended above rushing rapids. After a while I was so shaky that I crawled across these, barely registering the pastel profusion of orchids—half the world's species grow in the Macarena—clinging to the dripping walls. In one stream, we came upon a lumbering tapir. In another, we flushed a family of hundred-pound-plus rodents called capybaras. By then, I was foundering seriously. I realized that I was dehydrated, which seemed absurd, surrounded by so much moisture. But we'd exhausted the water we'd brought. I suggested to Jorge that we stop to drink, but he pointed out that the water was probably malarial. "I have a filter," I said.

"If we don't move faster, we'll be caught by darkness." Chagrined that I was holding us up, I plodded on. Abruptly, the terrain changed. We could again see the sky as we passed through a field of burnt stumps surrounded by wispy, lime-green deciduous shrubs. Then, just as suddenly, we were in forest again. After the third time, I realized through my toxic exhaustion that these weren't natural clearings caused by a lightning strikes, but *cultivos*.

"*Sí*," Jorge confirmed. "*Es coca.*" Just at that point, there was a rustling in the bushes, and we found ourselves facing a youth dressed in olive-drab, aiming a semiautomatic assault weapon at our chests. Apologetically, he informed us that we could go no further.

A six-man patrol relieved the guard of his two captives. We thanked the young guerrilla soldier, who had kindly shared his full canteen, and then marched in silence for an hour. At dusk we reached a sizable, orderly compound of thatched bamboo structures arranged around a drill field. We were led to a row of bamboo-plumbed showers and instructed to clean up and then report to *Comandante* Raúl Reyes. "Raúl Reyes," Jorge whistled.

Reyes, a national legend, had been a *guerrillero* for twenty-three years. A short, thickset former schoolteacher, he considered me with small, unsmiling eyes for nearly a minute before speaking. "I'm informed that you are a democratic journalist who will tell the world the truth about our mission," he said.

"Of course."

The encampment of the FARC's Eastern Forces had officers' quarters built from thatch and *guarumo* planks, a bamboo aqueduct drawing water from a stream that had been dammed to create a swimming pool, a field clinic, and a diesel plant for lights and a radio transmitter. About two hundred *guerrilleros* were stationed here. The entire camp, superbly concealed by the jungle canopy, could be evacuated in five minutes if necessary, diesel plant included.

Reyes was aware, he said, that the Serranía de la Macarena was an environmental marvel. He had personally interceded, he added, on behalf of politically enlightened ecologists who wanted to visit this repository of genetic history. I declined to mention the Peace Corps biologist who had been held prisoner for three years in this very camp. "These reserves are important to Colombia's future," he declared. "And Colombia's future is what we're fighting for."

What about the unnatural clearings surrounding his camp, I asked over a steak dinner that night at the outdoor officers' mess. "How does letting people cut down the forest to plant coca protect the environment?"

The table, replete with *comandantes,* grew silent.

"Because we protect humans first," Reyes replied. "Until the government provides opportunities for *el pueblo* to earn a living, this is the only one they have. We don't like drugs. But these people deserve to be defended. If the government won't, then we will."

"You don't make money off the coca *cultivos*?"

"The people make a contribution in exchange for our protection. In your imperialist country, you pay taxes, too."

For two days, while the *comandantes* considered my request to travel through the Macarena to see its fresh-water dolphins, spectacled bears, ocelots, and giant armadillos, I was allowed to wander freely. At the FARC's school for young *guerrilleros* from rural regions where education was barely offered, several asked about my country: Why did the United States force black people to live in urban concentration camps called ghettos? Were we really going to invade Panama to oust its democratic leader, General Noriega? I answered as truthfully as I could. About half were women, and I asked one nineteen-year-old how her parents reacted when she joined the guerrillas. The question surprised her. "They were proud."

With *Comandante* Joselo, a gray-chested, forty-year veteran of Colombian civil war, I stood waist-deep in a stream watching the guerrillas cavort at water tag. "It's good to play now and then," he said, "because most of the time, we are locked in struggle." Two days later, hiding in the boatman's house with the guerrilla guides that Raúl Reyes assigned me, I learned that only the week before, Joselo had been radioed the news that his *guerrillera* daughter was killed in a firefight in southern Colombia.

In propaganda and rhetoric, the guerrillas' struggle might sound romantic, but on the ground it meant the business of killing and dying. And now, smelling cordite and bomb smoke drifting over the jungle, listening to steady rounds of automatic gunfire just over the hill, I was in the midst of it. Each time a helicopter's malevolent shadow stretched over us, it occurred to me that I might very well die here. Strangely, I felt not so much afraid as guilty. What right did I have to be out here playing soldier, getting myself killed?

It was decided that young Lucho would try to run back to

camp to learn what he could about the army operation. All we could tell was that the airstrip where we were supposed to have camped, just beyond the rounded hill immediately south of us, was the target. An hour before dusk, he returned. At camp, they were amazed that we were still alive: At least thirty men were killed in the attack at the airstrip. The orders were to get Jorge and me out of there and report back to duty. *"Estamos en pie de guerra,"* Lucho panted; they were officially on a war footing.

José Antonio took us across the river. We headed back toward the main *trocha* at a trot. Several times we dived off the path when choppers swooped in to spray bursts of machine-gun fire that cut through the canopy foliage above us and sent the macaws and monkeys shrieking.

At one point in that dying afternoon, lying chest down in muck while a black snake as thick as my wrist oozed past, I felt a sudden, unexpected, stunningly clear sense of purpose. I'd come here, goddammit, because there was a war going on. It had nothing to do with Communists; it was beyond politics, and even beyond history. This not was a war to defend country or creed, but the earth itself.

I was watching World War II–vintage American-made bombers—the same kind that had roared over my father's head at Anzio—punch holes in what was possibly the most precious Eden left in the world. I had risked my own puny life to get here because I believed that the very soul of this living planet was suspended in a tug of cold war between systems so locked in their dogmas that they failed to see that, all along, they'd been wrecking the very foundation on which they stood. One day, when there was no more topsoil or ozone or potable water or enough trees, they would finally discover that their exalted politics were irrelevant.

"¡Ya se fueron—vamos!" hissed Anselmo, and I picked myself up from the slime and ran forward again, mindless of my raging blisters. Over the next several hours, dodging copters and tracers, I felt something I had never before known: what it meant to be imbued with a cause that justified putting my life on the line.

Days later, safe within the walls of my Bogotá apartment, I had the luxury of analyzing my own motives and wondered if I weren't just a forty-year-old child still trying to live up to my father's image. But in that moment back in the jungles of the Serranía de la Macarena, I had no questions. I knew. Saving the planet, I believed, was my own generation's just and noble war, worth dying for if need be. I had come to defend it with my words and witness, and I would never again feel small in my father's gaze.

CHAPTER 10

My father had landed on Anzio Beach a private. He left wearing sergeant's stripes, a Silver Star, the Combat Infantry Badge, the Good Conduct Medal, and two unit citations. His file bore a recommendation for a Bronze Star and contained letters from his company commander and his battalion commander attesting to his skills, leadership, bravery, intelligence, and sense of duty. Each ended with a recommendation for his appointment to the Judge Advocate General Corps Officer Candidate School. "It's all set on this end," he wrote to my mother on July 4, 1944. "Now it's up to the War Department, but if Nate and his congressmen can push from that end, we can be together by our anniversary."

That was only five weeks away. It had been a heady two months for him since the liberation of Rome. A birthday message he wrote my sister, explaining why he couldn't be with her, won first prize—a Bulova watch—in a letter-home-from-overseas contest, and was printed in local papers and read every night over the radio for a month. His victorious troops had an audience with the Pope, who blessed rosaries he sent to Catholic friends back home. And he ran into a soldier who miraculously pulled from his pocket a leather-bound, hand-tinted photograph of my mother and sister he thought he'd lost forever one murderous day at Anzio.

He returned with his division to a seaside training camp near Naples to await their next marching orders, which he hoped wouldn't come before his appointment to the Judge Advocate General Corps. While there, he saved two British soldiers from drowning, and there was talk of yet another citation. He also had high hopes of actually seeing Herman, whose convoy was due to arrive shortly with reinforcements for whichever turn the war would take next.

For the first time since Pearl Harbor, this was an encouraging notion, because the D-Day invasion of northern Europe had finally occurred on June 6. At last, the American forces in Italy weren't alone. My father prayed that the next turn of events would find him training to be an officer-attorney in Washington, reunited with his wife and daughter. But as July dragged on and there was no progress on his behalf, he got worried. "Nate and the congressmen had better act quick before the next round begins," he urged. "If this doesn't go through, I'll die of heartbreak."

Finally, he was summoned to see his company commander, only to be shown an unofficial Army communique indicating that JAG Corps preference was being given to lawyers with ten years' experience. It wasn't definitive, but the commander said he was real sorry.

Such lawyers, my father realized, were all senior, rear-echelon men. "This eliminates soldiers like me from combat units, and gives preference to the stay-behinds," he stormed. Again, he directed his wrath on my hapless Uncle Mike—"I'm interested in knowing what he's doing in this world-shaking conflict"—tormenting my mother, who thought he was long past all that. He added a warning:

> People at home better get to understand the front-line
> soldier if they want to get along with him. He is concerned
> about the kind of world he is coming back to, because he
> risked everything trying to save it. He expects that those at
> home lucky enough to be spared his experience should do
> what they can, and certainly desires to know whether they
> are. Do you think we're fighting just to give noncombatants

a chance to go on with their business as usual? There are things they can do at home, and by God, they'd better do them. And no one should feel indignant when a combat soldier asks for an accounting.

He also hinted mysteriously that requesting recommendations to the JAG Corps had been a gamble, because it meant passing up something valuable he'd been offered. He wouldn't tell her what. Two months later, she stumbled upon the answer in an Associated Press story. It described how one Bobby Brady, a former Jersey City featherweight boxing champion, had taken out four armed German soldiers with his bare knuckles. This deed was recounted to a journalist at the front by his platoon leader, Sgt. Simon Weisman.

"I sort of lost my head and tied into them," explained the embarrassed Brady, who added:

> "Say, Sergeant, why don't you tell him about your decorations and how you turned down a soft commission because you wanted to fight as an infantryman?"
>
> It was Weisman's turn to be embarrassed. "Decorations are a dime a dozen. And keep quiet about that other business. I've got a law practice to think about and no one will want a crazy man defending him in court."

It wasn't a soft job he'd rejected, he swore, trying to calm my mother, but a battlefield commission. It wouldn't have gotten him back with her and Cooky any quicker, as the now-lost chance at the JAG Corps might have. "Better get another scrapbook ready," he added glumly. "It looks like the next waltz is about to begin."

It turned out to be their anniversary waltz. On August 14, six years after their wedding day, the Third Division invaded southern France. The Nazis, squeezed from Normandy to the west and Russia to the east, now faced the prospect of being pushed back toward Germany from the south. Just before the landing, my father wrote:

The worst thing is that I will be cut off from your mail. For how long, I don't know. My yearning for you is more intense than ever. I have no control over the ache from being apart. But there is some compensation for this sorrow. My ordeal has opened my eyes, and I must confess something that you in your profound feminine wisdom probably long suspected. For a long while you have indeed had a rival for my affection. Green-eyed and seductive, she had a real hold on me, until this separation from you made me realize that only you mattered—that I could never be happy except with you. Who was she? This jealous mistress was my ambition and pride. I wanted to go places in my profession, to become known, to gain respect and esteem—there was no limit to my greed for that elusive entity men sell their souls for.

Because of that, I neglected you so much. That is why you spent miserable hours waiting for me, why so many good times we should have had together were deferred. Believe me, my darling, I have more than paid for this infidelity. To say I regret it is a wild understatement. Sweetheart, I swear by all that is sacred that if God grants us the wish to be together again, I'll have but one goal and ambition: to be with you and make you happy. My career can go hang.

I hope after you read this confession you will love me as before. Don't ever stop, because if you do, I'll die. Let us both pray for much happier wedding anniversaries in the years to come. So long, my gorgeous darling; take care, have faith in God and don't ever forget how much I miss, love, worship, and adore you. I am forever

Your loving Si

He enclosed his anniversary gift: a poem. "This is so beautiful," exhaled Cecilia, tears forming in her eyes. She stood before a gilded frame hanging in my parents' den, reading aloud the verse that my mother had preserved a half-century earlier under yellowed cellophane tape:

My Meshie

Everything worthwhile in me, you inspire;
To be worthy of your generous love, I aspire;
Everything about you, I love and admire;
To be close to you always, is all I require;
The very thought of you sets me on fire;
Because you are, and always will be, my
*   heart's desire*

"My husband sent that to me for our sixth anniversary, just as his regiment shipped off to invade southern France. He didn't think he was ever going to see me again."

"God, I can't imagine," said Cecilia. "You must have been so scared."

"Sweetie, you don't know the half of it. I was sure he wasn't coming back alive. I didn't see him for almost three years. Isn't that right, honey," she said, glancing around at my father stuffed in his recliner, squinting at the television. "Si?"

"What?" he asked.

She turned back to Cecilia. "You kids these days don't know what it's like to suffer. You have no idea what we went through."

❧❧❧

What *did* she go through while he was away? "I don't like you working so hard. You don't want to lose your looks," my father warned. He was still annoyed that she was at Mike and Sylvia's advertising studio, which had grown successful. (After the war and the advent of television, Mike's share would truly skyrocket with his most famous advertising coup: a slogan for a hair home permanent formula that asked all America which twin had the Toni. But by then, my father would have reaped more than enough glory of his own to bother being jealous.)

My mother and sister continued to live with Nate and Esther Meshbesher. Despite failing to keep my educated father out of

165

combat, Nate was having a good war. Rich men's sons and politicians came to him to fix things with the draft board. One rumor, unsubstantiated, was that his clients included Minneapolis's first post-war mayor, Hubert H. Humphrey. His clout extended well within the military: A friend of his son Buddy was astounded one day, while marching with his unit at St. Paul's Ft. Snelling, to be pulled out of formation by a general who drove up in a jeep with Nate Meshbesher seated next to him and ordered him to go visit his mother.

People called Nate for black market cigarettes, bolts of silk, nylon stockings, sugar, or extra gas ration cards. His main connection was underworld kingpin Tommy Banks, currently trafficking in anything traded at a wartime premium, for whom Nate served not just as bagman but bank. This entailed risks: During one torrential April downpour, opening the door to the basement where Nate hid the ammunition boxes stuffed with Tommy Banks' cash, my mother found a layer of soggy hundred-dollar bills floating like leaf litter atop four feet of rising water. Panicked, Nate had my mother, her cousin Shirlee, Aunt Esther, and even little Cooky pressing each C-note with a warm iron and hanging them on the line to dry all night long.

Once the waters receded, that basement began filling with the trophies my father sent: German helmets, knives, pistols, swastika-emblazoned flags, medals, officers' swords, and rifles. Crates of this booty kept arriving, making my father the idol of every Meshbesher child, who wrote him begging for more. Enthralled by Si Weisman's heroic example, sixteen-year-old Buddy lied about his age and enlisted in the Marines, only to be rejected because he was color blind. Scouring Minneapolis optical shops, he found a set of the isochromatic plates the military used to test for his condition. With my mother drilling him, he memorized which ones had which numbers hidden among the colored dots and successfully re-enlisted, this time in the naval air corps.

For two breathless weeks, my father dared to believe that he might emerge from the coming months alive. On the first day of their landing near St. Tropez on the Côte d'Or, his Thirtieth Infantry took more than 200 German prisoners. Within a week they'd captured Aix-en-Provence, then moved west to secure the valuable deepwater ports of Marseille and Toulon. The scattered, disorganized German divisions they met barely mustered resistance compared to what they'd known at Anzio, and the Third Division's prisoner count soon rose past 2,000. Sensing a crumbling enemy retreating before them, they raced ahead even faster.

"I've averaged two hours of sleep a day since my landing almost two weeks ago," my father finally wrote. They ate once a day, if that, because supply trains couldn't keep up with them. When there was food, there was no time to cook it: Once, when a horse was killed in a crossfire, his platoon fell upon it and devoured it raw. They had already charged an astonishing two hundred miles up the Rhone Valley, and in the next two weeks they would advance two hundred more. In Lyon and Besançon, liberated French citizens mobbed and embraced them. As my father entered these towns he held up the leather-bound photograph of my mother and sister, and the delirious French grabbed it and kissed it.

But now they were in northern France, with the Vosges Mountains between them and the Rhine. As September passed, it became obvious as they waited for fuel and ammunition to catch up with them that the Germans were entrenching themselves in the heavily wooded, complicated mountain terrain. With their homeland at their backs, the Nazis fought like cornered rats. By the end of September, the Americans realized that they might face another winter campaign.

October was a terrible slog through the Vosges, engaging the enemy repeatedly on steep slopes of a seemingly endless succession of forested peaks identified only by objective numbers. His regiment gained ground at a cost of sixty casualties a day. By October 20 they had lost 600 men. My father was among the survivors, but barely: After a night battle in the woods outside Le

Tholy, he emerged with shrapnel in his back and another Bronze Star.

"I am in the front of the front lines," he wrote. "The horrors of what I've seen mark my soul. When I look in a mirror, my eyes scare me." He didn't look in mirrors very often; it wasn't until mid-October that he had his first shower since leaving Italy nearly two months before. His letters alternated between ceaseless longing for my mother and mounting disgust for the damn slackers back home who didn't appreciate how men were dying for them.

Although half-insane with desire for her—in one letter, he disregarded the censor and went on for pages to describe a dream in which they made love—he was often exasperated over her failure to fully grasp his wartime ordeal. No, although he was fighting near the Swiss border he wouldn't have a chance to look up her neighbor's friends in Bern. No, the French girls in St. Tropez didn't look better than her in a bathing suit. Italy? The only females he got close to in Italy were sheep. How did he know they were female? For God's sake, Charlotte. No, even though he was in his third campaign, there was no way he could put in for a furlough, much less a furlough back to the States. Won't he catch a cold sleeping in a wet foxhole? No one pays attention to mere colds; men keep fighting with bullets in their chests. And, sorry, he couldn't sympathize too much over his brother-in-law Mike Gold's advancing hair loss after witnessing his buddies' arms and legs blown off.

He surely knew the terror such words would provoke. "I don't tell you these things just to cause you grief," he claimed, "but because knowing the truth is easier than not knowing it."

How could she respond to such monstrous truths? How could she match his journey through the darkest reaches, such as his eighty-six straight days of combat as they entered November? The snow came and the Germans, whose own supply lines had grown shorter, were far better prepared, with ample winter gear and wool clothing. Not only were the Americans still wearing summer fatigues, but to avoid giving away their positions after dark, they couldn't build fires, so meals were eaten cold. Men stood all day in foxholes filled with sleet that froze solid around them as they slept. Repeatedly, they were jumped by enemy patrols hidden in the forest as they moved after dark through the mountains toward the Muerthe River, which lay between them and the last thirty miles to the German border.

My father's assignment was to precede his battalion on reconnaissance missions, then join the ensuing attack itself. By night he kept H Company moving toward their next positions, saw that ammunition and supplies reached their destinations, and supervised the sixteen men in his platoon. Ahead of them, the Nazis were fortifying a line just west of Strasbourg-on-the-Rhine with zigzag fire trenches, machine-gun placements, and concrete bunkers. There the Germans expected to hold the Allies through the winter. But before that line was in place, the Third Division deployed prefabricated footbridges to stage a surprise night crossing of the Muerthe, so swollen by autumn rains that the Nazis believed no troops could wade across.

"We've broken through the formidable line the enemy expected to hold for months," my father exulted by Thanksgiving. "I've had little sleep, shelter, food, or drink for the past forty-eight hours in some of the ruggedest fighting and terrain I've ever been in, but we're clear of the damned mountains and have him on the run once more! And all my boys are unscratched." As was he: "My company thinks I'm made of iron, scared of nothing. They should only know how weak I really am and how much I pray on each of my missions—often ten to twelve of them a day. They probably would think twice before following me."

Reaching Strasbourg, he was promoted to full staff sergeant. He took a real bath, in the summer home of Napoleon III. They now had hot food and coffee, provided by French citizens tearful with gratitude, who insisted that the filthy, exhausted American soldiers sleep in their homes. The comfort and rest after scaling and killing their way across the Vosges was a wonder, but now they had momentum they didn't want to lose. They were at the Rhine, itching to wade across immediately. "We're headed to Germany. Nothing can stop us now."

Except they weren't. Two weeks passed, and no movement. My father agonized over this lost opportunity for a knockout punch. In the streets of Strasbourg he watched men with their wives and families and grew lonelier than ever. He wrote of lying on his mattress—a mattress!—at night and visualizing her. He wrote of missing Herman and his mother, and especially his daughter, who was changing so quickly in the pictures my mother sent. He even promised to forgive and forget his rancor with Mike and Sylvia Gold. He gorged on captured German sugar, butter, sausage, liverwurst, and beer. He bought souvenirs, sent them home, and waited with his men for the order to leap the Rhine and finally end the war.

It never came, and ten days before Christmas they found out why.

❦

On the way to Strasbourg, at Natzwiller, my father's regiment had liberated their first concentration camp. It confirmed, he wrote, every abomination that had been rumored. He would say nothing further, except: "I had to hold back some of my men, who, after seeing these products of Nazi culture and enlightenment, were ready to violate the rules of war."

In local university laboratories in Strasbourg, they discovered German experiments: tests of poison gas and disease cultures on human subjects. He and his men were now ready to swim the goddam Rhine, and when they learned that crossing it was not their mission after all, they only grew angrier. Like wind preceding a hurricane, my father's voice rose to a roar, echoing the terrible Old Testament wrath that had welled up in his prize-winning letter to my sister from Anzio, which declared that God was surely punishing them all for disregarding Him. Earlier, he had written of trying to fast on Yom Kippur, a day they chased the Germans thirty miles through central France, and of almost making it until sundown. He described how he paused in mid-battlefield to say *Kaddish* on the anniversary of his father's *yahrtzeit*. His allusions to prayer, I assumed, were typical of a soldier under fire, but as his outrage mounted I now saw not only the soldier, but the Jew.

I pity any Nazi who stood in his way in January 1945, as his regiment was forced to turn away from the tantalizing sight of Germany, just across the Rhine. Instead, they headed south into Alsace, where several German divisions were still braced in a pocket around Colmar, a small city tucked between the Ill River and the Rhine itself. My father had written how at times he had even prayed for enemy soldiers—wounded prisoners he had helped to the hospital tents, where he'd served as their interpreter. But now his entire division burned to avenge the atrocities they'd seen and to annihilate the pigheaded Germans who persisted in the face of inevitable defeat. The last great Nazi counteroffensive—the Battle of the Bulge, a surge into Belgium and Luxembourg to try to recapture the port at Antwerp—had been blunted. The Colmar pocket was one of Germany's only remaining strategic pieces of occupied territory in Western Europe.

Fanatically, the Nazis clung to it.

January 29, 1945
Somewhere in northeastern France
My dearest darling sweetheart Meshie,

This is my first chance to write in eight days. The last seven days have been among the most trying of all the unfortunate and miserable times I have had overseas. I can't give you many details, but I can tell you that our luck ran out—three of our boys are no longer with us. My grief at losing these wonderful kids is so great I can't collect my wits enough to write you a proper letter.

Except for getting quite wet in a 1,100-yard swim through an icy river and being half frozen to death, I am

171

none the worse off physically—except that I am getting too old for this horrible business. I have slowed up in the last thirty days, but we don't have the luxury to refresh our weary bodies or recharge our worn batteries—we have no choice but to go until we drop. I'm certain that if we had to take our induction physicals again, none of us would pass.

For five weeks, his regiment had been fighting with the First French Army in Alsace-Lorraine, seventy miles south of Strasbourg. They were part of a special task force that had engaged the Germans in steep woodlands above the Colmar pocket, penetrating along a mountainous salient that cut deeply toward the north. After a month of nonstop combat, often in blizzard conditions, they had accomplished their bloody mission of securing their position. My father's Thirtieth Infantry Regiment had been recommended for both a Presidential Unit Citation and a French Republic unit citation by General Charles de Gaulle.

Then, the assault on the pocket itself began. It was Anzio in reverse, this time with the Allies on the high ground, except the Germans were superbly fortified behind two natural barriers: the Fecht and the Ill rivers, which paralleled the Rhine. During a five-day break, my father's regiment trained in snowshoes and skis and practiced river crossings by night. On January 22, they made ready to charge bridgeheads over the two rivers. The Alsatian plain was covered in deep snow; the temperature never rose above 14°F. Trucks and armored vehicles were painted white, and the men camouflaged themselves in suits sewn of sheets and pillowcases. The tank and infantry battalions planned to attack at 9:00 P.M., force a crossing of the Fecht, then race two miles to the Ill, where they would secure the main bridge leading to the city of Colmar.

Using prefabricated footbridges heaped on rubber rafts, two entire battalions were across the Fecht within an hour. But there everything stopped, as they were met with enemy mortar and machine-gun fire. With his reconnaissance unit, my father crept ahead toward the Ill. German patrols were practically everywhere;

it took all night to crawl and wade the intervening two miles. By 5:00 A.M. his unit reported back that the low, wooden bridge at a narrows called Maison Rouge was intact; they had crossed it, and were now attracting enemy fire.

Behind them came the rest of their battalion, charging across gullies over makeshift footbridges until they reached the river's edge. All morning, forces from both sides amassed up and down the river, exchanging mortar rounds and small-arms fire, as they fought for the little Maison Rouge bridge. By noon it belonged to the Allies, and three companies were able to join my father's reconnaissance patrol across the river. Their tanks, however, couldn't follow, due to doubts whether the old wooden bridge columns could hold them.

That afternoon, American and French troops engaged in a tremendous battle with German armor and infantry on the east bank of the Ill River. By 4:30 P.M., when it was nearly dark and the outcome still undecided, the Americans decided to break the onslaught of German tanks by sending their own across. Army engineers who had rushed to reinforce the Maison Rouge bridge with metal treadway, however, were still fifteen feet short. Figuring that jeeps and other vehicles had already made it, they decided to chance it. They lay treadway on either end, leaving the fifteen-foot gap in the middle, and sent a tank over. It promptly crashed through and fell into the river, just as the truck bearing the remaining treadway sections appeared. The infantry troops on the east bank were now stranded without tanks against the heavily armored Germans. At that moment, the Nazis charged.

My father's battalion was caught in the open. Another squad began directing bazooka fire at the advancing enemy tanks to cover the exposed men. American and French field units lay down a huge sustained artillery barrage, blanket coverage that enabled nearly all Allied troops to pull back that night across a makeshift bridge laid over the partially submerged tank. But scattered elements were reported still pinned down on the other side. The men of my father's H Company realized that he was among them.

On March 24, 1958, my father took us to dinner at Sheik's, a Minneapolis restaurant. The occasion was my mother's birthday and mine: I was now 11—the same age, my father reminded me, when he arrived in America. The maître d' at Sheik's was a tall, balding German named Hans. That night, he stopped by our table, and in the course of conversation he and my father discovered that thirteen years earlier they had been firing at one another for control of the same bridge over France's Ill River, a few miles from the Rhine.

Listening to them, I tried to comprehend what could have been so important about a bridge—or anything—that these two friendly men had once tried hard to kill each other. My father and Hans apparently saw no particular irony in this grisly coincidence. In fact, they were clasping each other's shoulders and laughing.

"How can you even talk to him, Dad, if he was your enemy?" I asked after he'd left.

"Because the war's over now."

"I know, but still—"

"A lot of the German boys didn't want to be fighting. They had no choice. When I was interrogating prisoners, they told me that anyone who suggested they surrender was shot on the spot by their officers. You had to be there to understand, son. Now finish your steak. I want to see a clean plate."

"Yes, sir."

Around 9:00 P.M., by the glow of searchlights they spotted him, backed up to the river by advancing gunners. There was only one way out, and he took it, plunging into the swift, icy Ill and swimming for his life as German soldiers fired at him. The air temperature was −5°. The current dragged him a thousand yards downstream as he fought to reach the other side. "It was either that or never see you and Cooky again. How I made it against the current with a bunch of Krauts shooting at me, I will never know. You, my sweetheart, were never closer than at that time. Every ounce of my energy was gone and I couldn't move one arm—yet somehow I managed to stay above water. You pulled me through. If it weren't for the power of your love, I'd be turtle bait now."

No change of clothing awaited him. Immediately, he and his platoon marched seven miles, dodging artillery and skirmishing with enemy riflemen. Six hours later, he was able to pause and strip off his uniform, frozen so solid that in places it ripped his skin free as he removed it. After partially drying it over a fire, he put it back on still damp and continued on, his teeth chattering uncontrollably. The forced march probably saved him from hypothermia that would have killed him, but his companions weren't as lucky. Around midnight, an artillery shell landed on them dead center, blowing three of his boys to bits.

The fighting at Colmar continued at the same pitch for sixteen more days. There was no more battle strategy, only a slugfest. The French and U.S. armies simply heaped on more men until the Germans were finally driven across the Rhine and out of France forever. In that two-and-a-half weeks, 500 men died in my father's regiment, which was awarded the French Croix de Guerre. The entire Third Division received a Presidential Unit Citation. It was the end of February. Germany lay before them.

Two days after his icy escape at the Ill River, my father learned that his application to become an officer in the Army's Judge Advocate General's Corp was officially rejected. No reason was given in the mimeographed letter signed by a colonel in Washington, which arrived in a folder containing splendid recommendations, from his company commander all the way up to an aide in Eisenhower's office.

"Why is it everything I want so badly never comes to me?" he wondered. But, hell—he truly didn't care anymore, he wrote my mother during a two-day pass to Paris after the Colmar Pocket campaign. All that mattered were the boys he had lost in battle and getting home as quickly as possible. But nothing, he warned her, would accomplish that until the last Nazi Party official was dead. Despite what the papers printed about the Russians being within thirty miles of Berlin, the worst was yet to come. Hundreds of thousands more would die, he predicted, in the Armageddon God had planned for them.

Yet two months later—on her thirtieth birthday, March 24, 1945—he could write that "God has helped us achieve unbelievable success. What took Hitler years to build, God and our division have torn asunder in less than twenty-four hours. That's all it took us to puncture and rip to shreds that portion of the Siegfried Line which [General Patton's] armored divisions have poured through to surround the Krauts."

He had been in Germany just nine days. Back with the Seventh Army now, his Third Division was racing even faster than during their celebrated dash from Marseilles to northern France. With armored bulldozers, they pushed fill into the deep anti-tank ditches of the Siegfried Line and charged across. A week later they took Heidelberg, then Worms, then rushed due east from town to town, liberating Allied prisoners of war they found nearly starving to death in Reich camps. In early April they crossed the Main, then crossed it again as Patton's Third Army continued east and the Seventh veered south to Nuremberg, which they captured on April 20. It was Hitler's birthday, and they raised the American flag in Adolf Hitler Platz, which they renamed Eisener-Michael Platz for the Third Division's commander, General Iron Mike O'Daniel.

A week later, just as it looked like no one would again try to stop them, they met an unexpected artillery force on the Lech River, the likes of which they had only seen in Anzio and Colmar. Until that point, my father had grown so heady over their great victories that in his letters—when he had a moment to dash one off—his thinking had jumped beyond V-E Day: There were unnerving

176

rumors that the Third Division would next be sent to the Philippines via the Suez Canal to end the war with Japan.

He begged my mother to write to everyone in Washington on behalf of him and his comrades, who were now in their seventh campaign—one that wasn't over yet, as they learned when they encountered a spectacular last-ditch mass barrage of eighty-eight-millimeter guns at the Lech bridgehead. The firefight that raged all night and through the next day was so fearsome that afterward he sent a rare telegram to assure her he was safe.

The following night, they were camped on a rise, looking down at their final objective: Munich. Within hours, the lines of German prisoners stretched further than the eye could see.

On May 3, his daughter's third birthday, my father's regiment was ordered to march south until they crossed the border and liberated Mozart's beautiful city of Salzburg, Austria. In seven weeks in Germany, they had covered 700 miles and taken 25,000 prisoners. As they entered Salzburg, they found that an armistice commission representing Field Marshal Kesselring, commander of all German forces on the Western Front, was waiting for them. The war in Europe was over.

"I never expected to live through it or see you again," he wrote. But when would that be? From the way they jumped back into training, he feared demobilization would never come—that he'd be trading his snowshoes for tropical fatigues any day. In the meantime, he sent my mother boxes filled with more spoils of war: Luger pistols, his Spandau machine gun, felt-encased canteens, ceremonial swords, more helmets, German field glasses ("we'll use them at football games"), swastika armbands, and medals of the Third Reich. Another prize he kept with him: a German Leica camera, which he used to photograph Salzburg's castle and the U.S. Army marching through the streets, and to take hundreds of snapshots of his triumphant boys.

Now that they had become an army of occupation, the brass finally noticed that my father had other talents than merely being a killing machine. He was multilingual, and an attorney to boot. Since Anzio he had been the unofficial German translator for his regiment, and he amazed them all when he provided the same services in Russian when the Allied armies of the East and West began to mingle after they finally met at the River Elbe and split the Western Front for good. Now they put him to work as interpreter, investigator, judge, and arbiter of affairs between soldiers and civilians, as well as chief vegetable purchaser for the regiment.

He knew what was coming. With war crime trials already being discussed for the following autumn in Nuremberg, the army would need bilingual prosecutors. Sure enough, within days he was offered another field commission, this time finally as an officer with the Judge Advocate General Corps. But by then the demobilization program had been made public: Men who had earned eighty-five points—calculated by a combination of campaigns fought, decorations earned, and months of service—would be the first to receive their discharges. My father had amassed 112. "No thank you," he replied for a second time to the offer of a commission. He was going home.

But months passed before army bureaucracy got around to him, and his letters of the summer of 1945 plunged quickly from the elation of victory to the galling impatience of waiting, as he wrote my mother that their separation felt more maddening than ever. "I'm gaining weight," he fretted. "Better buy me pants with a size-36 waist instead of 34."

No, he promised, he wasn't drinking any more than an occasional beer. No, he didn't care what her friend's husband had done with a French woman, he was remaining true. "You should hear the stories we deal with," he retorted, "about soldiers coming home to the illegitimate children their wives bore while they were away." And by the way, why was she still working at Mike's, now that the war was ending? "I'm glad you've enjoyed it, but when I come back you will be too busy to be there," he informed her.

———

"You know," old Rabbi Schulman said to me at the funeral forty-seven years later, "I met your father at the train when he returned from World War II. That seems like barely yesterday."

Until just a few days before he stepped off that train, he'd written to her every night. Even with the shooting over, he was unable or too scared to stop communicating to this woman in the only way he had for thirty-one months. Reading the last rush of letters, I tried to imagine the scramble of their emotions—the excitement, desire, repressed wartime terrors, and now this: the reencounter. How had each changed?

My father once wrote of a battlefield dream in which he had come home and his tiny daughter was wise enough to tell everyone that "Mommy and Daddy need to be alone." And in the end, it turned out to be this daughter who diverted all their anxieties. That summer, a routine case of childhood mumps escalated to a mastoid infection, and suddenly at the end of July my victorious father was staring with disbelief at a telegram saying that his precious daughter had undergone emergency surgery that left her face paralyzed and her fate uncertain.

Two weeks of no news followed, two weeks in which his telegrams went unanswered and three years of war suddenly seemed like nothing compared to the hell he now knew. Somehow, during those frantic fourteen days he smashed through the bureaucracy and got the emergency furlough every other American soldier in Europe wanted. And somehow, the God to whom he'd prayed for years for a break finally gave it to him. On August 14, their seventh anniversary and the day Japan announced its surrender, he learned that it wasn't a furlough, but an honorable discharge. And while awaiting his ship home in La Havre, a cable reached him that read: "Cooky fine. Don't worry."

"I arrived safely in Boston," he wired.

"I'm in Camp McCoy, Wisconsin," he wrote. "I'll be discharged in three days, on Friday. I'll be on the Chicago-Milwaukee train that arrives in Minneapolis at 6:45 P.M. Can you get a pair of decent tickets for the football game on Saturday? Maybe Nate can help you."

He would see his mother and "everyone else on the welcoming committee" on Friday night, his letter continued. On Saturday, they would go to the game and go out to dinner. On Sunday, rest and take Cooky for a walk in Wirth Park. So simple.

"Oh, yes," he added. "Should I buy some you-know-whats at the PX?"

PART THREE

CHAPTER 11

On a Sunday in 1954 when I was seven, my father took me to the Orpheum Theater in Minneapolis to see Audie Murphy in *To Hell and Back*. It was the first time he and I ever went to a movie alone. It was a war film, he told me. "Not for womenfolk."

Audie Murphy, the most decorated U.S. soldier in World War II, played himself in the movie. Like my father, he fought in the Third Division, from North Africa to Italy, France, and Germany, where he won every medal the army awards to combat soldiers. My father, I knew, didn't win as many as Audie Murphy, but clippings in my mother's scrapbook called him the most decorated soldier in Minneapolis and the most decorated Jewish soldier in the Upper Midwest.

We sat in the maroon velvet theater seats I knew well from the Saturday afternoons when my sister, Cooky, would bring me downtown on the bus to see matinees. But with my father, there was no popcorn. "We'll eat later. I want you to pay attention to this." The plot moved through Murphy's early life in Texas—abandoned by his father and orphaned by his mother—to his enlistment and assignment overseas. Once we got to the part about Anzio, my father began shaking his head. "Aw, bullshit," he'd hiss through tight lips, as Murphy performed his heroics.

"What's wrong, Dad? Didn't you like him?" I whispered.

"Sure I liked him. He was very brave," he whispered back.

"But these goddam movie directors have a pretty soft idea of what war is like."

I was watching an impressive amount of gore, but I had nothing to compare it to. My father brightened during one scene when the men were eating K-rations while standing in a soaking downpour. "Now that's a little more like it," he said. "Except that's how most days were. They've got the sonofabitch backwards."

The movie's climax was a scene just east of the Colmar pocket, where Murphy won the highest decoration of all, the Congressional Medal of Honor. Although they were in different regiments, my father was quite near him that day, barely concealed in a sparse woodland outside the town. Just as Lieutenant Murphy crept ahead to man a command post, waves of German foot soldiers and tanks charged. At one point, the Nazis' artillery hit one of their own advancing tank destroyers, setting it ablaze. Suddenly, Murphy leaped forward, mounted the burning tank, swung its .50-caliber machine gun around and began firing at the advancing enemy. They were coming from all sides: up the draws, through the forest, between the tanks, and Murphy, completely exposed, kept mowing them down, seemingly oblivious to unceasing rifle and artillery fire that seemed certain either to kill him or blow the destroyer's fuel tank.

In the movie, the scene lasted only moments—where in real life, my father objected, he single-handedly repulsed the attack for nearly an hour. "And he was badly wounded, too. They knocked him off that goddam thing twice, and he kept crawling back on and firing again." The movie had ended, but we still sat there while he finished setting the record straight for me.

"And another thing: This happened in the dead of winter"— three days after my father's icy swim in the Ill River—"and the reason we were so exposed was that there were no leaves on the trees and the ground was frozen so solid we couldn't dig in. Believe me, the sun wasn't shining, the way they have it. Why the hell didn't they film it in January? Because they didn't want to freeze their fannies off like we did. That's why."

It was early winter dusk in Minneapolis when we finally left the theater, and since we were downtown my father decided to take me to the Standard Club. "Let's go have a steam bath."

"Okay," I replied, keeping my mixed reactions to myself. The Standard Club was a Jewish social club that my parents had joined when my father returned from the war. It had a bar and restaurant with green carpeting on its top floor, smoky card rooms below where men played poker and kids weren't allowed, and a men-only locker room in the basement, with a steam bath and four bowling alleys. It had been known for decades as the Gymal Doled Club, named for the third and fourth letters in the Hebrew alphabet (an older St. Paul club was called Aleph Beth). A decision in 1951 to Anglicize its name was angrily contested by the older generation who claimed correctly that it was a portent of assimilation, but younger members like my father had prevailed.

We often had dinner there on weekends. I was pleased to be going there alone with my father, especially since I knew we would end up at the bar, where the bartenders would mix me a house "kiddie cocktail" of ginger ale with a maraschino cherry when they served my father's scotch or bourbon. ("Take a sip and tell me which," he would say. They tasted equally acrid, and I only guessed right half the time. But I liked sampling them.)

The steam bath, however, was more complicated. I loved the sheer masculinity of the locker room, with all the big men stripped naked, wrapping themselves in white sheets that the black attendants handed out as we headed for the dry heat room, where we always began. But once inside, it became an ordeal that I had learned I must abide, lest I displease my father.

At that age, what might be relaxing about a room where my father hiked the thermostat to 150° F. and men in shower clogs drooped in wooden armchairs, sweat pasting their chest hairs together and their circumcised members shriveling until they looked like pink eggs in their curly nests, was beyond me. Our sheets smelled, and felt, as if they were about to burst into flame. There was a big round wall clock, whose minute hand I mentally willed to advance as fast as possible through the ten minutes my father liked to spend in there. But I knew not to complain.

"Who's this, Si, your boy?" the only other man in the room asked.

"My son, Alan. Alan, this is Mr. Winter."

I recognized him as one of the cigar-smoking poker players I'd see from the restaurant staircase whose brushed-metal art deco bannisters I liked to descend.

"Are you going to be as tough as your father?" he asked me. Four parallel streams of perspiration poured down his matted gray chest.

"Damn right he is," my father answered for me. "We even call him Tuffy for short." Already at seven, I'd had to learn to defend myself because of that nickname, which my father foisted upon me when I was barely a week old. When bigger neighborhood Gentile boys who reflexively beat up smaller Jewish kids heard it, it made normally bad things only worse.

There was a moment of blessed relief when we crossed the ten feet between the dry room and the actual steam bath, the temperature instantly dropping eighty degrees as we handed our sheets to the attendant. Then we were inside a cauldron of scalding vapor, through which I could faintly discern rows of pale male legs descending from the upper tiled tiers, where the heat soared much higher than I could tolerate. Even at the bottom, where my father mercifully let me remain, it was hard to breathe. I stayed quiet, though, staring up at his toes with their forests of black hairs, recalling that I had been here before and this, too, would pass.

Admittedly, there was something wonderful when it was all over and we stood under deliciously refreshing showers. I knew that my father was proud of me for enduring this ritual without complaint. In the shower he sudsed me down roughly, pulling me against his growing belly with powerful arms to nearly flatten my head with a bar of yellow soap. I avoided mentioning that my mother had taught me only to use shampoo on my hair—never soap, which was much too harsh. Afterward, he rubbed me so hard

186

with the towel that I thought I would shine like the bowling balls the black attendants polished for the evening men's league, whose members were just now arriving. My father didn't bowl, but he made it a point of knowing all the attendants and pinspotters by name, because they attended North High School where he'd graduated and played football. Colored people, as my mother called them, were now even living in the house on the North Side that we sold when we moved to the suburbs.

"We'd better get going home—your mother will start to worry," he said an hour later, after we'd downed a pair of kiddie cocktails and Johnnie Walkers. My hair was still wet, and outside in the Minnesota evening air it froze instantly. The windshield of my father's Pontiac instantly turned opaque as we settled our still-overheated bodies into the front seat.

"How much worse was the war than the movie?" I asked him, as we sat waiting for the defroster to take effect.

He snorted. "You'll never know, son, until it's your turn someday to go and fight one. God willing, you'll never have to. But if you do, you'll have to do your duty. Just like I did."

"Did you ever kill anybody?"

"It's not nice to talk about it. I just did whatever I had to so my men and I wouldn't get killed ourselves. But most of the time, it felt like the world was ending."

That intrigued me. "Do they know how the world will end, Dad?" Immediately, I knew I had asked the wrong thing. His lips tightened, and he started swabbing at the windshield frost with his overcoat sleeve. "Damn it," he muttered—not at me, really, but at everything in general that wasn't responding properly to him. He had been imparting something about his war, and I'd slipped away on my own tangent, taking a metaphor literally and turning it into a science question. Already I was mapping out my own world, and it was a lot different from his. Soon after learning to read, I'd realized that he couldn't answer most of the questions that interested me. As I grew older, it became increasingly rare that we enjoyed a real conversation.

187

We drove home in silence, my father in a distant cloud of disappointment, me wondering who I could ask about the end of the world. Not my first grade teacher, who, since the unit on birds we'd just completed, admitted that I knew more about natural phenomena than she did. Not my mother, whose knowledge veered more toward the supernatural than nature: She saw portents in the likes of itching palms, dropped silverware, and spilled salt shakers, and predicted dark consequences if we failed to heed them. Three years earlier, when my great-grandfather Jacob Meshbesher died at age ninety-one, she made sure every morning that I stood away from the tall elm in front of our house while awaiting the nursery school bus, so that *Zaydeh* could look down and see me from heaven. I was impressed that she knew precisely where the dead could or couldn't see, but I correctly guessed that her realm of understanding was beyond science.

When we got home I went to my sister's bedroom: In this new house, we each had our own. My walls were covered in tight brown burlap, and I had hung them with pictures of birds and pennants of college football teams, along with framed photographs of my dad in his army uniform. My sister's room was painted pale turquoise. She was sitting on her quilted bedspread, reading a book for her sixth grade class when I went in. "Did you have fun?" she asked.

"Uh-huh. Cooky, how's the world going to end? Do you know?"

"I think I read that the sun will fall. It will get much hotter and we'll all burn up."

That night I dreamt of soldiers firing at each other, then stopping dead in their tracks as they looked up and realized that the sun was getting bigger, and bigger, and coming to turn them to ashes and put an end to all their wars.

◦⟨👁👁⟩◦

"All our lives, the sun has meant life and rebirth to us," the bishop told us. "But now when we walk out and see the sunrise, it has become a sign of our death." Tomás González Morales, bishop of Punta Arenas, Chile, the world's southernmost city, had large, friendly, drooping jowls reminiscent of a basset hound, and a similarly doleful countenance as he described ministering to a flock that suddenly found itself living on the edge of the Antarctic ozone hole.

From Brazil, Cecilia and I had flown down the spine of the Andes to this city on the Strait of Magellan. In southern Chile, a pristine land where Andean condors circled over fabulous blue glaciers, rumors now swirled of sheep and rabbits going blind. Light-sensitive crops like roses and cucumbers were shriveling; melanomas and other skin ailments had surged; and children were turning pink as lobsters from a phenomenon hitherto unknown in these cold climes: sunburn. Ozone loss caused by man-made refrigerants was suspected. In just twenty years, the amount of springtime ultraviolet radiation hitting the Antarctic Peninsula, only six hundred miles to the south, had doubled, and Punta Arenas residents were now worrying that one day they actually might have to abandon their homes.

After days of interviewing doctors, ranchers, horticulturists, and naturalists, we realized that more research was needed to know what was causing such changes in this beautiful land of craggy fjords that snaked among mountains nearly as high as the Himalayas. But plainly, people here were scared. "We always thought this was the lost paradise, one step from Antarctica," a local journalist told us. "We thought nothing could reach us—like Chernobyl, which contaminated the food in Europe. But now we poor, underdeveloped people at the end of the earth, who are least responsible for this, may be one step from having the worst disaster ever over our heads. It doesn't seem fair."

The idea of such a cataclysm coming from the sky was shaking their very souls, she said. How, we asked the bishop, did he address this growing eco-spiritual crisis in his midst?

"There's a Bible passage I share with parishioners. It tells of a new heaven and a new earth," he told us. "It's in the Book of Revelations. The Apocalypse." I looked up sharply. I couldn't ever

189

recall hearing Catholic clergy refer to Revelations. He showed us where: in Verse 21:1, after the seven angels of the seven seals had unleashed their seven plagues on the land, as God wreaked His terrible vengeance, burning the sinners in a lake of fire and destroying the world, prior to resurrecting a new one.

> *And I saw a new heaven and a new earth;*
> *for the first heaven and the first earth were passed away;*

Did he really equate this ozone thing with *that*, we asked? Was Armageddon flickering just beyond the southern horizon?

He fingered his Bible silently before he finally responded. "Maybe this passage just means that rebirth comes about as a result of new respect for the earth. That's what I try to tell them in my sermons: That we have to be the earth's friends. When the Pope gave Mass here three years ago, he said that we who stand at the end of the earth are the hope of the future. We will either open the door of hope to a world that mustn't destroy itself— or close it."

As I unlocked the door and entered my house in the pine forest outside of Prescott, Arizona, for the first time in almost a year, the phone was ringing.

"That'll be Charlotte," I said to Cecilia, as I picked up the receiver.

"Alan," said my mother, "she's darling."

"I know, Mom. Cec is terrific." I winked at Cecilia. She was gazing around with approval at the open beams, skylights, and spruce paneling of the cabin that my former wife and I had modified, which she'd never seen before.

"Don't you think so, Si?" my mother said. "Si, did you pick up the receiver?"

"Don't I think what?" my father grunted.

"That Cecilia is darling."

"Who the hell is Cecilia?"

"You know: *Cecilia*. Alan's girlfriend. They came by here this morning on their way back from Costa Rica."

"They did?"

"Of course they did. They drove all the way. They're back to stay now, don't you remember? Oh, Alan, he doesn't remember anything anymore."

"It's all right, Mom. Dad, you were pretty tired. We woke you up from a nap."

"When?"

We'd returned from Chile to our Costa Rican base a day after Sandy and Nancy had arrived from their final trip, to Honduras. To celebrate the end of our field research, we drove to the Pacific coast and rented a pair of cottages at a small resort. After a blessed nap, we convened at the patio restaurant. Sandy produced two bottles of strong dark rum that we'd purchased in the Dominican Republic. In white slacks and shirt, he looked tan and handsome, but weary. We all were: I noticed that strands of silver now glinted in Nancy's long, lush black hair.

En route to the seacoast, Cecilia and I had argued in whispers in the backseat. It started because she was upset at Sandy over a misfired communication. When I kept insisting that she confront him, she redirected her anger at me for telling her what to do. Somehow, this turned into a fight, and suddenly I was screaming at everyone. I wasn't even sure why; the way my colleagues eyed me with alarm, they certainly didn't know, either. Finally, I broke down in tears. "I'm sorry," I apologized when I could speak again. "I'm so damn exhausted."

This was met with silence; they'd heard this from me before. "Everybody's tired," Nancy finally agreed.

Over dinner, we proceeded to get very drunk. For nine months, in a dozen countries, we had been documenting unprecedented societal dislocation. Refugees were nothing new: Merely a generation or two back, our own families had been pried from their respective homelands. But the world had never seen the like of these massive new dispossessed populations. Throughout the Third World, grand development schemes were pressuring the land to yield ever more resources. As ancient forests were mowed and farms converted to cash crops for export, entire peasant and indigenous societies were forced into unproductive marginal areas, or into cities where they became landless urban poor, raising a burgeoning worldwide generation of rootless children.

Sandy and Nancy had just spent a week on the outskirts of Tegucigalpa, in one of the misery belts widening around Third World cities everywhere, filled with exiles from a southern Honduras valley once known as the granary of Central America. It was now classified as permanent desert, beyond recovery. "It looked like southwestern Arizona," said Sandy, pouring us more rum. "Dozens of rivers have dried up. The hills are bald."

In our own lifetimes, environmental collapse had joined war and persecution as a threat to the existence of entire human cultures. In Chile, we'd begun to wonder whether everyone's homeland might be vanishing, if thinning of the ozone layer continued to spread. I recounted how, after interviewing the bishop, Cecilia had suggested we stop into the Punta Arenas parish school to record the sound of kids at recess. In the gymnasium, well-scrubbed, healthy-looking children in blue gym uniforms were playing indoor soccer on a beechwood basketball court. They were mainly fair-skinned—descended, like most southern Chileans, from Croatians who had fled when World War I broke out in neighboring Serbia, finding cheap land in this far corner of the Americas after the new Panama Canal diverted shipping traffic northward.

We'd been sitting in bleachers that were painted a candy spectrum, and I'd suddenly recalled once glancing up during a wrestling meet and seeing my father seated in rainbow-striped stands like these, watching me. . . .

Abruptly, I'd shoved my microphone at Cecilia and run outside. A moment later, she found me sitting on the steps, sobbing.

"What's wrong?" she kept asking, but it took ten minutes for me to compose myself. Finally, I explained. In one country after another we had met Indians, mestizos, and blacks being ripped from the places they loved. But—I was ashamed to admit—it wasn't until I watched a bunch of white kids who looked like me playing ball in a gym that looked like some school in Minnesota that I finally, truly understood.

In that moment I'd seen a mirrored image of my own home at the other end of the earth, and my very blood sensed that something terrible could be happening here. The invisible, deadly nightmare looming overhead kept getting bigger; everybody was telling us about crazy things happening in a gorgeous setting at the end of the earth, which wasn't some exotic rainforest but someplace shockingly similar to home. This stuff wasn't just happening to remote, forgotten people. It was happening to us all.

By the time I finished telling my colleagues that story, the rum was gone, but we all felt dead sober. Nancy broke the silence. "Speaking of home," she said. "I've got some news for everybody."

We'd planned to remain in Costa Rica to produce our NPR series from the tape we'd gathered in the field. But Nancy, our project administrator, had just learned from the customs ministry in San José that our vehicle permits couldn't be renewed. She had an appointment with an attorney the following week. "But don't get your hopes up. The customs brokers tell me you can't even bribe these people."

Unexpectedly, exultation welled within me. For months, we'd been hearing an endless litany of the troubles the United States had caused in Latin America during this century: first with its big stick, now with its big corporations and big banks. But in that moment, I didn't care what misdeeds my country was responsible for. Given the chance and the power, any nation on earth—at least any nation I'd ever been in—would probably exploit its neighbors just as greedily.

The United States might be making hash of the hemisphere;

it might have orchestrated coups to depose heads of state in Guatemala and Chile and financed a protracted war to do likewise in Nicaragua. But it was still home. I was one of the diminishing percentage of humans on the planet who still had a home. I wanted to go there.

CHAPTER 12

In 1946, journalist Carey McWilliams, author of several distinguished books about minorities in America, traveled to Minneapolis on assignment to *Common Ground* magazine. The article he eventually published, titled "Minneapolis: The Curious Twin," portrayed the town where I was born the following year as the "most anti-Semitic city in America."

Unlike neighboring St. Paul, McWilliams wrote, where German Jews had been among the city's founders, in Minneapolis Jews were restricted to specific neighborhoods. They were excluded not only from private country clubs but from local Rotary, Lions, Kiwanis, and Toastmasters chapters. Jews were not admitted to the board of Realtors, and couldn't even join the Minneapolis branch of the Automobile Association of America. Jewish doctors like my father's ophthalmologist cousin, Harry Friedman, had to take their postgraduate residencies elsewhere, and were routinely denied access to surgical theaters in Minneapolis.

Given recent revelations about the Nazi Holocaust, in 1946 such charges were particularly shameful, and the city's new mayor, Hubert H. Humphrey, commissioned a task force to investigate them. His blue-ribbon panel concluded that the problem was even worse than McWilliams had described. Fewer than 2 percent of the city's Jews were professionals. Although Jewish schoolteachers were common in urban school systems elsewhere, Minneapolis had just five, plus one Jewish principal. Jews were even barred from local chapters of labor unions whose founding members back in New York had been Jewish. Summer resorts on Minnesota lakes advertised in Minneapolis newspapers that they catered to "Gentiles only." Department stores such as Montgomery Ward wouldn't interview Jewish job applicants.

Unsurprisingly, the commission discovered that Negroes and Indians were similarly blackballed throughout the city. Vowing to expunge discrimination, Humphrey turned the task force into a permanent Mayor's Council on Human Relations. Over the next two years, the city council passed many measures outlawing anti-Semitic and racist practices in housing and employment. The image of Minneapolis changed quickly from national embarrassment to progressive leader, but its Jewish community, although encouraged, wasn't fooled. The teaching profession remained almost exclusively Christian; during my own kindergarten-through-twelve trajectory, I would encounter only one Jewish teacher, a substitute. The University of Minnesota was notorious among job-hunting Jewish Ph.D.s for its *yudenhein* faculty (literally, purified of Jews). The only solution to local bigotry in that other classic Jewish career, medicine, was to build a Jewish hospital, Mt. Sinai.

This was the civic ambience to which my father returned from the war, where his final duties included interrogating SS officers about Jewish concentration camps. A starving Minneapolis Jewish attorney before he enlisted, he returned to find the legal profession still largely a Gentile world. My mother's Uncle Si Meshbesher was among the few Jewish lawyers; my father harbored an indelible, sore memory of the one time Uncle Si had hired him to write a brief, then paid him just ten dollars. But now, he had no further need to subject himself to humiliation.

Even non-Jewish law firms were eager to add a highly decorated hero such as my father to their rosters, and astutely he joined one. The final entry of my mother's war scrapbooks was a news clipping stating that Minneapolis attorney Colonel Edward Kotrich, recently Judge Advocate of the U.S. Army in the United

Kingdom and winner of a Bronze Star, was forming a new law partnership with well-known local lawyer Fred Ossanna, who represented the Yellow Cab Company and Sears & Roebuck. Among the firm's junior associates was another noted veteran: Staff Sergeant Simon A. Weisman, graduate of the University of Minnesota Law School, holder of seven battle stars for European Theater campaigns, winner of the Purple Heart, the Silver Star, two Bronze Stars with oak leaf cluster, two Presidential Unit Citations, the Good Conduct Medal, the Combat Infantry Badge, and the French Croix de Guerre.

With World War II, my father had completed the passage begun years before on the football field. No longer was he just an immigrant. He had finally won his stripes as an American.

At thirty-three, he was ten years senior to the other associates in his office. One of them, Fred Ossanna, Jr., had studied law at the University of Texas and invited a classmate to apply to the firm. Charles Hvass, a tall, lanky Lubbock native with a cleft chin, visited Minneapolis during June and made the mistake of accepting the job before sampling a northern winter. My father was soon delighted that he did. During the war, he discovered, this young Texan had commanded a B-24, piloting bombing missions over France and Germany.

Charlie Hvass soon learned that his new best friend was one tough Jew. Early on, he saw my father win a barroom bet by ripping a Minneapolis phone book in half. The story of how Si had passed up a commission in the war was well known; the reason, my father told him, was that he wanted to prove that a Jew could fight. And everyone had heard that after Si Weisman quit playing college football because he had to study and drive his bakery truck, the second-string quarterback who played behind him on the freshman squad went on to lead the 1936 University of Minnesota team to the national championship.

My father took Charlie Hvass to see the house he was having built. His wife, Char, he explained, was seven months pregnant

and due in March, so he'd convinced the contractor to keep working through the winter. He drove Charlie up to Minneapolis's
North Side, past Nate Meshbesher's house—even new lawyers in
town knew who Nate was—and pulled over at a construction site a
block away on Thomas Avenue. As they walked in, the first thing
my father noticed was that in places the new plywood flooring
didn't quite reach the walls. He called over a workman and pointed
to the gaps along the baseboards. "What about that?" he asked.

The workman, who turned out to be the crew chief, had never
met him. "Carpet'll cover that. The owner will never notice." This
answer, Charlie Hvass knew, was a big mistake. Bodily, my father
heaved the man off the job, told him to take his goddam crew with
him, and added an explicit message for the contractor who hired
them.

The next day, the contractor called his office. "They said you
own a German machine gun and you were going to use it on me,
Mr. Weisman. I'm sure they were just kidding, of course."

"You heard right, you s.o.b. Unless you build that house the
way it was mean to be built." Which he did.

The house was atop a crest, requiring a stepped walkway to
the entrance. My mother insisted that this path be curved. The
luckless contractor somehow managed to build it straight. Sure
enough, three months before I was born she fell on the new steps
and—according to family lore—nearly miscarried. That evening
my father informed the contractor precisely what would happen to
him if those steps weren't ripped out and built correctly by the next
time he came by the building site. Which they were.

They moved in during January 1947. It was barely nine hundred square feet: a living room with green floral carpeting and a
flagstone fireplace, a dining room off the kitchen slightly bigger
than the table, a single pink-tiled bath, two bedrooms, and a staircase leading to a hot attic. The back door opened into a landing
that led up into the kitchen or down to a basement, where my
mother kept her washing machine and the hot rotating cylinder
she used to iron sheets. No one would ever accuse Charlotte Weisman of letting her family sleep on unironed sheets.

We lived there until I was six. Another family legend claimed that the first time my father held me, lifting me to eye level, I kicked him, bloodying his nose, an incident that resulted in the nickname that taught me to defend myself at an earlier age than usual. I don't remember that event, of course, but I recall another when I was still two: climbing the Victrola to make it play "Jambalaya" by Hank Williams and pulling it down on top of me. Mainly, I recall my terror at what my father would do to me when he got home.

"Just wait until your father hears about this. Then you're going to get it." That refrain of my mother's, more than one therapist later informed me, did my sister's psyche and mine no great favors. Aside from the fact that her role of snitch undermined her own authority and our trust in her, I was given to understand that by leaving the punishment to him, our mother presented us with a fractured parental front guaranteed to confuse our emotions and skew our loyalties. Still, I'm not sure that disciplining us herself would have mattered. To Cooky and me, the difference between our mother and father was no mere crack in the family foundation: It was a chasm.

Mostly, he was on one side, and the three of us were on the other. Occasionally there was some shuffling, such as when, over her protestations, he would take me out of school to go on hunting trips. But mainly, we were all terrified of this barrel-chested warrior who could lay waste to Nazi regiments and telephone directories, whose spankings left us still tender days afterward, whose regular threats to slap us silly if we transgressed were never to be doubted. Even as kids, my sister and I understood that deferring to him as the family sergeant-at-arms was our mother's futile attempt to be his accomplice, in order to prove their solidarity. He never bought it. He knew, as did we children, that what impelled our mother was not her will but his intimidation.

Every April, after the first lilacs confirmed the snow's end, my mother began planting the backyard rock garden she had built with lettuce, carrots, radishes, chives, rhubarb, peas, pansies, morning glories, and tiger lilies. From our nearby sandbox I would watch her bend with her trowel, impaling seed envelopes on popsicle stick markers, her dark hair wrapped in a kerchief. One May a truck delivered hunks of gray limestone and bags of cement. "I'm building us an outdoor barbecue," she told me. "Won't that be fun?"

A neighbor boy helped her mixed the mortar and construct the squat little fire pit. They finished late in the afternoon. My father returned just before sundown. Briefcase still in hand, he made a snarling inspection pass around it, then let her have it. Why the hell, he inquired in tones audible a block away at Uncle Nate's house, hadn't she waited until he got home, like he goddam told her to? When the hell was she going to finally learn? Placing a wing-tipped foot against one corner, he shoved against the hardening concrete, his face turning tomato-red, until the limestone rocks collapsed in a jumble. Then he marched past her sobbing figure into the house.

That night—I was perhaps six—I dreamt that she and I were in the yard together. She was wearing a kerchief and working so hard and was so tired. Suddenly bags of cement that were piled halfway up the side of the house toppled onto her. And then I was pulling on her arm, trying to get her out from under all that terrible weight, feeling so sorry for her, but I was too small and weak to help.

"You know, I really loved your dad. I thought he was the greatest. He was a hero to all of us. And your mother: God, how she loved him."

"I know."

"She was totally his wife. Totally. I remember the day he called to say he was going overseas, how she screamed that she had to take her baby to go see him before he left—I think he was stationed in Alabama—how she was going to him if it was the last thing she ever did. Remember, this was wartime. You couldn't just go get on a train. Nate got her on—Nate could do anything, of course. But it was so crowded that I understand she stood

200

for hours on that train in August in the South without air-conditioning, holding her baby girl. And she got to see him."

"I know. The trip to Alabama is yet one more epic family legend. Buddy, we all know how much she loved my father. But what did you really think about their marriage? Did you ever wonder about them?"

"You mean, would she ever leave him? Never. But I'll tell you: I once saw Si kick Char right in the ass. He'd asked her to do something—they were outside on the lawn, she was gardening, bent over weeding or something, and he got mad and kicked her. That was the only time I ever saw him get physical with her. But your dad could holler. I guess you know that."

"Oh, yes."

"And you know why he was like that, right?"

"I have my ideas. How do you explain it?"

"I knew it was from what he went through. Losing his father in Russia before his very eyes. Struggling over there, then coming to America just in time for a Depression. And on top of that, the war. Do you understand what he went through over there?"

"Some. I heard about it all my life. I've read his letters."

"Then you know why he was the way he was. It was a miracle how he survived World War II. I've come to understand there are some things you never get over, things that a human being can witness. So I always kind of thought he was entitled to flare up the way he did."

"That's an interesting concept: being entitled to cruelty."

"Not entitled to cruelty. I meant entitled to wrath. Think of what he saw, of the people he had to kill in order to survive. And he also saved so many lives. He was entitled."

Before he left for the war, my father had been vice president of the Mikro Kodesh, the Orthodox North Side *shul* that my great-grandfather Jacob Meshbesher had cofounded, where my mother's relatives attended. The Jewish enclaves on the South Side, mostly German and Romanian, had two synagogues: one Conservative, which actually allowed women and men to sit together, and the other Reformed—an even more radical departure, wherein Hebrew became merely a nostalgic garnish to a service conducted mostly in English. The North Side Russian Jews considered the former a disgrace and the latter a church, but then a group from my father's generation bolted from the Mikro Kodesh to form their own Conservative congregation, called Beth El.

Elders like my great-grandfather Jacob were stunned by these defections. To thwart the dreaded specter of assimilation, they started a parochial school called Torah Academy that lumped secular instruction into a Jewish context. When I got old enough, my mother promised her relatives, I would enroll there. But even faster than I was growing up, our home was changing. Although we spent every *shabbos* with my Meshbesher great-grandparents and Sunday with my grandmother Rebecca, during the week our place was known as Char's boarding house to the Gentile associates in my father's law office. Charlie Hvass ate over often, as did a young Catholic lawyer named Bob King, who would one day become my father's other partner. After Charlie married the obstetric nurse who attended my mother when I was born, Christmas morning meant going over to their house, where presents awaited us under their tree. Obviously, my father's colleagues didn't keep kosher, and when we dined in their homes, we didn't either.

In 1951, just before my fourth birthday, my great-grandfather Jacob Meshbesher announced that he had lived long enough. He went to bed and refused to eat. My great-grandmother called his doctor, who examined him and declared that *Zaydeh* had lived a long productive life, and that everyone should leave him alone and let him die. Nobody would, of course, and after nearly a week I was enlisted into the plot to try to get him to eat.

"You tell him he's teaching his great-grandchildren bad manners by not eating," my mother instructed, zipping my parka. I understood the gravity of this charge. Failing to finish everything on my plate was the biggest sin I'd yet been accused of in my short life. "Don't be ungrateful little snots," she scolded, whenever we tried to refuse frightening things she'd serve us, like borscht or pickled tongue. "Children are starving in Europe."

I walked the block from our house to see *Zaydeh*. The streets were so frozen that my sister and her friends could skate the five blocks to school. I wore buckle overshoes and mittens secured to my sleeves by my Uncle Mike's latest successful invention: chrome-plated clips connected by an elastic strap. Inside *Zaydeh* and *Baubeh*'s house I ascended the staircase, past the samovar on the landing, above which hung an oval photograph of their youngest daughter, Sara, in a frame filled with cuttings of her blonde baby curls. My great-grandfather was in bed, wearing a collarless white shirt and his *shtreimel*—a tall black paper yarmulke that only men his age seemed to use—and listening to *The Lone Ranger* on the radio. His beard was a snowy V that pointed at his sunken breastbone. "Zadie, you're supposed to eat something," I said. "Children are starving in Europe."

"*Hob im in bod.* You want to give me something, bring me my bottle of whiskey." It was on the table by the closet. I brought it over to him. He sat up on the edge of his sickbed, hawked into his brass spittoon, poured three fingers of umber scotch into a water glass, drank them off in two gulps, and handed me back the bottle. "There. Tell them I ate."

Two days later he died. After that, the smell of frying bacon began wafting through our own home. Henceforth, red felt Christmas stockings with my sister's name and mine spelled in silver glitter hung alongside our Chanukah decorations. We left the Mikro Kodesh and joined the Beth El, and I was saved from Torah Academy.

My father rarely attended the new synagogue. My grandfather Avraham's leather phylacteries, which his mother had carried from Russia so his eldest son could *davan* on his bar mitzvah with a remnant of his birthright, remained in their velvet pouch in a cabinet, no longer worn. The Sabbath became another day at the office, unless the University of Minnesota's football team had a home game, in which case my father knocked off at noon. The only times he appeared at the Beth El were each autumn for Rosh Hashanah—the Jewish New Year—and ten days later for Yom Kippur, the Day of Atonement. My mother still lit the *shabbos* candles every Friday night, but he was never present to chant the blessing with her.

Baubeh, now widowed, moved in with her daughter Jennie, whose husband Mandel owned a liquor store. Jennie's brothers Ben and Max also owned a liquor store, and several Meshbesher sons- and cousins-in-law were liquor salesmen. It was a world in which Jews now worked on Saturdays, so the day that all the Meshbeshers lined up to kiss *Baubeh* switched to Sundays, the Gentile Sabbath. I liked *Baubeh,* even though she called me and all the rest of her great-grandchildren *goyim* because we spoke no Yiddish. But she always smiled; seated in the pink overstuffed chair she rarely left, her swollen ankles protruding from under the shawl across her knees, this was a woman happy with the large clan she had spawned.

All day Sunday, while their wives played canasta at the dining room table, the liquor-selling Meshbeshers gesticulated with fat cigars as they argued in the living room. On the sublime occasions that the warring identical twins, Benny and Nate, showed up simultaneously, the arguing waxed into an uproar. Things calmed a bit after Jennie and Mandel got a television and everyone watched pro football. *Baubeh,* who had learned to play canasta in order not to be ignored, now did likewise with TV. In her nineties—she claimed to be older than *Zaydeh,* born when Abraham Lincoln was still president of the United States—she became a Green Bay Packers fan so she wouldn't be abandoned during the game of the week.

My father would make it through the first half of the game before two scotches-on-the-rocks knocked him out in his chair. He was reasonably uncomplaining about going there, though—football and Uncle Mandel's booze were adequate buffers between him and the Meshbesher men. Our alternate Sunday trips to my grandmother Rebecca's, however, were another affair altogether. There we huddled in stale gloom while my father stretched out on the red tufted couch and closed his eyes, opening them only when his mother asked questions that invariably seemed to upset him, because he would answer her in loud, irritated Yiddish, punctuating every word as if he were admonishing a child. My grandmother, now a round mass of colorless dough with rouged cheeks and gray curly hair, would sink back into her stiff chair as he'd yell, squeezing her plump hands together until she generated enough pressure to dare address him again.

During the war my grandmother Rebecca had wed for a third time, this time to a man who was also her brother-in-law. Back in the Ukraine, Louis Tockman had been married to my grandfather Avraham's sister Rivkeh. Shortly after their marriage, he'd been conscripted into Czar Nicholas's army. Facing the prospect of winter patrols in Siberia for the next quarter-century, he deserted, escaping with his wife on foot through the forests of eastern Europe, often hiding in caves. Many months later, they arrived in America. Rivkeh managed to pass the gauntlet of medical examiners on Ellis Island, who failed to detect the rheumatic fever, contracted in one of their subterranean refuges, which eventually killed her.

In 1942, six months after my Uncle Harold collapsed in the pharmacy and died, my grandmother agreed to marry her widower brother-in-law, who had three daughters. Perhaps she needed new children to absorb the ache. But during the first year, this third marriage didn't go so well. Within a few months there was a war at home to rival the one under way in Europe. "It's a terrible mess," my Uncle Herman told my mother in 1944 after a quick trip to Minneapolis between voyages, and shortly thereafter my grandmother threw her third husband out. They weren't apart very long, however, by the following January, Herman reported that "Mom and Uncle Lou seem to have arrived at a truce. I hope it will last."

Like so many other things in our family, the stories of my grandmother Rebecca's marital turbulence were concealed from my sister and me. By the time I got to know her, she was Grandma Tockman, married to Louis, a little white-haired geezer who owned a North Side kosher fish market and sat around the house in sleeveless white T-shirts, smoking Pall Malls. I thought he was a nice man. He played dragon by blowing streams of smoke through his nostrils, and talked to me in decent English while Grandma either feuded in Yiddish with my father or fidgeted in silence. From a pewter frame on the wall, Louis's dead wife Rivkeh gazed sternly down at us through dark, burning eyes. Nobody ever told me who she was, but I recognized her eyebrows and severe nose from my dad, her nephew, and sensed guiltily that she was accusing me for being oblivious to her generation's suffering.

The only time I ever heard laughter in that house was when my Uncle Herman visited Minneapolis. He would carouse with me on the carpet, pretending to be a green-eyed monster, so jealous of my parents for having me that he was going to devour me alive. We never missed visiting there when Herman, about to become a college professor, was in town—until suddenly the opposite was true. Whenever he was in Minneapolis, I once overheard my mother tell her cousin Shirlee on the phone, we were certain to steer clear of her in-laws.

But nobody ever told me why, until I learned it from Herman forty years later.

꒰◌꒱

Before the war, my Uncle Herman had gone to New York with two fellow graduates of the University of Minnesota's class of 1939, Joe Conway and David Raskin, to try their luck in theater. They shared a midtown apartment in the New Yorker Hotel on 34th Street, for which each paid five dollars a week. Failing to crack Broadway immediately, they soon sought day jobs. Herman's experience driving a bread truck back in Minneapolis landed him work in a Manhattan bakery that paid fifteen dollars weekly and all the cake he could eat.

Raskin soon gave up on New York, so Herman and Joe Conway

moved to an even cheaper place on 112th and Broadway. Joe, an oaken baritone, started landing parts in radio ads. Herman baked six days a week, wrote at night, and tried to peddle his scripts during his lunch hours. Depression-era Broadway proved a tough market for new playwrights. During his second summer, however, he was hired onto the stage crew at the Chapel Playhouse in Guilford, Connecticut, where he worked for the next two stock seasons. The casts included Buster Keaton, Diana Barrymore, Sidney Blackmer, and Faye Ray. Herman became drinking pals with them all and felt like maybe he was getting somewhere.

Where he got to instead was Europe and the war. After it ended, he remained in command of his ship for nearly a year, partying with the troops he ferried back home on French champagnes and cognac captured from the Nazis, and attending theater in Oslo, Naples, and London. In April 1946, he brought his boat, the U.S.S. *Alhambra,* into its home port of Brooklyn for the last time. He had won two battle stars for surviving dive-bomber attacks and was recommended for another for eluding submarines, and had made more than forty wartime Atlantic crossings. Rejecting a promotion to major, he mustered out of the army.

Before resuming his pursuit of a theater career in New York City, he went to Minnesota to visit his mother and to finally reunite with his brother Si. He found my parents and sister camped with my grandmother Rebecca, her husband Louis Tockman, and Louis's daughters—an explosive situation about to be defused, Si and Char assured him, by the house they were finally building. To celebrate Herman's return, my parents took him to dinner at the Nicollet Hotel.

"Why don't you stay home and settle down already, Herman?" my mother beseeched him. "Plenty of nice Minneapolis Jewish girls would love to get fixed up with a cute guy like you."

"Sorry, but my brother got the best one in town. Anyone else around here would be a big disappointment."

"Oh, go on," she said, blushing. "You're just too choosy. You're not getting any younger, you know. You're nearly thirty."

"Leave him alone, Charlotte." My father was sharing a bottle of victory scotch with his brother, and was beating him to the bottom.

"Well, it's true. What are you going to do in New York? You think you're going to become a famous actor? It's not so easy, kid."

"I want to write plays."

"*Kuk eh suhn.* Who's going to pay you to do that?"

"I'll just have to get lucky. Or," he said, raising his glass to his brother Si, "convince my successful relatives to support me."

"*O vu dehn,*" replied my mother, smirking. "That will impress all your little Broadway *shiksas.*"

"Charlotte," said my father, raising his voice slightly, "let him do what he wants. He was a troopship commander, for Chrissake. He's earned the right to live his own life."

"Well, that doesn't mean he doesn't have to grow up sometime. I know the kind of people he'll be running around with in New York. They're all a bunch of nuts."

"I said that's enough, Charlotte."

Herman was hired back at Guilford's Chapel Playhouse as a summer stock stage manager, and was accepted into Actors Equity. But by the end of the run, something had changed for him. Charlotte was right: He *wasn't* getting any younger, and the struggle had lost its romance. That summer, he'd been in charge of Guilford's apprentices, and found he enjoyed teaching them. Eligible for the G.I. Bill, he reasoned that a master's degree in theater education would keep him in the world he loved, yet afford him a stable income.

"I still intend to write," he wrote my parents. "In fact, script writing will be part of my course work at NYU."

"Good for you, Herm," my mother replied. "Now you're making sense. But you shouldn't stop with a master's degree. Get your Ph.D. Then you'll be a real *mensch.*"

Through his best friend and old roommate Joe Conway, now performing in radio soap operas, he stayed connected with the entertainment world. They hung around mainly with two other

Minnesota boys: Larry Gates, who later played on Broadway in *Teahouse of the August Moon,* and Charles Irving, who had once portrayed Falstaff in a university production of *Henry the Fourth* in which Herman played Lord Bardolph. Irving would often appear later as a judge on television's *Perry Mason* show, but in the late 1940s he could be heard on live national radio, proclaiming that "the Norwich Pharmaceutical Company, makers of Pepto Bismol and other fine products, is proud to sponsor Dashiell Hammett's most exciting character, *The Fat Man*"—a program based on Hammett's parody of his own *Thin Man.*

One evening at a party, Gates told my uncle he wanted to introduce him to a woman named Hester Sondergaard, who was also from back home.

"Hester Sondergaard? Any relation to Gale?"

Back in 1939, Herman had accidentally met Gale Sondergaard, winner of the first Academy Award for best supporting actress for the 1934 film *Anthony Adverse,* in which she starred with Olivia de Havilland and Frederic March. He and Joe Conway had boarded an elevator in a theater on their way to an audition, and there she was, long-lashed, lovely, and sultry as she was on screen, standing with her husband, director Herbert Biberman. "We're from Minnesota, too," Herman had blurted, and she had smiled and shaken their hands.

Petite Hester Sondergaard wasn't as stunning as her tall, brunette sister Gale, but she was bright, had a dancer's body, and wore flowing dirndls that Herman liked. A radio actress, she sometimes took character parts on Broadway and in the new venue of television. Although she was ten years his senior, Herman found her a pleasant antidote to his latest fizzled romance.

Soon, however, their dates didn't involve dinner and movies as much as attending meetings. Like many of his friends, Hester belonged to the American Federation of Television and Radio Artists. At her AFTRA sessions and his Actors Equity meetings, discussions suddenly concerned Washington, D.C., more than Broadway. In the deepening Cold War, the House of Representatives' Special

Committee on Un-American Activities, fairly dormant for years, had gained permanent status and subpoena power, and was currently playing a major villain's role on the American stage, screen, and airwaves. As a graduate student who had let his theater career lapse while he worked on his master's degree, my Uncle Herman didn't feel personally threatened by the accelerating events. But his friends and his girlfriend did.

✿

In 1938, when the House committee first began probing New Deal programs for subversion, my Uncle Herman and his intellectual New York friends dismissed it as a clan of ignorant, Roosevelt-hating rednecks. The committee was mostly comprised of rural southerners incensed by the American Communist Party's growing Depression-era popularity, with its Robin Hood-style brigades that moved families and furniture back into homes from which banks had just evicted them, and its electricians who pirated power back into houses unplugged for nonpayment. Then, confirming warnings by U.S. conservatives that Communism was just a facade for totalitarian dominance, Stalin signed the Nazi-Soviet pact of 1939. The committee's chairman, a Texas congressman named Martin Dies, Jr., realized that his mandate had suddenly widened.

Intellectual ridicule turned to alarm as Dies and his colleagues focused suspicions on two targets. The first, resurrecting old post-World War I slurs against foreign-born labor organizers, was resident aliens: Dies demanded that immigration cease and aliens be deported, both for anti-American tendencies and because they competed with hungry American workers for jobs. The second was the entertainment industry, beginning with the WPA's Federal Theater and Writers projects, which employed hundreds of out-of-work actors and writers. The liberal social agenda pervading their works, Congressman Dies charged, was influenced by radical thinking and perhaps even directly by Moscow.

The notion that foreign intruders were snatching the bread

210

from real Americans was nothing unusual to my uncle, who grew up in Minneapolis hearing that Jews should be shipped back to where they came from. The attack on the arts was new and disturbing, especially when President Roosevelt capitulated to critics and canceled the Federal Theater Project. But before it was clear what this red-baiting portended for writers and intellectuals who, like many other Americans during the Depression, had joined the Communist Party, World War II interrupted. Russia, heretofore the evil fomenter of subversion, was suddenly the object of American sympathy and gratitude, as the Soviet Union bore the murderous brunt of the European war against the Nazis practically alone until the 1944 D-Day landings.

My Uncle Herman had never been a Party member, but the wartime rehabilitation of his homeland Russia's reputation cheered him. One night shortly after D-Day, he was in Philadelphia while his ship underwent repairs. That evening, at a restaurant with a date, he recognized the olive woolen uniforms with red epaulets worn by two diners at a nearby table. Rising, Captain Weisman went to shake hands with the Soviet army officers. Having left Ukraine when he was just five, he remembered only a smattering of Russian, but managed to communicate his pleasure that, in this war, his old and new countries were allies.

His gesture was received warmly. Peering closely at one of the officers, Herman took a chance and addressed him in Yiddish. He'd guessed right: The Soviet major was Jewish, and suddenly everyone was communicating excitedly. Herman brought his date over to their table. They poured vodka all around and toasted their alliance against the common enemy. Herman explained how he had come to America two decades earlier after a pogrom in which General Anton Denikin's White Army slaughtered his father and other members of the family. The Communist officers sympathized; they knew well how many Jews had died at the hands of czarist loyalists who had opposed the Bolshevik revolution.

But just three years later, with the incandescent war against Nazi fascism over, a new cold one had begun. Soviets were again the enemy, and the now-permanent House Un-American Activities Committee had embarked on a consummate anti-Communist crusade. Again, it stalked entertainers. This was not a random choice: The movie industry in particular had been built largely by immigrants—mainly, Jewish immigrants—whose huge success had earned them jealousy and distrust as well as money. Many well-known stars had also dabbled in leftist causes during the 1930s, such as civil rights, relief for sharecroppers, and the Spanish Civil War. Name recognition of Hollywood celebrities was the perfect means for the HUAC committee to gain the public's attention, and it went after them.

⁘⦿⦿⁘

A frightened Hester Sondergaard told my Uncle Herman that her brother-in-law Herbert Biberman, who had been a Party member, and her sister Gale expected to be called before the committee. Herman was incredulous that this could happen in the country whose freedoms he had gone to Europe to defend. Herbert Biberman had written and directed one of the most intelligent films of the war—*The Master Race,* about the difficulties facing Europe after the Nazis were finally defeated. Along with John Ford and Howard Hawks, Biberman was a cofounder of the Directors Guild of America.

Although in the end Gale Sondergaard did not testify, the prediction of a subpoena for Herbert proved true. He and nine others, together known as the Hollywood Ten, were summoned before the panel in October 1947, where he attempted to read a prepared statement. "This committee," Biberman asserted, "is in the course of overthrowing not Karl Marx, but the constitutional way of American life." He was shouted down by committee members. The new chairman, Congressman J. Parnell Thomas, warned him to cooperate.

"Mr. Chairman," Biberman replied, "I would be very suspicious of any answer that came out of my mouth that pleased the committee."

212

Congressman Thomas, who later went to federal prison for accepting bribes, was not amused by this response, nor by the refusal of each Hollywood Ten colleague to answer a question that would become familiar to American ears over the next six years: "Are you now or have you ever been a member of the Communist Party?" They had assumed that the First Amendment, assuring free speech, would protect their choice not to name names nor discuss their political affiliations, which, after all, were not outlawed. Their inquisitors, however, rejected this constitutional defense, and after a loud ensuing quarrel all ten were declared in contempt of Congress. On that charge they were tried, convicted, and sentenced to prison.

"What is the country coming to," my uncle wrote to my lawyer father, "if such a mockery of personal freedom and justice can be condoned in a court of law?" But to his surprise, instead of agreement from my father, he received a terse reply alluding vaguely to "Communist troublemakers."

Herman didn't have time to worry about his brother: All his friends, certain that they would be next, were trying to simultaneously preserve their acting careers and their principles—an increasingly complex proposition. Stunned by the government's apparent disregard for the First Amendment, film producers feared further censorship if they resisted HUAC. Already nervous over the recent emergence of the movies' first real competition, television, Hollywood studio owners decided that defending left-wing employees wasn't worth the risk. Jointly, they announced that the ten writers and directors cited for contempt were fired. Henceforth, they would not hire Communists, and would pressure screen unions to identify and expel them.

The liberal film business thus became the first American industry to bar alleged subversives without a trial. It was the beginning of the Hollywood blacklist, which would wreck the careers of hundreds of writers, actors, and directors, including Gale Sondergaard and her husband, Herbert Biberman. Although no studio admitted its existence, everyone knew how the blacklist operated. Invoking the Fifth Amendment before HUAC, or refusing to name

213

others who might have a history of Communist involvement, resulted in an automatic presumption of guilt—and unemployment. The only way out was for writers to toil under pseudonyms, but always for far less pay than they'd formerly earned.

That option, of course, wasn't open to actors. One by one, my Uncle Herman watched his friends grow frantic, then resigned, then drop away altogether. His old roommate Joe Conway announced that he was leaving radio soap operas and New York.

"But you were never in the Party," Herman protested.

"I'm a known liberal. These days, that's enough." Conway became a pilot. During the ensuing reign of Senator Joe McCarthy he moved to Mexico. Only after the 1954 televised army hearings finally discredited McCarthy and calmed anti-Communist vigilantism in the United States did he return to acting, appearing in television shows such as *Sky King*.

Though not officially blacklisted, Hester Sondergaard knew that by association she was through. Her brother-in-law Herbert Biberman, released from prison after five months, would never get studio work again. Banned from the Directors Guild he had helped create, in 1954 he and a blacklisted producer formed their own company and, using all blacklisted writers and actors, filmed *Salt of the Earth*, a true account of a New Mexico mining strike. During production they were barred from film laboratories and sound studios and denounced in Congress, and even by the press, for allegedly making a Russian propaganda film. The Mexican star of the movie was arrested and deported, requiring them to complete the shooting south of the border. Awarded the 1956 International Grand Prize for Best Film by the Acadèmie du Cinèma de Paris, *Salt of the Earth* was banned in the United States until 1965. Years later, it was listed by the Library of Congress among the one hundred most important American films.

Following her husband's death from bone cancer in 1971, more than twenty years after her own blacklisting, Gale Sondergaard finally resumed her career, which concluded with the 1976 film *The Return of a Man Called Horse*. But that was long after her

214

sister Hester, shaken by the events that had ruined her family and so many colleagues, left New York and the acting business for good. She moved to the Pacific Northwest; for a while she and Herman remained in touch. The last he heard was that she was getting married.

"So you asked my father about all this First and Fifth Amendment business?"

"Sure I did. From time to time I would send Si literature to convince him."

"What kind of literature, Uncle Herman?"

"Things I picked up in support of actors who were getting blacklisted. Once I sent him a copy of the *Daily Worker*—"

"You sent him the *Daily Worker*?"

"We'd gotten into an argument, and later at meeting I noticed some exposé in the *Daily Worker*. So I sent it to him."

"I can just imagine my father's reaction to receiving a copy of the *Daily Worker*."

"I simply thought that, considering where we came from, my brother should feel as I did."

"Where you came from? You mean Russia?"

"I mean that we came from persecution."

In early 1948, however, my father was coming from a decidedly different place than my Uncle Herman. Far from feeling persecuted, for the first time since his life changed so tumultuously back in the Russian Ukraine when he was six years old, he was learning what it meant to feel secure. In barely two years, he had acquired standing in the community as a war hero and a job with a good law firm—a non-Jewish law firm that afforded him entrée into previously closed realms. He had a good income and his own house. He believed, as he often lectured us children, that he had fought for and therefore deserved these things.

Now that he had them, he wasn't about to risk them. Doubtless the legal implications of the HUAC hearings troubled him, especially the denial of explicit constitutional assurances of the right to express unpopular beliefs. But these weren't normal times: By ringing down an iron curtain around Berlin with its blockade, the Soviet Union had clearly severed its alliance with the West. As this curtain proceeded to envelop all of eastern Europe, Communism's aspirations of world domination were even more evident. Then the Soviets exploded their own atom bomb. Having just defended his adopted country against one armed totalitarian regime, my father knew that with the prospect of aggression, the rules changed.

War, or even an emergency state of alert, must prevail over civil law. Just as he would one night silence my sister with arguments justifying a rapist's entitlement to legal defense, surely he recognized the same right of accused Communists to counsel as they filed before HUAC and various appellate courts. But as lawyers for these defendants increasingly incurred the same suspicion and embargos as their clients, and as local Minnesota bar associations were urged to screen their membership for radicals and to cooperate with HUAC and the FBI, I doubt that he would have willingly risked his newly won earnings to be numbered among them.

Minnesota's populist tradition, born of survivors who eked success from a harsh climate, had long been represented by the Farmer-Labor Party, a perennial contender in state elections. During the Depression, American Communists had especially targeted states with third-party histories, and Minnesota, with a third party devoted to issues of land and labor so dear to the left, was considered especially vulnerable.

With the war over, with Roosevelt dead and an unknown named Harry Truman in the presidency, international Communists sensed that America was ripe for ideological expansion, particularly Minnesota. The popular, populist mayor of Minneapolis, Hubert Humphrey, had just crafted a merger between the Farmer-Labor Party and the Democrats that sweetened the prospect. The former third party was now firmly wedged into the state's political foundation, transforming Minnesota's Democratic Party henceforth into the DFL: the Democratic-Farmer-Labor-Party.

Except the Communist Party underestimated Humphrey's ambition. Hubert Horatio Humphrey, a former political science teacher, had not united two parties merely because they blended his personal convictions. He did it for votes and power, which he had no intention of sharing with anyone taking orders from elsewhere—least of all from Moscow. The Republicans had always controlled Minnesota's congressional delegation, and Humphrey had a plan to end that, which first required consolidating the opposition.

His eventual triumph involved a curious but shrewd gambit, one that both earned attention and assured him credibility in a suspicious age. Although a fervid New Dealer who had held several federal appointments during the Roosevelt years, Humphrey began his career in politics by running for mayor without party affiliation. The reason, he declared, was that even though he was a DFLer at heart, too many Communists lurked in the party.

Very soon, he promised upon being elected in 1945, he would do something about that. Which he did—just as my father, whose own star was about to rise in Minneapolis, had arrived home to watch.

CHAPTER 13

One summer evening in 1972 I sat, rather uncomfortably, with my father at a Formica-topped table in the restaurant section of the Lincoln Delicatessen. Its all-American name notwithstanding, the Lincoln was a kosher-style deli. It had opened during the mid-1950s in the Minneapolis suburb of St. Louis Park, the successor to delicatessens that had once lined the North Side's Plymouth Avenue, before so many Jews like ourselves abandoned the city when suburban pleasures finally became our due.

From age six, I had grown up in St. Louis Park, the first suburb to succumb to the pressure of Jewish money and Hubert Humphrey's politics of equality. But the Lincoln Del where my father and I shared a dismal silence was even a farther cry from the old North Side, where the only remaining synagogue buildings now housed black Baptist churches. This was a *new* Lincoln Del, in the next town over, Golden Valley. In 1953, when we left the North Side, my parents had looked at a home in a maple-covered Golden Valley neighborhood called Tyrol Hills. But after repeated calls to Realtors failed to be returned, they finally apprehended the message: Despite considerable progressive leaps since 1948, Minneapolis's new housing and employment opportunities had yet to spread very far beyond the city limits.

Only St. Louis Park on the city's western edge, my parents learned, was permitting Jews to purchase. Just to the south, for instance, in elegant Edina—against whose high school football team my own would later wage grim, epithet-strewn wars—deed covenants explicitly restricted Jews and Negroes (Indians didn't even rate mention). "You tell your boss that either he finds us an available listing or I'm hauling his ass into court. There are laws against Nazis in this state," my father thundered over the phone at some quaking real estate agent.

But that never happened. In this rare instance, my mother prevailed. "Just forget it, Si," she'd pleaded. "We don't want to go where we're not wanted."

"I'll be damned if I'm ever going to forget it," he vowed, and he didn't. Eighteen years later, with their children grown and gone, my parents built themselves a smaller home in Golden Valley's Tyrol Hills and were among a handful of Jews who belonged to Golden Valley Country Club. Now even the Lincoln Del had arrived. Why we were there together, I can't recall, because it was at a time when my father and I rarely spoke. Possibly my mother had sent us out together to talk. "Talk to him, Alan," she would beg me.

"*Me* talk to *him*? He's the one who doesn't want to have anything to do with me. He takes one look, shakes his head, and walks away in disgust like I'm some kind of roach."

"Well, it wouldn't hurt you to put on something nice for a change. Or do something about that hair. Oh, Alan, is this the way we brought you up? To go around looking like a slop-can all the time?"

Our biggest upheaval—there had been several aftershocks—had occurred four years before, on the August night when he and I briefly met as adversaries on the streets of Chicago during the 1968 Democratic National Convention. He was there politicking for Vice President Hubert Humphrey, then running for president, while I had come to protest the Vietnam War—whose end was championed by Humphrey's former Minnesota senatorial colleague but now detested rival for the nomination, Eugene McCarthy.

On that occasion we'd exchanged just enough words to establish that I would never again accede a point merely because he was my father. My insubordination thus confirmed, he returned, tight-lipped, to his friends and I returned, trembling but swaggering, to mine, and from that point our relationship continued to fray and was now down to a shred. But that night in the Lincoln Deli-catessen, I was the one who broke the silence. Until that moment, I had been concentrating on finishing my grilled cheese-and-sauerkraut sandwich so we could get the hell out of there. The meal had quickly jumped to a bad start when I'd ordered a grilled Reuben but stipulated that I wanted no meat in it.

"I know, don't ask me, he's crazy," my father had made it a point to tell the waitress.

I hadn't bothered to defend myself, knowing where it would lead. But now, looking over his shoulder, I noticed something that would interest him. "There's your pal Hubert, Dad."

He swung around to see that Hubert Humphrey, the former vice president of the United States, who had lost in 1968 to Rich-ard Nixon because of—I'd often been reminded—anti-war trou-blemakers like myself, was standing at the counter filled with bagels, *challah,* and kosher pastrami, shaking hands and greeting his longtime Jewish constituents. My father stood and caught his eye. He beamed as the famous politician waved and moved toward our table. Then he glanced down and remembered who he was with. "My son, Alan," he said in a tone that could be charitably characterized as resignation, as he presented me to Humphrey.

"Nice to see you," I muttered, locking this warmonger's friendly eyes with an accusing glare.

Hubert Humphrey took in my hair, jeans, moccasins, chamois shirt, and my father's pained countenance. "Good to see you, Si," he said, releasing my hand and clapping my father's shoulder. "I guess we've all been through plenty these past few years."

❦

In 1948, my father couldn't help but be excited about Hubert Humphrey and his political protegé, a Guadalcanal war hero named Orville Freeman, who were giving voice and action to his own beliefs. Two years earlier, the DFL convention had turned into the brawl for party control that Humphrey had anticipated. At one point the Communists tried to tempt Freeman into their camp by offering him the office of party treasurer. "Go to hell," he replied. Instead, the Humphrey forces elected Freeman party secretary as the Communists petulantly stormed out of the convention. Beginning with his war on anti-Semitism in Minneapolis, Humphrey had earned statewide attention. Now he lifted his sights to the nation.

That summer, at the 1948 Democratic convention in Philadelphia, Humphrey thrust himself and civil rights into the national spotlight by waging a platform fight against southern Democrats. For years, they had thwarted liberal Democrats' attempts to take a stand on racism by invoking the right of states to choose for themselves. President Truman's advisors warned Humphrey that the party would split over a strong civil rights plank and likely lose the election.

Ignoring them, he pushed for a floor vote. In his high, piercing voice, he proclaimed to the packed convention: "There are those who say to you that we are rushing this issue of civil rights. I say we are a hundred seventy-two years late." It was time, Humphrey concluded, to "leave the shadow of states' rights and walk forthrightly into the bright sunshine of human rights!"

Exactly as the Communists had filed out of Minnesota's DFL convention two years earlier, the southern Democrats stomped from the convention hall following his speech. Just as surprising as Truman's election defeat of Thomas Dewey a few months later, Humphrey's motion carried, vindicating his judgment and propelling his election that November to the U.S. Senate.

Over the coming years, Humphrey would mend relations with the Democrats' southern flank by balancing his soft spot for minorities with a hard line against Communism. As founder of the Americans for Democratic Action, a national anti-Communist liberal organization, he and Orville Freeman attacked Reds in

221

campaigns all over Minnesota, hotly refuting the notion that anyone who preached equal rights must be a Communist. Liberals, they claimed, had been defending poor people, farmers, laborers, Jews, Negroes, Catholics, Italians, and all deserving Americans long before left-wing extremists showed up to co-opt their issues with half-baked foreign ideologies. They'd be damned if they were going to let them get away with it.

His combination of progressivism and patriotism was a perfect fit for a Jewish immigrant like my father, finally making good on the strength of a spectacular wartime record, in a city where his kind were at last being recognized as Americans with all attendant rights and privileges. Humphrey's politics, he believed, combined the humanity of the New Deal with pragmatic postwar reality—as opposed to, for example, the Progressive Party, recently formed by New Dealers loyal to ex-Vice President Henry Wallace, dumped from the 1944 ticket in favor of Harry Truman by conservative Democrats for his alleged extreme liberalism. Although my father admired Roosevelt, he found the Progressives, who claimed to be the true heirs to Roosevelt's New Deal, at best naive. Such as his brother Herman, for instance.

To the family's relief, Herman had finally left New York, accepting a doctoral fellowship at the University of Denver. Far from that known hotbed of subversion, the theater, Colorado seemed much safer. Nevertheless, in my father's opinion Herman had managed to find trouble anyway, by volunteering to organize for Henry Wallace's 1948 third-party bid for the presidency. Now Herman was sending his brother more literature, this time from the Wallace campaign, about Harry Truman's cold-warmongering, which he believed was pointlessly raising tensions with the Soviets that doubtlessly would spread to places like China and Korea.

"That's a lot of damn foolishness," my father told him. At a terrible cost, they had just defeated two bloodthirsty enemies of the United States. Why sit back and let another one get strong? American isolationists had done that with the German Reich after

World War I, he reminded Herman, and with the Japanese as well by selling them the scrap iron they'd converted into ships, planes, and guns. Hadn't they learned anything? Communists were dedicated to bringing down capitalism, that very expression of American freedom that allowed people to work as they chose without taking orders from a central government. Henry Wallace's Progressives, he opined, were a soft bunch of pacifists who had no more inkling of the danger they would allow to spread than of how many card-carrying Reds were in their midst.

Herman decided it was better to avoid the subject. When he wrote again, it was to say that he was engaged to be married to a lovely coed he had met in an English literature seminar, named Margaret Cohen. "Good," my father told my mother. "Now maybe he'll settle down and stop all his goddam nonsense."

By some measure, following the 1948 elections, the whole country settled down, into a sustained confrontation with Communism. Democrats—including President Truman—had branded Henry Wallace and his followers as pinkos, a strategy that boosted Truman to his upset victory over Republican Thomas Dewey. A year later, the Soviet Union's successful A-bomb test and the triumph of Mao Zedong's Red forces in China squelched most remaining public debate over whether the United States had anything to fear from Communism, clearing the way for sending U.S. troops to Korea when fighting soon commenced there.

Stalking Reds became America's newest spectator sport. Having wrecked the careers of hundreds of actors and writers, HUAC turned its attention toward government and science. It accused Roosevelt's former assistant Secretary of State for Far Eastern affairs, Alger Hiss, of having been a Communist spy. His perjury conviction, based on murky evidence provided by a self-styled rehabilitated former Party member named Whittaker Chambers, to many symbolized the demise of the New Deal's social priorities. Depression-era terrors of economic ruin had been replaced by fears of an external menace that could snatch away America's World War II triumph, and few people objected when HUAC began investigating scientists who might have shared data about the atomic bomb with the Russians.

In fact, some had, believing that atomic energy was so dangerous that the best way to guarantee that no aggressor would use it was to make sure its enemies could retaliate equally. A Communist Party member named Julius Rosenberg and his wife, Ethel, were convicted in 1950 of passing alleged atomic secrets to the Soviets that Julius acquired through his brother-in-law, a machinist at the New Mexico headquarters of the American atomic bomb project. When Ethel, found guilty mainly by association, was sentenced to death with her husband, tremors shot through the American Jewish community. First all the Jewish actors, directors, and writers—like Zero Mostel, Martin Ritt, Lillian Hellman, and nearly half the Hollywood Ten. Now the Rosenbergs. Were Jews once again becoming scapegoats, being purged and even executed in order to purify society?

"My God, Si. Will they really kill her?"

"Damned if I know, Charlotte. If the court convicts them of spying, they very well could."

"*Vay iz mir.* This McCarthy sounds just like Hitler."

The same year the Rosenbergs were tried, Joseph McCarthy, a junior senator from Wisconsin, had given a speech in Wheeling, West Virginia, in which he claimed to possess a list of two hundred hard-line Communists employed by the U.S. State Department. The fact that he never actually produced his famous list barely seemed to matter. The wilder McCarthy's claims about Communists infiltrating all walks of American life, the more America seemed to listen.

"I think it's just a way for those no-good *goyim* to get rid of the Jews. Where are they going to stop?"

We had our first television, a Motorola in a heavy blond maple cabinet. Every day, I hoped that cartoons would end before my father came home and switched on the news, replete with congressional hearings. I was just four years old, but I knew who Joe McCarthy was.

"This isn't about Jews, Charlotte," I recall my father saying.

"It's about Communists. If these sons-of-bitches sold out their country to the Russians, they deserve what's coming to them. It'll teach the rest of them a lesson they damn well won't forget."

But in the way that a four-year-old senses so clearly despite understanding so poorly, I knew that my father was worried, too. At that age, I had already learned that it was us Jews against the world. Did I know this because the inconceivable-but-true Holocaust, perpetrated just before my birth, had changed the tenor of every Jewish conversation henceforth? Or was this knowledge far more ancient, braided into my DNA over generations of persecution, of which my grandfather's murder and the six million newly dead in Europe were just further confirmation?

As I now reopen tiers of memories long shelved for their apparent irrelevance to my life—a life that diverged as far as I could transport it from my parents and the suburban *shtetl* where we Jews could afford to buy respect for the first time in centuries— from the vantage of years I understand now that my father simply wasn't taking any chances. By the early 1950s, he and Charlie Hvass had begun their own law partnership. Starting in a one-room office, facing each other across a desk, within a year they were doing well enough to add more rooms and more partners. Soon, my father was active in many Minneapolis civic groups where Jews previously were rarely seen. At a Jaycees Americanism rally, held in the same North High School where a football coach had begun to transform him into an American, he gave a fiery speech about the "gentlemen's agreement" in Edina, the suburb where no one would sell property to Jews.

"I'll be damned," he concluded, "if I laid my life on the line to fight injustice in World War II, just to tolerate it when the war is over."

❧

His doctorate nearly complete, my Uncle Herman applied for teaching jobs. He had two offers: from a college in Yankton, South Dakota, and from the speech department of Manhattan's Hunter

College. The choice seemed easy. He loved New York, and his wife, Margaret, was from Brooklyn. Only after they'd moved did Herman learn that his job was a temporary position. Obtaining tenure, he was told, meant getting his appointment listed as a line item in the New York City budget. Some faculty were still temps after working several six-year stints in a row.

And his annual salary was just three thousand dollars. One day he saw an ad in the *Times* for a technical writer. The employer was a microwave electronics research and development branch of the Brooklyn Polytechnic Institute. Herman called. They'd tried having engineers write their instruction manuals with poor results, they told him, so now they were looking for an English major. He assured him that he was one. Did he have any technical writing experience by any chance?

He recalled his old WPA job developing geographical abstracts for U.S. government texts, producing blurbs on things like farming and fishing in Africa—but anything having to do with geography, he decided, qualified as technical writing experience. He was offered a position, and at a considerably better salary than he was earning at Hunter.

First, though, he had to submit to a security check. At Brooklyn Polytechnic, he would be teaching and writing for the research and development division, which had defense contracts for Air Force and Navy surveillance equipment. The prospect made him nervous: Throughout America, teachers were being fired for failing to meet current political criteria. The National Education Association recently had barred Communists from its membership. Although never a Party member, my Uncle Herman had been in the arts, and therefore had associated, dated, lived, and slept with well-known New York lefties. And besides organizing for Henry Wallace in Colorado, he had also campaigned against entry into the Korean War.

Nevertheless, despite what in 1951 qualified as a shady background, he passed and was issued secret government clearance. Within three months, he headed Brooklyn Polytechnic Institute's technical writing division, supervising and editing a team of illustrators and engineers, as well as teaching English to future scientists. He hadn't been there quite a year when a tall, thin Jewish physicist he worked with named Sid Deutsch stopped by his office.

"Herman, aren't you from Minneapolis?" Deutsch asked him.

"I sure am. Why?"

"Because I'm going there to present a paper at a conference of radio engineers."

My uncle felt a twinge of nostalgia. He had a baby son now, whom his family back home hadn't even seen. It had been a while since he'd written my parents; even though Si ridiculed the articles he'd sent, he missed him. "When you're there," he told Sid Deutsch, "give my brother a call and say hi for me. He'll probably treat you to a good lunch."

The meal turned out to be supper, Deutsch reported, when Herman saw him ten days later. "Wonderful. How did you and my brother get along?" Deutsch hesitated. "What's the matter?" Herman asked.

It had happened after dinner. Deutsch had ordered a cup of coffee. My father was having another whiskey. "My brother Herman's doing all right at that place where you work?" he asked. Very well, Deutsch replied, a little puzzled. This was ground they'd covered early in the evening's conversation. Everyone liked Herman Weisman, he repeated.

My father leaned toward him. "So tell me," he asked. "Is he still a Communist?"

"He said *what*?"

Deutsch reddened. "He asked me if you were still full of commie ideas. I told him I didn't know that you had any, but even if you did, he shouldn't talk about it. I mean, he didn't know me from Adam. I might have been FBI. You're involved in secret military work."

Dumbstruck, Herman nodded.

"You'd better tell that brother of yours to be more careful. These are dangerous times."

Which is exactly what Herman did, by telephone. My father refused to back down. The conversation ended with both receivers slamming.

The following spring, Herman traveled to Minneapolis to visit his mother. My grandmother was aware of the rift: For months, the two brothers hadn't talked or written. She had gotten nowhere with my father, and was now prepared to plead with Herman to call his brother and reconcile. "I already did, Mom," he said, to her surprise. "I knew this was making you upset." He and Si had agreed, he told her, to go to lunch and talk things out.

They met in downtown Minneapolis in the Nicollet Hotel. My father brought along his law partner Charlie Hvass. Herman didn't object; he liked Charlie, and figured his presence might have a calming, judicious effect on both. My father, seemingly in reasonably friendly spirits, ordered roast beef with hot creamed horseradish for everyone. But before Charlie could eat much, the two Weisman brothers were locked in battle.

"How could you have been so stupid," Herman demanded, "to jeopardize your own brother's career and family by telling his colleague that I might be a commie?" Especially now, he added, with this nut McCarthy presiding over kangaroo-court sessions in the Senate that made the HUAC witch trials seem decorous by comparison.

"If the shoe fits, it's not my goddam fault," my father retorted. Herman was a naive bastard if he didn't realize that his theater friends were pinko fellow travelers sabotaging the country that had saved them. "You want to move back to Russia? Go right ahead."

The louder they became, the less they heard. Charlie got the check. He shepherded them outside, both now shouting as they marched up Nicollet Avenue—Si publicly branding his brother a goddam Communist, and Herman, beyond trying to reason with him, attacking my father's self-serving opportunism in reply.

From that day, Charlie Hvass never heard his partner Si mention his brother Herman again.

CHAPTER 14

The freighter *Erebus* threaded through the Gerlache Strait, holding course about a quarter-mile off the bony Antarctic Peninsula, which intermittently flickered into view through swirling gusts of snow. This was December 1991, the end of the austral spring. Periodically, the deck thermometer edged above freezing, until sudden, directionless zephyrs engulfed the ship in whiteouts. In seconds, the temperature would plunge 30°F. Then, just as swiftly, atmospheric eddies would suck away the flying avalanche, revealing jagged white mountains off the port side, their seaward cliffs draped with coppery lichens resilient enough to endure even in the farthest stretch of earthly existence.

All along the peninsula, and on the parallel archipelago of rocky islands that framed the Gerlache, glaciers were calving. We chugged past towering white walls collapsing into thousand-ton shards, filling the strait with giant tabular ice anvils that capsized under the massive weight of their snowy heads. Slowly, their metamorphosed bottoms would bob to the surface, exposing ancient ice from which all the air had been compressed, leaving crystals of solid water so pure that light passing through them turned a rich indigo, as though refracted by the polar sky. In past seasons, Antarctic researchers had cross-country skied safely across the tops of these white cliffs, but now they were crumbling at an unprecedented rate, as the Antarctic icecap shrank back to reveal patches of bare earth. In places, grayish clumps of grass were growing.

On this voyage, the *Erebus* was contracted to the U.S. National Science Foundation to bring meat, fresh fruit, and vegetables to the United States' scientific base on Palmer Island, just off the peninsula. Besides provisions, the cargo included journalists: Each year the NSF was required to bring down press, so that Americans might know what their tax dollars were purchasing at the bottom of the world. Officially, I had come to learn about ozone loss—but also to escape, preferably as far away as I could. Antarctica seemed just about right.

During the previous six months, my partners and I had been in Prescott, Arizona, laboriously extracting a documentary radio series from five hundred hours of tape we'd brought back from Latin America. Cecilia and I lived in my house, and we'd rented another for Sandy and Nancy with a basement that served as our studio. Added to the strain of being together almost constantly for fifteen straight months, my relationship with Cecilia now bore the scars of collaborating on scripts against the incessant pressure of deadlines.

After taking her to meet my parents on the way back from Costa Rica, they'd soon learned that if they wanted to see us, they had to come to Prescott, two hours away by car from their house in Scottsdale. "Sorry to make you do this, Mom. We really need to be here."

"I have to take your father for a two-hour ride every day anyhow. Otherwise he drives me nuts. What difference does it make if I drive around Phoenix or up the highway? At least here, it's cooler. You were smart to buy up here, Alan," my mother said, admiring the tall, long-needled ponderosa pines of the Prescott National Forest through my picture window. "It's so hot in Phoenix in the summer, even the devil heads north."

"So go back to Minnesota for a couple of months. Everyone would love to see you."

"Who's going to pay for it? Your father pished away everything."

"C'mon, Mom," I said. My father sat grimacing on my couch,

not entirely sure where he was, sensing that she was berating him but unable to defend himself. Lately, even the act of breathing had become a labor to him. His doctor called it congestive heart failure, a frightening term that, he assured us, didn't portend imminent death as long as my father remembered to take handfuls of blood thinners and assorted other prescribed pills five times a day.

"How's he going to remember all that?" my mother had protested. "He can't even remember where his *tuchis* is half the time." It had fallen upon her to mix the correct combination of drugs every three hours and hand them to him in little paper cups, whose multicolored contents he'd swallow in a single gulp.

I'd given up arguing that it wasn't true that they couldn't afford to go to Minnesota. We could easily fly them up there. My sister and her husband owned a thriving infant furniture business, inherited from my brother-in-law's parents after he shockingly quit my father's law firm. My Aunt Sylvia and Uncle Mike frequently begged them to come to their summer home on Lake Minnetonka. They had parlayed Mike's advertising success into Las Vegas TV and radio stations; like the money they'd given my parents for their retirement home, airfare wasn't an issue. The real reason my mother refused to go was embarrassment. The last time, on their fiftieth wedding anniversary, my disoriented father had ended up waking everyone, hollering curses in Sylvia and Mike's hallway where he'd gotten lost, knocking pictures off the wall as he flailed in the dark and peed himself trying to find the bathroom.

"We're going to lunch with Alan and Cecilia now, Si. Do you have to use the biffy first?"

"I don't even know where the damn thing is."

Like all women, Cecilia liked him. "You should get him on tape, Alan, while he's still around. He's led such an interesting life."

"He can barely remember anything."

"That's short-term. They keep their long-term memory. You have to coax it out of him."

At lunch, prodded by Cecilia's nudges, I tried to get him to talk about life back in Ukraine. "What do you remember about my grandfather, Dad?"

"Who?"

"Your father."

A dollop of ketchup spilled from the roast beef sandwich held an inch from his mouth, landing on the napkin my mother had tied around his neck. "The sons-of-bitches killed him when I was pretty young," he said.

"Which sons-of-bitches?"

"The Russians."

"Which Russians?"

"What do you mean, 'which Russians?' How many goddam kinds of Russians are there?"

"I mean that during those times there were Cossacks fighting, and Bolsheviks—the Communists. You know."

No answer, as he was distracted by his sandwich, half of which he'd stuffed into his mouth. I looked at Cecilia. Keep trying, her big green eyes encouraged.

"Do you know who killed him, Dad?" I asked when he finished chewing. "Or why?"

"Who?"

"Your father."

"That was so damn long ago. What do you want from me?"

"I just want to know about your life. What our family was like when you were living in Ukraine. Did the Communists take over your village?"

"In Yelisavetgrad they did."

"That's where you went after your father was killed. What was it like, living under Communism?"

"It was a unified system. It's hard to explain."

His face was clenched against the bombardment of questions. My mother was giving me warning signals to back off before he started hollering. "Why don't you leave him alone, Alan? Dad's tired." I looked at Cecilia. She shrugged.

Listening to our Chile tapes, we'd both agreed that our ozone piece needed more hard science to respond to the frightened citizens of Punta Arenas. Our travel budget was exhausted, but I called the *Los Angeles Times Magazine* and, to my relief, got an assignment to interview key ozone experts in Antarctica. It wasn't just the story. Cecilia and I needed a break.

Recently, we had unexpectedly reached, and crossed, a watershed. Although it hadn't ended our liaison, without admitting it I knew that as a couple we were doomed. It was a simple but huge thing: For a while, we thought she might be having a baby. Two weeks passed, then three, and one night we finally acknowledged out loud what was happening, or failing to happen. It was a relief to openly voice the anxiety each had separately harbored, but there was no simple resolution. We would come to the brink of confronting what pregnancy would determine about *us*, and back away, waiting for nature, or even human nature, to make a decision for us.

But before either did, something she said one evening revealed to me the inevitable result of all this, no matter how we arrived at it. We were lying on the carpet. I had listed our options. On the list was marriage. Cecilia smiled sadly. "You know, Alan," she sighed, "something like this shouldn't be the reason to get married. I want getting married to be a celebration. A party."

There was so much, I understood, in that utterance. Whether she realized it or not, she was telling me that she would not be marrying me—not now, and therefore not later, either. If carrying my child were not reason enough to celebrate, nothing would ever make her love me enough. I shut my eyes, tasting the sting of this pronouncement. This was not, however, a time to think of myself. Already coping to accommodate this lonely new truth, I rationalized that she had moved us toward a hard decision, should we need to make it, that would absolve me of a gigantic new responsibility in my precarious life.

Once, during college, I had driven to the south side of Chicago with a girl without whom, I then believed, there was no reason to keep living, although she was already through with me. In the waiting room of a clinic, I'd sat among big game trophies that included African gazelles and a stuffed Alaskan grizzly— the doctor's practice, then illegal, afforded him this expensive

233

hobby—while she saw the man who, with unexpected gentleness, she said, pried my child from her womb. Aided by the palliative of a bottle of pink-and-white pills, I preserved her secret, sealing this loss within me until, over time, the pain dissolved in its own acids and dissipated into my system. But how could I do that with Cecilia? How could I knowingly aid and abet, at this time in my life, the deliberate extermination of my chance to have . . .?

Yet I knew what, if pressed, we would do. And then she wasn't pregnant after all. The anxiety was behind us. But our future was cast.

For three days at Palmer Station, a clump of blue prefabricated steel buildings at the edge of an enormous glacier, I talked to scientists who had set out to learn whether stratospheric ozone loss was attacking life on earth. The previous October, as the sun was rising after six months of darkness, they'd suspended plastic bags containing plankton samples at various depths in the ocean, some shielded from ultraviolet rays, some exposed. The ozone hole, an elongated depression bigger than the United States, rotated invisibly above them like a propeller every two weeks, giving them three full cycles to chart plankton growth both inside and outside the hole. It was soon clear that every time the ozone hole passed over, reproduction vividly declined.

After each interview, I would don the polar fleece sweatsuit and squall parka I was issued and go out to stare at the sky, trying without success to discern the cosmic rip that was possibly causing this place to die. It would take years to know exactly what their data signified. Would those numbers tumble through the Antarctic food chain, resulting in even greater losses of the shrimp-like krill that fed on plankton—which in turn, became the staple for whales, penguins, and herring? Would the plankton toll become the aquatic equivalent of burning rainforests, depriving the earth not only of food but of even more plant life to convert carbon dioxide back to oxygen?

Above me, cape petrels with wings like scimitars sped between the sun and moon, bobbing on the lavender northern horizon.

234

South Polar skuas the size of eagles hovered over pods of elephant seals as big as Volkswagens. Out in the bay, humpback whales slapped their flukes as they circled rookeries of thousands of nesting Adelie penguins and blue-eyed shag cormorants. All these world champion survivors, thriving in perpetual chill. The notion that something invisible could tip these stalwart creatures toward oblivion was unspeakable.

Sleepless on my final night, I paced through the frigid midnight sunshine thinking about a pair of married biologists I'd met who had a grant to study diminishing populations of krill. Since tracking the tiny creature's reproduction cycle required an entire year, the husband had just spent six months in Antarctica, while his wife taught at their university back home. Now they'd be changing places. "We have three whole days to tell each other everything," they'd said.

I kept trying to fathom what kind of love sustained a marriage whose partners could only spend three days and nights together all year—and most of that time to debrief each other about little crustaceans, at that. It had to combine, I guessed, devotion both to each other and to a cause they mutually cherished. I heard enough from each to know that this common cause involved more than their careers: It was the belief that what they were doing mattered—mattered enough to sacrifice a year together. Noting the glances they exchanged, I was pretty sure that they had that kind of love, and pretty convinced that I didn't. I would have given anything for what I imagined they shared. By the time the next annual ozone hole formed, I would have reached my mid-40s. I was in love with someone wonderful but much younger, from whom I would eventually, inevitably part. Then I would be approaching 50, alone and childless. How had this happened?

※ ☙ ※

Enrique, the young desk clerk in Punta Arenas's little Hotel Mercurio, ran to the door to help me with my duffel. *"Recibió un llamada telefónica urgente de la señora Cecilia."*

235

Señora. Enrique remembered Cecilia from when we had stayed here eight months earlier. He assumed that we were married. Her message read: *"Llámame inmediatemente."*

Still hauling my South Polar gear, I headed for the lobby phone booth. I waved through the window at Enrique, who dialed the long-distance operator for me. In a minute I was listening to my phone ringing in the United States. Neither Cecilia nor the answering machine picked up. I tried our studio, but got Sandy and Nancy's machine. Damn it, where was she? I looked at my watch. It was nearly midnight. Chile was directly south of the U.S.'s east coast, so it would be 10:00 P.M. in Arizona. I called my number again. This time Cecilia answered after the first ring. "God, I was hoping that was you. Did you try to call about three minutes ago?"

"I did. Why didn't you answer? Why didn't the machine pick up?"

"The power's out. We're having a huge snowstorm. I couldn't figure out why the furnace went out, too, until I realized that the thermostat's electric. It's freezing here. I was out at the woodshed getting logs. I heard the phone ring, but by the time I got to it, it stopped."

I felt ashamed at my irritation. "I got your message. Enrique said *urgente.*"

I could feel her hesitate, seven thousand miles away. "It's your father," she said.

I walked out into the long austral dusk. Six hundred miles north of the Antarctic Circle, night would actually fall here for a few hours, but even at midnight there was still enough light to discern colors: new green cypress boughs in the central plaza, the deep blue capes of naval officers, the olive uniforms of the white-gloved *carabineros.* A half-mile away, the waters of the Strait of Magellan glowed pink. My father wasn't dead. I knew, however, that a process had begun that would gradually take bigger chunks of him until one day, there'd be nothing left. This time, literally: His right leg was choked with phlebitis. Only in the operating

236

room could the doctors determine if an artery transplant was still feasible. If not, they'd have to amputate.

My poor terrified mother. How would she get him in and out of the car for the daily ride he insisted on? Already, he practically grew violent whenever she protested that she didn't feel well enough to go out. Two years earlier, her chronic anemia had been diagnosed as low-grade lymphoma. Technically a leukemia, the doctors assured her that if she took her medication, she'd die of old age long before the lymphoma got her. But she still had days when all she wanted was to remain in her chair with a Danielle Steele novel and an afghan pulled over her knees.

My father. I'd been watching this rock crumble slowly for several years now, this formidable icon whom even all the divisions Hitler threw at him couldn't crush. A boy who grows up with a father like that can't imagine him weakening and one day actually dying, much more than he can imagine the earth giving way underneath him. Yet eventually, even the things we count on most give way. I'd learned that while living in Mexico, during my first earthquake. Suddenly the thing we take most for granted—solid ground beneath our feet—turns traitor. Gravity itself loosens and panic instantly seizes, as something utterly fundamental fails. After a while, the shaking subsides, the rattling in the windows fades, the chandeliers stop swinging, and the earth reverts to silent immobility. But you never trust it—or life—the way you once did.

"There's something else, Alan," Cecilia had added. My father needed the operation promptly, lest a blood clot dislodge and flow fatally to his brain. But the surgeon had agreed to wait a few more days if it meant that I could get there.

"Why would he wait for me?" I asked, puzzled.

"It's a she." She paused long enough for me to wonder if she were angry over this male assumption. That wasn't it. "The truth is, Alan, that it's not just whether they can save his leg. Even if they can, at his age he might not be able to tolerate the anaesthesia."

Meaning he might not wake up. I looked up, toward the tattered layer of ozone. It was all so fragile. In Antarctica, the huge jagged icebergs on the watery horizon had resembled mountain ranges rising out of the pearly flatness like a white-and-blue version of my country's southwestern desert. But now I flashed on a vision of my Arizona home as if entombed in cold—so still, so chilled, frosted blue like a cadaver. Spaceship earth, spinning dead in the universe.

How much, I wondered, was my perception of the world dying simply a reflection of dawning personal loss? I recalled my breakdown at the parochial school here months earlier while watching innocent children who might have been me playing under an imperceptibly fading sky. I remembered being seven years old, lining up in a school gymnasium that doubled as a cafeteria, secure in the presumption that, like hot lunch, a long full life lay ahead. Even my father, at that age already a refugee, had no inkling that he had anything harder to survive than his own father's assassination and a country in turmoil. The earth itself wasn't going anywhere—in fact, there was another, safer side of the planet waiting for him, just across the ocean.

How was it possible, a mere three score and ten years later, there was no safe place left anywhere on that planet for a person to stand?

PART FOUR

CHAPTER 15

Cooky met my flight in Phoenix. I wasn't expecting her. I practically lunged at her.

"Of course I came," she whispered, as we kept hugging. "Did you think that you can come all the way from the South Pole, and I can't even make it from Minnesota?"

"I don't know. I wasn't thinking at all. You look terrific."

"God, I'm such a mess. It's so dry here my skin cracks off in sheets."

Her skin was perfect. My lovely sister, who elicited gasps of disbelief when people learned her age. In mere months, I realized, she would be fifty, five years older than me, and easily looking ten years my junior. Barely five-foot-two, her luminous skin flowed smoothly over the fine cheekbones she'd inherited from the sainted Aunt Frieda we never knew, whom she'd resembled even more before her hair darkened and straightened after bearing her first child. It now hung smartly at the collar of her blue wool sweater, no gray and no faking it either. I noticed a couple of servicemen on leave for Christmas scoping out the sagging guy around whose neck one of the best-looking women in the airport had just thrown her arms.

I hugged her tighter, my sister who'd always been there for me, the only relative who had never scorned my decision to be anything but a lawyer. My sister who once, entirely unsolicited, sent me two hundred dollars when I was down to my last fifty—how had she known? She had always known, and here she was again. I shook my head to clear the soup from my brain. Of course: This was her father, too. I wasn't in this alone.

"Where's Mom?"

"Waiting in the car outside baggage claim. I'll bet you have tons of luggage."

I had a black canvas carry-on slung over each shoulder. "Just this."

"Christ. Don't tell me you went all the way to Antarctica with only carry-on."

I lifted the back of my jacket, revealing a large fanny pack I routinely smuggled past the flight attendants, containing two tape recorders, three microphones, batteries, a camera, and four steno pads. "Wow. My little brother, ace reporter."

We stepped onto the moving passenger conveyor. "Have you seen Dad yet?" I asked

"Last night. He was actually in a decent mood. I'm not sure he's exactly aware of why he's in the hospital. In fact, I know he isn't. Mom made me swear not to say a word to him about having an operation."

"God forbid any of us should ever be burdened by the truth."

"Except her, of course. Bearing every burden is her job. She's the only one on earth who can handle it. You know what she always told us."

Together, we recited: "What you don't know won't hurt you."

In the baggage area, she turned to me. "You know, I was really hoping that Cecilia would be here. I looked forward to finally meeting her."

"She's spending Christmas with her mother in New Jersey. She's always made it a point to do that since her dad died."

"I know, Mom told me. It's too bad that you couldn't be there with her. I know how disappointed you must be." Translation: *I'm* really disappointed—and a little pissed—that Cecilia didn't cancel her Christmas plans so she could be with you when your father is

242

about to have life-threatening surgery. Is there something wrong between you two? I know—Mom told me that Cecilia's ticket to New Jersey was nonrefundable. But does this mean I shouldn't be getting my hopes up too high, again?

Poor Cooky had always wanted a sister. I didn't take that personally: Our love, forged early as we sought shelter with each other from parental ballistics, was mutual, fierce, and unconditional. Much of this yearning, in fact, was to see me happy and accompanied. Even though she and my biologist ex-wife had little in common, Cooky loved her because I was no longer alone, and our divorce had grieved her. But she also longed for female company in this family. Our mother was the only woman among us she could talk to, a situation with its limitations.

Much of their interaction seemed hilarious in retrospect, but surely was exasperating in the moment: Charlotte insisting that Cooky wear a panty girdle under her leotard so she wouldn't jiggle provocatively in aerobics class, or tugging at the sleeve of a customer my sister was waiting on in her store and demanding, "What do you think of a daughter who doesn't call her mother?" She had always given us plenty to laugh about, this mother who would holler urgent directives up from the basement like: "Quick: Go whatchamacallit the thing!"—or who once bought us cemetery plots for Chanukah. But it wasn't easy on my sister, I knew, to be held throughout her marriage to our mother's unmatched standard of wifely devotion. Many of Cooky's compromises in life had derived from either trying to satisfy my mother, or to keep her at bay.

Only ten years earlier, the area where my parents now lived had been a cactus-rich expanse of Sonoran Desert just north of the Pima Indian Reservation. I would sometimes jog there with a buddy who knew the trails, and we'd chase packs of wild horses that still roamed the palo verde washes and jump over diamondback rattlers that slithered among the spiny saguaros and chollas.

When my mother first described the location of their new place, I didn't believe her. In a blitzkrieg of development that had coincided with years I was away living in Mexico, the Pimas had found themselves encircled by senior citizen complexes, faux Venetian bridges arching over artificial watercourses, miles of thirsty imported sod, and redundant orange-tiled, white stucco subdivisions with names that maimed the Spanish language.

Next appeared mock-adobe shopping centers surrounded by melting asphalt parking lots, followed by that other commercial enterprise demanded by local demographics: new hospitals. Minnesota's venerable Mayo Clinic cloned itself two miles from my parents' new house, but any similarity to the distinguished original—hallowed back home as a state treasure—escaped me. This one mainly seemed to have followed retired Midwesterners like my parents down to the Sun Belt to hook itself into their new Arizona savings accounts as though by gigantic IVs. Its cavernous waiting room was practically a community center to the elderly who limped through regularly en route to tests and blood work. The lucky ones would be sent back to their subdivisions to wait until next month. The rest, like my father, were referred for advanced care to one of several surrounding health care facilities colonizing the newly scraped desert.

In one such shiny new monolith, we followed our mother through a bewilderment of carpeted halls, not realizing how familiar they would become over the coming months. "There's Daddy," my sister said, as we rounded a final bend. He was in a wheelchair in the hallway, dressed in pale blue pajamas, unshaven and haggard.

"H'lo, Alan," he mumbled.

"Oh, no!" my mother gasped. "Quick, Alan, get a nurse."

"Why? What's wrong?" I was encouraged that he'd recognized me.

"Can't you see? Look at his face."

She snagged the arm of a passing doctor. "Look," she said, gripping his lab coat. "My husband's supposed to have surgery tomorrow. But he's had another stroke."

The doctor, a young resident with thick red hair, peered at my father, who returned his gaze forlornly, and then flinched when the doctor peeled back his left eyelid and shined a penlight on his pupil. "Be right back," the doctor promised, and headed off at a trot. My mother, in the meantime, turned on Cooky and me. "What's the matter with you two? Can't you see how he's talking through his teeth? Like he's clenching them?"

My sister and I exchanged a look that said: So what's new about him clenching his teeth? But now I saw what I hadn't noticed at first—that the left side of his face was drooping, like a candle just starting to melt on one side. "Honey," my mother was saying to him, "honey, are you all right?"

"How the hell do I know, Charlotte?" he slurred.

An hour before his operation was scheduled, the surgeon arrived. She was blonde and tiny, with large, dark-rimmed glasses. We stood in the doorway while she stretched to bend over my father, who was easily twice her size, lying in his hospital bed. "See?" my mother whispered to my sister. "See how much cuter she'd be if she did something different with her hair? And those glasses make her look—"

"Mother! Shhh!"

The surgeon was holding the results of the EEG they'd run on him while we had picked at lunch in the basement cafeteria. "He's definitely suffered a stroke," she confirmed. "You were really sharp to catch it, Mrs. Weisman."

"See?" said my mother, spearing each of us in turn with a glance. "Don't tell me I don't know my own husband."

"Not a major stroke. He's coming out of it fairly quickly. But I can't operate on him like this. Not until the EEG shows that his brain has stabilized."

"How long will that take?" asked my sister.

"We don't want to wait too long for his operation. Maybe a week. Maybe two."

"Oh, shit," Cooky groaned.

"God, I hate to do this to you," my sister said on the way to the airport. In the midst of the Christmas season, she had taken off

245

three days from the two stores she and her husband owned in order to be here during the operation. She couldn't remain any longer.

"Don't worry about it, Cook. I'll stay here with Mom until they operate on him."

"That's what I'm worried about. You'll go nuts."

The doctors agreed to operate on December 30. I called Cecilia to let her know I wouldn't be spending New Year's with her. On January 2, she was going to Miami to do a segment for a special public radio series on Latino AIDS. We agreed to meet in Washington, D.C., in mid-January, when she'd be editing it at NPR and I would be finishing our ozone research nearby at Goddard Space Center. Depending, of course, on my father.

"*Pucha*, Alan, we'll have gone nearly six weeks without seeing each other. Doesn't that seem strange after being together so much?" I wasn't sure if she was sad or relieved.

I spent the next few days at the desk in my father's den that he never used, transcribing tapes from Antarctica. At night my mother and I watched videos. The day of the operation she was too tense to eat, but after his gurney disappeared behind the brushed stainless steel doors of the surgery, she confessed to being ravenous. "Let's go to dinner," I said. "Doctor Brown says that the operation will probably last five hours."

"What if something goes wrong and I'm not here?"

So I ordered us a pizza. Domino's didn't think it at all strange to deliver to the anteroom of the surgical theater. "You'd be amazed at how many calls we get every night from intensive care," the delivery man said.

"I'm not going anywhere, Alan. I have to stay home to take care of him. Who's going to take care of him if I'm not there? You? *O vu dehn.*"

I ignored her reflexive thrust at my guilt plexus. My father had survived. Fifteen minutes earlier, the doctor had emerged, still in her blue surgical scrubs, her offending hairdo safely concealed from my mother's appraisal by a plastic cap. The operation had gone easier than expected. "He's a pretty tough guy, your father," she'd said to me.

"Tell me about it."

"That's right," said my mother. "You tell him, Dr. Brown. Do you have any idea what this man has survived in his life? My son doesn't appreciate that."

"Even Dr. Brown can't cure my lack of respect, Mom. Let's thank her for saving Dad's leg and let her go home and go to bed."

My mother threw her arms around the surgeon and sobbed.

It was nearly midnight when we drove the two miles back to my parents' house. "C'mon, Mom," I said, resuming our earlier argument. For the past eight years, her only relief had been twice-weekly evening art classes at the local community college. I'd practically had to drag her to enroll, but she returned so happy from the first session that she hired a retired woman to babysit my father and never missed a class. She'd become Grandma Char to a bevy of younger artists and received an "A" every semester. Now, however, she claimed that she was quitting to take care of my father during his expected lengthy convalescence.

"You can't, Mom."

"Oh, can't I?"

Wrong choice of words; she would rise to that challenge, just as she had all her life. "Of course, you *can*. But you don't want to live your whole life for him."

"Oh yeah? What the hell do you think I've done all my life?"

"Exactly. Which is why you have to think about yourself a little, while you still have time. You've done everything for him."

She snorted. "Honey, you don't know the half of what I've done for him. You have no idea what I've put up with from your father."

I had more idea than she knew, from things people had let slip over the years, possibly intentionally. Looking back, I wonder why I didn't know as a child, because it all added up. Possibly a child isn't sophisticated enough to—no. Wrong. That's my mother's voice from the grave, telling me I'm too young to understand. The real reason was a conspiracy of silence in our house. The conspirators were my father and mother—even when he did her wrong, she would always cover for him, and he knew it.

There was a spring evening in 1958 when I was eleven. My sister and I had a piano recital in an auditorium downtown. Dressed in uncomfortable clothes, we waited until the last possible minute for him to arrive home from the office. My mother, wearing a sleeveless chemise with a white patent leather belt, paced in her brown-and-white high heels. Torn between fury and fear—his terrible driving was legendary among his law partners—she finally piled us into her station wagon. Less than a block from our house, we met his gold Buick coming toward us. He braked sharply, causing him to visibly lurch at the wheel. "Where on earth have you been, Si?" my mother demanded through the car window, pulling up next to him. "You know very well that the kids have a recital—" then she stopped, because she could see very well where he'd been.

His head rolled loosely on his neck and his face was flushed. "Stop your nagging, goddammit. I can't stand it when you nag me like that, Charlotte."

"Stop yelling. The entire neighborhood can hear you. Who's been kissing you?"

"I don't know what the hell you're talking about."

"Then you should take a good look in the mirror." Craning my head forward from the backseat, I could see the lipstick smudges. My dad didn't look so well. His head seemed sort of rubbery. "Where the hell were you?" my mother demanded.

"None of your goddam business, that's where I was. I'm here now, so quit bitching."

"Well, you're not coming with us looking like that. You're going to have to change that shirt."

"If you don't like it, to hell with you." He hit the accelerator and was gone.

"God, he makes me so mad sometimes," my mother muttered under her breath.

Somehow, I actually forgot the entire incident until hours later when we returned. As we pulled into the driveway, my Aunt Sylvia's eighteen-year-old daughter Margie, who was staying with us that year, came running out of the house. "Uh, oh," said my mother.

"Aunt Char, I have to tell you!" Margie squealed, the long-lashed dark eyes she inherited from Aunt Sylvia blinking rapidly. Margie and her boyfriend had arrived home two hours earlier. Through the garage window, they'd noticed that the dome light in my father's car was lit. The driver's side door, they could see, was ajar. When they went to close it, they saw his feet hanging out. "We were sure he'd had a heart attack."

"Oh my God," wailed my mother, leaping from the car. "Simon!"

"Wait, wait." Margie stepped in her path. They'd called an ambulance, she explained, whose siren naturally lured all the neighbors to our driveway. Everyone—"God, *everyone* was here"—watched as the medics ran in with a stretcher, and saw them return with it empty.

"Aunt Char, he was drunk! Dead drunk!"

I have a recollection of my mother's embarrassment that night being so powerful it overwhelmed her anger. "He's a wonderful guy," she said over and over to my cousin's boyfriend—who, after all, wasn't family. That a stranger should witness this shame was far worse to her than my father's behavior that sparked it. "He's a wonderful guy," she repeated.

"I know, Mrs. Weisman."

"But when he drinks, I just don't know what to do with him. Thank God," she fibbed, "he doesn't do it very often."

By the late 1950s my father had become a prominent Minneapolis attorney—not a wealthy one; his clients were individuals, not corporations—but we had a fine suburban house and lacked for nothing, as far as I knew. (Later, I would learn that we lacked for savings. But as long as he was working, this was not an issue.) He no longer represented a roster of lowlifes as when he'd just started to practice, although he had a reputation as a courtroom pit bull who would clamp his jaws around a prosecutor's leg and not let go until due process was thoroughly discharged, even for the most unappealing defendants. He now belonged to so many civic organizations that he had a lapel pin to inspire the trust of practically any juror as he approached the box during his arguments, including the Purple Heart and Silver Star pins he wore especially for veterans, whom he always favored during jury selection.

Both in criminal and personal injury trials, he frequently had to cross-examine police and detectives called by the prosecution. With officers of the law, he softened his bulldog tactics, disarming them with deference even as he nudged their supposedly hostile testimony inexorably toward bolstering his client's case. As attorney for the Minneapolis Brotherhood of the Police, most of them already loved him anyway. Over the years, he represented many cops through their own travails, their DWIs and divorces, and eloquently defended their honor in letters to the editors of Minneapolis papers when other lawyers festooned their pretrial publicity with accusations of police brutality or incompetency.

His success in the courtroom, his associates agreed, derived from his credibility. He argued his cases on principles of fairness and justice codified in the American Constitution and Bill of Rights. My immigrant father believed so strongly in these standards that he would invoke them without embarrassment as he orated before a jury. Once, while defending a suspended suburban police chief in a misconduct case the press characterized as an unwinnable, the town attorney alleged that the defendant made patrolmen use the town's sole squad car to deliver liquor to his girlfriend. Any use of the vehicle for purposes other than police duty, he argued, was a violation worthy of dismissal.

"Any use?" my father made him repeat. Thereupon he revealed that the town attorney himself had requisitioned the same car to chauffeur Hubert Humphrey during a recent visit. Was it fair, my father asked the jury, for the pot to call the kettle black? His client was reinstated.

His passionate conviction that his clients were innocent amassed him a fantastic record of acquittals—juries often assumed that anyone with someone as honorable as my father vouching so strongly for him simply couldn't be guilty. We heard this from his colleagues and grateful clients often, but hearsay was our only source. We were never allowed to see my father in court. My mother's terse explanation was that early in his career she went to see him try a case, and he lost. Therefore, it was deemed bad luck for anyone in the family—other than that perennial court lizard, Nate Meshbesher—to see him in action, and that was that.

We didn't see him all that much outside of the courtroom, either. During those years he was out the door no later than 7:00 A.M.—a formidable presence to reckon with at that early hour, from whose path my sister and I leapt back into our rooms if by mischance we happened to be in the hallway when he strode, briefcase in hand, toward the kitchen where my mother would have prune juice, coffee, eggs, and bacon waiting. I remember the fear in her eyes one rare morning when she was running behind when he appeared at the breakfast table. Amazingly, he didn't scream. He just drained his juice glass and held it out, telling her to give him his eggs raw. Obediently, she handed it back with two yolks suspended in the thick transparency of the whites; I watched in awe as he downed the nauseating thing in a gulp.

He never returned before dark. We didn't question the hours he worked. We'd heard his "Who the hell do you think earns the money around here?" often enough, anyway, without having to evoke it unnecessarily. For Cooky and me, that was fine. We got to eat what we liked for supper—often, breakfast cereal—and could read at the table, something forbidden on the rare occasions we sat down as a family. By the time he came home to be fed his nightly steak by my mother on the second supper shift, we were safely in our rooms.

251

I never suspected an alternative explanation for his late hours, or for why he fell asleep in his recliner directly after eating, remaining that way until my mother would awake him at 11:00 P.M. to go to bed. Only as an adult did occasional comments by his acquaintances begin to pierce the image so ingrained by my mother that, even though by then I knew better, I still had trouble accepting the obvious. Which was, of course, his string of girlfriends. Minneapolis was not that large a city, and it was statistically predictable that he couldn't entirely conceal this double life.

One of my mother's best friends' sister worked at J. C. Penney, and would see him come into the store to pick up the *shiksa* who worked at the perfume counter, who later showed the other salesgirls the gifts he bought her. Then there was the time he had a taxi deliver a new television set to a resident of a well-known prostitution crib he apparently frequented; unbeknownst to him, the cabbie lived next door to his cousin. That episode inevitably leaked back to my mother, who instigated a screaming bout of her own, demanding to know why he was sending TVs to whores. "Just keep your big trap shut when you don't know what the hell you're talking about" was his typical reply in what I now realize were several such instances. The law firm, he claimed, often gave presents to clients. Was Char aware of every bit of business his firm did, and with whom? Was she?

This would usually shut her up, as she wasn't privy to the inner mysteries of the temple known as the office. "Do you know what he would say to me when I would call him there?" she once told me toward the end, after her rage finally began to pour forth. " '*State your business.*' In that voice of his. You know that voice. Can you imagine? Not 'Hi, honey, what can I do for you?' or 'Is something the matter?' but 'State your business.' God, the nerve of that man."

Mostly she cried, but on the occasions that she yelled back her replies, once unleashed, would soar quickly and dissolve in pure scalding noise, overwhelming our synapses as my sister and I huddled behind the closed doors of our rooms. (Their fights often spilled into the hallway, along which all our bedrooms were strung, and we didn't dare emerge while they were in progress.) If the bomb unexpectedly went off before we could retreat to our individual sanctuaries, Cooky and I would be stranded together, usually in her room where we listened to records. Only once did we make the mistake of raising the volume of her 45 rpm portable to drown them out. In seconds, he was attacking the door.

"Turn off that goddam screaming! I can't stand hearing such NOISE!" That was the epithet invariably elicited by rock 'n' roll, but this time we were listening to Mario Lanza singing *The Student Prince*. I yanked the tone arm off "Gaudeamus Igitur" so quickly that the needle gouged a deep notch across the grooves. We sank back on her rug, miserable, and waited for the cyclone to pass.

Two or three days of terrible silence would follow. Each was capable of hissing, "I'm not talking to you. Remember?" when the other tried to suspend the war in order to address some inconvenient but unavoidable matter, such as joint signatures required on a bank card, or a dinner engagement with a judge and his wife.

"I don't care, Si. You can go by yourself, for all I give a damn. You don't want me around, fine, I don't have to be there."

"Please, Charlotte," he'd growl, "don't be that way." Eventually he would buy his way back. Flowers were one option, although he was in competition with himself with the incremental roses he heaped upon her with each new anniversary. Usually, all it took was a heavily embossed Hallmark card, the schmaltzier the better, signed "Your Bobe." What it was in these canned sentiments that appealed to her so much that she instantly forgave him, we could not imagine. She would read the florid verses over the phone to her friends as if he'd penned them himself, as he once had done in the poems he tucked into his war letters. Going through her final effects, we found that she had saved every one.

She quit speaking, forever, to one of her best friends who once dared to inquire into the latest rumor about them getting a divorce. Lest her former friend miss the point, after slamming the receiver my mother actually got through to my father at his office and made

253

him call, a task he performed in language and decibel levels never forgotten by his staff. Most of my mother's acquaintances knew better than to touch this taboo subject, having heard her deny it so often. No matter what happened at home, never did she publicly accuse my father of any sin or even of any error. Nor did she acknowledge her grief with him to my sister or me until the end. And even then, it was hard for us to believe, because we'd been raised on the myth of her perfect marriage. Didn't every father holler at the top of his lungs, every day? Wasn't that normal?

This routine denial was so ingrained in us that not only would a child ignore lipstick on his father's neck, but as even as an adult—an adult journalist, no less—he would, at first, utterly overlook the most flagrant evidence.

"You have to go to the gynecologist? Aren't you a little old for that, Ma?"

"This is different."

"Different from what?"

"From having babies. This is a growth I have to have removed."

"A tumor?" I got alarmed. I was calling from San Juan after being trapped for three days by Hurricane Hugo during an assignment on an island off Puerto Rico. The airport had just reopened—could I get back to Arizona in time for her surgery?

"It's not a tumor. I've had these before."

"These? What are they?"

Her reply was so low I couldn't make it out. "What?"

"Warts," she repeated.

"You have vaginal warts, Mom?"

"I just said so, didn't I?"

Relieved, I proceeded to tease her. "Getting some on the side, Mom? There's only one way of getting vaginal warts that I ever heard of. Don't worry, I'll cover for you with Dad." Sensing that she didn't find this funny, I backed off. Even then I simply didn't get it, chalking it up to yet one more geriatric infirmity. It wasn't until long after she was gone that my Aunt Sylvia enlightened me when I asked what she knew about my father's philandering.

"I never wanted to believe it," she said, "because your mother didn't want to believe it. I never thought he'd be unfaithful to his Meshie. He wrote her beautiful letters; he bought her gorgeous gifts inscribed with beautiful sentiments."

"Did something make you change your mind?"

"Sure. Fifty years later, I found out about those warts she would get. I took her to the doctor. It was terrible. What pain she went through. They had to burn them off."

"You mean my father gave her—?"

"Where else would she have gotten them? Could you see your mother sleeping around with other men?"

There is a brief, shattering moment in every boy's life, right after he learns where babies actually come from, when he realizes that his own mother must have done *that* with his father. It's a shock that soon transforms into amused skepticism: How could those two old farts ever get it on, anyhow? So it is far, far harder to imagine one's own mother with a venereal disease. One's own Jewish mother who preserved her daughter's virtue with threats of banishment or worse. How many years did she hide this ache and shame from us? Why, enduring something like that, did she need to convince the world that he was the most flawless husband who ever graced womankind?

It wasn't simply a matter of showing her cousins that she, the foster child who once sought shelter with them, could get the best husband of all—a lawyer, no less. She wanted, I suppose, to be rescued by a prince. Later, when the prince's dallying evoked her own father's waywardness, she again must have known the old visceral dread of being abandoned. So she made her stand and refused to be budged, opting to endure any and all to preserve her marriage. Mainly to convince herself, she set out to persuade everyone that not only would he never leave his wife, but that this man simply could do no wrong.

Maintaining appearances wasn't hard during those years. We had the biggest home of any of our relatives. My father's law firm moved to hardwood-paneled headquarters in the newest office building downtown. To hear my mother tell it, Si Weisman's

255

success single-handedly made this possible. In truth, the move was mainly financed by Charlie Hvass. As a former pilot, it made sense for Charlie to handle any personal injury cases involving aviation that came their way. In 1960, one of the biggest in U.S. history did: a Northwest Airlines Lockheed Electra en route from Minneapolis to Miami that crashed at Tell City, Indiana.

Following Charlie's successful multimillion-dollar suit on behalf of the captain and crew, few major air accidents in the country didn't involve the law firm of Hvass, Weisman & King—and some from beyond, including the 1977 collision of two jumbo jets in the Canary Islands, the worst air industry disaster ever. The firm was profiting hugely from these claims, but although my mother benefited directly, she was not entirely happy about it.

"I see Charlie Hvass's got his name in the paper again. Why do you let him grab all the headlines?"

"Charlotte, you don't know what you're talking about. So shut up, please, will you?"

"I don't care. You're just as important as he is. Why the hell should he get all the glory?"

Her husband, she told her friends, was so modest that he let Charlie take the big cases, because Charlie was a big shot who liked to see his name in lights while Si could care less about that sort of thing. Once, overhearing her, my father grabbed the receiver and warned, "Charlotte, if you keep saying that, I'm going to kill you. Charlie Hvass is one of the best damn plaintiff attorneys in the country. He's my best friend. He and his wife are two of *our* best friends. And you damn well know it."

She did. Nevertheless: "I don't care. He doesn't have to hog all the publicity. That office would be nothing without you. If it weren't for you, Charlie would still be running errands for Fred Ossanna."

At that point he'd say, "I don't know what you want from me, Charlotte," then throw up his hands and walk away, knowing it was useless to point out that leaving the Ossanna firm to start their own had been Charlie's idea first.

What more did she want from him? He had risen from orphaned poverty to having his own distinguished law firm, one that was getting so many personal injury cases that their third partner, Bob King, a tax and estate planning specialist, had to help out with them. Besides criminal law and his specialty, car accidents, my father was counsel to labor unions and continued to represent the Minneapolis liquor industry, from local distillers to bar owners. As both Bob King and Charlie Hvass's wife were Catholics, my father also took on divorce cases that came their way. Women divorce plaintiffs especially liked how this big, solid man stood up to their husbands in court.

Whenever I walked down a Minneapolis street with him, I never failed to be struck by how many people greeted him, and with such pleasure. "Your father," my sister and I heard constantly, "is such a wonderful, generous man." People told us of the adoptions he refused to charge for, and the dollars and hours he donated to, apparently, every charity that asked. Few outsiders seemed to be aware of his white rages—other than caddies who sometimes had to chase the putters he threw, whom he later would put through college. An attorney who knew him well once was surprised when I referred to his volcanic temper. "Si? He's so restrained and formal in the courtroom. I'd even call him soft-spoken—albeit very persistent."

Could this beloved man be the same person who kept his family suspended in such terror? His public persona was that of a consummate charmer, the guy who picked up every tab. His simmering tensions evidently did sometimes boil over in the semi-private confines of Hvass, Weisman & King, driving at least one secretary to march into his office and tell him at some length, by way of resigning, that he was the most unpleasant human being she'd ever worked for. He absolutely had no idea what she was talking about, and remained baffled about it thereafter.

He desired much more to be regarded the way he was by another young woman in the secretarial pool, whom the partners one day decided to let go. My father, drawing the short straw, had to deliver the bad news. He called her into his office. Her sobs could be heard through the door. A half-hour later she emerged, beaming. Not only hadn't he fired her, he'd given her a raise.

❧

Some years after my parents' funerals, I visited Minneapolis again. It was June, a season so flawless, so swaddled in fresh foliage that it never failed to redeem the long despair of the Minnesota winter. Each morning I drove to one of the city's tree-lined lakes and ran around its perimeter. By afternoon, the placid blue waters would fill with bright, billowing triangles of sailboats while Minnesotans exuding good health strolled and sunned themselves along the grassy shores. I had spent much of my youth fishing and swimming these lakes, whose names for me conjure summer itself: Lake Harriet, Lake Calhoun, Lake of the Isles, Cedar, Nokomis, Wirth, Brownie—all in bicycle range of my house. Just beyond lay lakes named Medicine, Christmas, Waconia, Minnetonka—and so many others that Minnesota stops counting at ten thousand, although there are actually thousands more. From the air, they glitter like silver coins displayed on green velvet.

Many of my father's best friends—his law partners, clients, and judges—owned lake cabins in Minnesota's north woods. Much as I yearned for one, my mother never would abide it: It was not, I was informed, something that Jews "did." (Years later, I would learn about the Catskills. "Those pushy eastern Jews—*hob im in bod*," my mother sniffed.) I was outnumbered, anyway. My sister had once attended summer camp, and announced afterward that she'd had enough of nature to last a lifetime. My parents didn't sail. My father's earlier interest in fishing gave way to golf; I inherited the fishing tackle and was often packed off to his friends' cabins by myself.

But I learned the city lakes from him: Wirth, where we would feed the wild swans when we still lived in north Minneapolis, and, afterward, Cedar and Calhoun, where he took me for dawn dips in the spring to teach me to tolerate numbing water barely reclaimed from the ice. Later, I lifeguarded at beaches on these lakes, as he had done. During that visit after he died, it was impossible to slip into the coolness of Cedar Lake, or canoe Lake of the Isles, or buy an ice cream cone at the Lake Harriet band shell without thinking of him.

That week, nearly everyone had the same pilgrimage planned for me: a meal at Murray's, a downtown Minneapolis restaurant locally famed for steaks so tender they could be sliced with a butter knife. It would be incorrect to say that my father held court at Murray's, because there were always too many actual judges present who could make that claim. The first time in nearly two decades that I walked in, they were still there.

"My God," I said to Ron and Ken Meshbesher, Nate's two lawyer sons. "Nothing has changed." Murray's decor was, in a word, pink. Heavy pink satiny drapes framed mirrored paneling that traded pink reflections with the opposite wall; the pink ceiling was patterned with pink drop acoustic circles; all the heavy cloth table linens were pink. Pat Murray, the smooth-cheeked, smiling owner and manager, greeted me warmly. His parents had founded the place; like mine, both were now dead, a fact upon which we commiserated as we shook hands. Now, he acknowledged, the rose-tinted legacy was his.

"Place looks great," Ronnie said to him. "Nice job remodeling."

"Thanks, Ron," Pat replied. "Nice seeing you, Alan. We sure miss your father."

"What remodeling?" I whispered. "Not a napkin has changed."

"He and his folks have always remodeled every few years. They do it the same way every time."

Ken Meshbesher, who had started his career in my dad's office, had retired from law in his early sixties, but his older brother Ron, one of Minnesota's most celebrated criminal attorneys, was still in practice. As we moved toward our table, lawyers and judges stood to greet them. How, I marveled, had a place this pink

259

become *the* male bastion of my childhood? From the time I was eight years old until I left for college, every Saturday in autumn when the University of Minnesota Gophers had a home football game, my father would bring me to his office, where, surrounded by rows of leather-bound state and federal statutes, I'd read in the library until noon. Then we'd come here for a lunch of Mrs. Murray's oversized game-day hamburgers and irresistible garlic toast, then board shuttle buses that Murray's chartered to the stadium, where my father and I had season tickets. After the game, back here for a drink, or to the Standard Club for a steam bath.

Just as on those bygone game days, I was once again shaking hands with Judge Scott, Judge Stone, and Judge Fitzgerald. Across the restaurant, Judge Minenko and Judge Lebedoff were too steeped in conversation to interrupt. Except for my father's funeral, the last time I had seen most of these men was in this same place. I looked around for him. The only conceivable explanation for my father's absence was that perhaps he was in the bathroom, using one of the wall-to-floor porcelain urinals, then touching up his hair with the comb and brush from the glass urn filled with green disinfectant by the marble washbasins. Any minute now, he'd be joining us, pausing at every pink table along the way to shake hands, then sitting, tucking in his napkin, and calling over Marie Murray to send drinks with his compliments to the people he'd just greeted.

Becoming part of the Minneapolis legal pantheon that took their martini-and-steak lunches at Murray's was ample proof that, by the early 1950s, my father was firmly established in his career. It was not a raucous place, but one where big men with alcohol and cigars basked in unlikely elegant equilibrium with pink textiles. Only once did my father nearly violate Murray's steady decorum. He was drinking in the back room one afternoon with Pat Fitzgerald before he became a judge and one of Pat's Irish friends, Cos Eagan, who owned a plumbing and heating business. Somehow, Eagan managed to offend my dad. Since Cos was known to like to hit people, my father offered him the chance then and there.

"Cos," he said, "I'll let you throw the first punch. But if you do, either you or I will not walk out of this place alive." The blow did not get thrown.

"Your dad," Judge Fitzgerald said, his eyes moistening, "was a pretty tough guy."

"He was a big teddy bear," said Coke, his wife. "I'd always get such a big hug from him. That man had so much warmth."

"You're both right," I agreed. "When he wasn't yelling at us, he was hugging us. Even though we were scared as hell of him, we always knew that he loved us."

"He had a gentleness about him, but I could see his torment," said Coke. "Like he had something on his mind and was chasing after it but it was one step ahead of him. You know?"

I knew.

Judge Fitzgerald took his wife's hand. A balding man with a friendly Irish mug, he hadn't changed much since my father's surprise sixtieth birthday party at Lake Minnetonka, at which my mother had served only wine, hoping that my father would drink less because he didn't care for it. He and Pat Fitzgerald had rifled my Uncle Mike's kitchen cabinets until they found a bottle of whiskey, and spent the first half-hour of the party in there, pouring shots.

"When we got married," Judge Fitzgerald said, "there was a stag party for me in the back room at Jennings Liquors in St. Louis Park. All the lawyers were there. There was a big poker game. Your dad never touched cards, so he was taking care of the rest of us. About 1:30 A.M., in comes the St. Louis Park Police Department, five of them, raiding a tippling house. The guy leading the squad looks around and sees the table piled with high stakes, but then notices that the players include the county attorney, the city attorney, and a couple of state supreme court justices. Then he sees your dad. 'I think we'd better leave, boys,' he says to his men. And Si stops him. 'Why don't you have a drink before you go?' he says. He made sure each cop left with a bottle of champagne. Si always knew exactly what to do."

"I adored him," said Coke.

CHAPTER 16

"How's he doing?" I was in a phone booth in Maryland, outside Goddard Space Center.

"Oh, Alan, it's so sad. All he does is sit in his wheelchair with a bunch of old *kackers* watching television. They're supposed to make him get up and walk. Do you think they do, unless I'm there? I keep telling them: If he doesn't get exercise, he's going to die. *Ach*—what do they care? I should have never taken him there. I feel like I'm just digging his grave."

"Stop it, Mom. What choice was there?"

For the first time since World War II, they were living apart— only this time he was never coming home. My father now resided at a care facility three miles from their house. This had not been the plan: In the hospital, he had responded surprisingly well to physical therapy, hobbling up and down corridors with an aide on each arm, and a week after his surgery, we had brought him home. Once back in the house, he'd negotiated the few steps to his recliner by himself and settled in with a grunt. Later, leaning on my arm, he'd walked down the hall to bed.

That night, I awoke to a thump. I was in the spare bedroom off the den. I leaped from bed, looked out there, and saw nothing. I tried the living room, where my Aunt Sylvia, who had flown down from Las Vegas to help, snored softly on the foldout couch. I nearly turned back, thinking it had been a dream, when I saw a movement. One by one, my father's bare legs emerged from the doorway of my parents' bedroom. Apparently he had fallen and, unable to rise, he was stretching himself out on the floor, naked.

I bent over him. "Dad," I whispered, trying not to wake the women. "Are you all right?"

He opened his eyes. "Damned if I know."

"Give me a hand, I'll help you up." Weakly, he extended an arm to me, then groaned in pain when I pulled. I attempted to put my arm around him, but there was no room: His shoulders were nearly wedged in the doorway. Next I tried from behind; his two hundred thirty pounds were like dead weight. I woke Aunt Sylvia. "My father's on the floor," I said.

Together we got him to a sitting position. "Wait! Wait! Wait!" he moaned, awakening my mother.

"Oh, my God, what's going on?" she cried. She and Sylvia wore identical gauzy pale blue nightgowns.

The three of us finally got him to his feet. "What were you doing, Si?" my mother wailed.

"Trying to go to the bathroom. I still have to." He took a step toward it, and tipped sideways. I caught him, and the wall caught me, saving us both from toppling.

"Alan, help him to the toilet! He can't walk by himself."

Together, he and I limped to the bathroom. "Let me sit," he mumbled.

"Okay," I said. "I'll wait here by the door. Call me when you're ready."

I sagged against the doorjamb, desperate to fall back asleep to escape a mounting sadness. "Alan," he called from behind the door.

"Right here, Dad. You ready?"

"Alan. I'm sorry I'm such a mess."

It was the most coherent speech I'd heard him utter in months: an actual recognition of what was happening, coupled with actual consideration.

My eyes stung. "Don't worry, Dad. It's okay. I love you."

"I love you, too."

In the morning, my mother, Sylvia, and I met in the kitchen. During the night, he'd fallen again. It was clear that his sense of balance was gone. It was also clear that my mother, at half his weight, would never be able to pick him off the floor by herself. She confessed that this had happened once before. "In the shower. I didn't tell you, because I knew what you'd say." On that occasion, she'd had to call the fire department to get him back on his feet. We didn't have to tell her she couldn't do that every time, any more than we could always be around to help.

Head in hands, suspended over her cup of Sanka, she said, "I swore I'd never put him in a home. Never."

"I know, Mom."

"*Gracias,*" Cecilia mumbled, barely looking up as I arrived at NPR with a pizza. She had a long, doleful night ahead of her in an editing booth, distilling a week of interviews of Miami Cuban-American women undone by the double shock of their sons dying of a disease incurred during sexual encounters with other men. Soon, I knew, Cecilia wouldn't be in such hot emotional shape herself, relistening to all of that. Not good: We had to talk first. "Make it quick," she said. "I've got to get back to this." Already I could see her soft features locking into the mask that presaged a ferocious deadline. Even so, in the sweater of multicolored Chilean wool that I'd bought her in Punta Arenas, she looked fabulous.

We had both arrived in Washington three days earlier. After an awkward encounter at the front desk of the hotel, it suddenly felt good to be together again. That night, we held on to each other— but no more. It was enough. Maybe it was all. We hadn't talked about it, nor much of anything: We were both too busy. But now I needed her input on the interviews I was doing for the ozone piece. "It's not just my story, Cec, remember? It's both of ours."

She closed her eyes. "Alan," she said very softly, "just tell me whatever you need to tell me in the next ten minutes while I eat. I cannot, I repeat cannot, deal with any more than that at the moment. Do you understand?"

"I'll make it real fast."

My first stop in Washington had been at the White House, to see President Bush's science advisor, a white-haired physicist in a striped bow-tie. A half hour later, I was back outside, shaking my head. I'd asked if he knew that NASA had recently detected even more man-made chlorine over New England and eastern Canada than they'd found in the Antarctic four years earlier. He did. Any plans to phase out CFC refrigerants more quickly, I asked, now that ozone was vanishing over our heads, too? No, he said: Fortunately, the recent eruption of Mt. Pinatubo in the Philippines had thrown enough dust into the air to deflect dangerous ultraviolet rays back into space for the next four years, giving them more time to study the problem before implementing drastic controls that might negatively impact the economy.

"Excuse me?" I'd asked, incredulous. "After the Pinatubo debris settles back to earth, will you then prescribe pumping air pollution into the sky to protect us from ozone loss?"

At Goddard Space Center, a collection of late-fifties red brick buildings scattered over a thousand acres in Greenbelt, Maryland, every scientist I spoke to rolled his eyes at this alleged dust shield—airborne volcanic grit actually worsened the problem, they said, by providing a platform for deadly chlorine reactions. None, however, was ready to sound dire alarms just yet, although they admitted that for years they had disbelieved their own satellite's data showing a gaping hole in the ozone layer, until a British ground observer in Antarctica reported it. But more research was needed, I heard repeatedly, to learn how humans would be affected.

"From there," I told Cecilia, "I went to the University of Maryland to see this botanist who Al Gore's people recommended. The guy was scary. All these new experiments indicate that pine forests, rice, and other crops like cassava decline under increased ultraviolet—"

"Oh, great. Rice and cassava make up the total diet for half of Brazil."

I nodded. "Know what seems to be the most sensitive species they've identified?" She glanced at the clock and shook her head. "The common garden variety of cucumber."

The cucumber question had arisen during an unsettling discussion with our editor at NPR's science desk, who was dubious that a cold, sun-poor region like southern Chile, where a horticulturist showed us withering cucumbers, would actually experience visible effects from ozone depletion. Recalling that disagreement, Cecilia's jaw began to tighten. "Look, Alan," she said, "I've got to get back to this. Thanks for bringing me dinner. I really appreciate it."

In the cab to the airport I told an exhausted Cecilia about my surprisingly detailed discussion of atmospheric issues with Senator Albert Gore. (Years later, it would result that none of the measures he'd proposed in our talk would be implemented during his vice presidency. But for a moment that afternoon in his office, I'd dared to believe that the American political system that I had once thrown back in my father's face in the streets of Chicago might actually work after all, if men this well-informed were still allowed in Washington.)

I then described my encounter with an EPA deputy director, who'd told me that even though I'd seen ozone-eating CFC refrigeration systems still being marketed aggressively throughout Latin America, the phaseout of this equipment would be swift once it became illegal to manufacture chlorofluorocarbons. "We'll cut them off at the source," he assured me.

"The same way we stop cocaine production, right?" I asked. Wasn't he aware, I demanded, that clandestine factories in Mexico, Brazil, and Russia were already cranking out black-market CFCs? And that so many were now being smuggled into Miami International Airport that they were about to overtake cocaine as the most common illicit chemical import?

"The guy had no clue," I told Cecilia. "Him and the president's science advisor. Fucking jerks."

"You know, Alan, that attitude really comes through a lot when you talk about this stuff. We're going to have to sound more controlled when we put together the story. NPR's editors are going to want balanced reporting."

"I'm sorry. That's bullshit."

"There you go. One word, and you blow up. Do you realize how that'll go over in our editing sessions?"

"Jesus, Ceci. What am I supposed to do? I look at all this evidence and—"

"Is it evidence, or just theory? You said they're just now starting to do experiments. I think we may have to interview some people who don't think this means that the sky is falling."

We pulled up at American Airlines. I was sitting closest to the curb. "Let's go," she said.

"Wait," I replied. Jesus, why didn't she see this? "Just listen, okay? Balanced reporting isn't necessarily accurate reporting. In fact, it can be the complete opposite. Suppose this story were about lung cancer. Do we give equal space to some whore doctor who pockets half a million a year from the American Tobacco Institute, just to achieve fucking balance? Should we do that now with right-wing assholes who insist that the ozone hole doesn't exist, just like the Holocaust never happened—that it's just some tree-hugger plot to undermine poor defenseless DuPont Chemical?"

The Senegalese cabdriver had turned around to stare at me. I guess I was yelling. "Listen how angry you are," Cecilia said calmly. "You're furious with the government. You're convinced that our editors are stupid and you're always the one that's right, and I get blamed if I don't support you against them. You argue over every decision Sandy Tolan makes as our executive producer. You can't wait to get George Bush. Has it ever occurred to you that you have a real problem with authority?"

"Now wait a—"

"Look," she said, more loudly. "Maybe you're right about all this. But we don't know it yet. We're not fortune-tellers, we're journalists. We have to write our story like journalists. Now can we please get out of this fucking cab before we miss our flight?"

She slept all the way to Arizona while I sulked. Granted, I'd become pretty emotional about this story. Maybe even a little obsessed. Again, I wondered how much of this sense of everything collapsing was simply because a sizable chunk of my personal world was on the verge of breaking away? But how *was* I supposed to react to potential worldwide catastrophe, for God's sake? And where did all this crap about authority come from, all of a sudden?

After three hours, the pilot informed us that we were over Lincoln, Nebraska. When I was eight, my family had driven to California, and the first night on the road, we'd stayed in Lincoln. I remembered every stop along the way: Colorado Springs, Santa Fe, the Grand Canyon—then, just before Las Vegas, my mother had remarked that she hoped we could still find a motel with a swimming pool for us kids, since it would be nearly sundown when we arrived.

"Charlotte, I'll do my best," my father said. "But if we don't, we don't. It isn't going to hurt them to do without. They think they've got the whole world coming to them as it is."

"Oh Si, don't start. We're on vacation."

"I'll start whenever I damn please. If you don't like it, you know what you can damn well do about it."

"Would you please tell me what I said that was so bad—" And then they were off. In back, Cooky and I sneaked a glance at each other and looked away, knowing that spotting our eye contact in his rearview mirror could draw us into his range of fire as well.

At Aunt Sylvia and Uncle Mike's place in Los Angeles, our cousins trembled for a week because their Uncle Si was always ready to whack anyone who got out of line. The only respite was at night: Despite my mother's pleas, he refused to stay with the Golds and checked into a hotel by himself. But each morning he was back to inspect the tautness of the military corners of our beds, warning what would happen if we didn't pass muster. These weren't empty threats: For failing to express sufficient gratitude for a trip to Knott's Berry Farm, which I hated, he summarily quashed the Disneyland excursion I desperately wanted. "You get just what you deserve in this world, Mister," he reminded me. "Nobody owes you a living."

Stop it, I told myself, realizing how tightly my jaw was clenched over these thirty-five year-old memories. At times, I'd noticed the same thing during the previous week in Washington, as I smoldered over men in high places who dared to risk the very air we breathe for the sake of their precious economy. It made me so livid that—

Uncurling my fists, I willed my fingers to relax. I took some deep breaths. I looked at Cecilia, frowning in her sleep. I checked my watch. In an hour we'd land in Phoenix, then drive straight to the rest home to see my dad.

❀

My mother was waiting at the curb outside the baggage claim. A coughing spasm hit her just as she started to hug Cecilia, causing her to back away with her hand over her mouth. I put my arm around her shoulders to steady her until the hacking subsided.

"You sound like hell, Mom," I said.

"I know. I thought I was over this lousy cold, but the cough just won't go away."

"Then what are you doing out of bed? We could've taken the shuttle to your place."

"Oh, don't be silly. What do you think I do—lie around all day? If I don't go check up on your father, who knows what the hell could happen to him."

"Mom. You're paying professionals to take care of him."

"Professionals, my *tuchis*. Oh Alan, you should see those *gonifs*. If I didn't stand over them all day, they wouldn't exercise him so his leg gets better, they wouldn't even change his clothes. Do you know how far I had to drive last week to find him double extra large diapers? If it was up to them, they'd let him pish his pants and sit there in his chair until he drowns. I don't know how much longer I can take it. Wait till you see, Cecilia."

I got behind the wheel. A brief skirmish ensued while my mother insisted that Cecilia sit in front, next to me. My mother won, of course. Despite the balmy Phoenix winter—sunny, temperature nearly seventy—I noticed she was wearing two sweaters.

Cecilia turned around to face her. "Do they keep him stimulated, Mrs. Weisman?"

"Stimulated? *O vu dehn*. You've got to be kidding, dearie. He sits like a lump in front of a television set all day."

"That's all he did at home, Ma."

"Well at least he wasn't surrounded by a lot of old *kackers* who're so *fahrmisht* they don't know where they are, most of them."

"Does Dad?"

"I don't know what he knows anymore."

"Man," breathed Cecilia. "I'd live here." It did look rather like a resort, with terra-cotta patios, Spanish-style fountains, inlaid Mexican tile, and bougainvillea shade. It was mainly to impress visitors, of course. Most of the residents were too far gone to notice, or, if still self-aware, too depressed to care. They knew why they were here, and that they were never leaving.

As we walked to my father's room, my mother shook her finger at every nurse and aide we encountered, making them swear that they wouldn't just leave him lying in bed. The second afternoon he was here, that's exactly how she found him, she reminded them. "I know, Mrs. Weisman, I know," protested a young black physical therapist whose name tag read *Bill*. "You already told me. Twice. Remember?"

"So? It doesn't hurt to tell you again."

We found him in the television room. A semicircle of wheelchairs were grouped around a 48-inch floor console, tuned to

270

NASCAR racing. My father watched with the identical absence of expression I'd seen on my grandmother Rebecca's face when I first visited her nursing home.

"Hi, Bobie," my mother said, bending to kiss him.

He returned her kiss automatically. "Hi, Moke." Over the years, his old nickname for her, *Meshie,* had segued to *Molka,* from her Hebrew name, *Malcha.*

"Look who's here, Si. It's Cecilia. You remember Cecilia."

"Mom, people are trying to listen," I said, though probably we were far more interesting than the vehicular blur on the big screen. We wheeled him down the hall, onto one of the patios.

"Cecilia," my mother repeated, grasping Cecilia under the chin and pointing her at my father's puzzled face. "*Cecilia.* You remember, Si."

"I do?"

"Of course you do. Alan's girlfriend. We had Thanksgiving dinner together."

He shrugged. "I donno, Charlotte."

"Yes you do, Si."

"Leave me alone, will you?"

I squatted next to him. "Dad."

"What?"

"Cecilia's from Argentina, but her last name is the same as ours. Only they pronounce it *Vaisman* instead of Weisman down there. When you lived in Russia, how did you say it?"

"Where?"

"Russia. Where were you born, Dad?"

"Mala Viska."

"And where was that?"

"Russia. The Ukraine."

"Exactly. How did you say your name there?" His face blanked, so I tried again. "You spoke Yiddish there. How do you say your name in Yiddish?"

"*Shimon Vaisman.*"

"See!" said my mother. "He knows. All he needs is someone to

271

talk to him, to keep his mind active. You're good for him, Alan. Talk to him. Talk more."

I took Cecilia's hand and brought her to face him. "Shimon Vaisman, meet Cecilia Vaisman. Her grandfather came from Ukraine, too. We're all probably related."

My father looked. "What's your name?" he asked her.

"Cecilia *Vaisman*. Just like yours."

He beamed. "Well, what do you know about that."

I was sequestered in our studio, transcribing the cassettes I'd recorded in Washington, when Cecilia came looking for me. I removed my headphones. "I just checked our answering machine. There's a message from your mother, saying to call. She sounded like she was crying."

My father, was all I could think. But Lillian, the woman who used to babysit him when my mother went to her art classes, answered the phone. "Your mother was feeling so weak she called me," she said. "Her doctor says it sounds like pneumonia and to get her to the hospital."

"I have to go to Phoenix," I told my partners. "I'm sorry," I added, seeing the alarm in Sandy's face. We were so far behind. "Look," I said. "I'm almost through my Washington tapes. I'll take them with me. Let me just get her situated in the hospital. If I have to stay down there a few days, I've got the ozone magazine article to do, anyhow."

Three hours later, I was at Scottsdale Memorial Hospital. In my mother's fifth floor room I found her lying on her side. Her eyes fixed me a little wildly. "Oh, Alan," she muttered.

"Mom, how're you doing?" I said, kneeling to kiss her. She didn't respond, except with a low moan. "Mom?" Her eyes were open, but again no reaction.

I went for a nurse, who checked her temperature. It was rising rapidly, she told me. "Who is her doctor?" she asked. I found a phone and called the oncologist at the Mayo Clinic who treated her low-grade lymphoma. "I'm sorry, he isn't available," his receptionist told me. I asked how soon I could speak to him. "His appointment book is full for the rest of the day."

"Look," I said, "My mother is one of his patients. He had her admitted to the hospital. She's taken a sudden turn for the worse. A doctor needs to see her. So what do I do?"

"I'm sorry, I can't interrupt him. A lot of patients need to see him. And he's leaving town after work. If there's an emergency, the nurses know how to reach him."

"Tell him," I said, "that if he doesn't want to hear his name and reputation dissected on national radio, he'll page me within the next hour at this nurse's station."

Within ten minutes we were speaking on the phone. "There's something wrong here," I told him. "She recognized me when I came in, but now she doesn't seem to even register my presence. She keeps repeating something over and over. I think she may be saying 'Oh, Sylvie, oh, Sylvie,' over and over. Sylvie's her sister, the person she's closest to in the world. But I'm not even sure, because she's talking as if her tongue were swollen."

The doctor was silent. "Hello?" I said.

"I guess I'll be there in a while," he finally said, in an irritated voice.

You arrogant bastard, I barely refrained from replying. "Thank you," I said. I hung up and went back to her. Now she was chanting the phrase, clearly delirious.

"Doctor, should I call my sister and tell her to come down here?"

"Where's your sister?"

"Minnesota."

"Wait. Let's see if she responds to the antibiotic we're dripping into her. It should do the trick." This wasn't her regular doctor. "He had to go out of town," the new doctor had apologized when he arrived. "I'm covering for him this coming week." I visualized a few things I might do to him when he returned, then quickly put them out of my mind. I liked this new guy.

273

From the nurse's station, I called Cooky. "I don't think it does any good for both of us to be missing work, Cook. If the doctor thought it were that serious, he'd have told me to get you down here right away. She's raving because her temperature was so high, but it's already spiked and is coming down. She's still moaning, but she's starting to doze. I think we're past the worst."

We agreed that I would call her first thing in the morning. "What about Aunt Sylvia?" Cooky asked. We decided to wait until morning for her, as well. I hung up, feeling very alone. I returned to my mother's room. Her head was lolling back and forth, slower than before. I tried to talk to her, but she didn't hear me. "Oh, Sylvie," she whispered. I sat in a vinyl armchair facing her bed, opened my laptop, and tried to concentrate on the disintegrating ozone layer.

I awoke to the sound of nurses doing something at the foot of her bed. This had gone on all night; at times I'd awakened and heaved myself out of the chair, waiting until they changed her catheter—when had they inserted that?—before I'd ask how she was. The night nurses didn't volunteer much. "She's restless," one of them told me. They'd given her a sedative, which would wear off by morning when the doctor came.

Now it was 8:00 A.M. I bent over her. Her eyes opened. "Hi, Mom," I said softly. No answer. Her eyes flicked back and forth, as if in fear. "Mom," I said, a little louder. Her eyes found me. That was better, I thought. "Mom, how do you feel?" Her lip trembled, and she exhaled a puff of rotten air. "Can you say anything, Mom?" She groaned, and her eyes started jumping again.

I went out into the corridor and ran into the doctor, who was just arriving. He was tall and had short-cropped salt-and-pepper hair. He watched her for a moment, spoke to her with no clear response, pried up an eyelid, listened to her heart. "I'm not sure what we're looking at," he said. "Something more than pneumonia, maybe. I'm going to have a neurology resident look at her."

"Neurology?"

"I don't think we're seeing a stroke here. But I want him to check. I'll be back shortly."

The neurologist, a slim young resident named Faisal, was accompanied by a pale, crew-cut intern. Faisal shook my hand shyly, then sat on her bed. She was partially propped up against the pillow. Again, as best as I could make out, she was calling for Sylvie.

"Mrs. Weisman," Faisal said. "Mrs. Weisman!" He got her attention. He held a finger up in front of her nose. "Follow my finger," he requested, moving it to one side. She followed it, then flicked her eyes back and forth as he moved it the other direction. He reversed again, and she rolled her head, moaning as she tried to keep up with the digit moving before her eyes. He tapped her forehead; suddenly, her body arched, lifting away from the headboard, and her wail rose up the scale and sharpened into a stream of staccato *ooohs!* that resembled no normal human sound. As if stretched by invisible hooks, her face appeared to flatten and elongate diagonally from her lower left jaw to her upper right brow. Her arms stiffened and lifted from the sheet like a marionette's, her fingers growing straight and rigid as her arms jerked in slow motion, as though a carving of Nefertiti had come to life and was trying to lurch free from the wall of a pyramid.

We gaped at her; I was certain that I was witnessing her death dance. The neurologist barked an order at the intern, who fled. Within seconds the room was full of doctors—seven of them working over her, hiding her from my view. I could hear Faisal explaining the procedure he had followed when she suddenly was gripped by her seizure. Without looking up, a doctor assured him he had done everything right. He looked visibly relieved, then glanced over at me, remembering that I'd witnessed everything. "She's coming out of it," I heard someone say. I dared to look, and saw my mother again, her features no longer protracted like rubber, but slick with perspiration. Her breathing was rapid and shallow. "Let's get her into intensive, NOW," a doctor ordered. In seconds she was on a gurney and being raced out of there.

The doctor who was her oncologist's replacement reentered

the room and turned to me and Faisal. I put my hand on the shaken young neurologist's shoulder and said, "Thank you for reacting so quickly." He looked at me with gratitude.

"What do you think?" the doctor asked him. A conversation ensued in language I couldn't follow. "We're going to do a spinal tap," the doctor said to me. "I'll let you know in an hour what we're looking at."

"Spinal meningitis," he told me an hour later.

"How the hell would she get meningitis?" I asked.

"It's commonly a result of a bacterial or viral infection like pneumonia. How old is she?"

Our mutual birthday was coming up in less than a month. I would be turning forty-five. She would be—"Seventy-seven next month."

"You know what we call pneumonia?" I shook my head. "The old man's friend."

"Is she dying?"

"Maybe not. But I think you might want to call your sister now."

Several hours later he looked for me in the waiting room. I was sitting in a lumpy upholstered chair, my laptop in its case next to me, magazines on the table in front of me. I was unable to look at any of them, nor at the television that flickered soundlessly from its perch near the ceiling. Nothing except the clock. He took the chair next to me. His square jaw was now flecked with a day's growth of dark whiskers. "Has your sister arrived yet?"

"She should have been here by now." After talking to her, I'd called Cecilia, who'd driven immediately down from Prescott, offering to meet Cooky's plane so I wouldn't have to leave the hospital. But they'd never met before, and Cecilia didn't know Phoenix, so any number of things might have gone wrong. They might have been hit by a drunk on the freeway. That was probably what had happened—if they were merely lost, they would've called and had me paged. "Her plane got in nearly an hour ago. I checked."

"Okay. We've got ten minutes to go yet. I don't want to wait too much longer." An hour earlier, he had told me that it didn't look good. "There's one more thing we can try. It's risky, and even if she survives it, it may not work." It involved sticking a tube down a vein in her neck and injecting an antibiotic directly into her heart. "You'll have to sign this release, acknowledging that you were informed in advance that this is a—"

I held up my hand. "It's okay. But I'd like my sister to read it, too."

Where were they? The pay phones were around the corner and down the hall, and I didn't want to be somewhere else if they came in—

"God, that was so funny."

"I know, can you believe it?"

My sister and Cecilia were upon me, hugging me and laughing over how they'd gotten lost and sweet-talked some man into guiding them all the way to the hospital. I was so relieved to see them, I laughed too. I knew we had ten minutes, then a long wait.

I explained to my sister. I held up the form we had to sign. "Where is she?" Cooky whispered.

I pointed to a closed door. "We can go see her. But I have to prepare you, Cook. If I didn't tell you first, you might not recognize her."

Our mother was encased in clear tubes and metal; it was as if clamps and bindings were holding her together. Her face, all that was visible, was so crumpled and shrunken that I wouldn't have known her myself. Cooky gripped my arm. She was unconscious, but we talked to her anyhow. "I'm here, Mom," Cooky assured her. "We'll see you in a little while." We touched the white linens covering her arms. There was no way to kiss her through all the forbidding hardware. We stood there, holding each other, as they came to wheel her away.

"I never, ever thought that she might go before he did," my sister said. "Never."

"I know," I replied.

"I mean, it just never occurred to me. What do we do if she dies? How can we just leave him in a rest home in Phoenix with nobody coming to visit him every day?"

"What other choice do we have? Bring him to your place? I don't know if he could survive the trip, let alone the staircases in your house. There's nowhere to put him in mine. Neither of us can quit work to take care of him. Neither has a spare room for a nurse."

"I just can't stand the idea." She looked out the car window at a bank of pink oleanders. "God, this is amazing weather for February," she said glumly.

"Hi, Daddy," said Cooky, hugging his head and kissing him.

"Hello." He nodded pleasantly at each of us in turn. He was in his wheelchair, dressed in one of the extra-large sweat suits my mother had bought for him, as instructed by the nursing home. His double rack of suits; all his sport coats, whose colors had grown strangely wilder through the years; his total spectrum of alpaca golf sweaters—all now reduced to this.

"Let's go outside, Dad," I suggested. He shrugged. I wheeled him into a courtyard. "I don't know if you remember Cecilia," I said. I told him again who she was, and what her last name was, and why.

"What do you know about that?" he said, appraising Cecilia with approval. "Isn't that nice?"

"You know who I am, don't you, Dad?" Cooky asked.

"You bet I do."

"What's my name?"

He pointed at her. "Milstein!"

"Who?" whispered Cecilia.

"I think he thinks she's our Aunt Frieda Milstein, his half-sister who died," I whispered back. "Cooky's supposed to look just like her."

My sister, who'd never seen him this far gone, didn't know whether to laugh or cry. I put my arm around her. "It's okay, Cook."

278

Addressing him, I asked, "And can you tell these ladies my name, sir?"

He was having fun, enjoying the attention. "Sausage!" he exclaimed.

This was a new one. We all laughed, and let the subject drop. Except there wasn't much else to talk about. We were still drained from a midnight vigil in the hospital, during which my mother had hung on. "Sorry we can't stay longer, Dad," I told him ten minutes later. I knew that it didn't matter much—his sense of time was long gone. "We have to go to the airport to pick up Aunt Sylvia. But we'll be back."

"That's okay, Herm," he replied.

Outside the rest home, we said goodbye to Cecilia. "Thanks for coming down," I told her.

"*Ay*, Alan, you don't have to thank me," she said.

"I know. But thanks anyway. It meant a lot."

My sister hugged her for a long time. "She is such a doll," she kept saying to me in the car. "I know I shouldn't say anything, but if there's any chance that you and she might—"

"One day at a time, Cooky. We're not making any plans."

I had finally reached Aunt Sylvia at her home in Las Vegas just before our mother went into surgery. "I tried to get you all day, Aunt Syl. I'm sorry to shock you with this, but it doesn't look good."

"I just got in this minute. What do you mean, doesn't look good? I just saw Charlotte last week." I explained. "No, sir!" Sylvia told me. "She is not going to die. I know these things. Your mother is going to pull through."

"I hope you're right. The doctor wasn't very—"

"What do they know? Why, do you know what the doctors told me fifteen years ago?" I actually listened to the whole thing, not wanting her to stop. It was the closest thing left to my mother's voice I might ever hear.

"See, I told you she'd still be alive," she said at the airport. "I knew she'd make it."

"She hasn't made it yet, Aunt Sylvie," my sister said.

In the hospital, my mother was still almost invisible behind all the paraphernalia. Sylvia bit her lip, but then scolded the supine, unconscious form. "Charlotte, we're going over to see Si. Then we're coming back. I expect you to be awake. Do you hear me? You'd better."

"He'll remember me. You wait and see," Sylvia declared. Her hair, so jet black when we were growing up, had never been allowed to gray, diverted instead over the past several years to a pale ocher blonde. She still looked great.

"Just don't get your hopes up, Aunt Syl," Cooky warned her. "He thinks I'm his sister Frieda and that Alan's his brother Herman."

"What, is he crazy?"

"Well, kind of. He's getting there," I said.

"He's really losing it, Aunt Syl," Cooky said. "He didn't even ask for Mother when we saw him. Didn't even notice she wasn't there."

"That ungrateful so-and-so. Do you know all your mother's done for him? What she's put up with from him?"

"Aunt Syl, I don't think he's being this way on purpose."

"Well, he'll know me. You'll see."

"Hi, Sylvie," my father said.

She shot us a triumphant look as she bent to kiss him. But then he saw my sister over her shoulder. "Hi, Cookybelle," and Cooky's eyes filled with tears as she hugged him.

"Hi, Dad," I said.

"Hi, Herm."

Two out of three wasn't bad, and I was too happy that he had given that little gift to my sister to care.

"See," Sylvia said. "He's doing much better. I think he just had a bad stroke, and it's taken this long for him to come out of it."

"Do you feel better, Dad?" Cooky asked.

He shrugged. "Are you married?" he suddenly asked her.

We all looked at each other. "Yes, Dad. My husband's name is Gary. Remember?"

"Gary?"

"Gary."

"Isn't that nice? Do you have any children?"

"*Oy,*" Sylvia said. My sister's two sons, Brian and Peter, had been my father's chief interest in life since each was born.

Cooky fished in her purse, and produced Brian's college graduation picture. "Who's this, Dad?"

He scrutinized it while we waited. Finally he looked up and said, with the sorriest expression I'd ever seen on anybody's face, "I don't know who it is. But I know he's someone I love."

We settled into my parents' house and waited: Sylvia, Cooky, and myself. I had all my notes with me, and all the tape transcripts, and knew what I needed to do. Except I couldn't write. Every day, I went in the morning to the intensive care unit to see my mother, who was still listed as critical and unresponsive, though the doctor told us that each day that she was still alive, her chances improved. Then I would come back to the house, open my laptop, and stare. Nothing. The screen and my mind remained equally blank. I called my editor at the magazine. "I'm trying," I said. "It's a powerful story. I've got strong stuff. I just need some time."

"I understand," he said. "But try to write—maybe it'll take your mind off it. It's scheduled as a cover story. How does *Naked Planet* sound as a title?"

"Fine. I'll try." How could I tell him that a story about the potential loss of the earth's natural defense system was not an ideal distraction from the potential loss of my parents, my own natural protectors?

Ten days after her emergency procedure, we stood around her bed as the doctor examined her. The tubes were gone, and she was propped on pillows, weak but fully conscious for the first time. And ornery. "Alan," she said, "I'll bet my house is a mess. You've probably got your things thrown all over the place, if I know you. Honest to God, doctor, I don't know if you have kids, but getting mine to pick up after themselves—forget it, brother."

He removed the stethoscope from his ears and sat on her bed. "Now be nice, Mrs. Weisman," he reproved. "Do you have any idea what good kids you have? They've hardly left your bedside since you've been here."

That evening, while we were watching the TV program Sylvia had switched on, I caught my mother gazing at us. "What are you looking at, Mom?" I asked.

"My good kids," she said.

That night, back at her house, I started to write.

Four days later, just two weeks after she'd teetered at death's edge, we took her home. Even the doctor was amazed. She insisted on driving back herself. But first, she drove straight to the home to see my father.

He was in his chair, his face as distant and unreadable as a cat's. My mother burst into tears. "Why are you crying, Moke?" he asked her.

"Didn't you miss me, Bobe?"

"Why? Did you go somewhere?"

"Honey, you haven't seen me for weeks!"

"I haven't?"

CHAPTER 17

✺

At 8:00 P.M. on Sunday, August 25, 1968, I pulled the rowboat onto the main beach at Lake Harriet, chained it to the lifeguard stand, and called it a summer. I drove over to the main guardhouse at Lake Calhoun, changed in the locker room, and turned in my trunks and whistle.

An hour later I was climbing out of my mother's car near the highway interchange where I'd asked her to drop me. "I can't believe I'm letting you do this," she said. "Why don't you drive? You have a car."

"Bye, Mom," I said, blowing her a kiss as I stuck out my thumb.

"Remember to call your father to let him know you're all right. At the Conrad Hilton."

"Right." Immediately, a Volkswagen van pulled over. I saw her face craning out her window as I climbed in, her mouth wide open.

I couldn't have articulated to myself why I wanted to hitchhike. Two nights before, I'd made plans to check out the antiwar demonstrations at the Democratic convention in Chicago with a friend from college. During the previous school year—I attended Northwestern, just north of the city—I had evolved from aloof bystander to chary participant in the rallies that increasingly disrupted our formerly placid North Shore campus. Following my freshman year, an upheaval in the admissions office had apparently eliminated Northwestern's unwritten quotas for Jews, Catholics, and blacks, all of whom promptly appeared in unprecedented numbers. Many of the new Jews, from the East Coast, resembled neither my clean-cut, football-playing Jewish friends back in Minnesota nor the Chicago Jews I knew at Northwestern, still flaunting the tight pants and pointed shoes of their nearby high schools. As these easterners staged sit-ins and defiantly grew their hair, I remember wondering whether they had parents. How else could they get away with such behavior? My own father would have slapped me silly.

Many, I eventually learned, had parents quite unlike mine: They were New York Communists, whose kids had grown up attending socialist summer camp in the Catskills, and who weren't rebelling against their parents, but conforming to them. Although I felt an attraction to their polemics—against war, for equality— they intimidated me, eliciting the same response I still have to Hasidic Jews on Manhattan streets: a sense that I had somehow grown up wrong.

Oddly, I found it easier to get acquainted with some of my new black classmates. Before 1966, Northwestern barely had enough for a basketball team. Suddenly, a hot core of brilliant urban ghetto survivors had bored through campus like a volcanic extrusion, appearing with Afro hair and something to prove. I knew even less about them than about the Jewish red diaper babies from New York, but we had one thing in common. During my last year in high school, I had discovered jazz. Then, a neighbor in my freshman dorm turned out to be a jazz pianist. He explained the music theory underlying how Miles, Monk, Coltrane, and Bill Evans were driving me so wild and led me to the best jazz record store in town.

A year later, some new black students at Northwestern discovered me and my record collection. "You hip," they told me. I wanted to be. I smoked their dope and listened spellbound to conversations that bounced among them like scat singing. We had codeine cough syrup parties in my apartment and got woozy to Mingus, Bobby Hutcherson, Ornette Coleman, and Freddie

Hubbard. We went to see Miles himself when he played Chicago's Plugged Nickel. And when they commandeered the registrar's building one day and refused to leave until their list of demands was met, I was in the Caucasian sympathy picket outside on the steps.

This was a big step for me, because I was still wary of the antiwar demonstrations fomented by the radical Jewish campus pacifists. Once, I actually played devil's advocate with my roommate's appalled date, defending the U.S. moral position in Vietnam as the lesser of two evils.

"But the killing, Alan!"

"Do you have any idea how many people Communists have killed?" I retorted. "What about Stalin? The Chinese Cultural Revolution?" Before she could reply, I delivered the *coup de grace*. "Communists," I declared, "murdered my grandfather," effectively ending the discussion.

But now I'd found a way to have my protest and my father, too. Surely he would support me upholding the rights of Negroes, as he still called them: Many labor unionists he represented were Negro railroad workers. I'd been raised on B'nai B'rith Anti-Defamation League books that condemned racial discrimination as fiercely as they opposed anti-Semitism. So it was unsettling to receive a clipping from my father by commentator Paul Harvey, about the "tantrum" thrown by black power students at Northwestern University demanding increased financial aid, more Negro enrollment, black counselors, black studies, chitlins and collard greens in cafeterias, and more black faculty.

After these impudent Negroes occupied the building for thirty-six hours, Harvey fumed, the university had ceded all these points and refrained from punishing them. "The undergraduate majority," he assured his readers, "was dismayed," and quoted one of my boorish white classmates to the effect that he'd have been thrown out of school had he tried something like that.

My father's accompanying note said that he was "one of those old-fashioned naive Americans who feels that occasionally the

285

majority's rights should not be ignored when the majority happens to be right." It was soon followed by another column, by Negro columnist Carl T. Rowan (*Negro* here being Rowan's own term), who advised that when these "anarchists and nihilists resort to illegal mob tactics, they ought to be expelled—pronto!"

"I don't think anyone can accuse Carl Rowan of being a white racist," my father wrote. As usual, his letter had been dictated to his secretary. His initials appeared in caps, separated by a colon from hers in lower case, with a notation that a copy was being filed. "I'll appreciate your thoughts and comments," it concluded, and as always, was signed, "Affectionately."

It was thrilling to stand on the edge of the great concrete network that connected all America, able just by pointing to make hurtling cars and trucks stop and take me where I wanted to go. My last ride, a Chevy Impala just outside Rockport, Illinois, took me right to the Evanston apartment of my friend Steve Weber. It was 6:00 A.M. I banged on the door, and Weber opened it immediately, his thick blond hair swathed in a bloody bandage. "Jesus! What happened to you?"

"The fucking Chicago Police Department happened to me," he said. But he was grinning. "You're not going to believe this scene."

He'd been bludgeoned the night before in Lincoln Park, north of downtown on Chicago's lakefront, where amassing antiwar demonstrators had intended to camp overnight—until dozens of Mayor Richard Daley's police began swinging billy clubs at them. This attempt to crush protests before they began proved a tactical blunder: The following evening, thousands of war resisters poured into a site much closer to the official action, where we joined them: Grant Park, directly across Michigan Avenue from the Conrad Hilton Hotel, where delegates to the Democratic National Convention were ensconced. And my father.

He was not a delegate himself this time, as he had been eight years earlier in Los Angeles when Kennedy was nominated. Now the attorney to the Minnesota Teamsters Union, he was in town to muster labor support for the candidacy of the current vice president of the United States, Hubert H. Humphrey, whose nomination wasn't really in question. The Democratic presidential primaries that year had been split between two antiwar candidates, Minnesota senator Eugene McCarthy and Robert Kennedy. Humphrey had avoided the primary route, however, instead cashing in party chits he'd accrued over two decades to gain enough pledged delegates well before the convention to assure himself victory— and outraging millions of young Americans in the process.

That Monday afternoon, Chicago seemed occupied more by competing carnivals than two warring camps that would shortly lay battle lines to divide America for years to come. In Grant Park, luminaries abounded among the hippies, yippies, and their kindred seekers. Over there was William Burroughs. Here was Allen Ginsberg, walking barefoot and holding hands with Jean Genet. The guy with a guitar case who bummed matches from us was Phil Ochs.

Across the street, the Conrad Hilton was festooned with bunting and placards. Fresh-scrubbed campaign volunteers and paunchy delegates flowed in and out of the hotel, and no one stopped us when Steve and I entered the Hilton's rich dark red lobby. We took an elevator up to McCarthy headquarters. A few subdued college-age staff members stood behind tables covered with thick white hotel linen, halfheartedly distributing peace leaflets. They were the troops who had gotten "clean for Gene," trading beards and dungarees for coats and ties to take McCarthy's campaign door-to-door around the nation, and now they had nothing left to do. Eugene McCarthy had no chance at the nomination, and earlier that day he'd failed to get his antiwar plank wedged into the platform. His children's crusade had withered to this funeral in a windowless room in the Conrad Hilton.

"He's a traitor to his party," my father had told me over the phone after McCarthy's surprise New Hampshire primary victory. "All that goddam fool is doing is making it harder for Hubert to win. He's going to hand the election right over to that son-of-a-bitch Nixon. And then," he told me, "you damn kids will be sorry."

Until that moment when he lumped me in with my generation, I hadn't realized how much my own sympathies had been energized by McCarthy's audacious challenge to party authority. Having been raised in a home that valued obedience, not independence, the idea of someone thinking for himself was an exotic concept for me. As a boy, I had heard Eugene McCarthy discourse with impromptu elegance in my family's own basement amusement room, my father then among his appreciative audience. He hadn't sounded like a goddam fool at all.

Four intoxicating months had followed his New Hampshire win—a great national ballooning of excitement, only to be punctured by the bullets that first felled Martin Luther King, then Bobby Kennedy. Whereas McCarthy was a symbol, Kennedy had been a real threat, a charismatic, electable heir to his dead brother who likely would have beaten both Humphrey and Nixon. After he bled to death in Los Angeles, it was evident that the symbols remaining to us weren't nearly enough to fix what really ailed America.

On the way down, the elevator stopped at the Humphrey campaign headquarters. "Let's check it out," said Steve. "There may be food." He headed for a table laden with glass bowls of iced shrimp and began filling a napkin.

The room was in high celebration, many people wearing ersatz straw skimmers with HHH bumper stickers as hatbands. Posters read "HUBERT, THE HAPPY WARRIOR." His campaign slogan, "Politics of Joy," in a nation that tuned to the news each night for the day's body-bag count, infuriated me. A young man about my age holding a microphone jumped onto a bandstand and sang. "Will everyone here kindly step to the rear, and let a winner lead the way? Humphrey for president's the one we adore. . . ." Even with its original lyrics I hated that song, but I listened, rapt with disgust that any peer of mine could possibly want this bloodthirsty fascist for president.

On the way out, I used a pen at the front desk to leave a message for my father. Thirty years later, I discovered it among his papers.

Father,

Am in Evanston, alive and well. If you wish to speak to me, I'm at 869-1813. Affectionately,

A.

I never called him "Father," so the chill must have struck immediately. The following morning, he called me. "I'm glad you're safe in Evanston," he said. "I'd like to see you, but I don't think it's a good idea for you to come down here. There's a lot of trouble brewing. Stay up there and watch the convention on TV."

"We're headed down there right now."

I could picture his jaw working as though he were trying to swallow something disagreeable. "I'll be gone during the day," he said finally. "Try me in my room if you're still here tonight. But be careful. You had your mother plenty damn worried with that silly idea of hitchhiking. I don't know what the hell's gotten into you, anyway."

Waiting for him at the front desk, I heard my name called. Vernon Ford, a guy I knew from college, was standing in the lobby in a lightweight cable-knit sweater and pale olive slacks, looking lithe and slick, accompanied by some friends from Chicago's South Side. "These are a coupla good dudes," he said by way of introducing Steve and me around. "They cool, brothers."

We'd just finished slapping and shaking hands when I saw my father emerge from an elevator. I nudged Steve and nodded. "Kind of looks like a hamburger," he observed.

He kind of did: big, beefy, and red. He hadn't spotted us yet, but he was already scowling. Not only didn't he know how to mask disapproval, but it would never occur to him to try. "Dad," I called.

Weber didn't wait for me to introduce him. "Hi, Mr. Weisman." Steve was husky, with a snaky little blond moustache—my father despised facial hair—and wore a red bandanna and an untucked U.S. Marines shirt with rolled-up sleeves over blue jeans. Eight years hence, the Minneapolis newspaper would report how my father raised a ruckus in a downtown barbershop that was celebrating the U.S. Bicentennial with red, white, and star-spangled blue sheets to catch customers' hair clippings. But by his reckoning, equally sacrilegious as flag desecration was disrespect for a military uniform. His lip predictably curled when Steve stuck out his hand, but then he noticed Weber's name stitched over the pocket.

"This is Corporal Steve Weber, Dad," I interjected. Steve had recently returned from six months of Marine reserve training. I'd been anticipating this moment.

"You should be grateful to be serving your country in the reserves," he told Steve.

"I am," Steve agreed. "It gets me out of the draft."

Next, I introduced him to Vernon Ford and his friends. "Well," he said, finding himself at an unfamiliar disadvantage, outnumbered by an insubordinate Marine and a passel of young blacks accompanying his son. "Are you boys all here for the convention?"

Bad start. "You here for the convention, *boy*?" one of the blacks said, turning to another.

"Yeah I is, *boy*. What 'bout you, *boy*?" he said, to the one next to him, and so on around the circle. My father wasn't sure what he'd said wrong, but he sensed that something wasn't quite right as all eyes turned back to him expectantly. Vernon kindly let him off the hook. "Actually, we live here. What brings you to town, sir?"

"The convention. I'm doing some work for Hubert Humphrey's people."

"Ah," said Vernon.

"Da Hump," said one of his friends. "He workin fo' da Hump, brother."

"Hump da Hump," the others echoed. It was extraordinary to see my father flustered. Before he could summon a response, another black man wandered over. Unlike the rest of us, he wore a sport jacket and necktie. "Wait a minute," he said, "wait a minute." We turned and looked at him. "How come? I mean, how come," he asked, addressing my father, "you for da Hump? I mean, why is that?"

"Because I like what he stands for. He'll make a good president. You people don't want to see Nixon elected, do you?"

The man looked around at us. He was swaying a little, but he didn't seem drunk, just puzzled and out of his element, as if someone had made him dress up to talk to white folks. He seemed to be trying to decide who my father meant by "you people." I was glad when he let that question go. "We not talking bout Nixon. I ast bout da Hump."

"What about him?"

"Well, man, he gonna keep all the brothers fighting over there. And tha's what we got to *stop*. Ain't it?"

"Sorry," my father said. "I just don't agree with you."

The man tugged on his sleeve. "Yeah. But why is that? Because, man, that's the difference between you and me. They ain't going to make *you* go over there."

My father removed his hand. "I'm sorry—what was your name?"

"Charles."

"Well, Charles." He looked around at the rest of us. "I've been over there."

"You been to Nam?"

"No. I fought in Europe. And if guys like me hadn't, you boys wouldn't be here discussing these issues freely today."

"*Freely.*"

"That's right. I'm not saying that everything's the way it should be in America. You people have legitimate grievances. But everyone

291

here is free to make something of himself if he tries. I was given that opportunity, and I fought so my son here could have it, too."

"But listen," Charles said. My father waited, but Charles was having trouble pinpointing the right reply to my father's patriotism. "Listen to me, man."

"I'm listening. So whatever it is you want to say, say it already."

He was trying, but too many ideas were battling for his tongue at once. "Wait a minute. Wait a minute," he said.

"Okay," my father replied, "I'm waiting."

Charles knit his brow and squeezed out his thought. "We ain't talking about no Europe. Nam is a bunch of gooks, man. They din declare no war on us. They din bomb no Pearl Harbor. And LBJ and da Hump is making all the brothers go get their asses shot off. Why you for that, man? You tell me." He wasn't challenging my father so much as expressing genuine stupefaction over why a human being would do such a thing.

"Because if we don't make a stand and defend Vietnam, we'll be handing Southeast Asia to the Communists on a silver platter."

"Listen to me, man."

"I'm listening, damn it. Talk."

Charles took an involuntary step backward, then swayed back toward my father. "The Communists," he said. "The Communists isn't what it's about. It's about *us*, man. It's about black men. We the ones getting put over there. We the ones getting put down here. We always getting the shit kicked out of us. An' tha's gotta stop."

"Pitying yourself isn't going to make it stop. And let me tell you something, young man. You think you have it bad now? Try living under Communism. I did. I watched those sons of bitches kill my father. Nobody showed him any respect. You want respect, you've got to earn it. Nobody promised you a—"

"Those little yellow mothafuckers kill your father?"

"Not the Vietnamese. The Russians."

"We ain't fighting the Russians."

"Who the hell do you think you're fighting?"

292

"I ain't fighting nobody. Everybody been fighting me all my life. Fucking pigs over there," he said, as two of Chicago's largest and finest strolled by, slapping billy clubs into their palms.

My father, the police federation lawyer, visibly jerked at that choice of words. "Look," he said, "I don't know where or how you were raised, mister. But when I came to this country my father was dead and—"

"My father was dead on the day he was born in this mothafucking city," Charles muttered, looking at the ground.

My father looked around at me, helplessly.

"Hey, brother, what's going on?" Another classmate of ours, his name long forgotten to me, came up and clasped Vernon Ford's forearm. He gestured with long, elegant fingers at the little scene we were making.

"Mr. Weisman there got stuck with some brother without any sense," I heard Vernon reply. "Can't say what he's trying to say."

"Even if that brother had any sense, you think that white man could hear him?"

The following night, Wednesday, August 28, I stood among three thousand others in Grant Park with Steve Weber. Another college friend, Jeff Schatz, had joined us. A small-boned, elfin-faced Chicago boy, Schatz would be teaching elementary school in the fall to avoid the draft. His own father was president of a Chicago association of Jewish attorneys. "You don't have to tell me what it's like to be the son of a high-powered Jewish lawyer," he would say to me. It was an empathetic bond between us that remained intact until the day when I met his father and discovered that he was only 5'4".

The thick August air had cooled. Behind the Conrad Hilton, the sky slid from blue to cobalt to violet. Weber had picked up a cheerful, stoned hippie girl in a blue denim jacket named Bonnie, who was hugging him around the waist. As the tally coming over portable radios confirmed that the convention was about to nominate Hubert Humphrey, and thus—at least in our minds—commit the country to more war, protesters started climbing the park's flagpole to tear down the star-spangled banner hanging limply above us. That was when the line of blue-vested Chicago tactical squad policemen in riot helmets and Plexiglas shields, who until that moment had stood taut with fury on the sidewalk, facing a barrage of verbal abuse—that was when their rage cracked.

"Oh-OH-OHH!" The banshee howl of the shocked crowd was like nothing I'd ever heard before. For a moment we stood riveted, as though the large uniformed men rushing toward us, swinging clubs the size of small baseball bats, couldn't possibly be real. When one of these connected with a protester's body and his ribs audibly snapped, Schatz and I started to run. Where was Weber?

A white puff exploded in front of me, and I thought they were shooting until I started to gag. Plastic eggs of tear gas powder were falling all around us, blinding us as they cracked open. Through the stinging haze, we stumbled toward the wedding cake shape of Buckingham Fountain. As we scooped water into our faces, some-one yelled, "They're coming!" and the cops were behind us, bear-ing down. They chased us up Columbus Drive, away from the Hilton. The next two cross-streets that connected back to Michi-gan Avenue were blocked by Illinois National Guard troops perched atop olive green urban troop carriers. We kept running northward, and inexplicably Jackson Street was open.

Ahead, the air was clear, but at the corner of Jackson and Michigan we collided with a stupendous snarl of humans, ve-hicles, and animals led by Dr. Ralph Abernathy, heir to the South-ern Christian Leadership Conference after Martin Luther King's murder three months earlier. Hundreds of hymn-singing black marchers were following him and three mule-drawn wagons down Michigan Avenue. I grabbed Schatz's arm and we ducked between two mule teams, then started marching with them, next to a griz-zled black man in a clerical collar bearing a sign that read "SCLC POOR PEOPLES' CAMPAIGN." Soon the street flooded with thousands more protesters, all descending toward the Conrad Hilton amid the nonviolent parade that momentarily halted the police on-slaught.

We stopped directly in front of the hotel, exactly where the policemen hadn't wanted us. A tall Australian journalist had just started to question us when a blocky sergeant approached and jabbed two fingers the size of Polish sausages into my solar plexus. As I doubled over, I scooted underneath his upraised club. Another cop attacked the reporter's photographer companion who had shinnied partway up a lamppost, batting the camera from his hands and smashing his knuckles. The Aussie slid down the pole, leaving a streak that glinted in the lamplight.

A megaphone barked. They charged, coming and clubbing from three sides. Behind us, through large plate glass windows of the Hilton's Haymarket Inn, I glimpsed people absurdly enjoying cocktails. The crush grew so intense that my feet left the ground, but I remained upright. Suddenly, the big windows shattered, and Jeff Schatz and I spilled inside, upturning a round cocktail table as a woman in a black shift staggered back in horror. The police rushed in, swinging at everyone, felling the woman in the black shift, smashing trays of thin-stemmed wineglasses. We raced through the lobby where the night before I'd been with my father—*where was he? Where was Weber?*—and bolted from the hotel back into the bedlam of the street.

Later that night, thousands of us ended up back in Grant Park. Incredibly, I saw Steve Weber and Bonnie emerge from under a cement bench. They had crept under it when the police first charged, and simply stayed, fucking fiercely as civilized order collapsed around them. We remained until dawn. "The whole world's watching!" we chanted, knowing it was true. A podium was rigged from amplifier boxes, and one by one, the famous rose from the crowd or descended from the hotel to voice their solidarity with us. Phil Ochs sang "I Ain't Marching Anymore," and everyone shouted the words. Next came Mary Travers and Paul Stookey, sans Peter. Repeatedly, we called on people inside the Conrad Hilton to flash their lights if they were with us. At one point, it occurred to me that my father surely wasn't among those who did. Then I dismissed him from my thoughts for the rest of the convention.

The following night, two thousand of us tried to march on the Chicago Amphitheatre, where Hubert Humphrey was accepting his nomination. We were chased by riot squad policemen and National Guardsmen bearing rifles and bazookas back to Grant Park, where they barraged us with tear-gas cannisters. By now, the grass had been trampled away; with every step, stinging, powder-soaked dust rose in our faces, and more wasn't going to make things any worse. We held our ground—a motley, hacking crowd, defiant of the uniforms that seethed at our perimeter. Someone started singing "America the Beautiful." It may have been to mock the police and Guardsmen, but as the crowd took it up, it turned serious. Nearly everyone was weeping, and not only from the gas. We were crying over what had become of the beautiful land we'd been promised as children, a land where my father raised me to believe that policemen were our friends, soldiers our defenders, and the president our wise leader.

Instead, it had come to this.

CHAPTER 18

"I promised my mother we'd stop by before we headed home," I told Cecilia when I met her flight from Rio de Janeiro. She was returning from covering the Earth Summit—the United Nations Conference on Environment and Development. Two weeks earlier, NPR had called, wanting her knowledge of Portuguese, Brazil, and environmental reporting. Although it set back our production schedule further, we'd agreed that after pulling our ozone story over editorial differences and selling it to another network, it was politic for her to go.

"I'm really tired," she said. "I'd think I'd like to get straight up to Prescott."

"I think she's got a birthday present for you, Cec."

"Oh, God." She shut her eyes.

I was pretty sure I didn't want to know what that reaction signified. Our two phone conversations while she was in Brazil hadn't gone well. Mainly, she'd grumbled about more editorial struggles. Intending to sympathize, I'd critiqued one broadcast I'd heard, but she recoiled as though I were attacking her work. Attempting to explain only worsened matters. I hung up, hoping she was merely exhausted, like me. For months, our main recreation had been walking a block from our studio to a granite outcropping, where we would take our squabbles instead of inflicting ourselves on our partners. The previous fall, we'd briefly seen a counselor, but after all the intervening travels and troubles, we hadn't gone back. With the relentless pressure to produce scripts under deadline, it was too tiring to work on our lives.

Cecilia was silent on the way, but when we met my parents at my father's rest home, she was sweet and gracious. My mother had bought her a linen sunsuit that she really liked. "Thank you, Mrs. Weisman. It's great. You really didn't have to do that."

"Don't be silly. You know we wouldn't forget your birthday. We love you. Don't we, Dad?"

My father, who was having an agreeable day, looked up from the apple he was devouring and nodded. "Yup," he said. Cecilia kissed them both.

"We're very happy you're part of our family," my mother said, squeezing Cecilia's cheeks. "*Shayna punim!* You know what that means, don't you?" She didn't. "It means gorgeous face."

We were a half-hour from Prescott when she spilled it. "Alan, I don't want to go to the house when we get there."

"You want to go to the studio?"

"To a motel."

She'd timed her announcement well. By the time we pulled into town, I'd tried all the ways I could to talk her out of it. For another hour, we sat in front of the motel. By then I wasn't trying anymore, but in her decency Cecilia didn't just grab her bags and run. She was angry with me—even decent people resent it when you entangle their feelings—but she acknowledged that she still cared. Not enough, however, to continue.

The following night, I was home, contemplating life alone again, when she drove up.

"Alan," she said through the screen door, "I have no right to ask you, but I'm having big trouble with this script. I don't want to hassle Sandy or Nancy with it, but I really need—"

"Come on in."

We sat at the kitchen table with our laptops. About 2:00 A.M. she went to sleep on the futon couch downstairs and I climbed up to my loft and fell into bed. And that's how we got through the next two months. Mostly she stayed at a friend's cabin, but sometimes in my guest room. With the pressure of our romantic liaison finally released, our professional partnership actually flourished. Which was a good thing: We now had an inviolable deadline to finish our series. As a result, I didn't get down to Scottsdale to see my parents during that time. Besides working sixteen-hour days, I wasn't ready to spring the news about Cecilia and me. But one morning my mother called, fairly hysterical. My father had tried to escape the nursing home.

"Escape? He can't even walk by himself anymore. Did he hide in a laundry basket?"

Somehow, he'd managed to wheel his chair out the front door, through the parking lot, and over a curb, and was nearly halfway across a busy thoroughfare when a male nurse spotted him and yanked him back. "He could have been killed. Alan, you have to come down and talk to him. When I say something, he just screams at me. Right in front of everybody. It's so embarrassing, I can't take it. You should hear him."

"I've heard him. Mom, he never listened to me when he had all his faculties. Why would he listen to me now?"

"Please, Alan. Try to explain to him."

I went, of course, not that it would do him any good, but because she was watching her husband crumble all by herself. "As soon as we're done, I'll come stay with you for a week," I promised her. Surprisingly, she wouldn't go with me to see him. After some searching, I found him on a service ramp that led to the rear entrance. He was in his wheelchair, creeping slowly toward the door by pulling himself hand over hand along the railing.

"Hi, Dad."

He looked around. "Hi, Herm," he said, and resumed pulling.

"Dad, where are you going? Come on," I said, wheeling his chair around. "You're not supposed to be out here."

"Goddammit, you let me alone! If that's the way you're going to be, get the hell out of here. NOW!"

"Dad." I squatted down and faced him. "You can't go out by yourself. It's not safe."

He refused to say another word. Why, I silently asked a negligent deity as I drove away, couldn't You have let him get hit by traffic and go on his own terms? He may have lost most of his mind, but his will is intact and it will stay that way until his body finally falls.

God was not forthcoming. There was nothing to do except hope that I myself went someday before they put me in diapers and a set of wheels and exiled me to adult daycare. Everything I ever imagined about the indignity of being sentenced to die in a rest home was not merely true: It was worse. My father barely had any words left to articulate a thought, let alone defend himself as he had once so brilliantly championed his clients. But that didn't mean that he didn't know. He knew. He knew what his life had come to.

So what the hell was I supposed to do, I asked myself en route back to Prescott that evening. Take him in myself? Isn't that what used to happen? His aged grandmother had lived with his family, at least until they—the Communists or the Cossacks—killed her and my grandfather. In the old country, that's what families did. But our traditions had been plundered along with our land, and now this was America, where we were barely rooted. I tried to picture how different my life was from the generations of Weismans before me. Like the hapless Indian and peasant protagonists of our radio series, my family had been severed from its history. Eventually, we'd landed in a strange place with so much to distract us that we couldn't go back to who we were, any more than Guaraní hunter-gatherers could remain very Guaraní once exiled from the forest and dropped at the edge of some burgeoning city. And now, who was I? Forty-five, living alone, no children to continue the lineage that got twisted by dispossession and flight. Was I a cultural refugee, too?

⁂

Following the 1968 Democratic convention, a federal conspiracy trial was held in Chicago of ringleaders of the antiwar demonstrations. The presiding judge's contempt for the defendants colored his rulings so flagrantly that the proceedings became a mockery. The radical defense attorneys easily got the verdicts against their clients quashed on appeal; impressed by their defiant success, I deluded myself into thinking that law might be my calling after all.

I was still looking to somehow have life both ways: to be my father's son *and* be myself, but that was not to be. During high school, I'd tried. Although my weight never topped 150 pounds, I scrapped my way to a starting position on a football team that—discounting me—averaged 210 pounds per man and finished second in the state. The thought of doing anything other than excelling at the game had simply never occurred to me. My approving father had his secretary send newspaper clippings about my team to his colleagues. He missed the part my mother saw, however: the trips to the emergency room for stitches, the rounds of physical therapy after the periodic shoulder dislocations. She endured all this simply as one more burden females must bear: that men, apparently, are congenitally obliged to expose themselves to injury.

"Alan, you're going to kill me," she announced whenever she had to fetch me from practice, towels ready to preserve the car's upholstery from bloodstains. Yet she didn't dare protest that perhaps football wasn't a ritual mandated by God.

"A little blood never hurt anybody," snapped my father, muzzling her involuntary yelp the first time I came home with my nose streaming, and she never forgot it. I made him proud, but ever since the November night of my final game, when I leaped into his arms after we won the conference championship in a come-from-behind thriller, I never again fulfilled his dreams for me. I was too small to play in college, which came as an unexpected relief. And unlike my hungry immigrant father, I had no professional ambitions whatsoever. I simply liked books, and I spent my college education absorbed in them.

"I'll never forget," Charlie Hvass recalled, "you coming home for Thanksgiving your freshman year and mentioning over dinner that you were majoring in philosophy, and your mother bursting into tears."

It was true. Over the next three days, every time she looked at me she started sobbing. "What the hell are you going to do? Become a philosopher? *Er iz knacker!*"

"I could get a Ph.D. and be a professor."

"He's just like his goddam Uncle Herman," my father spat.

"Dad's right. You won't make *kasha*, kiddo. You won't have a pot to piss in. You'd better listen to your father, if you know what's good for you."

The next term, I took a psychology course. I wrote my parents that I was considering becoming a psychologist. On my next visit, my father called me into his den. Surprisingly, Dr. Barr, the gynecologist who lived next door, was there with him. My first thought was that something was wrong with my mother, who saw him professionally. Beyond that, my parents and the Barrs rarely mixed. But here was my father, claiming that Dr. Barr had just dropped by, and in fact they were just talking about me.

"Have a seat," he said, rising and pointing to his own recliner. "I'll just let the two of you talk," he said, easing out the door. I sat, wondering what the hell was going on. Moments later, I found out: Dr. Barr had been conscripted to talk me out of psychology.

"You'll only be frustrated. You'll waste all that time getting a Ph.D. and then find out that the psychiatrists make all the money. What you should do is go to medical school."

I had no interest in, and even less aptitude for, medicine. "Wouldn't it be a bigger waste of time for me to spend four years taking science and anatomy classes I'll never use? A psychologist does his grad work in his field. It's a better education than psychiatry."

With a wave, Dr. Barr dismissed this faulty thinking. "Alan. Listen to me. Anybody can learn that stuff. It doesn't take seven years. Believe me, psychiatrists get all the respect. And all the gold. You're going to want that."

I became an English major. It was a way to get credit for what I did all the time anyway: read. It also got my father off my back, because, as he frequently reminded me, English was supposedly a good preparation for law school. But during my senior year, slightly panicked because (1) all my classmates seemed to have futures in mind and I had none; (2) being unemployed was the quickest route to being drafted; and, (3) because by then my father was barely talking to me anymore, I decided to take the law boards just to see how I'd do, which turned out to be well enough to be accepted wherever I applied. There seemed to be no escaping the fate my parents had chosen for me. I gave in, enrolling at Berkeley, where, I rationalized, I could at least become a radical lawyer like the ones defending the Chicago Seven.

By December, I'd bombed out and returned a dope-sodden failure. To my father's credit, when I called with the news, after a moment of bottomless silence all he asked was when I was coming home. "I thought I'd finish out the semester. That way they'll give me a leave of absence."

Except I was never going back, and my father understood that. "Why bother, if you're quitting? If you can make it home by Sunday, the Vikings are playing for the NFL championship, and there's a ticket for you."

Sunday was three days away. I left the next morning, driving twelve hours to Salt Lake City. The day after, I made Minneapolis in twenty-three straight hours. My dad and I poured a pint of Courvoisier into a quart thermos bottle, topped it off with hot coffee, and sat in 7°F snow flurries watching the Vikings beat the Cleveland Browns. By the end of the game, the thermos was empty.

CHAPTER 19

"Good night, Alan," Cecilia said from her side of the room.

"Night, Cec. Want some aspirin?"

"Good idea."

I handed over aspirin and a glass of water. In the window, a long triangle of moonlight floated atop Buzzards Bay. *"Qué linda, la luna,"* she said, hiccuping. After stumbling in from a Cape Cod restaurant where we had worked our way through a few dozen steamer clams, two large lobsters, and one pitcher of beer too many, our hosts had replenished our blood sugar with watermelon, and we now felt exquisitely tranquil. *"Gracias.* This was nice," Cecilia murmured, reaching across the space between our beds, taking my hand. "I'm glad we came."

I squeezed back. "I know," I said. "Thanks."

Two weeks before, on August 31, 1992, we had parted in Arizona. Our series finally done, all my colleagues had left for Massachusetts: Sandy and Nancy to Harvard, where Sandy had a journalism fellowship, and Cecilia to produce a pilot documentary for a Boston public radio station's series on racism. "I feel terrible leaving you all alone here," Cecilia had said.

"I'm fine," I lied, wanting her gone already. I had visions of sleeping for a month. After awaking, I'd worry about being lonely. I headed into the mountains and camped at a creek. One morning, I was aroused by rustling in the sycamore branches. A female brown bear, half raised on her haunches, was exhaling steamy clouds that nearly reached my face. "Hi," I said. That same day, I hiked to my truck and drove to town for supplies. I called my recording machine and learned that a friend in Boston had died of AIDS. That was when the loneliness hit.

The day after attending the memorial service, I called Cecilia. She didn't sounded too thrilled to hear from me: She had just moved on to a new life, and here I was again. "I can maybe meet for coffee—"

"Don't worry about it. I'm headed to Jay and Tina's for the weekend," I told her.

"You are?" Jay Allison and Tina Egloff, veteran radio producers who lived in Woods Hole, had been our script consultants. They were wonderful, talented people with beautiful children, and we all envied them. "Can I come?" Cecilia asked.

Arriving, there was a note saying that our hosts were at a birthday party. So we'd found a lobster shack and eaten—and drunk—dinner together. "I can't believe we're here doing this," Cecilia kept saying. We kept doing it all weekend: being friends. Once, awakening from a nap in a lounge chair, I found her looking at me. Her eyes were full of warmth, but I knew that what we shared wasn't what we'd once tried to achieve. "It's like we really are related," she said.

Surely we were: Over time and oceans and continents, the branches of our family tree had groped and grown toward each other and intertwined once more. We embraced farewell like brother and sister. I flew back to Arizona and stopped through Scottsdale to see my parents. They had put an electric bracelet around my father's ankle that triggered an alarm whenever he tried to escape, my mother told me as we drove the nursing home.

"He's always setting it off. I try to tell him not to do it, and it goes in one ear and out the other. Alan, he doesn't understand a thing."

I wondered. To me, trying to escape that ambulatory cemetery smacked of pretty alert thinking.

"Dad, let's play a game."

He turned to consider me with round, baggy eyes, his hands gripping the padded arms of his wheelchair. He wore a new royal blue sweatshirt, one of three my mother had bought him just the day before because his others were now permanently food-stained. Later, I withheld these sweatshirts from the Goodwill pile, and I still wear them on cool days. His hair was untrimmed and lifted in twin gray tufts above either temple. His lower incisors were worn down toward the gum in an uneven parabola. No one had shaved him that morning, and he looked like an old man. In a week, I realized, he would turn eighty.

"We'll start off easy, Dad, okay? State your full name."

"Simon A. Weisman."

"Correct. And who's this?" I pointed at my mother.

"Molka."

"Two for two. And do you know who I am, by chance?"

Knitted brows. I gave him a hint. "Is she your wife?" I asked. He looked at her and smiled. He nodded. "And I'm related to both of you. So who would I be?"

"Our son?"

"Bingo." We shook hands. "And my name?"

"Herman."

"Oh, Si," said my mother, "this isn't Herman. You know who Herman is."

"Isn't Herman a son?"

"Herman's your brother. This is Alan. *Alan.* Our son."

"Oh. I'm sorry, Alan."

"No problem, Dad. You always told me I took after Uncle Herman. Now c'mon; we're just warming up here. Do you remember where you were born?"

"I was born in Russia. In Mala Viska."

"Excellent." He beamed. I took him through the name of the city in the United States he moved to after emigration. He remembered that football was his favorite game. When I asked him if he'd been a soldier, he told me he'd fought at Anzio under General Iron Mike O'Daniel.

My mother was ecstatic. "See, Alan, he remembers everything. It's just that these *schtunks* here don't stimulate his mind. All he needs is someone to talk to. Right, Bobe?"

He nodded vigorously. But as we moved closer toward the present, he needed more prompting. "Dad, when you used to work, what did you do?"

He thought for a while, but was stumped. "I'm sorry, I just don't remember."

My mother's smile faded. I hushed her before she could tell him that he did so remember. "I'll give you some clues. Let's see how soon you can guess. Do you remember your friends Don Barbeau and Pat Fitzgerald?"

"Sure. Judge Barbeau. Pat Fitzgerald. They're judges."

"And you would see them sometimes when you were working, right?"

"Right. In court."

"So if they were judges, and if you were in court with them, that would make you . . ."

". . . an attorney!"

We all applauded. I next asked him his law partners' names, and with a little help—"it starts with *chhh*, Dad"—he got Charlie Hvass. But then he tired, and when I asked him who was the president he'd helped get elected he neither produced the name John Kennedy nor seemed to recognize it when I told him.

"I wish you could come every day," my mother said as we drove away. "You bring him back to life. It's so hard to see him like this, Alan. I'll never forgive myself for putting him in there."

I paused at a stop sign. Blinding afternoon light glared off the concrete boulevard. "Mom. Look at me." She did, reluctantly. "Mom, what alternative did you have? Your house is too small for a live-in nurse. And you see him every day. How many people in there have someone like you? You're giving him the best that your money can buy."

307

"Lot of good that does."

I knew what was worrying her. Recently, Cooky and I had calculated how long she could keep him in a private nursing home at three thousand dollars a month. That was a thousand more than what they got from social security and disbursements from the IRA she'd set up with my father's pension fund. In nine more months, she would have to start dipping into the principal. A lawyer explained that in another year we should take legal steps to separate his finances from hers, lest there be nothing left to support her. By splitting their holdings, at the point when he became indigent she would not be held responsible for his care, and the state would take over.

"You mean I'm going to have to divorce him like those elderly people on Oprah have to do? Forget it. I'm not getting any divorce and that's final."

I explained that in Arizona couples no longer had to divorce to legally separate their finances. "They did that so people like you wouldn't be turned into paupers, just because you're married."

"Oh sure. I suppose they're going to keep him right where he is, where at least it's pretty. You know what will happen. They'll throw him into some state hospital and he'll lie around in dirty sheets that he's pished with a bunch of crazy people. I'll die first. I'm not doing it. It's his money—he earned it. I'm not going to deprive him of one red cent."

"Jesus, Mother," Cooky had interjected. We were sitting around the dining room table, eating microwave popcorn as we went over our parents' finances. "You don't think you earned it too? Who did his laundry so he could go to the office every day? Who gave him a nice home? Who fed him and cleaned up after? Who waited on him hand and foot? You don't think you're entitled to half of his paycheck? He couldn't have accomplished anything without you."

"That wasn't work. That was my duty. I was his wife. I *am* his wife."

"Mother," Cooky wailed, "listen to what you're saying!"

"Your father was wonderful to me. To all of us. And don't you forget it."

"Oh, right. He'd come home from work, hit us first, then ask you what we'd done wrong that day to deserve it. He screamed at us every day of our lives."

"Big deal. So he hollered a little. Your father had a very hard life. And I'm going to make sure he gets the best for whatever's left of it, if it's the last thing I do."

"And it will be," said Cooky. "He won't be satisfied going to the grave unless he drags you along to iron his underwear."

Could he live four or five more years and wipe her out? The nursing home aide who caught him before he wheeled his chair into traffic attested that my father was still strong as a grizzly. "That dude grabbed those spokes in those ham fists of his and wouldn't let me *move*. I had to call two other guys to carry him and his chair back inside."

❧❀❧

The evening after I returned to Prescott following my Boston trip, I had dinner with friends. Afterward, I found a message on my machine. "Alan, call me. I think Daddy's dying."

I called. "Yesterday afternoon," she said, "I went to see him. I brought my portable radio so he could hear you." A program that Sandy and I produced in the Dominican Republic had aired on NPR's *All Things Considered*. "I always do that when I know you're going to be on. All these old geezers sit around in a circle and listen to you. Dad is so proud, though I have to keep explaining to him that it's his son on the radio. 'It is, it is?' he keeps asking me. But this time I could tell that something was wrong with him. He was having a hard time doing every-thing. I thought maybe he was constipated. But you can't ask him if he's gone or not—he doesn't remember. So I called Dr. Waldman."

309

Dear Jay and Tina,

Today we learned that after a long, sad decline, my father is finally dying. For no specific reason, his kidneys have slowed, almost to a halt. Like dusk dissolving, his body is quietly shutting down. The doctor says it will be peaceful: a lot of sleep for a few, maybe several days. Then he won't wake up.

I really loved him, and I was scared to death of him. I don't recommend you try this combination on your beautiful kids. The love gave me something to live up to, true. But the fear held me back in all kinds of ways. And yet, both love and fear sensitized me, slit open whatever taut membrane holds a boy's incipient emotions, and, ever since, feelings have poured from me—sometimes like blood from a wound, sometimes like poetry. Sometimes, of course, like both.

There are better ways. But this is my legacy from him: a frightened eleven-year-old boy when he came to America, who saw his father murdered during the Russian Revolution. All my life he told me it was the Communists who did it. My uncle, whom he didn't speak to at all while I was growing up, says it was really marauding Cossacks. At the time, though, I imagine that all that mattered to an immigrant boy, selling newspapers on frigid Minneapolis street corners to keep from starving, was that his father was gone.

He arrived just in time for the Depression. Then a war, soon after which I was born. I was not so much raised like a child as steeled and disciplined like a plebe. His war memories became my lullaby: I heard his stories of European combat and of doomed companions left behind, and I now can only marvel at what pulled him through. I wonder if he relived his own father's monstrous death as he hunkered in foxholes, waiting—or if he sensed other horrible fates met by ancestors whose collective memory brims in our blood. How many generations of enemies was he really firing at?

Somehow, a man who loved justice emerged from those

whirlwinds and storms. He taught me to believe in it, too. I thank him for that, even though it backfired on him when I began to accuse as unjust some elementary American institutions he had adopted as sacred. We never really got over that. He'll never know, though, that my refusal to trade my convictions for easier beliefs is also his legacy. I am—I am because of him, and in spite of him. We had our small communions, with safe, denatured sacraments like football, but we were mostly lonely together. Late in his life, not long before the strokes began, he read things I wrote and began to understand. It took us both too long to reach that point, but at least we reached it together, however briefly. I was his son after all.

Don't wait too long. Listen to your children, and not just to hear your own echoes. Love their voices, no matter what they say. The most beautiful things in this sweet world lie far beyond words, anyway.

Thanks for opening your house and hearts. Much love—A.

The nursing home had a hospice wing, and by the time I arrived my mother had already transferred him. Besides receiving special care, hospice patients paid a rate far below what long-termers were charged. The fact that this had not escaped my mother amid her burgeoning grief I interpreted as an encouraging sign that she was thinking beyond her imminent loss.

"*Hob im in bod,*" she said. "We've paid them plenty already. *Plenty.*"

"Doctor," I asked after a week, "how long can this go on?" My father was sleeping much of the time, but he still took nourishment. Whenever he didn't seem alert enough to chew, my mother slipped chips of ice into his mouth.

This was a hospice physician we hadn't met yet. He had the tormented, dark good looks of a television actor playing doctor. He flipped through my father's chart, took his vital signs, and then un-hooked his stethoscope. "Frankly, I don't understand why your dad's still alive. Anyone else would've been dead by now. He must have an enormous will to survive."

"You don't know the half of it."

"You know," he said, "some of these old war horses have been fighting for their lives for so long, they just don't know when to quit. Over the years, survival behavior becomes a reflex action for them. The body is so accustomed to fighting pain it forgets to die."

"Sounds like the father I know."

"Suppose we give him a little morphine along with his glucose. Relax him a little bit." He read my look, and added, "Not enough to do anything damaging. Just to ease the stress he's been carrying with him for God knows how many years."

"Since he was six, I figure."

"Just to relax him. His body will know what to do."

His eyes opened. "Dad?" They flitted toward me. His lips parted. I held a Dixie cup in front of him. "Dad, would you like some ice cream? It's chocolate."

"Please."

It was the last word I ever heard him say. With a wooden spoon, I fed him his last sweet meal.

The call came that night. My mother and I picked up extensions simultaneously.

"Your husband isn't doing so well, Mrs. Weisman," said the hospice nurse. I recognized a Native American accent. "I think he may be getting ready to go."

We were there ten minutes later. It was just past midnight, the early minutes of September 23, 1992. His eightieth birthday. "Dad made it to eighty, Mom."

The nurse was a heavyset Navajo woman named Pat. She lifted the light blue knit cover to show us how the skin on his legs was becoming puffy and mottled. "It starts below, and rises to his heart. It doesn't take too long. His blood pressure's pretty low."

"He's eighty years old today," my mother said.

"I know," Pat said. "We sang 'Happy Birthday' to him a few minutes before you arrived. Talk to him. They can hear you, you know." She addressed him. "Si, your family's here. Si?"

Sure enough, his eyes opened as my mother and I leaned over and peered at him. His expression was the same as my grandmother's when she stayed alive long enough to verify that her son Herman had come from Washington to say good-bye: a filmy, uncertain, almost skeptical gaze that we wanted to believe was registering us.

"Talk," said Pat. "The hearing is the last thing to go."

"Hi, Dad. I love you."

"I love you, Bobie."

I bent close to his ear. "I love you," I repeated. My mother, on the other side, smoothed his brow and kissed him.

We straightened up. He was asleep again. Pat lifted the sheet. "I need to clean him up a little."

"I'll wait outside," my mother said, hugging her light sweater against the desert night chill. I lingered for a moment, watched the ease with which Pat expertly rolled his big body on its side, heard him grunt with the effort, the same familiar grunt he always expelled at any exertion. It was a comforting sound.

I followed my mother. "C'mon, Mom, we can sit over here," I said, leading her to a bench, but before we reached it Pat was back.

"He's gone."

He was so still. I had never, ever, seen him be still. Even when he slept, he had always made huge sounds: big throaty breaths, angry gasps when sleep apnea further complicated his ills toward the end of his life, and snores so violent that his partner Charlie Hvass had once fled their cabin on a hunting trip and taken refuge in a barn, only to awaken again convinced that my father had followed him, until it turned out to be a cow.

He looked no different than he had moments before, except for this enormous, motionless silence. He had become a statue to himself, in repose. We kissed him again. My mother touched his hair but didn't cry. "You can call anywhere you like," Pat said, pointing to the phone. My mother told me the name of the Jewish funeral home in Minneapolis. Within minutes, everything was arranged: A Jewish mortuary in Phoenix would arrive shortly to collect the body, for which a plane reservation back to Minnesota had already been made.

My mother took a last look and went out to wait until they came for him. I lingered. He was already changing, yellowing, his cheeks hollowing to form faint dimples. I noticed he was now as static as the other things in the room: the semi-collapsed heavy-duty wheelchair with a blue leather seat my mother had bought him; the stuffed brown recliner he'd never used; the vinyl cupped chairs with chrome legs. A television hung like a giant blind eye from a wall brace high in one corner. One pink curtain held a small dried bloodstain.

A touch lamp, a glass shade, a white phone, my father in white pajamas with a dotted blue pattern, a call button clipped to his pillow. At the foot of his bed, a calendar of hospice activities for September: Sensory group. Reminisce. Sports time. Bingo. Surprise bag. Bible study. Favorite movie. I watched him. Was he breathing? It looked like he was breathing. But I knew that this was the sensation of walking on dry land after a day of sailing and still feeling waves underfoot. I had seen this body breathe all my life, and I couldn't yet imagine that it had finally stopped.

I kept walking in and out, noting and clinging to more details: his hair, gray and black, against the pillow. Death's smell—slightly acrid, not yet unpleasant—steadily increasing. The water pitcher and the package of baby wipes. I pulled back the cover and touched his hand, bent down, put my ear to his nostrils and listened for one last time to the sound of his utter absence. Why hadn't I been in the room when he slipped away, to witness that final moment of his existence? I should have known that when she had to clean him it meant that his sphincter muscle had loosened its grip at last, and that he would follow accordingly. Now I felt my own heart sphincter opening, letting out regret, anger, frustration, and pain. My big father, finally silent.

314

"Go check on them," my mother said when they arrived, two black men pushing a gurney. They donned rubber gloves, counted to three, and then—half pulling, half sliding—transferred him. Just before they wrapped him in their burgundy cloth, tying it across his big stomach that rose like an Indian mound from a plateau, I looked one last time at his face and ruffled his hair. They rolled him away. His brown leather slippers were still under the bed, but it was over. As my mother and I drove home, a thick yellow slice of moon was rising over the desert.

❦

Eight years before my father died, his office received a call from a court reporter in St. Paul, saying that twice while taking depositions that afternoon, Mr. Weisman seemed to have blanked out. Afterward, he had refused a ride home, insisting rather angrily that he was fine and could drive himself.

Next, he forgot a court date. Then, during a pretrial hearing, he began spouting gibberish. One afternoon, his partners at Hvass, Weisman & King asked his secretary to stay after hours. Opening his files, they discovered three pending cases in which he'd allowed the statute of limitations for filing motions to slip. In another, involving a motorcyclist who lost a leg when a cement truck crossed in front of him, my father seemed ready to accept a modest settlement offer. His partner Charlie Hvass stepped in and won a judgment for ten times the amount.

His partners braced themselves for the eruption when they informed him that his career was over. It never came. His docile acceptance of this verdict confirmed that a major hunk of the man they knew was missing. He never spoke of this, but my mother sensed his terrible humiliation, because except for one brief visit the year after they left, when the mayor of Minneapolis proclaimed November 18, 1985, to be Si Weisman Day, he never again wanted to return to his beloved adopted city.

But his funeral was a triumphant posthumous homecoming.

315

The same rabbi who waited with my mother to greet her returning Jewish hero husband at the train after World War II officiated, even though my father had insisted on being buried not at the Jewish *bet olom* with his mother, brother, and sister, but at Ft. Snelling National Military Cemetery. Hundreds of his Gentile friends and associates wore yarmulkes and stood silently as we recited the *kaddish* in the gleaming autumn afternoon. An American Legion honor guard fired rifles over his grave, then presented my mother with the folded flag from his coffin as a bugler played taps.

His partner Charlie Hvass delivered the eulogy. As he recounted the struggles of an eleven-year-old immigrant boy selling newspapers on freezing street corners after Communists murdered his father, I exchanged glances with Cecilia, who stood next to me, holding my hand. She had called the day before. I was touched by her request to attend, but I had hesitated. For a year, my mother had told everyone in the family about my talented, beautiful Jewish girlfriend, omitting the detail that her mother was Catholic and adding that, amazingly, she was Cecilia *Vaisman:* also a species of Weisman—as though I had snagged some Jewish royalty, just as my mother had always tried to convince herself that she had done.

Requiring no explanation, Cecilia offered not to complicate matters and to temporarily be my girlfriend again. Courteously, she submitted her cheek to my relatives for lipstick smears and pinches, and listened politely as they expounded their theories about the similarity of her surname and resemblance to my father's family. "Incredible," exclaimed my father's cousins, Dr. Harry Friedman and his sister Bertha, each taking one of her hands. "I still remember the day your father arrived at our North Minneapolis house from Russia," Bertha said.

The day following the funeral, I showed Cecilia the houses where I had lived, and drove her past the gray bleachers of my high school football field, where boys in scrub uniforms were banging into the blocking sled and mauling tackling dummies. It was where I had made my father happiest, I told her.

Under glowing oaks and maples that showered us with petals

of orange, red, and saffron, Cecilia and I walked around Lake of the Isles. We sat on a bench alongside the empty Lake Harriet band shell, closed after Labor Day, watching the moored sailboats bob gently, the reflections of their naked masts pointing toward the false sky that concealed the lake's murky depths. We climbed a brick-cobbled street to Lowry Hill, where my sister lives overlooking the green patinaed dome of the Basilica of St. Mary—which, long ago, a young immigrant engineer named Sam Friedman had helped build in this graceful heartland city to where his Russian relatives had followed, one of whom we'd just buried. We sat up late with my sister, still berating herself for not flying to Arizona to see our father one last time.

"It was like when you called to tell me that he'd survived his leg operation and I told you, 'Of course: He's indestructible,'" Cooky said, wiping her eyes. "I couldn't admit to myself that he could actually die." Cooky was also having trouble accepting that Cecilia was now just my friend. And, truth be told, that weekend I almost . . . no. It was only heightened emotions, Cecilia and I agreed at the airport when we embraced chastely before she flew off, after which I drove back to Lake Harriet, stripped to my running shorts, and ran around it until I was sure that I would sleep profoundly that night, albeit alone.

I had magazine assignments in New Mexico, Trinidad, and Colombia. I begged my editors' indulgence for a week to get my mother settled. Back in Arizona, we sifted through finances, insurance policies, and old photographs. Charlie Hvass sent us a column from a Minneapolis weekly, adapted from his eulogy for my father. It tempted me to raise the matter of my Uncle Herman's version of events back in the Ukraine that contradicted my father's saga. While my father was still alive, there was no point bringing it up to my mother: Her marital reflexes were conditioned to defend unequivocally whatever he said and did. But now it might be different.

I was in no hurry; she was still grieving. There would be plenty of time, I told myself. My sister and I had great plans for her,

317

now that she was no longer tied to an invalid. "Don't bother me," she kept saying, but we knew that, amidst her sorrow, the funeral in Minneapolis had revealed prospects for life after my father. Friends and relatives she hadn't talked to in years had mobbed her. "Your mother looks so good," they exclaimed to me, and she did: At times she seemed actually relieved to be finally liberated from his long, pathetic decline.

"I'll be back in a week, Mom," I said, kissing her through my truck window as I pulled out of her driveway, headed to New Mexico. "Lillian'll take good care of you." We had hired the woman who babysat my father during my mother's art classes to help with cooking and light housework—although true to form, my mother cleaned the house herself before she came.

My assignment was in New Mexico's boot heel, where an unlikely coalition of ranchers and environmentalists had defeated a common enemy: developers bent on turning some of the wildest open spaces left in the West into five-acre ranchettes and golf courses.

"It's beautiful here, Mom. It's good to write about something hopeful, for a change."

"That's nice, honey. When are you coming back?"

"Three more days. You sound tired, Mom. Haven't you been able to sleep?"

"I've been sleeping all the time."

That didn't sound good. That sounded like depression. I had only seen her cry once since my father died, on the plane to his funeral. Not even at the cemetery, where she'd commandeered the shovel and made sure that each male relative fulfilled tradition by taking his turn at covering the coffin with a few spadefuls of soil. But mourning was unpredictable. For six decades, my mother had defined herself as the companion of a man who—I could barely believe it myself—no longer existed. "If you can get her through the first year, she'll be fine" was the home truth Cooky and I heard repeatedly, and we'd vowed that we would.

Three days later, Lillian met me at the door. "Alan, I'm worried."

She was asleep in her living room recliner. I stood over her, stunned. She seemed to have imploded, reduced by grief and exhaustion to a shade. I went to the phone and called my sister.

"She has an infection," said her oncologist. My mother adored him, but recalling how he had been unreachable earlier that year when she developed meningitis, I didn't trust him. Her hemoglobin was way down; he recommended she go to the hospital for a transfusion to bring it back to normal, followed by an intravenous antibiotic.

The day after the transfusion she looked like she had gained twenty-five pounds. Color again filled her cheeks, and she was ordering my sister to bring her tweezers so she could pluck her eyebrows. Two days later I took Cooky to the airport. "Thank God," she said. "I would have never have forgiven myself if I hadn't come this time."

"Cooky, what are we going to do? You live in Minnesota, and I travel. Next week, I fly to Trinidad. Ten days later, on to Bogotá."

"What can we do? She's so damn stubborn." She had already announced that she wasn't moving back to Minnesota. She likewise refused to live with either of her sisters while their husbands were still alive. "I'd feel like a fifth wheel," she told us, and we refrained from correcting her arithmetic.

"We can't push her, I guess," Cooky said as we hugged at her gate. "I'm just glad we pulled her through this."

I tried to ignore how quiet my house seemed. This was only for a week, I reminded myself. But within two days I was so anxious to get away that I found myself already packing bags, one for the hot Caribbean, the other for Colombia's chilly Andean highlands. Every day, I called my mother in the hospital, where she was finishing her antibiotic treatment. On the morning she was to be released, she called me.

"Hi, Mom—are you home already?"

"Alan, something's wrong. You'd better check it, Alan."

Check it? "Check what, Mom?"

"I don't know. I can feel something's wrong."

She sounded like her tongue was covered with fuzz. I penetrated her doctor's deep interference by informing the receptionist that I was on assignment to a major magazine—completely true, albeit having nothing to do with the purpose of my call. For five seconds, I let him vent his annoyance over my disrespect for his protocol, then suggested that he cut to the chase and tell me what was going on. "I'm not certain," he admitted. "She still has the infection. I'm no longer so sure we can knock it out."

"There must be something you can do."

"There's one more antibiotic I can try. The problem is that the antibiotics lower her resistance to lymphoma. If I increase her lymphoma medication, that, in turn, lowers her resistance to the infection." He was telling me that she was caught in a cross fire of conflicting treatments. Separately, either the low-grade lymphoma or the infection would be easy to control. But like wildfires, attending to one caused the other to flare beyond control.

"But I just saw her on Sunday," I protested. "She looked terrific."

"Sure she did. I had just transfused her with healthy hemoglobin. The infection went right after it. I have to be frank: If the other antibiotic doesn't work, I don't know what else to do."

The calendar read Wednesday, November 10, 1992. For a long time I stared at my bags for Trinidad and Colombia. Then I packed another, with woolens and a down coat for Minnesota, and drove to Scottsdale Memorial Hospital.

She was lying quietly, looking at the ceiling. The television was on with no sound. I tapped on the doorjamb, and she turned and smiled through colorless lips when she saw me.

"Hi, honey. You came down."

I kissed her forehead, sat on the edge of her bed, and took her hand. The slight bulge of her form under the woven cotton hospital blanket seemed so tiny. "Well, I figured that since I'm not leaving until Monday," I told her, "why not bring my work down here and stay at your house for the next few days, so we can spend more time together?"

"That's nice." Her voice sounded tranquil but oddly thickened. I explained that her doctor agreed with her that something still wasn't right and he was switching her antibiotic. She nodded. "I thought so. Alan, make sure that if you use the washer and dryer that you clean up real good and empty the lint trap. And don't dirty up my kitchen. Use the dishwasher."

I smiled. "No, Mom. I'm going to make a big mess for Lillian to see."

"Don't you dare, you slop-can."

"God, I love it when you talk dirty to me. Mom, how do you feel?"

"Not too bad," she said. "But something isn't right. I don't know how to explain it."

I squeezed her hand. "Mom, are you scared?" It was the kind of question that no one in our family ever asked when serious illness was concerned: one that went directly to the truth.

"Sometimes," she answered promptly. "But then I think, if something happens to me, I'll just be going to where Dad is."

"You've got all eternity to be with Dad. He's not going anywhere. You stay here with us for a while. We'll have some fun."

"Okay, honey." She yawned. "I'll see you in the morning. Remember, don't mess up."

I was headed to the door when she called me back. "Oh, Alan?"

"What, Mom?"

"Do you see what I see on the ceiling?"

I looked up at the acoustic tiles. "What do you see?"

"Are those bugs crawling around up there?"

"No, Mom. Just little holes in the tiles."

"Oh." She settled back. "I thought that might be what they were. But I keep seeing them move."

My Aunt Sylvia kept insisting that my mother was fine. "Aunt Syl," I said over the hospital pay phone, "I'd like to believe that, too. The doctors aren't very encouraging."

"What do they know? Last time they were giving her up for dead, and you saw what happened. A week later she's driving her car and fighting with all of us like she always does."

"I know. But I think this is different. Cooky just got here, and she agrees that it doesn't look good. And Aunt Ellie's on her way."

"My sister Eleanor? You're kidding. You mean she's coming all the way from Florida? What does *she* know?"

"Maybe more than the rest of us." Ellie's mystical treatment of her husband's cancer, still in remission, had been written up in the annals of the Tallahassee Mayo Clinic. People in her retirement village outside Tampa regularly consulted her for healings. My mother swore that Ellie was smarter than all the doctors in Florida put together.

"The Mayo Clinic was ready to bury your Uncle Chick," she'd told me. "Then Ellie started up with her meditation and chanting and *chotz clotz!*—he's back on the golf course. He's going to dance on those goddam doctors' graves."

"When I called Ellie," I told my sister as we drove to the hospital from the airport, "she immediately said she was coming."

Cooky winced: Eleanor also claimed to be in communication with the beyond. "That's a bad sign. What about Aunt Sylvie?"

Sylvia, who was in Las Vegas for the winter, an hour's flight away, continued to deny it for another day. "I know," I agreed when I called again. "It was sort of like she was crying wolf last time." Last time, my mother had made Sylvia stay three weeks, as she'd done when we put my father into the rest home. My Uncle Mike, still conducting his businesses in his mid-80s, was forced to be a

322

bachelor half the time because his wife kept flying to be with her sister in Arizona.

"Look, Aunt Syl; she's going in and out of consciousness. Whenever she wakes, the first thing she asks is when you're coming. I know you just saw her last month, and she looked fine. But the doctor just saw her five minutes ago. And he says she's dying."

"Is she coming?" my sister asked. Cooky, who had flown back to Minneapolis only five days earlier, had needed no convincing to return immediately.

"I think so. She was calling the airlines. Ellie's plane arrives in two hours. You want to come to the airport with me?"

"I think one of us should stay here with Mom."

I turned to glance at our mother. She was face up, motionless, the head of her hospital bed slightly raised. "Still asleep?"

"She hasn't awakened once. I hope she'll be able to talk to Aunt Ellie and Aunt Sylvie. Do you think she's in a coma?"

"I don't know." I realized that we were trying to converse over the babble of the television in my mother's hospital room. That sound had been so normal, and annoying, in the house where we grew up that ever since I left home I had refused to own one. "This goddam thing is driving me batty," I snapped. "Can we turn it off? Oprah Winfrey, for God's sake."

"So turn it off. What the hell do I care about Oprah Winfrey?"

There was a sound somewhere between a rumble and a purr, so peculiar that at first we looked around to identify its source. It was emanating from our mother's bed. Her eyes still closed, she was straining to speak. It took her nearly half a minute: "I . . . love . . . Oprah!"

Cooky and I sank into chairs, trying to stifle our laughter. "No problem, Mom," my sister gasped, wiping her eyes. "It's staying on."

She was awake when I returned with Aunt Eleanor, alert enough to exchange kisses and inquire how she was. Ellie, who taught aerobics and yoga at her retirement complex, was the cutest seventy-two-year-old I'd ever seen. "That's sweater's a nice color on you," my mother murmured. "You should put on some lipstick."

She never asked why Ellie happened to be in Arizona: She knew. As Aunt Eleanor chattered on, my mother quickly tired. From time to time she asked for Sylvia, and we promised her that she was coming. By afternoon her speech grew so thick that we could barely decipher it; her tongue and the inside of her mouth were coated with a black mucus that intrigued the doctors, who swabbed a culture out of curiosity. We fed her ice chips, which seemed to soothe her. Clearly, she was fighting to stay conscious long enough to see her older sister. I called Sylvia back. "You have to come." She would be there in two hours, she said. "Hang on, Mom," Cooky was begging as I headed out the door for the airport.

I raced Sylvia to the hospital. "Sy'vee!" my mother wailed, just once. They embraced.

"Now let me tell you, Charlotte," Sylvia began to say, but stopped as she realized that my mother was already asleep.

For a half hour we watched her. Outside, it grew dark. "Maybe we should get some food," Eleanor suggested.

A discussion ensued regarding what or where, who couldn't possibly eat, and who didn't care, she was starving. "Maybe we should go into the hall," Cooky suggested, as our aunts kept interrupting each other in ten-decibel leaps. The debate had just resumed outside the door when Cooky and I simultaneously recognized a strange sound. Each of us clamped a hand over an aunt's mouth.

"I'm . . . sor . . . ry!" my mother struggled to expel, lest she be unable to hang on until we returned from dinner.

We rushed back into the room. "Don't be silly, Mom," we reassured her.

"It's all right, Char."

"Really, Mom. It's all right."

"We'll be right back, Charlotte. Don't you dare move."

Later, when my sister and I returned to Arizona to pack up their house after we buried her next to my father's still-fresh grave, we would understand what she'd meant. Even worse than the un-remitting assault of hospital bills was the daunting task of confronting the accumulation of their lives. All his framed diplomas and membership certificates. Her sterling that no one would ever use. A ceramic bust of me she had sculpted in her art class from an old book jacket photograph. Boxes of borax dating to the 1940s that had inexplicably moved with them through four houses. The revealing stack of greeting cards and letters she'd chosen to save over the years.

During the estate sale, as familiar old items were carried away by strangers, I would gaze around the void that was formerly an inhabited room, carpet indentations marking the ghost furniture, and cling to the sight of a lone lamp still in its rightful place, still bearing witness to what once was. It recalled those final hospital hours when, each time I looked, there was a little less of them, until they were gone.

"I'm sorry." Those were our mother's final, guilt-drenched words—but she didn't get the last word on the subject of her own life, which must have been awfully frustrating for her. During her final hours, practically her entire life passed before her ears, as her sisters disgorged stories across her deathbed that Cooky I had never heard before—stories of what these three women had endured after their own mother died and their father fled, leaving them to be shunted from aunt to aunt, where they were always the stepsisters to the cousins into whose territory they had encroached. Stories that explained so much to us, so late.

Everyone wept as these memories welled up and spilled forth, except when we were nearly incapacitated from laughter. "Charlotte," my Aunt Eleanor sobbed, "I remember how I used to hide from you in *Baubeh's* pear tree and you never thought to look up—"

"Eleanor," Sylvia interrupted, "you don't know what you're talking about. *Baubeh* didn't have a pear tree."

"She most certainly did. I climbed it. Hundreds of times."

"Oh, please, Eleanor. It was an apple tree. Big, green baking apples."

"Sylvie, I know there was a pear tree. I would eat them while I was hiding."

"Apples. *Apples,* Eleanor."

"Pears!"

"Oh, Ellie, what did you know? You were just a baby."

"See how they treat me?" Ellie appealed to Cooky and me, gesturing at my Aunt Sylvia and at my comatose mother. "All my life, like a baby."

Cooky, practically gagging, was temporarily unable to reply. "Really, Mom," I scolded. "Stop picking on poor Aunt Ellie. She's only a baby."

My mother didn't answer. Her breathing had grown so soft. Throughout the day she hadn't regained consciousness, but at times seemed to grow agitated in response to choice parts of the chronicle that pulsated between her keening sisters like alternating current. But now she was visibly withdrawing from her role in our family pageant. A little earlier, there had been a pause in my aunts' saga while my Aunt Sylvia was in the bathroom, and Eleanor, out of her earshot, resumed doing something that had been driving Syl crazy: stroking my mother's arm and crooning softly to her about entering a long tunnel.

"There's a beautiful golden light ahead of you, Char. Look for it. Go to it. They're waiting for you. Our mama's there waiting for you. Our little brother, Marvin. Go to them."

As she droned on, the lines around my mother's eyes and mouth tightened. Her fingers clenched slightly, and her head moved, just barely, from side to side. I bent until my cheek touched hers. "I love you, Mom," I whispered in her ear. Almost imperceptibly, her discomfiture heightened. I straightened, and saw that a nurse had entered the room.

She was a dignified, graying presence. "Is this your mother?" She asked.

Cooky and I nodded.

"She's so beautiful."

We all looked. With her silver hair flowing back on the pillow, she truly was.

"I can see that she's restless," the nurse said.

"Does that mean she's in pain?" I asked.

"Possibly. Would you like me to give her something to ease her discomfort?"

"Like what?" Cooky asked.

Her eyes became strangely brilliant as she uttered that simple, clinical term: "Morphine."

My sister looked at me. I nodded. "Please."

"A wise decision," the nurse murmured. She produced a plastic pouch, whose tubing she routed into our mother's intravenous hookup. It confirmed what I'd already suspected I had done to, and for, my father—something that merciful doctors and nurses did routinely and the world pretended not to know. I hoped that my parents each understood this final peace offering from their son whom, as they had so often complained, they never quite understood at all.

As my mother's breathing wound down, so did her sisters' stories. They had exhausted their resentment for all those aunts and uncles who had been their stepparents, who were now gone as well—all except for Nate Meshbesher's wife, Aunt Esther, in her nineties and still playing her daily canasta. Esther, everybody figured, was holding out as long as possible before she had to rejoin Nate. Until the day he succumbed to one heart attack too many, Nate had never stopped. From his winter retreat in Miami, he conducted everyone else's business in Minneapolis via his WATS line; before they buried him, his sons placed a telephone and the Minneapolis phone directory in his coffin.

Her breath grew ever shallower. I lifted her sheet and saw how the edema had already discolored her legs and was now seeping under her hospital gown into the place from which, impossibly, I had emerged forty-five years earlier. Such horrible déjà vu: just seven weeks after my father. We rose and fell with her breath, now only the merest trace of movement, as, little by little, she disengaged from her surroundings, from her sisters and children, and from the body she had tended and clothed and perfumed so carefully for so long, now of no further use.

She inhaled and froze. "That's it," exhaled Eleanor, but then my mother shuddered and breathed again. Moments later, once more her flattened chest rose and stopped. "That's it!" Ellie repeated, and again my mother's lungs released the tiny puff of air they held. Transfixed, we watched her inhale, and—

"That's—"

"Eleanor, would you shut up!" Sylvia hollered.

My sister and I couldn't help it; we erupted with laughter. I hugged Aunt Ellie and told her not to pay any attention to Sylvie; we still loved her. Sylvia sank into a chair, looked around, then saw my mother's overnight bag on the floor and suddenly started pulling things off the night table and packing the bag—my mother's eyeglasses, her purse, a package of tissues.

"Aunt Syl, what are you doing?" Cooky gasped.

"I can't stand this anymore. We're letting her die. I won't do that. Your mother's going to need these things when she gets out of here and—"

"Aunt Syl, please. Look," I said, and something she heard in my voice brought her back to her senses, and to the bedside. "Look," I repeated.

My mother, whose eyelids had been half-closed throughout the day in a semi-stupor, now squeezed them shut. Her lashes still looked young and full. The barest, faintest trace of struggle lingered beneath them. "It's all right, Char," whispered Ellie. "You can go now."

"It's all right, Mom," said Cooky, pulling me close. "We'll take care of each other."

From her left eye, a tear leaked down her cheek. She exhaled, and it was done.

"Bye, Mom. Say 'good-bye, Mom,' " I said to my sister, gripping her hand.

"Good-bye, Mom."

"Good-bye, Charlotte," my aunts echoed, just in time for us to see *something* rush from her body, fill the room, and then go. It took just an instant—and then we were all talking normally. What remained in the bed was just a husk, not my mother at all. We barely noticed it.

"Now," Aunt Ellie said, turning to my sister and me, "you're orphans just like us."

CHAPTER 20

Alone, I walked around Lake of the Isles. The leafless oaks and maples were black and skeletal against a lowering sky. A film of ice was forming along the shore. The day before my mother died, Cecilia had reached me at the hospital. She was in Mexico. I didn't ask what she was doing there, nor how she had known. I thanked her for calling, and told her not to think of interrupting her trip to come this time.

"*Ay*, Alan, don't give up hope yet," she'd told me. But now, watching the last Canada geese of autumn flee southward from the land of my birth, it felt like hope would never be the same again. By early afternoon, when we carried her coffin up the short hill to lay her next to my father, cold rain was falling and old Rabbi Schulman hurried through the *Kaddish*. By dusk, I knew, the rain would freeze into sleet and, sometime during the night, turn to snow. Winter would settle over the military cemetery, and our pain would gradually cool as well.

His marble headstone, which would now be theirs, was not yet in place. It was taking a while to carve the long list of his medals in the space beneath his name, my sister learned when she called Ft. Snelling. "Where does our mother's name go?" she asked. On the back of the stone, she was told.

"The hell it does!" I grabbed the phone and called back. "Our mother's name goes on front," I told some major.

"Wives in back," he repeated.

"Come on. She doesn't belong stuck in back, like some after-thought."

"Army regulations. No exceptions."

"Fuck your army."

"If you have a problem with military procedure," he replied be-fore hanging up, "write your congressman."

The same limousine driver drove us over the identical route we'd taken merely seven weeks earlier. This time, when I pressed the tip into his hand, he shook his head. Inside my sister's house, the same faces from last time blurred around me, with one excep-tion: Uncle Herman flew in from Washington. Having missed my father's funeral, he'd felt he couldn't stay away again. Touching as it was to watch Herman and his cousin Harry Friedman embrace for the first time in a quarter-century, I kept seeing two time-shrunken, depilated images of their former youthful selves. At one point I had a grisly vision of fleshless death's heads in animated conversation.

Stop being morbid, I told myself. Although nearing eighty, both were healthy and sharp: Dr. Friedman still taught on the Uni-versity of Minnesota ophthalmology faculty, and Herman had re-cently brought out his latest edition of *Basic Technical Writing*. What was gnawing at me had nothing to do with them: It was the old cliché that a man's father is the barrier between him and his own mortality. Underscored by my double loss, it was a cliché no longer—or maybe I had learned that life eventually comes down to a few weary clichés, like stumps that remain where a forest of ex-pectations once sprouted.

But no one had ever explained it quite like this: All my life, my parents had been there. Now they weren't, and everything hence-forth was different. It was that simple. Life would never be the same. I'd spent a major part of my youth escaping them, and a smaller but satisfying amount of my adulthood working back to-ward resolution. During years of cool distance, I had made my way without them, and that independence, I'd believed, had strength-ened me. But now I smashed headlong into another trite-but-true bromide: that parents are our archetypes of security. With mine suddenly gone, my nights filled with long-forgotten childhood nightmares, in which ghastly things chased me while I could barely make my limbs move. Gradually, these faded, but for weeks I continued to awaken before dawn, sad and troubled.

Flying home after a glum Thanksgiving with my sister and her in-laws, I arrived in my vacant house and realized that I could not tolerate being there. The next morning, I spoke to a friend in Gloucester, Massachusetts, north of Boston. An hour later he faxed me rental listings from the local newspaper, with an old fisherman's cottage circled. Just before Christmas, I met my sister in Scottsdale, where we packed up my parents' house, gave away most of its contents, and handed the keys to a Realtor. I leased my place in Prescott to a college student, loaded my vehicle to capacity, and drove across America in four mindless days. Beyond a few magazine articles, whose deadlines my editors had kindly extended yet again, all my plans were floating just beyond my grasp. Like ashes and dust, they would eventually settle, I figured.

I moved into my drafty wooden house on the north shore of Cape Ann in January. It had painted floors, old linoleum rugs, a huge granite fireplace, and a sleeping porch that hung practically over the water. The room upstairs where I wrote overlooked Ipswich Bay, filled with arctic ducks and lobster-trap buoys. At low tide I harvested mussels in front of my place, amid boulders on which I would huddle in a slicker against the cold salt spray, watching seals and dolphins surface offshore. If I cranked my head eastward, I looked to empty ocean. The wintry seascape comforted me: It felt exactly right to be poised on the edge of the continent. By night, however, I still tended to startle awake with a big freight train of sorrows roaring right over me. This, I knew, was called grief. It hurt, just the way it was supposed to.

❧

"You're not going to Colombia, and that's final," my editor at the *Los Angeles Times Magazine* told me over the phone.

"Mary, I need the money."

"Fine. But we're not sending you anyplace depressing." Originally, we'd planned an investigative story based on a radio piece Cecilia and I had done about the pesticide perils of the Colombian cut-flower industry. "Forget it," she said. "Pick something fun. Anywhere. Go to Mardi Gras. Go to Carnival in Rio."

Carnival. Anywhere. I chose a thousand-year-old hamlet in western Spain called Laza, where the pre-Lenten celebration of Carnival had existed long before Lent was invented—an extended pagan ritual to vanquish winter's stagnation and arouse spring's potency. During Carnival week in this village of unmortared slate walls surrounded by turnip fields and vineyards, any behavior short of manslaughter was not merely permitted but encouraged, to shock the heavens and jar awake the new season.

At one point on the final evening, as I swigged homemade *aguardiente* laced with mint and danced a drunken *paso doble* in Laza's cobbled plaza with two dark-eyed sisters, a donkey cart appeared piled with dripping fertilizer. Suddenly, everyone was slinging handfuls of muck. The air filled with fragrant grime, coating us with the earth's sheer essence as we smeared each others' cheeks and hair with ooze primeval. We leaped atop a pile of humans writhing and shrieking happily on the old paved stones, as the street lamps were snuffed and the Milky Way blushed at the bedlam below. Lying under the starlit Spanish sky in the warm, alcoholic embrace of a mass of strangers steeped in ecstasy, I released months of tears, replacing them with more sweet *aguardiente* until I felt the cycles of the earth move within me.

"God, it sounds amazing!" Cecilia said. She was in Boston for a meeting. We'd met for lunch.

"It was. It's sad, though. Traditional Spanish agriculture can't compete with slick European Community agribusiness. Except for old men in berets and black-stockinged widows, nearly everyone now leaves for cities like Madrid, or to factories in Germany or Holland. The people make an annual pilgrimage home for

Carnival, but they live so far from the soil that their ancestral rites have been reduced to mere nostalgia and entertainment fodder for tourists."

"Only you, Alan, could turn Carnival into a vanishing homelands story."

"Sorry." There was something she wanted to talk to me about, she said. I made it easy on her. "I already know, Cec." Nancy had let this information slip recently, regarding a *Chicago Tribune* correspondent Cecilia had met at the Earth Summit, whom she was about to visit in Buenos Aires. Strangely, although I missed her company and often missed having a lover, I felt no particular jealousy. Lately, I wondered if I still felt much of anything at all.

"I wish she'd waited until I said something," Cecilia said.

"Don't worry about it. Really. And don't say anything to her. Looks like Nancy and Sandy have enough troubles of their own lately."

"Something's really wrong with them, ¿verdad? Ay, Alan, what's happened to us all?"

"Well, we spent one year watching the world get torn apart and another year trying to figure out how to tell people, and now we still have to deal with our lives while the sky keeps falling in slow motion. No wonder we all ended up in therapy." We had.

"And on top of that," Cecilia added, "your parents. I still can't believe it. Promise me you'll have fun in Trinidad."

"I promise."

I did, although my departure was a little disconcerting. Sandy was also at the airport, headed to Bosnia. Things were going so badly with him and Nancy recently that a Monitor Radio assignment in Sarajevo seemed to him like a vacation. I had seen a lot of them lately—each had come up from Cambridge, seeking retreat from an inexplicably degenerating domestic situation. Now, as he headed off to war, Sandy looked ten years younger. Not a good sign.

In Trinidad, I passed some tranquil days, courtesy of *Condé*

Nast Traveler, on the wooden verandah of a nature retreat, sipping rum punches and watching violaceous trogons, purple honey-creepers, bearded bellbirds, blue-crowned motmots, and ruby-topaz hummingbirds. At night, I would go to hear a marvelous Trinidad invention: steel pan music, performed on velvety-toned instruments fashioned from fifty-five-gallon oil barrels. A place that alchemized the detritus of the petroleum industry into or-chestras that played everything from calypso to Mozart gave even me hope.

After ten days, I flew home, wondering why I wasn't a travel writer all the time. Back in my cottage on Ipswich Bay, the light was blinking on my machine. Ominously blinking, I told myself melodramatically, already depressed to be back.

It was a message from an editor, asking if by any chance I were available to go to Chernobyl.

PART FIVE

CHAPTER 21

There was a moment in Moscow when it dawned on me where I was. It was in the great, grimy Belarus Station, where hundreds of sullen men and babushka'd women waited for the train I was about to board to western Russia, on my way to Ukraine and Chernobyl. Gazing up at the high translucent ceiling, through which weak gray light filtered past decades of pigeon droppings and soot, I realized that here, seventy years earlier, my father had boarded a train to the Baltic coast to catch a boat for America.

They had spent months in Moscow, while my grandmother Rebecca made the rounds of the new Communist bureaucracy, filing forms and leaving bribes financed by money her sister had borrowed in Minneapolis to bring them across the water. One afternoon, squadrons of soldiers paraded by their window for hours, in the midst of which came an open car bearing bald Vladimir Lenin, arms folded, gazing over his minions. My father bristled when he described it, but his eyes also had betrayed an emotion I rarely associated with him: fear. Moscow was not a place to remember, he said, but one to get the hell out of, as quickly as possible.

My own impression of the city had not been not much brighter. In June 1993, eighteen months after the collapse of the Soviet Union, it was a capital still stunned by defeat, not a land basking in the glow of new freedoms. If I often felt as if the firmament had been yanked from under me with the deaths of my parents, it was nothing compared to the dazed Russian people I met, whose entire universe had proved to be a fraud.

"The collapse of the USSR," a scientist at Moscow State University told me, "left us like the man whose wife honestly admits her adultery—wiser but less happy." That didn't begin to describe the shock engraved in the faces of people lining subway passages, desperate to sell roses, cucumbers, cheap Georgian champagne, and assorted contraband. The Soviet promise of full employment and cradle-to-grave security had been their state religion, a covenant whose breathtaking dissolution was to them like a Christian learning that the New Testament was really a novel. At an ex-military college where I stayed, now a center to retrain officers in the arts of capitalism so they could do business with their former enemies, a few younger students approached to ask about investment opportunities and jobs in the West. Mostly, however, I'd seen in people's eyes the resentful mixture of accusation and deference that the vanquished hold for the victor. It was not unlike being a white man on an American Indian reservation.

In the western Russian district of Novozybkov, I stood in a potato field with Vitaly Linnik, overlooking a peat bog. The brook winding through it marked the border with Belarus. The secret Soviet decision after the 1986 Chernobyl accident to seed any clouds headed east so that contaminated rainfall would not reach Moscow had filled the rich, undulating landscape before us, 150 miles from the destroyed reactor, with invisible poison.

Three years later, rumors began to surface about widespread fallout in western Russia that the Soviet government had tried to conceal. For months, Vitaly, a husky blond physicist and expert in heavy metals pollution, had taken readings in forests, bogs, and leaf litter, sampling soil at depths of two and five centimeters, in the center and each corner of every field in Novozybkov. These fine collective farms where we now stood, he discovered, were the most contaminated places in the republic. Immediately, they were evacuated. Vitaly Linnik, I was told by his colleagues at Moscow State University, was a genuine hero. In whispers, they added that as a result of prolonged radiation exposure, he suffered bouts of irrational behavior. They also feared he had leukemia. He refused to discuss it.

His Geiger counter showed that we were receiving from 200 to 300 micro-roentgens per hour: ten to fifteen times more radiation than normal. "I thought you said this place was evacuated," I said. Thousands of Novozybkov villagers had been exiled to public housing in the city of Bryansk, a hundred miles to the northeast, but I could plainly hear the voices of young children. In front of what supposedly was an abandoned brick farmhouse, we could see a skinny woman in blue sweatpants holding a small boy in a checkered cap. A barefoot girl in a flowered skirt stood alongside them. A big bay horse munched at a hayrick heaped against one wall, next to a vegetable patch with the biggest rhubarb leaves I'd ever seen. A man joined them, shirtless and sweating from digging potatoes. One of his eyes was blackened, as though he'd been fighting.

Anatoly Bynya had brought his family here nearly two years earlier, he said. Vitaly winced. Didn't they understand, he asked, that this place was considered too hot for human habitation? Anatoly and his wife looked at each other, then nodded. I glanced at the children.

"We didn't have much choice," Anatoly said. This house had belonged to his father, who, during the 1950s, was sent to Kazakhstan as part of a five-year-plan to open new agricultural land. Anatoly was born and raised there. But with the breakup of the Soviet Union, Kazakhstan became an independent Islamic nation, and ethnic Russians were no longer welcome. So they returned.

"But it's radioactive here," I repeated.

"It was there, too."

Kazakhstan was the site of Soviet nuclear weapons testing, Vitaly reminded me. "Hugely contaminated. No one knows how much. Top secret."

That afternoon we met three men who were breaking the law by milking a radioactive cow. "I'd rather die early here than grow old in the housing project where they put us," one told us. I couldn't blame him. The fields were filled with robust stands of fat corn and wheat, the apple orchards were bursting, the danger was so insidious because it couldn't be seen. I had a vision of southern Chile, with its ozone hole lurking invisibly overhead.

We entered a woodland of fragrant red pines intermingled with white birch, bordered by clumps of blueberry and raspberry. Because forests form natural windbreaks that catch and hold moisture, Vitaly explained, they were the most tainted of all. This was particularly sorrowful in the Russian countryside, where picking forest mushrooms and berries was a favorite pastime and a significant source of vitamins. Gathering them from this sweet-smelling glade, or anywhere in Novozybkov, was now strictly forbidden. Vitaly set his counter on some moss. It clicked wildly. "I wonder if it will hit 400," he mused. It went to 500. He whistled. It kept going, and he quietly stared at it. I heard a woodpecker. The Geiger counter finally held at 857 micro-roentgens per hour. It was the highest reading Linnik had ever seen here. "We should go," he said.

Down empty highways lined with giant purple lupine that appeared to be thriving in the surrounding radioactive haze, we drove to the western Russian city of Bryansk. That night we attended a banquet at the Bryansk Pedagogical Institute, where scientists from Moscow State University and the University of Oregon had just installed an interactive information center for Russians living in the contaminated zones. There, local citizens doomed to a radioactive future could learn to minimize their radiation intake with computers that graphically traced Chernobyl fallout as it flowed through soils and waters around their homes and fields.

At one point during dinner, my translator, a good-natured frizzy-haired blonde named Galena, gave me an 8x10 glossy photograph of her even blonder teenaged daughter, in a pose that emphasized her remarkably long legs. Perhaps I could circulate it to modeling agencies in America? Her husband, a local television journalist, presented me with a diploma certifying my election to the Order of Lenin. After Communism fell in Bryansk, someone had found a blank stack of these high honors in an abandoned office, which they now gave away like party favors.

During the dessert of berries and cream, Vitaly Linnik started shouting uncontrollably, and had to be led away by one of his colleagues. The rest of us poured more vodka and continued what we'd been doing: toasting this U.S. and Russian cooperation, born of the Chernobyl disaster—one that, if repeated, would inexorably unite us even further.

That night, on the train to Kiev, I nipped more vodka, trying to push everything I knew back beyond the perimeter of my consciousness. As I collapsed in my sleeping berth, however, that perimeter did likewise, and knowledge rushed back, engulfing my dreams. "Just wait till I tell your father," I heard my mother say.

In the middle of the night came the screech of metal brakes. Boots clanged in the steel passageway, and I heard a sharp knock. The woman in the lower berth opposite me didn't move. The knock was repeated, this time more insistent. I jumped down, parted the curtain, and slid open the sleeping berth door. A soldier in an olive-gray woolen uniform that looked too heavy for June uttered several rapid commands. I shrugged with incomprehension. The woman in the bunk stirred. The soldier repeated his orders and she pulled a plastic folder from the folds of her blouse and handed them over. He turned to me again, and I gave him my passport. Twenty minutes later, he returned it. I had entered Ukraine.

I lay back in my narrow vinyl-upholstered pallet, covered by a heavy sheet. Throughout his life, whenever anyone would suggest it, my father vowed that he would never return here. Had I betrayed him by coming, I wondered drowsily. When I dozed again, I was revisited by my old childhood dream in which I was six years old, playing outside while my mother weeded her rock garden, which, I now noticed, was filled with rhubarb. Again, bags of cement piled against the house toppled and buried her, and again I tried to pull her free but they were too heavy. But now the dream changed, as my father entered the scene. I couldn't see him so much as sense his contempt for my helplessness, as he reminded me how, as a six-year-old, he'd helped drag his own father's big, bullet-ridden body to the grave they'd dug him.

Waking before dawn, I left my berth and stood between the sleeper cars, watching Ukraine materialize from the fading night. Gradually, it revealed itself: Flat, gray-green. Larch trees, lindens. Laundry hanging behind unpainted cottages facing away from the tracks, power lines filled with hooded crows. Ukraine, taking on dimension as it filled with diffused light under a putty-colored sky. An actual physical setting for the most resonant myth of my childhood.

The track multiplied into many tracks, and we pulled into Kiev. I knew I was somewhere north of my father's village. In two days I was going to Chernobyl, then I would have another week to complete my research—and maybe find a way to get to Mala Viska, to learn what I could about my family.

As I picked up my bags, I noticed that my hands were unsteady. I was about to set foot in the land of my fathers. Did I really even want to know what had happened here?

✶✶✶

Мала Виска, the sign read in Russian. In Ukrainian, Volodya Tikhïi told me, Mala Viska would be Малая Виска, Malaya Viska, but Ukraine had a ways to go to expunge the remnants of Soviet rule from its countryside. Restitution of the Ukrainian language was part of that recovery, a dream for which Tikhïi's own linguist father had died in the Gulag.

And now, Volodya was taking me to learn which injustice— that of the Communists, or of Cossacks led by a general named Denikin—had resulted in the death of my own forebear, my grandfather Avraham. Like Vitaly Linnik, Volodya had risked his own life after the disaster, collecting water samples as Chernobyl's spreading stain seeped from the tainted Pripyat River into his country's alluvium. Thus far, medical tests revealed no apparent repercussions, and he had since fathered a healthy daughter. "There's nothing I can do," he said, "but live on." Nevertheless, he had left government employ as a nuclear physicist to work for Greenpeace.

For five hours and two hundred kilometers, we had bumped over roads that partly explained the former Soviet Union's inefficiency at distributing its harvests, through collective farms whose fields of grain, sunflowers, and hops flowed over every horizon, headed toward Mala Viska, a town he'd never heard of until he found it on his map. The sign we saw with an arrow pointing south was in the rail junction of Novomirgorod. Twenty kilometers later, at the end of a sea of sunflowers, we came to a concrete pillar with the name embedded in red-glazed wrought-iron letters: Мала Виска.

Would my father have recognized this place? Mala Viska had been Sovietized—its center razed and replaced with a linden-lined parkway devoid of buildings, except for a small department store and one of the dull, instant cream-brick tenement housing projects of the Brezhnev era, ubiquitous throughout the former USSR. We drove past two statues of Lenin, a vintage armored tank on a pedestal slab, and a monument to heroes of the Nazi occupation. A freestanding cement wall bore a plaque honoring local schoolteachers, whose photographs were displayed.

It was Sunday and it was raining; nearly no one was on the streets. Volodya located the soviet, a featureless concrete structure in the middle stages of neglect. We were hoping to find the town historian, who would probably know where a mill had stood in 1918, but everything was locked. Next we tried the police station. Inside, two men with thick blond crew cuts wearing brass-buttoned uniforms were barking into telephones. Behind them was a large wall map of the district. Inexplicably, I felt a chill of slick terror. As one of them gave Tikhïi directions to the historian's house, I looked into his pale blue eyes, wondering if his grandfather had killed mine.

345

The old village of Mala Viska still existed after all, tucked out of sight behind all the public works. Grigory Nikolavich Perebenyev, retired school director and unofficial local historian, lived on a rutted dirt lane of zinc-roofed brick and wooden cottages, each with a vegetable patch and a coal bin. The rain had stopped; his wife, Olga, and granddaughter were outside tending a bed of white lilies. Grigory Nikolavich, Olga told us, was bedridden with the grippe. Volodya explained that I had come all the way from the United States. She rose, patted the bun of her hair into place, and went inside. A few minutes later, she returned.

"Grigory Nikolavich will meet you," she said.

He had donned slippers and a blue sweat suit to receive us: a man whose face was all vertical creases, with thin gray hair combed back from a point above the bridge of his nose. He sat in a red stuffed chair, and we seated ourselves across from him on an orange foam sofa. The room was warm, and Tikhïi removed his denim jacket. I explained why I had come. Perebenyev told us that in the early part of the century there were four mills in or near Mala Viska. All had long since burned. Two of them—water mills—were noted by Pushkin when he passed through the village, he added proudly.

"That would have been before my grandfather's time."

"Da." Of course. But the other two were more likely what we were seeking, anyway, because they were near the Jewish quarter. The bigger one, which was on the river, very well might have been Avraham Weisman's. He recalled reading that the manager during the early Soviet years was a Jew named something like Lipschinsky. He didn't recognize my grandfather's name, but that meant little, he said. Records were very sparse. "It was extremely complicated here during the period of the Civil War. The White Guard, then the Red Army, Makhno's anarchists, the Grigoriev Gang, the Austro-Hungarians, the Don Cossacks. So much was destroyed. It wasn't until 1920 that it was possible to say that the Soviet powers overwhelmed all the rest."

"The Cossacks?"

"Certainly. Cossack troops moved through here from Novomirgorod, during the summertime when people had begun harvesting. Many Jews were assassinated."

"Are there any Jews left? Someone who might remember my family?"

His thin face filled with sympathy. "The only Jews here now are newcomers. All the others were killed during World War II. No one survived." He thought a moment. "There's someone who might know, though."

We were looking for Lenina 91-A, the home of Varvara Spak. Lenina Street was near where the mill once stood, Grigory Nikolavich had told us. We stopped to ask directions from an old woman in a white wool babushka, gathering eggs from a chicken coop in her yard. Nearby, a goat was tied to a tree. A flatbed truck drove by, followed by a horse-drawn cart.

She asked why we had come. Tikhïi explained about my father and grandfather. She hadn't lived in Mala Viska until 1927, she said. She pointed to the houses around her. Nearly all her neighbors were Jewish, she said. All her daughter's childhood friends. "Killed by the Nazis. All the Jews and their children. It was impossible to do anything for them." She reached for my hand. "I'm sorry," she said.

I explained that I hadn't expected to find any relatives here. I only wanted to see it, maybe learn exactly what had happened.

"Varvara remembers many things. Her daughter is a teacher. They should know."

Varvara Spak's cottage was faced with whitewashed ceramic tiles. The windows were trimmed with green wooden shutters. No one answered when we knocked, but presently she came up the path, walking with a cane. She wore a black kerchief patterned with roses. Her daughter carried kindling.

We sat on a bench under a chestnut tree. It was the daughter, Daria, a mathematics teacher, who knew the name Avraham Weisman. She had heard it in a history lecture on the sunflower-oil press factory. That was him, I said.

Her mother was sorry that she didn't remember my

grandfather herself, though she wasn't surprised, because she would have been a little girl then. She was two years older than my father. It occurred to me that I was talking to someone who might have seen him when he lived here. Suddenly this felt very real.

She did remember the mill, and explained where it was, very close by. When she was in her teens, she said, it was run by an accountant named Lischinsky. Then it burned. Her teens: That would have been after the Russian Revolution. Lischinsky, the Jew, might have been my grandfather's employee, kept on by the Communist government because he knew how to manage the mill. It made sense. Varvara thought so, too.

"After the Bolsheviks took over, Jews lived here like everyone else. Until the Nazis."

"When exactly did the Bolsheviks take over?" I asked.

"Not until after 1920."

That was what Grigory Nikolavich, the historian, had said. "Then who killed my grandfather?" I asked. She looked at Tikhïi, who translated. Then she turned back to me.

"When did you say he died?"

My grandmother's and father's naturalization documents, and my father's school admission papers and passport applications gave the date as 1919. They had celebrated my grandfather Avraham's *yahrtzeit*, the anniversary of his death, in September.

The old woman shuddered. "Then it was Denikin. General Denikin killed many Jews. I met him myself. He came to our house and demanded that my older sister come to work in his kitchen. When my father refused, he nearly killed him, too."

I walked through a glade of willows down to the river. The hillside above, where my grandfather's mill, his house, and a small synagogue that Varvara Spak also remembered had once stood, was now planted in cabbage, potatoes, and sugar beets. *Mistechko*, she had called this: a word meaning an enclave where Jews—*mistechkovyj evrayij*—lived. Bigger towns were often surrounded by *mistechka*, busy little hubs of local economy. The pogroms and the Nazis wiped them out.

348

I stood at the end of a low wooden dock so Volodya could take my picture. A green film of algae ribboned the water's surface where reeds grew along the bank. Some geese floated by. Later, I would ask myself why my father had lied about what happened here—surely, like my Uncle Herman, he had heard his mother's curses—and finally I would figure it out. I would also see how that lie was magnified as it passed to the next generation—it was part of my birthright, and now, knowing the truth, I must answer for it. But in that moment, all I did was look up from the river to the cloud-hung sky and ask:

Dad, did you play right here? Can you see me? Do I have your expression on my face? Did you stand by the edge of this river? Yes, you did. You were here. This is what you lost. I am so sorry.

CHAPTER 22

From 1917 to 1921, while Eastern Europe's Jewish Pale of Settlement churned and heaved and finally disappeared along with the Russian Empire, a Jew from Kiev in his mid-thirties named Elias Tcherikower embarked on an obsessed journalistic rampage, one that produced enough material to occupy the rest of his life. Tcherikower was part of a group of Jewish intellectuals who, prior to the Russian Revolution, were in the vanguard of an incipient Jewish renaissance. All over Ukraine, Poland, and Lithuania, small presses were publishing Yiddish poetry, essays, fiction, and news. But beginning in 1917, one story overwhelmed the rest, and Tcherikower became its greatest chronicler.

That his efforts survive is something of a miracle. I first learned of him when I ascended to the eleventh floor of a West 57th Street office building in New York and entered the cramped, temporary quarters of YIVO—originally, the Yidisher Visnshaft-lekher Institut, known today as the YIVO Institute for Jewish Research. The existence of YIVO is itself fairly miraculous. The result of symposia held in Berlin and Vilna, Lithuania, in 1925, YIVO was formed as a repository of anything Jewish—from rabbinical texts to Yiddish vaudeville scripts—that survived the Russian Revolution. A library was established in Vilna (today, Vilnius) and, by the beginning of World War II, it had amassed more than 50,000 volumes and rare editions. Elias Tcherikower was named research secretary of its history section. A second YIVO branch, founded in 1928 in New York City, began assembling a parallel collection of American Judaica.

In 1941, the Nazis took Vilna, and, after an initial ransacking, realized the future historical significance of this library. The YIVO building became an occupation headquarters where thousands of documents were catalogued by a staff of coerced YIVO archivists and meticulous Germans, then shipped to the Institute for the Study of the Jewish Question, a Nazi research facility near Frankfurt.

Jews would have to wait until 1989 to learn that the YIVO scholars who were forced to select materials for transport to Germany had actually hidden some of the rarest materials, including Torah scrolls, in the basement of a Vilna church. Long before that, however, the Allies had defeated the Germans in World War II, and the American army of occupation stationed in Frankfurt had discovered the Nazis' abandoned Institut zur Erforschung der Judenfrage. Inside they found hundreds of thousands of Jewish books and periodicals plundered from Vilna, which Hitler had one day intended to incorporate into an archaeological museum to a vanished race. Under the direction of the commander of U.S. troops in post-war Europe, these books and papers were all shipped to YIVO's American branch in New York, which had become its world headquarters during the war.

Because Elias Tcherikower was working on a multivolume history of the Ukrainian pogroms, many of his own papers had remained with him in Berlin, where he'd fled in 1921 after the Bolsheviks finally gained control of Ukraine. In 1933, the rise of Hitler required Tcherikower to flee again. He next settled in Paris, lugging along what amounted to a large chunk of YIVO's historical collection. But in early 1940, the Germans marched on Paris, and once more he had to escape. Hurriedly, he shipped his documents to southern France and followed with his wife. But now, no place in France was safe. The Tcherikowers managed to arrange night passage to Lisbon in neutral Portugal, an escape valve to America that was briefly open to a few lucky Jews before the Nazis effectively sealed French borders. But this time, they had to leave everything behind.

Tcherikower never saw his life's work again. Arriving in New York, he retained his position as research secretary of YIVO's history section, but the vast account that he had single-handedly compiled remained in a Marseille warehouse. He died in 1943, a year before my father's U.S. Third Division invaded the French Riviera. I have no way of knowing if his Company H paused long enough when they seized the ports along the Côte d'Or for him to have liberated the building that contained the Tcherikower archive. It is more likely that my ship's commander Uncle, Herman—as he continuously ferried fresh troops and supplies across the Atlantic and returned home loaded with prisoners and captured materials—transported them to New York. In 1944, in the midst of the war, crates of Tcherikower's papers arrived at YIVO, into the care of his widow, Rebecca, who remained chief YIVO archivist until her own death in 1963.

And now I confronted them: eighty-one linear feet of documents that Tcherikower had risked his life repeatedly to amass during five years of civil war in Ukraine, documents attesting to pogroms in which a quarter-million Jews were slaughtered and a million more raped, maimed, robbed, ravaged, and orphaned. Except for two bound volumes that Tcherikower was able to complete before his death, the documents were still raw, stored in gray cardboard boxes filled with files containing frail onionskin carbons, the faded purple block text of ancient mimeographs, thousands of brittle news clippings, and dictated eyewitness accounts—often in Tcherikower's own intense handwriting that jumped between cursive Yiddish and Russian.

Except for the few times he veered into the Roman alphabet—usually in French, when he was poring over some military document left by France's occupying navy in Odessa after World War I—I could understand none of it.

Sitting at the heavy oaken tables in the windowless YIVO

reading room, surrounded by boxes of what I now knew to be my heritage, I finally understood—in the same visceral way that comprehension dawns on me in the field whenever I find myself at last confronting the naked, beating heart of a story—that a crucial portion of my birthright was not what I had been given, but what I had been denied. The Cyrillic and Hebraic characters formed languages that my grandmother read incessantly in Yiddish and Russian newspapers. My father also knew them. But no one had taught me these tongues of our people, and now this fabulous repository of my legacy was all but lost to me.

YIVO provided a list of translators. I had used interpreters before in foreign lands and in indigenous America. But at YIVO I was chagrined to need someone to lead me through the language of my own family. With deepening embarrassment, I watched pale Yeshiva scholars, Jewish studies grad students in their wool yarmulkes, and New York Jews simply trying to track their genealogy switch effortlessly from English to Yiddish when they addressed the research librarian. She was a white-haired wisp of a woman named Dina Abramowicz, who had been the reading room librarian of the Vilna Ghetto Library. Since 1947, she had held that position at YIVO–New York. She regarded me kindly but with frank pity as I flailed through YIVO's card catalogue that held listings in six or seven languages that were all transparent to her.

"You know no Yiddish? Nothing?" she asked, sadly shaking her head at me.

"Only Spanish," I replied, ashamed.

Spanish seemed such a puny offering to my formidable ancestors who had struggled and died on the Russian steppes. Each time I requested Dina Abramowicz's help, I apologized furiously, inanely intimidated by a woman who barely weighed ninety pounds. I wanted her absolution and forgiveness for my childhood in a safe midwestern U.S. suburb where Judaism was a social denominator but barely a way of life.

As a child, I'd endured the usual five years of Hebrew education that Conservative Jewish parents in Minneapolis inflicted on their children, glumly boarding an orange bus with "Talmud Torah" painted on the side in the afternoons following public school. There, Holocaust refugees drilled us in Hebrew, the official mother tongue of the new state of Israel—but a language used by Jews everywhere else only for religious, not conversational, purposes. Nearly everyone I knew attended only until turning thirteen, our bar mitzvahs being the main object of this misery. For that rite of passage, we would have to read a portion from the Prophets called the *haftorah*—which most of us memorized, uncomprehending, from recordings the synagogue's cantor would sell us.

Following my own ceremony, I refused to set foot on that bus ever again. My mother was more than happy to stop paying the tuition. As for my father's spiritual priorities: When I was ten, I'd found his copy of *Exodus*, Leon Uris's novel of the birth of the state of Israel, and feigned sickness to stay home from school and read it in two days. Evangelized by the epic storytelling, I ventured into my father's den to ask why we didn't move there. Lowering his newspaper, he removed his reading glasses and impaled me with a stare.

"Do you have any idea how hard I've worked to make it in this country? And now you want me to throw it all away to go someplace new?"

"Israel isn't new," I stammered. "It's the promised land. Jews from everywhere are going back there."

"Well, this Jew sure as hell isn't. Our promised land is right here. I fought for this country, and this is where we're staying. If you don't appreciate it, go there yourself when you grow up."

❦

"I know the Yiddish and Cyrillic alphabets," I told Nikolai Borodulin, the translator Dina Abramowicz found for me at YIVO.

In the former Soviet Union, I'd memorized Cyrillic phonetics in order to decipher the subway stops in Moscow and Kiev. Yiddish employed the same characters as Hebrew, and I still recalled its vowels and consonants. I spent the next two weeks scouring hundreds of documents in the Tcherikower archive for words I recognized in both languages: *Mala Viska, Yelisavetgrad, Weisman* or *Vaisman, pogrom*. Nikolai, meanwhile, did his best to determine which of the hundreds of boxes and folders might contain papers that referred to the place and time of my grandfather's demise. In his mid-thirties, thin, soft-spoken Nikolai Borodulin had emigrated from Birobijan, a region bordering on China that the Soviet government designated in 1928 as a resettlement district for Jews. In that desolate land thousands of miles from Moscow, Nikolai had managed to learn five languages.

I didn't expect that we'd find much. Since I'd visited Mala Viska on a Sunday, I'd had no opportunity to examine town archives, but afterward I'd contacted a Ukrainian researcher from a nearby city to search for whatever records of my family, if any, still existed there. After several weeks, I received a reply accompanied by several notarized and embossed certificates.

Dear Alan Weisman,

In the Civil Records (ZAGS) of Mala Vyska there are no records at all for the period of 1919–1920. In the *rayon* archives they have data only after 1944.

On the territory of Mala Vyska there was one sunflower oil press built before the Bolshevik revolution. It was burnt down in 1923. There are no documents as to who was the founder or owner of the press before the revolution. It is known that in 1920 a certain S. M. Lashynsky was appointed manager of the press by the Soviet authorities.

There are no exact pieces of data as to who might shoot Jews in Mala Vyska. In 1919–1920 Mala Vyska was taken over by different fighting forces 6–7 times! Any civilian could be shot down on the spot if he showed resistance, irrespective of his nationality. Jews might be killed by soldiers of General Denikin's army, Nestor Makhno's, Grigoriev's, or Simon Petlyura's warriors. There were no centrally planned exterminations, similar to those during the Nazi occupation. Whenever anyone was caught at the wrong place or time he could easily be killed by any force. According to the museum guide, Jews could be killed by any of the above forces except the Red Army.

Relatives could bury the dead. The Jewish cemetery where A. Weisman might be buried stopped its existence in 1991. The last burial in it was done before WWII. During the Brezhnev era the cemetery was totally neglected. People began stealing the tombstones for construction needs. The cemetery became a garbage dumping place. At present they are building a car service station and a parking lot on the former cemetery site.

A. Litvinenko

Makhno, Petlyura, Grigoriev, Denikin. As I combed the YIVO archive, these names clanged like sledgehammers and echoed back like memories I didn't know I possessed. Denikin, of course, was the general my Uncle Herman heard his mother curse as my grandfather's assassin, whose presence in Mala Viska at that time was corroborated by an eyewitness. Possibly I had heard my grandmother Rebecca mention him myself, but hadn't understood, because my father had never taught my sister or me the Yiddish they spoke.

To understand who these Jew-killers were and why they did what they did required me to review history that at first seemed alien, except now I knew that this history was mine. I had inherited its consequences directly. It was the story of my forefathers, who were decidedly not the founding fathers of the United States of America. In 1776, while Washington, Jefferson, and Franklin were plotting independence, my people, after centuries of fear and subjugation, had shaken off the latest bloodbath and were finally pursuing some liberties of their own.

356

By the sixteenth century, when the major Jewish migration to Ukraine began, a pattern of Jews being shoved from one European land into the next was already long established. Entering a country as refugees, they would strive to overcome poverty, and arouse jealousy when they succeeded. Inevitably, this led to persecution. Eventually, the survivors again moved on.

But Ukraine, recently conquered by Poland, at first was different. Since these wandering Jews were rarely allowed to acquire land, over centuries they had developed great business acumen as a survival skill. When Polish noblemen opened Ukraine as a grand frontier between eastern and western Europe, in the Jews they found exactly the middlemen, business agents, and absentee landlords needed to administer their properties and ensure that their bounty was profitably traded. By 1600, more than 100,000 Jews were managing dairies, distilleries, mills, farms, and lumberyards in Polish Ukraine, and also serving as judges, tax collectors, and overseers of the peasantry in villages belonging to great agricultural estates.

Unsurprisingly, Ukrainian serfs resented these bossy foreigners who observed their own non-Christian Sabbath, jabbered in their own arcane tongue, and enforced everyone else's peonage. In 1648, their rancor finally detonated. Serfs across Ukraine rose up against the landowners—but since most lived far away, their Jewish surrogates became the focus of their hatred. Tens of thousands were attacked, beaten, and killed. The survivors had little choice but to stay: The next country beyond was Russia, where they were unwelcome. A little more than a century later, with their numbers approaching a half-million, it happened again: This time an estimated 50,000 Jews perished.

Yet not long thereafter—about the same time that the American Revolution was fermenting half a world away—Jewish fortunes finally seemed to shift. In another of Eastern Europe's constant border shuffles, Poland was cleft in two. Half went to imperial Russia, which found that a huge Jewish population came with the territory it had just acquired. Even as it moved to contain them, the Russians decided to treat them as a resource. A line was drawn around the areas where most Jews resided, which became known as the Pale of Settlement. Jews were encouraged to apply their economic skills to develop this newly acquired hinterland, but they were forbidden to dwell beyond it. To better enforce this edict, they were required to take surnames, a dictum also being applied elsewhere in Europe.

Until then, Jews had identified themselves solely by their patronymics (e.g. *Shimon Ben Avraham*: Simon, son of Abraham), an obstacle to today's descendants of northern European Jews who try to chart their genealogies prior to 1800. Three centuries earlier, Spanish Jews hoping to disguise their religion during the Inquisition had taken innocuous geographic identifiers such as del Río, or animal names such as León, or permanently adopted their Spanish patronymics (Ben Martín = Martínez). Similarly, in the Pale of Settlement appeared appellations such as Rosenfeld, Wulf, and Mendelssohn (Mendel's son).

My own family's designation became, blandly enough, Weisman: *white man*. Behind this plain facade, generations of my people recede into an untraceable past: I can only sense who they might have been. All anyone could tell me was that my great-grandfather Shuel, father of my grandfather Avraham, managed a wealthy man's estate and allegedly acquired his own—although, as Jewish ownership likely wasn't legal, no record exists of a Weisman owning land near Mala Viska. Likewise, my mother's people, the Meshbeshers from Medzhibozh—a name dating only to Ellis Island—fade behind my great-grandfather Jacob's headstone, which reveals his father's name as Mordecai. What surname Mordecai used is lost. No one ever asked.

The Jewish cemetery in Medzhibozh has, however, fared better than Mala Viska's, now entombed beneath the cement aprons of gasoline pumps. In honor of their founder, the Kabbalistic healer and exorciser of demons Baal Shem Tov, Hasidic Jews have lately returned to preserve his Medzhibozh burial place and the gravestones of other Jews that surround it, elaborately carved with unicorns and serpents. Some of them, doubtless, are my forebears, but no one remains to tell who was who. In YIVO, I was shown a volume published by Israel's Holocaust memorial, Yad Vashem, grimly titled *The Blackbook:* a roster of nearly five thousand towns whose Jewish populations were annihilated by Nazis. In the barest possible typeface, its alphabetized listings reduce the once-living to columns of ciphers alongside their vanished towns. Among the M's, the dead branches of my family stop only two inches apart: Malaya Viska. Medzhibozh. Exterminated. Gone.

That reference in *The Blackbook* was one of the few I would find to Mala Viska, and even then, the number of Jews murdered by the Nazis was not noted. In nearly all other cases, sickeningly precise death tolls were given, such as for Medzhibozh: 4,614. But no one in YIVO had ever heard of my father's village; nor did it readily appear in any of the databases maintained by Jewish genealogical societies. Clearly, my grandfather had taken his bride to live in a comparative Jewish backwater, where he or his father before him had seized an opportunity to make their fortune. But the names of many of the *shtetls* surrounding Mala Viska resounded in the YIVO archives, and from them I pieced together a history that conformed tellingly to what little I'd been told about my family.

❧❀❧

During the nineteenth century, Jews in Russian Ukraine found themselves yanked first one way, then another, by a succession of czars. Under one, they could own sugar mills, tobacco processors, factories, distilleries, and sawmills. The next one banished them from cities and forbade the public use of Hebrew and Yiddish. The next one restored these freedoms and allowed Jews to serve as army officers, attend university, raise grains and hops, refine sugar, and bottle spirits. Many grew quite wealthy.

That czar was Alexander II, who also abolished serfdom and floggings, promoted self-directed local government, and revamped the judiciary. For such pains, he was assassinated in 1881. His son, Alexander III, immediately set about dismantling his liberal father's reforms. As repression resumed, a rumor spread that the popular Alexander II had been killed by Jews. That Easter, riots by torch-bearing anti-Semites began in Yelisavetgrad and quickly enveloped surrounding towns. No one moved to stop them. The vandalism soon escalated to include murder and rape, and lasted three years. Not until 1884 were any rioters actually tried and convicted, but Jews were also penalized. Mandatory Russian language was again imposed on them. They were banned from living in Moscow. Strict quotas were set for the numbers of Jewish university students, doctors, and lawyers. Jews were again forbidden to own land, and even lost their licenses to sell liquor.

These pogroms were not yet the equal of 1648, when as many as 100,000 Jews may have been murdered in peasant uprisings. That would come later. But there was another compelling difference from that era: Now there was once again a place where Jews could flee—America. They began to trickle away, even without exit permits, sneaking through the border into Poland and Romania. The deserters were rarely stopped: Imperial Russia wanted them out. The dribble of refugees became a roaring stream.

Just as an onrush of Central American refugees a century later alerted North Americans to sustained atrocities in El Salvador and Guatemala, this sudden Jewish inundation made the world aware of the plight of tormented Russian Jews. In 1891, one of the richest men on earth, a Jewish banker from Brussels named Baron Maurice de Hirsch, contrived a solution. Recently, his bank had foreclosed on huge tracts of land in a distant, undeveloped frontier called Argentina. With these he attempted to launch history's grandest relief effort: transporting all three million Russian Jews over a quarter-century to *shtetl*-like agricultural colonies on the Argentine pampa.

Baron de Hirsch failed to take into account, however, the formidable obstacle that the combined Russian and Argentine bureaucracies presented to whisking 125,000 Jews annually across the Atlantic and the equator. He also neglected to factor natural reproduction rates that would have largely replenished the population of Jews in Russia in their wake. Over the next two decades, his Jewish Colonization Association managed to relocate no more than 25,000 Jewish émigrés in any given year, which nevertheless made Argentina the Jewish capital of Latin America. Among the arrivals were my putative great-great-uncle and aunt, Cecilia Vaisman's grandfather Mauricio and grandmother Leah.

It was now the twentieth century and the czar was Nicholas II, who would be the last czar of all. A weak-willed man, in response to the growing socialist revolutionary clamor in his country Nicholas encouraged and courted reactionaries. Having lost nearly all their freedoms over the previous two decades, many Jews were among the political rebels, and reactionary elements had little difficulty in equating patriotism with anti-Semitism. An attack against fifteen hundred Jewish homes on Easter Sunday, 1903, in the Ukrainian town of Kishinev was a direct result of lurid press accusations of Jewish political conspiracies.

Beginning with a disastrous 1904 war against Japan over remote territories, Czar Nicholas II soon managed to lose Manchuria, Korea, Russia's entire Pacific fleet, and control over his populace. By 1905, he had no choice but to establish a parliament and a constitutional monarchy. Jews widely rejoiced over this democratic development—which led, in turn, to Jews being marked by the right-wing press as perfect scapegoats to blame for Russia's woes. According to thousands of tracts circulated by an anti-Semitic cabal known as the Black Hundreds, Jews had pushed their way into the Duma—the new parliament—to undermine the nation with their growing internationalist Zionism movement. Conversely, Jews were denounced as socialist ringleaders who scorned the Duma as a tool to placate the exploited masses. Jews were the Antichrist, kidnappers of Christian babies for their blood rituals, and plotters of a godless conspiracy to undermine not only the empire but the world, as described in books whose publication the czar personally financed.

Among these was a forgery concocted by czarist police titled *The Protocols of the Elders of Zion*, which revealed how Jews intended to destroy Christianity and dominate the planet. A generation later and across the world, this book would be reprinted in Minneapolis to explain the 1929 stock market collapse as yet another orchestrated step in the grand Jewish drive toward world rule. But the *Protocols'* impact in Minnesota would be nothing like what anti-Semitic presses helped ignite in Russia in 1905, where 690 pogroms exploded.

"Why didn't you leave?" I whispered out loud in the YIVO reading room. Didn't you realize, I asked inwardly, that much worse was soon coming? How could you possibly not sense that?

Whom was I addressing? The ghost of this grandfather Avraham I never knew? "Why?" I demanded silently at night, lying in bed on Manhattan's Upper West Side, sleepless over the terrible saga I was absorbing in the Tcherikower archive. "Why didn't you have the good sense that even your brother-in-law Sam Friedman, the ritual slaughterer, had to get the hell out of there while there was time and take our family to the United States?"

I was blaming him, I suppose, for all the repercussions that had tumbled through time and landed on me. Sure, the 1905 pogroms finally waned, after prominent *goyim* like Leo Tolstoy grew so disgusted that they spoke out. And, sure, the Duma eventually conducted an actual honest investigation and correctly fingered the administration as the prod goading the peasant riots. "But, *Zaydeh* Avraham, couldn't you see where this was leading?"

It led to the czar effectively dumping the Duma and empowering the satanic monk Rasputin in its stead. And then World War I broke out, and it was too late. Nobody was migrating anywhere after 1914.

"Couldn't you see that staying was suicide?"

"Your grandfather was a businessman," my father's cousin Bertha Aronson, née Friedman, reminded me. "I can remember him, so tall, strolling into our yard to court your grandmother." We sat in a kosher restaurant on Pico Boulevard in Los Angeles, eating tuna fish sandwiches, as she told me this. At ninety-two, Bertha, a rabbi's widow, still walked a mile a day. "Your grandmother was closer to my age than to her own sisters. They all married *shochets*, like my father. But she always insisted that she wanted a businessman. And she got him. He was handsome. We would all sit around the samovar together and take tea on *shabbos*."

A businessman with land, with too much to lose, would have stayed. And, after all, there were Jews in the Duma, Jews among the Bolshevik revolutionaries, and—after Czar Nicholas II was deposed by the Reds in 1917, and Ukraine momentarily broke away on its own—there were even Jews in the new Ukrainian parliament, the Rada.

Maybe you thought all you had to do was hang on long enough, and among the winners there would surely be some of your own kind.

Of course, there weren't. But I have to remember that when the first spasm of revolution jolted Russia, back in 1905, Avraham Weisman would have only been eighteen. Around then, he went to Hungary to study milling, returning to marry my grandmother in 1911 and to set up a mill and sunflower press in Mala Viska. What can a young man in his twenties—gifted with business talent and land, blessed by a marriage to a rabbi's daughter—see except for great opportunity? What menace out there can he not outlast or outsmart? A Jew, but a Jew with imported rugs on his floors, with a governess and tutors for his sons. There was simply no walking away to America, where he would have nothing.

Or so I speculate. Because what happened next was so appalling that not only can't I imagine how he still remained, but I cannot fathom how he managed to stay alive as long as he did. Because beginning in 1918, for the next three years, no Jew in Ukraine drew a safe breath.

CHAPTER 23

❧

"These," said Nikolai, indicating yet another rolling cart stacked with gray boxes full of blue folders.

I sank into my usual chair at the oak table. For several days, I had been sifting news clippings, photographs, meeting minutes, handwritten notes, and legal documents that Tcherikower had amassed. I read down long foolscap strips of Hebrew characters, containing ledgers of the dead, painstakingly sounding out the *gimels, lameds, daleds, mems, nuhns,* and realizing with a start that, for instance, the name I just read—גולדמן—said Goldman. Somehow, it made the past terribly real to pick my way through this ancient alphabet and discover names so familiar to me. Goldman had been my great-grandmother Bessie Meshbesher's maiden name. Goldman, Schwartzman, Rosenbaum, Blumenfield: Seeing these names in the old tongue made me feel like I was related to them all.

Cyrillic was harder, but one day in two separate news clips I ran across the name Вайсман—*Vaisman*. Excitedly, I called Nikolai, who was cataloging manuscripts in an adjacent office. He ran his finger across the pages. Both, it turned out, referred to the same man named Weisman who lived near Odessa, who had been robbed of everything in a pogrom but survived to tell one of Tcherikower's associates about it. "Not my grandfather," I told Nikolai, after he translated. He shook his head sympathetically.

Nikolai returned to his work, and I continued my search. At random, I selected a folder that held a large yellowed envelope. The index sheet simply read "Torah." I opened it; the contents came sliding out on the table, and I jumped back. As grisly to me as if they'd been shreds of human skin, I was looking at a pile of Torah scraps.

I am not an observant Jew, but a Torah is hallowed thing. Each scroll, executed in flawless, solemn calligraphy, represents years of a scribe's work. The parchment fragments that lay before me had been gathered by some sorrowing Jew after *goyische* infidels in seconds had ripped apart a Torah easily hundreds of years old, over which untold generations of bar mitzvah boys had chanted the blessing, just as I had once done. One swift pogrom had severed that lineage. There was no indication which one: In their very anonymity, these remnants stood for them all. Feeling sick to my stomach, I gingerly replaced them in their box, labeled "1919"—a year when "which one" became irrelevant. The pogrom was everywhere.

❧☙

Czar Nicholas II had assumed personal command of the Russian army in World War I with disastrous consequences. Supply lines soon failed, and thousands of soldiers, desperate for ammunition and food, deserted for home—only to find that under Czarina Alexandra and her bizarre counselor Rasputin, their country was no better off. Starving workers in Petrograd—St. Petersburg—amassed outside the czar's winter palace, demanding food and wages. Soldiers sent to disperse these strikers ended up joining them instead. The day following his March 1917 abdication, the czar and his family were arrested and led off, never to be seen again. A provisional government formed, and a thirty-seven-year-old moderate, Alexandr Kerensky, became prime minister. Kerensky immediately set about suppressing the radical Bolsheviks, but promised political freedom to everyone else. Even Jews.

This must have given my grandfather a taste of sweet vindication. Kerensky spoke not only of full Jewish civil and political rights, but even of Jewish autonomy. His social democracy might even have worked, and the twentieth century might have turned out very differently, but for one fatal mistake: The new prime minister tried to keep his nearly wrecked nation in World War I, in which more than a million Russians had already died. The demoralized survivors were easily swayed by Communist revolutionaries who promised no more war. Where Kerensky spoke of eventual land reform, the Bolsheviks pledged immediate expropriation of the hated nobility, and army deserters who rushed home after the czar's abdication happily began seizing lands. In late October, a coup removed Kerensky and put Trotsky, Lenin, Rykov, and Stalin in power.

With this turn of events, Ukraine—along with Georgia, Armenia, Finland, and the Baltic states—tried to bolt from Russian rule. Their independence went unrecognized by the Bolshevik government, which sent in occupying troops. But just as suddenly they withdrew, as for an instant in history all those lands fell into the possession of Germany, ceded by the Bolsheviks in a humiliating separate peace they signed to rid themselves of the world war. Ignoring Ukraine's new national assembly, Germany moved its own forces into Kiev and placed a *hetman*, a regional governor, in command.

Soon, however, this *hetman* found himself quite stranded, as the Allies won and the Germans were forced to withdraw their occupying troops. At that point, five flags were raised over Ukraine, each heralding forces at war with the other four. They were:

- Ukrainian nationalists, again claiming their independence;
- Bolsheviks, reiterating their intentions to include Ukraine in their Soviet Union;
- Galicia, a former Polish-Ukrainian principality, seceding to form its own republic;
- The Poles, whose country lay historic claim to Ukraine's Galician territory;

- and, a loyalist "White" army, rising from the ranks of the once-proud Imperial military, financed by rich landowners to defeat the Reds and to reinstitute the monarchy of Holy Mother Russia.

All these opposing forces agreed on one thing: The great belt of rich black earth of central Ukraine, replete with grain and sugar beets, would be critical to their future. All swooped in to seize it. During the subsequent civil war, which lasted until 1921, Ukraine's capital, Kiev, changed hands fifteen times.

As I tracked the fate of Jews through this bloody maze, I tried to imagine the choices now facing my grandfather. Several Jews—including Trotsky himself—had helped engineer the Bolshevik revolution. My agro-industrialist grandfather Avraham logically would have opposed nationalization of property. Yet early in the revolution, to avoid the food shortages that helped depose the czar, agriculture was the one private enterprise the Bolsheviks permitted to continue—especially in loamy Kherson province, home to most Jewish farmers and where Mala Viska lay. So perhaps my grandfather felt secure there, and, since his lands were doubtlessly still in some nobleman's name, maybe he surmised that nothing would really change at all. Even if his holdings technically transferred to the state, they would still profit from his expertise.

And something else: Later, when the pogroms began again, Jewish presence in the Bolshevik movement and Lenin's initial sympathy for Jews as an oppressed people provided a shield for the Jewish populace—the histories I found and the Tcherikower archive attributed few Jewish deaths to the Red Army. So, did my grandfather feel more protected by the Bolsheviks because he was a Jew, or more threatened by them because he was a businessman?

In the Tcherikower archive there was compelling evidence upon which to make a good guess. My good guess is that my wily, successful grandfather did whatever it took to be useful to whoever happened to be in power on any given day, because he must have known that every day could have been his family's last.

The Ukrainian nationalists, whose fledgling independent government in 1917 had been easily thrust aside by the Germans, rushed back when the German Hetmanate collapsed near the end of 1918. The head of the Ukrainian armed forces that took Kiev from the scattered remaining German troops was a short man of thirty-nine named Simon Petlyura, a former journalist and propagandist for Ukrainian independence. Not long after the Germans were defeated and the new Ukrainian National Republic was declared, Petlyura became president.

He would not hold that office for long; by mid-1920 the Bolsheviks won Ukraine and stayed for the next seventy years. But Simon Petlyura's name would again resound worldwide. In 1926, while the deposed president sat in a restaurant on Boulevard St. Michel in Paris, where he published a tabloid for other exiled Ukrainians like himself, a graying man named Sholom Schwartzbard would step up to his table and carefully shoot him in the head.

Calmly handing his revolver to a gendarme, Schwartzbard explained that he had just rid the world of a mass murderer. In the ensuing trial, the true defendant turned out to be not Schwartzbard but the dead Petlyura, as dozens of Jewish men and women testified how their loved ones were raped and disemboweled and murdered in their beds, and their homes looted and burned by Petlyura's troops. After a while, the French jury forgot that a man was being tried for a cold-blooded killing in broad daylight that he didn't even deny, but grappled only with one question: Could Petlyura be held responsible for 50,000 Jewish deaths perpetrated by his legions? Yes, they decided, and acquitted Sholom Schwartzbard of murder. What he had done, the jury ruled, was slay something so evil it was surely inhuman.

During the trial, it was argued in Petlyura's defense that Jews were Bolshevik ringleaders out to undermine the Ukrainian National Republic, and hence fair targets. Actually, in 1918 fewer than 1 percent of Ukraine's Jews were Bolsheviks, but it is true that their first choice wasn't an independent Ukraine. After decades of pogroms by Ukrainian patriots, most Jews preferred the Russians, Czarist repression and all—Russian, not Ukrainian, was usually their second language after Yiddish. They had also heard how Petlyura's Ukrainian troops massacred many German officers, who had treated Jews with refreshing courtesy during the hetmanate.

And, in 1918 they were also hearing even worse. This time, Petlyura's men were coming after them.

The first pogroms of the civil war, in the spring of 1918 in northern Ukraine, had been isolated robberies and crimes against property attributed to scattered Bolshevik units withdrawing as the German troops advanced. Back in Russia, the Soviets vowed severe measures against any pogromists in their ranks, a discipline that not only held thereafter, but belied the later protestations of Petlyura and Denikin that they had no way to control deplorable acts perpetrated by their own forces. But if the Communists themselves weren't the marauders responsible for the ocean of Jewish blood spilled in 1919, their presence in the land was its foremost cause. The German hetman was barely gone when the Bolsheviks invaded Ukraine again, scoring a series of quick victories. As defeated Ukrainian nationalist troops evacuated regions they had previously won, they vented their frustration by taking vengeance on the hapless, helpless Jews.

It began on New Year's Eve, December 31, 1918, in the town of Ovruch, which one day would know the added misfortune of being situated due west of the Chernobyl nuclear power plant. Shouting "Kill the Jew Communists," retreating Petlyuran soldiers that night shot, stabbed, and clubbed to death twenty-six Jews. To the same battle cry, over the next ten days they hit a dozen more *shtetls,* exacting revenge for the beating they were taking from the Red Army. They went as far south as the Hasidic center of Zhytomir, where they killed fifty-two. Two months later, *pogromchiks* returned there to kill fifteen hundred more.

The Bolsheviks kept advancing. By February, they had seized Kiev. Nationalist strategy quickly degenerated into attacking the civilians under the guise of stamping out "Communist sympathizers"—a handy twentieth-century euphemism that in various places would later refer to Vietnamese and Nicaraguan peasants, Guatemalan Indians, Colombian banana-pickers, El Salvadoran fishermen, and North American entertainers. But here it meant only one thing: Jews.

The Petlyurans swept into Novomirgorod, dangerously close to my father's town of Mala Viska, but after killing one hundred Jews they followed the railroad the opposite direction: north toward Kiev, throwing Jews from windows of speeding trains and strafing railway platforms in each town. On February 14, Petlyura sent his most trusted ataman, or commander, a lieutenant named Semosenko, to head off a rumored Bolshevik coup in Proskurov, a city of 50,000 inhabitants, half of whom were Jews. Ataman Semosenko saw a wonderful opportunity. First he gathered leaders of the Proskurov Jewish community and exacted a fine of three hundred thousand rubles for their alleged pro-Bolshevik conniving. Once paid, he went to the town council. All Jews, he ordered, were to be shot—especially children, so that "no more Bolsheviks in Proskurov would reach adulthood."

On *shabbos* morning, Proskurov's synagogues were machine gunned. Hospital patients were bludgeoned to death. After being raped senseless, Jewish women had their breasts and buttocks sliced off with bayonets. Years later, at the Paris trial of Petlyura's Jewish assassin, survivors described old Jewish men flung by their beards from windows, children burned alive, eyes gouged, fingers chopped to collect rings, and streets littered with beheaded corpses. That Sabbath, the death count may have reached 10,000.

Others now joined the slaughter: renegade atamans who had broken from the Bolsheviks and hoped to return Ukraine to imperial Russian rule, self-styled patriotic saviors of Ukraine, or simply apolitical freebooters. Inflamed with centuries of anti-Semitic resentment and assured that Jews and Communists were synonymous, loose peasant armies hung Jewish "spies" as warnings to others who might favor the Bolsheviks. Jews were stuffed down wells and locked in rooms that were then torched. The price of ammunition having inflated to fifty rubles per cartridge, bayonets were the weapon of choice; or, as happened in one Sunday in Zhytomir, Jewish men were packed in a line to see how many could be killed with a single bullet (reportedly, six).

The most notorious brigand leader, the Ukrainian ataman Grigoriev, managed to wage civil war from all sides before staking out his own position. He began in the economic section of the German hetmanate, but left to organize insurrectionists for Petlyura. After World War I, realizing that the stronger Bolshevists would regain power, he joined them, but his troops robbed the civilian population so often that the Soviets declared him an outlaw and disowned him. With that, Grigoriev issued a manifesto demanding that "foreign elements from the ever-hungry land of Moscow and from the land where Christ was nailed to the cross" be expunged from Ukraine.

On May 15, 1919, Grigoriev's 16,000 troops entered Yelisavetgrad. As usual, he released all imprisoned criminals and incorporated them into his ranks. To foment Jew-hungry fervor among local Christians, he had the former mayor, shot earlier by the Bolsheviks, disinterred and given a patriot's funeral. Yelisavetgrad's Jews, however, had coexisted peacefully for years with the Christian community. Many belonged to the local Peasants' Assembly and the metalworkers' trade union. When the pogrom commenced, their fellow unionists took up arms to patrol against looters, and sent delegations to Grigoriev's staff, imploring them to cease. When they were assured that "only Jews would be attacked," many Christians hid Jews in their cellars and barns. Later, the Russian Red Cross reported that wherever the *pogromchiks* found Jews hiding, they tossed in grenades.

For three days, Grigoriev's men shot their way into Jewish houses, killed anyone inside, and carried off whatever gold, silver, or jewels they saw. Behind them came civilian mobs that carted away everything else, including beds and furniture, and smashed whatever remained, continuing until the arrival of four Soviet regiments forced Grigoriev to withdraw. Although heroic efforts by their neighbors held the number of Jewish dead to two thousand, 50,000 Jewish survivors lost everything they owned. Among them was a cousin of my grandmother's named Shika, who would somehow shelter my father's orphaned family when they arrived in Yelisavetgrad that fall, just four months later. Considering that out of several hundred Jewish stores, only five were left standing, it is difficult to believe that my grandmother fled there for safety. But she had little choice; pogroms were everywhere.

From Yelisavetgrad, Grigoriev moved to Novomirgorod, barely twenty kilometers from my family's home. There, Jews were made to dig their own graves, line them with lime disinfectant, and then were buried alive. Again, courageous Christian neighbors came to the defense. Advised that Grigoriev's gang was approaching, they arrested more than a thousand Jews and crammed them into a house of detention for eight days until the pogromists had gone.

According to records in the local soviet, Grigoriev's forces also controlled nearby Mala Viska in mid-May. If so, how my grandfather escaped death that spring is incomprehensible to me, unless my family was among those hidden in the Novomirgorod jail, or unless he paid an enormous bribe. Possibly he was protected by his employees—who, my father and uncle recalled, numbered more than a hundred. Probably the richest man in his village, he was doubtless powerful and canny enough to cut all kinds of deals. But even with Grigoriev?

As it happened, before my grandfather died, Ataman Grigoriev would be assassinated by an anarchist named Nestor Makhno— another leader of yet another army roaming the Ukrainian countryside. Makhno justified this deed because of Grigoriev's excessive pogroms, but his demise brought Jews no relief. Grigoriev's peasant legions were simply absorbed into Makhno's own ambitious campaign, responsible for scores of Jewish deaths in southern Ukraine.

But both Makhno and Grigoriev's names would soon pale in comparison to what came next.

"Scotch or bourbon?"

I tasted. "Scotch," I answered.

"Right you are. Come here, son, I want to show you something." I'd been summoned to my father's den, where we often spent Sundays together watching pro football. This, however, was a school night. Taking an oversized book in a shiny gold jacket from the shelf where he kept his World War II histories, he motioned me to the couch.

"I bought this today. I think you might find it interesting."

It was about the American Civil War. "All the techniques of modern warfare—use of trains, telegraph, repeating rifles, armored ships, submarines—were developed during our Civil War," he said. "Understanding it is critical to military scholarship. You know, son, before long you'll be going to college. Have you ever thought about West Point? I can ask Senator Humphrey or Senator McCarthy to get you an appointment."

Until that point, I'd assumed I would probably become an ornithologist. That same year, an eighth-grade science teacher who disliked Jews and an English teacher who loved me would permanently alter my future trajectory. A military career had never been a consideration, but not wanting to disappoint my father outright, I replied, "Maybe," and tried to show interest in his book, as we didn't often share moments like this. Years later, it proved useful, too; while researching my own writings, I learned that the training grounds for those innovative Civil War generals was the 1848 Mexican-American War, where Grant, Lee, Sherman, and Stonewall Jackson all served as young officers.

Later still, I would also learn that, as my father had characterized it, our Civil War was indeed considered an incubator of modern battlefield strategy. It was studied not only at West Point but in

European war colleges—such as the officer candidate school in Kiev, where an excellent student named Anton Ivanovich Denikin graduated in 1892.

ꙮ

During the early twentieth century, Anton Denikin served with distinction in two humiliating wars. By the end of the 1905 Russo-Japanese debacle he rose to lieutenant colonel, and in World War I he became a highly decorated general. When Czar Nicholas II assumed command of the armed forces, Denikin was selected to head Russia's Eighth Army. After the monarchy collapsed, he was named chief of staff to the provisional government's minister of war.

To his disgust, however, the new Soviet-pressured government was permitting soldiers' committees elected from the lower ranks to share decisions with officers, many of whom were being purged. When Commander-in-Chief General Lavr Kornilov protested, he was jailed under suspicion of planning a coup, and Denikin was among the loyal generals imprisoned with him. After the Bolshevik revolution, realizing they would be executed, they managed to escape to southern Russia. There, Kornilov began to muster a volunteer army from a few thousand former czarist troops, to seize the country back from the Communists.

His natural allies, he believed, would be the Don Cossacks, who were the first to take up arms against Lenin. The Cossacks were old Ukrainian and Russian peasant societies, noted for their abilities as warriors and horsemen. Over centuries, Cossack communities had developed into virtually autonomous regions, most notably in the southern valleys of Russian rivers that flowed to the Black Sea. Gradually, the Cossacks lost their autonomy to the czarist empire, but maintained their status as military castes. Especially distinguished as soldiers were the Cossacks from the Don River. When not off repressing uprisings against various czarist regimes, the Don Cossacks had also become successful, often wealthy farmers.

Naturally, they detested Bolshevik land expropriations, but their alliance with Kornilov's volunteer force quickly disintegrated over purposes: The Cossacks were mainly interested in defending their property and homeland along the Don, while Kornilov wanted nothing less than to reclaim from the Soviets everything from Ukraine to Siberia for Mother Russia. Discouraged, he retreated south of the Don, where his volunteers were surprised by a Red Army ambush. As he lay dying from a grenade blast, Kornilov passed command of his remaining tattered loyalist force to General Anton Ivanovich Denikin.

Unlike his predecessor, who had Cossack blood, Denikin was born a Polish peasant. Yet it was Denikin who finally forged an uneasy pact with the Don Cossacks against the common Bolshevik foe. Two developments brought their armies together. The first was a victory by Denikin's Volunteer Army of only 8,000 men against some 30,000 Red Army troops in the Kuban steppe, Cossack territory that was the gateway to the Black Sea. Deftly, Denikin had parlayed his underdog forces along railway lines, capturing key stations that effectively cut off the Red Army's communication with the rest of Russia.

This tactic impressed the Cossacks, as did another surprise: Germany lost World War I. The victorious Allies based a small force under French command in the southern Ukrainian port of Odessa. Concerned by Bolshevik boasts of incipient world revolution and indignant over their confiscations of French and British property in Russia, the French Allied commander pledged the Volunteer Army Allied support. With that, the Don Cossack ataman decided that the best way to rid the land of the Communist menace was through an alliance with Denikin.

In December 1918, the Don Cossack ataman delivered 50,000 blooded, disciplined, and well-armed warriors to General Anton Denikin, commander-in-chief of the combined armed forces of Southern Russia. Denikin's own Volunteer Army had grown as war prisoners were given a choice of serving in its ranks or facing execution. They had tanks, artillery, and ammunition furnished by the British. But the Bolshevik army, newly rejuvenated by Trotsky via purges and forced conscription, was now a huge fighting force of nearly 800,000 men, and the front that Denikin needed to maintain would also have to expand.

Denikin's Volunteers and Cossacks—known together as the White Army—worked their way north to Ukraine, where Petlyura's army and Grigoriev's and Makhno's gangs were circling each other. As they advanced, more joined their ranks, sometimes through inspiration but more often by coercion. Throughout the civil war, all sides experienced the same: Soldiers on the losing end would save their selves and their villages by switching allegiances—often in mid-battle—to the apparent victors. As long as an army maintained momentum, it was guaranteed reinforcements, albeit not especially loyal ones. In this war, commanders had little choice. Loyalties were spread too thinly among too many options; soldiers and citizens were demoralized to the point of stupor after years of governmental disarray and a world conflict in which Russia lost nearly two million men, and now with the generalized uproar of civil war.

A professional like Denikin knew the chance he was taking with conscripts faithful to little cause beyond their own survival. Worse still, all the adversaries were supplying themselves on the march, which meant requisitioning or simply seizing provisions and war taxes from the populace wherever they were. It was an unruly way to run a war that practically sanctioned soldiers to loot and pillage, but in the short run it seemed necessary, and it worked. By mid-1919 Denikin had won a succession of victories that melded into a tremendous forward surge. His growing forces took cities controlled by the Petlyurans, and maintained a line that stretched for hundreds of kilometers across Ukraine and southern Russia. Anton Denikin began to dream of Moscow.

Soon, however, he would pay for the compromises in military standards and discipline he'd accepted to achieve all this—but not nearly enough.

In June 1919, a delegation of Ukrainian rabbis, lay leaders, and Jewish businessmen sought an audience with General Anton Denikin at his seaside field headquarters, just west of the mouth of the Don. Only a month earlier, most Jews had believed that the advancing forces of the White Army were a godsend to rid them both of the savage Petlyuran pogromists and the Communist extremists. Jews had even enthusiastically joined Denikin's troops. But something, it was now apparent, had gone terribly wrong.

They were received by the broad-chested, beribboned general himself, his shaved bald pate gleaming above his upswept eyebrows, full handlebar moustache, and inverted pyramid of a goatee. They congratulated him on his army's stunning progress. However, they reported, the Whites' success had brought no end to the pogroms, but exactly the opposite. Volunteer and Cossack soldiers were joining in the plunder and gore. In Podolsk province, for example—birthplace of all my great-grandparents and untold generations that preceded them—Jews had been doused in oil and set ablaze. Cossack troops had buried Jews up to their necks, then galloped horses over their exposed heads.

Deniken heard them out. "Gentlemen," he replied, "I will be honest with you. I don't like you Jews. But my attitude toward you is based on humanity. I, as commander in chief, will take steps to prevent pogroms and other acts of lawlessness, and will punish severely those who are guilty. But I cannot guarantee that in the future there will be no excesses."

Denikin, in fact, was genuinely concerned—because, as he later wrote in his memoirs, the pogroms "struck at the troops' own morale, corrupting their minds, destroying discipline, causing disintegration." He was leading a fighting force, he complained to the Jewish delegation, comprised in part of the "dregs of humanity." He directed the Volunteer Army's commander to issue a proclamation guaranteeing the inviolability of life, home, and property of all citizens, regardless of race or religion. His assistant also penned a memo expressing gratitude for help that Jews had extended to the Volunteer Army, and—in reference to universal *pogromchik* dogma that all Jews were Communists—an assurance that they would never "hold an entire race responsible for the faults and crimes committed by separate irresponsible individuals."

With no other hope to cling to, some Jews at first believed him. As White Army troops neared Kiev, they were greeted as saviors. A schoolteacher from suburban Fastov assured Elias Tcherikower that only a fraction of the Jewish proletariat agreed with the Communists: "The other sections of Jewry, consisting principally of merchants, artisans, and persons of liberal professions, had rather a bourgeois frame of mind and were awaiting with great impatience the arrival of Denikin's troops, being persuaded that they are the bearers of principles of ownership, of free trade, of freedom of word, and in general of all that order characterizing a middle-class public. They had to pay dearly for their mistake."

The pages containing schoolteacher Isaac Berland's Yiddish eyewitness testimony were long, legal-sized yellow sheets, with attached copies in blurry Russian, tied together with hunks of brown string. As I gradually apprehended their contents, at times I felt myself hearing his language coming faintly through my genes. The scene he described, unlike anything I had seen in this life, seemed nevertheless familiar, and I found myself nodding in recognition. Of course, I kept thinking. Of course.

A Cossack White Army regiment, Berland recounted, had arrived in August. In groups of ten, they systematically visited every house in town. In each, they wrapped a cord around the head of the household's neck, strung him from a rafter, and threatened to leave him that way unless the family gave them all their money. If there was no place to hang a rope, they shoved his hand between door and jamb and warned that fingers would be lost if cash wasn't produced.

As this was obviously an organized plunder, a Jewish committee protested to the Cossack commander. He charged them ten thousand rubles for protection; nevertheless, the pillaging continued, interrupted only when a passing detachment of Bolsheviks briefly attacked. The following day the Cossacks announced that

378

a female Jewish spy had betrayed them to the Communists, and must be avenged. They began torching houses, forcing people back inside at saber-point to burn to death. Children had to sing and dance as their parents were eviscerated with bayonets. Any Christians found concealing Jews met the same fate, which persuaded others to turn out the Jews they were hiding. The streets of Fastov filled with feathers from mattresses ripped apart by soldiers looking for hoarded kopecks and gold. No one dared to bury the corpses piling up in the streets, which became meals for dogs and pigs.

Berland himself hid in an orchard behind a school, struggling to remain motionless while he watched Cossacks first rape, then kill high school girls among the apple trees. The pogrom finally ebbed just before Yom Kippur. The sorrowing survivors convened for services—until Cossacks swarmed into the synagogue, demanding more tribute. No one, of course, had money: To carry it violated the rules of abstinence on the Day of Atonement. While men in the main sanctuary pleaded with the invaders to wait until nightfall, other White Army soldiers climbed the stairs and burst into the women's gallery. Soon, women were throwing themselves off the balcony, as others were seized and defiled in the synagogue on the holiest of days.

General Denikin had raised considerable Jewish money for the Volunteer cause, and his officers were often quartered comfortably and at great expense in Jewish houses. In the midst of the Fastov pogrom, wealthy Jews vainly tried to appeal to these White Army officers. In their presence, one colonel admonished his troops that not only was the looting and bloodshed inhuman, but all Europe was watching. He was interrupted by his hooting men, who reminded him of things he'd said when no Jewish witnesses were listening. Berland, pleading with a White Army major, was told that Jews had brought this on themselves. "Why do Jews fight with the Bolsheviks?" he demanded. "Why is there not a single Jew in the Volunteer Army?"

Probably, Berland said, because they weren't allowed to join. "Probably true," the major agreed.

In fact, many Jews had enlisted in the Volunteer Army. But the chief physician in Denikin's field headquarters hospital soon instructed doctors not to admit wounded Jewish soldiers, under the pretext of lack of space. Shortly thereafter, an order expelling all Jewish officers from the White Army came from Denikin himself.

⁘⌢⌣⌢⁘

By September 1919, Denikin's armies had driven nearly all the Bolsheviks from Ukraine. The international press reported that the Communist revolution was tottering before the White general's march toward the Russian heartland, ever nearer to Moscow. His astounding progress was interrupted that fall, however, when Petlyura's Ukrainian nationalists declared war on the White Army following a collision of both forces in Kiev. As Denikin's Volunteers and Cossacks turned west to push the Petlyurans back, they were also engaged by the pesky anarchist troops of Nestor Makhno, still at large in the steppes. All this prolonged the fighting in Ukraine— and thus, the pogroms continued as well.

In early September, General Denikin was sent a memorandum from an organization identified as the Main Committee of the Alliance for the Regeneration of Russia in Ukraine. It is an odd document. By its title, the committee that produced it would not appear to be Jewish. Deferential to the point of being obsequious, it reaffirms the committee's faith in Denikin and the "honor and esteem of the Volunteer Army." But it then delineates the grievances of Ukrainian Jews in such detail, and argues in such pragmatic terms for drastic measures to halt the carnage, that a Jewish hand was unmistakably at work.

The memorandum's list of pogromized towns describes a wide swathe of the countryside. It notes the participation of White Army officers in violations "everywhere" of women in the presence of their parents and husbands, following the extortion of every last

380

kopeck. It catalogues demolished banks and synagogues, dese-
crated Torahs, systematic murders of revered rabbis, the destruction of Jewish schools down to the last book, and repeated
shootings of delegations of respected Jewish citizens who had gone
to welcome the Volunteer forces as delivering heroes. "Unquestionably," the authors assure the general, "said outrages are done
by non-intelligent elements of the army, in striking contrast to the
spirit of self-sacrifice of the best men in the Volunteers. All organizations which serve the cause of the Volunteer Army, among them
ours, are well informed that the responsible commanders are
grieved at these events and condemn them strongly."

They mention a meeting with Denikin's aide-de-camp,
Lieutenant-General Bredov, during which he vowed "the harshest
punishment" for zealots who continued agitating against Jews—yet
mysteriously, neither military companies nor local populations had
apparently ever received such an order. Next, the authors appealed
to Denikin's grasp of economics, describing how ravenous
Cossacks, after exhausting all Jewish sources of booty, often
turned their hatchets on shops belonging to Russians. Continual
harassment of Jews in trains and railway stations, they noted, was
disrupting the country's industry and enterprise, to which Jews
made such a vital contribution. Devastation and death in the Jewish merchant community, they warned, would assure shortages of
food and heating materials in the coming winter for everyone.

Finally, aiming at Denikin's sense of strategy and history, if not
his conscience, they also reminded him: "The news of these outrages that stain the real character of the Volunteer Army, strikingly
in contrast to [its] principles of lawfulness and tolerance, could
reach the West, and cause there general condemnation and draw
the attention of the Allied Powers."

This last point surely gave General Denikin a good laugh.
After just winning at terrible cost the most horrific war in history,
the Allies, he knew, weren't about to intervene in Russian affairs;
even if they did, it would be squarely on his side. Compared to
how alarmed they were by Communism—with Lenin and Trotsky

pontificating about first European, then world domination—the Allies didn't give a damn about Jews. All their hopes, too, were embodied in the White Army, which, their press was excitedly reporting, was now turning the tide on the Reds. The West wanted Denikin to win, at whatever cost.

In the streets of New York, thousands of horrified Jewish immigrants demonstrated in frantic support of imperiled relatives left behind. They pressured U.S. President Woodrow Wilson, who commissioned an American inquiry into alleged anti-Semitic atrocities in Russia. "The situation of the Jews," it concluded evasively, "is evidently precarious but will naturally improve greatly when order is restored."

A report by the head of the British mission in Odessa to the prime minister, in response to similar marches in London, was far more blunt:

> By continuing to supply General Denikin with arms and identifying ourselves wholeheartedly with the Russian National Cause, we shall be constantly in a position to exercise a modifying influence upon what are, after all, some of the most terrible hatreds which have ever afflicted mankind.
>
> It must be realized on the one hand that the Jews are identified in the minds of the great majority of the people of Russia with the hideous tyranny from which they are now finding deliverance, and on the other hand that the one who has the keenest sense of the responsibility of the Government to safeguard the lives, property, and civil liberties of the Jews, and is doing his utmost to ensure that the obligation is fulfilled, is General Denikin . . . so much so that he has been attacked by disgruntled Ukrainian elements as the protector of the Jews and has been accused of being bought by them.
>
> I cannot too strongly emphasize . . . the fact that

> Bolshevism is daily proclaiming itself more clearly . . . as the
> most diabolical anti-Christian movement that the world has
> yet seen, and . . . that a tide of feeling against the Jews is
> being piled up which will be impossible to control much
> longer, unless there is a radical change in the behaviour of
> the Jew commissars.

The Jews responsible for the memorandum of the Alliance for
the Regeneration of Russia were not "Jew commissars"—they were
Ukraine's remaining Jewish capitalists, about to lose everything
they had. I can imagine them arguing amongst themselves whether
they should stop equivocating and just let Denikin have it. Finally,
their patience clearly waning, they noted that not only had
the general neglected to personally order a stop to the pogroms,
but via the right-wing press, the Volunteer Army was actively pro-
moting Jewish genocide. They quote one such paper, *The Kievlianin,* in which Jews are characterized as "Communists and
executioners who drink from the bowl of retaliation to the last
drop."

The Kievlianin—in case Denikin needed to be reminded—was
edited by one of his own advisors, and was distributed directly
to officers and soldiers. Among its principal contributors was
A. Savenko, known for an internationally famous 1913 trial in
which he accused a Jewish brickmaker named Mendel Beilis of
murdering a Kiev boy to mix his blood with Passover *matzoh* flour.
Savenko was now the White Army's chief propagandist.

As I read this desperate document, its language proceeding
from unctuous to furious, and grasped the risk its authors had
taken, I kept wondering if my grandfather Avraham might have
been among them. Had he attended the meeting in early September with Denikin's aide, Lieutenant-General Bredov? He was one
of the shrewd, resilient Jewish capitalists who had prospered despite the oppressive restrictions against Jews in the Pale of Settlement. He had somehow lasted through successive waves of the
Red Army, of Grigoriev's gangs, of Nestor Makhno, and of Petlyura.

But just as it seemed that things couldn't possibly deteriorate further, here was Denikin, riding a crest of military glory atop a wave of foaming hordes of madmen. Avraham Weisman must have known that this time he and the remaining Jews were pressed to the wall.

On the few occasions that my father shared his memories of my grandfather Avraham, what he most recalled was his temper. "My old man," he told me once, chuckling humorlessly, "was plenty damn strict. He could be a real mean son-of-a-bitch."

Was that the irascibility he had inherited, which perhaps he clutched as one of the few shreds that remained of his father's legacy—irascibility that, given those appalling times, was certainly understandable? Over what matters had my grandfather roared in anger—anger at his wife, for instance, that later would reignite in my father's mindless rages at my mother? Did my grandmother Rebecca berate him for not getting them out of there in those final days, like her sister's husband Sam Friedman had with his family? Did he bellow back that if she didn't like it, she should have listened to her rabbi father and not been so set on marrying a businessman, only to find out later that he couldn't just get up and walk away from his investments like her *shochet* brother-in-law, a ritual slaughterer who didn't own *kasha*?

Was this, in fact, why my grandmother later turned down the proposal of a rich jeweler whom everyone urged her to marry—because she'd learned how fragile the security of money was in a world that hated Jews? Had she therefore instead chosen Milstein, a pauper junk peddler but a religious mystic, as an atonement, fearing that perhaps God had punished her for disobeying her Talmudic father?

Confirming the testimony of the old woman in my father's village, town records show that during the same month that the Main Committee's futile memorandum languished on some White Army bureaucrat's desk, General Denikin's troops arrived in Mala Viska. Both the local soviet and the history museum in Kirovograd—formerly Yelisavetgrad—date that invasion as occurring during August 1919, according to the Julian calendar still in use at the time, which bled into September in the new Gregorian system. The date of my grandfather's *yahrtzeit*, the anniversary of his death, according to the Jewish calendar—an ancient semi-lunar confusion whose relationship to western calendars gyrates substantially— generally coincided with early September.

About my grandfather, the regional archives were mute. He was not listed as a landowner, although that was no surprise. There was a reference to the sunflower oil press and to the mill, both in a Russian's name—again, to be expected—both of which were confiscated and nationalized by the Bolsheviks the following year, 1920. "Because of the turbulent events in the country from 1914 to 1919 and loss of records," concluded the researcher I'd hired, "it is impossible to trace anything related to this period. Weisman could have lived in Mala Vyska or Elisavetgrad without being registered as a household owner or a business owner."

In New York, as I looked for a name I recognized in the Tcherikower archive, I was told often that during those times Jews disappeared and left no trace, as if they'd never existed. The thought filled me with panic—how could my father have died without leaving me more memory of who we were? How doomed were we to act out traumas inherited from our forebears, without understanding that those ancient sorrows were the hidden cause?

But one morning, the Tcherikower archive finally yielded something. It was a Russian Red Cross list naming tiny Mala Viska as one of the villages in Kherson province to be rocked by a pogrom. No details: just enough of a time frame to place it in the realm of Grigoriev or Denikin. But that same afternoon, Nikolai added yet one more shard he'd discovered: a handwritten transcription of an article from a Kiev Jewish newspaper, *Hebrew Thought*, dated September 20, 1919. It described the unnamed author's journey from Kiev to Odessa earlier that month, and mentioned an immense pogrom around Yelisavetgrad by Denikin's White Guards. The situation was finally improving in the city, he wrote, but it was getting worse in outlying places. In one hamlet called Mala Viska, where there was a railway stop and a sunflower oil factory, a post-pogrom auction had been held of valuable articles that had been plundered.

Again, no names. But who else's could they have been? Who else had owned anything of sufficient value to warrant an auction, other than my grandfather: mill owner and purveyor of sunflower oil, the biggest employer in the village? Who else of means would have lived in that backwater, with so few Jews it was barely even mentioned in Holocaust archives?

By the end of September 1919, Denikin's troops stretched over a huge, crescent-shaped line more than a thousand kilometers long that bulged through Ukraine toward Moscow, barely two hundred fifty miles away. But it remained the goal they never achieved. Like avenging ghosts, the thousands of pogromized Jewish dead came back to haunt the commander of the White Army. Greed, plunder, and wanton savagery had corrupted his troops far beyond his ability to maintain the discipline necessary to confront an early winter and the replenished, more battle-wise Red Army that awaited them. Frostbite, typhus, and fighting on northern Russian soil weren't nearly as attractive to the Cossack army as the chance to grow rich off booty, plucked as easily from Jewish bodies as apples in the fall. Deserters melted away by the thousands, carrying their loot back to the Don.

At the same time, a mindless, tenacious charge by Makhno's anarchist hordes at the Volunteer Army's rear was first an annoyance, then a serious diversion that gave the Red Army time to seize the initiative back from Denikin. Trotsky had conscripted new recruits and had built a cavalry as well, and faced Denikin's 100,000 shaky troops with nearly twice as many men. In the end, a lack of reinforcements spelled the difference. Stalled by winter, attacked from ahead and dogged from behind, Denikin's forces disintegrated almost as miraculously fast as they had come together. By early 1920, Trotsky's Red Army ruled Ukraine, and Denikin relinquished his post as commander of the White Army.

That spring, my grandmother, now barely surviving with her sons in Yelisavetgrad, would return to Mala Viska at Passover to find the mill and sunflower oil press nationalized. The Communists would not return them to her, but they gave her bags of flour with which she made *matzohs* for her family and neighbors. Within a few months, the outcome of the entire war was decided, and Soviet Communism held sway for the next seventy years.

According to the Russian Red Cross and the Kiev Central Committee for Aid of Jews, nearly a quarter-million Jews perished in Ukrainian pogroms during the civil war—more than half of them, including my grandfather, at the hands of General Denikin's troops. It was a staggering figure, but barely remembered by the time I was born, because it had been so colossally trumped by the Nazi Holocaust.

Like Simon Petlyura before him and Nestor Makhno shortly afterward, Anton Ivanovich Denikin fled to Paris. He passed his days there in relative peaceful boredom, gardening and writing his memoirs about the exciting first half of his life when he nearly became the savior of Mother Russia. Later, in his dotage and after World War II had passed, he would resettle again, this time in a country distant from the recent unpleasantness of the Holocaust and the forthcoming Nuremberg trials—which perhaps he feared might recall earlier Jewish carnage, for which he continued to absolve himself in his writings.

He needn't have worried. Except for the single-handed justice that Petlyura's Jewish assassin took into his own hands, and the trap set by Makhno for his rival Grigoriev—"two scorpions in a jar," Denikin had called them—no *pogromchik* was ever tried for crimes of genocide against the Jews. Denikin emigrated to a country whose freedoms a stalwart foe of Communism like himself was welcome to enjoy: the United States.

There he would die in bed, in Ann Arbor, Michigan, in 1947, the year I was born.

CHAPTER 24

There are truths we are told and congenital truths we only sense. My father's account of his own father's murder was fundamental to my upbringing, yet, as it turned out, I was shaped even more by hidden undercurrents he was trying to escape. In this, I am not alone. Especially in my land called the United States of America, for reasons that my father's bewildering deception eventually led me to understand, children inherit not just the legacies our elders impart but a void left by what they withhold. Instinctively, we yearn to fill it.

As I stayed up nights with my sister after our parents' deaths, going through papers and photographs, confronting the knick-knacks of a lifetime—so invisible until the decision to keep or toss onto the miscellaneous table at the estate sale—it began to dawn on me how often in my career I had chosen to write about the themes of their lives: immigration, orphans, violence, and displacement. But it was only later, when I returned from Ukraine and attempted to unravel the reasons for my father's fabrication, that I began to grasp that it was no accident that I became who I am. My journey to Mala Viska had led me to the truth. Yet instead of ending a search, the answer I exhumed there began one.

In the windowless YIVO reading room, surrounded by boxes of the Tcherikower archive and holding those frail scraps that formed the fragmentary record of people and places from whence I sprang,

I began to see how the dramatic narrative of each era becomes wrapped around the double helix of genetic inheritance and bequeathed to the next generation. Whether we know their history or not, it is our legacy. But like so many to whom meaningful history begins only with their own births, I had never understood to what extent the consequences of displacement are my psychological heritage, passed from an immigrant forebear to his children. And in this inconstant nation and upheaving world, I am far from alone. Our roots, once torn away, run shallow. Easily, they loosen and wither, or blindly wander the surface.

This understanding came gradually. For months, I felt mainly numbed, my system overwhelmed by grief for one parent after another, by the shattering revelation in Mala Viska that had belied my family's creation myth, and by sorrow that, like Chernobyl's taint, settled invisibly but inevitably over a world of vanishing homelands. And there was loneliness: I had no one with whom to transmute these multiple anguishes into a possible tomorrow. An attempted liaison with a woman in New Hampshire dissolved away in unreachable silences. Several evenings I guided my canoe along the rocky Cape Ann shore and dared myself to follow the current to open sea, where I imagined tossing the paddle and drifting beyond sight of land, toward oblivion.

Late that fall in an unlikely setting, I had an epiphany about why my father had emended our family chronicle. One night I'd received a distressed phone call from Mexico. I called an editor, and a week later, I was in a meadow high in the Chihuahuan Sierra Madre, sitting in a drizzle and watching a Tarahumara Indian elder named Agustín Ramos roast corn. A leather band held his thick inverted bowl of gray hair around his walnut-brown forehead; he wore single-thonged sandals and a breechclout secured by a tassled girdle around his loins. By the reckoning of some anthropologists, Tarahumarans had been dressing this way and harvesting corn—or its genetic ancestor, *teosinte,* which still grew here—in this place for nearly 10,000 years.

According to Agustín Ramos, Tarahumara had always been

there. The Sierra Madre, a hulking jumble of colossal barriers interrupted frequently by profound chasms, had isolated them for millennia, making the Tarahumara one of the earth's most enduring cultures. I was there, however, because their lands had lately been invaded by growers of heroin poppies, who coveted this secluded, fertile nook of northern Mexico that was just an hour by single-engine plane from the United States. The *narcos* gave the Indians a choice: tend poppy fields or get out. Those who refused were shot, at a rate of about four per week.

Entire Tarahumara families were now doing something so unthinkable that their language barely had words to describe it: leaving home forever. Some huddled in Catholic churches and evangelical missions; others fled to the ring of detritus shacks surrounding Chihuahua City. "How will your people survive if you have to go?" I asked Ramos. At that very moment, their survival depended on a squad of armed *federales* with whom I'd arrived the day before—a tenuous shield, because entire regional police forces were routinely purchased by drug dealers.

Ramos knew that; what he didn't know was the answer to my question. To leave would change the meaning of life itself, and he groped to imagine what that could possibly entail. Among his replies was: "We would have to tell our children new stories."

In that instant, I understood that telling their stories is how the cells that compose a society collectively breathe, the reflex that propels human culture forward and carries life with it. When the chronicle is interrupted, we are left dangling without meaning, until we reweave the slack thread of the narrative into some new fabric—or splice it to whatever lifeline we can.

"But do you know why your father lied?" Cecilia asked.

"I think I've figured it out."

We were sitting atop a granite boulder in front of my rented fisherman's cottage. Above our heads, locust branches were beginning to leaf. Just offshore, a galaxy of black-backed gulls orbited

390

above two lobstermen cleaning their pots. Through the late afternoon spring air we could follow Ipswich Bay to the point where Massachusetts blended into New Hampshire: at the gray dome of the Seabrook Nuclear Power Station, four miles from where my biologist ex-wife was raised. The previous summer while writing about Chernobyl, I would watch Seabrook's winking red light from my second-floor office and recall her stories of high-school classmates invariably zonked on marijuana and more, as they labored on the nuclear plant's construction.

"So tell me," she said.

"I will. We need to sit and talk awhile. But don't you think we'd better get back to them now?" Inside my house, Sandy and Nancy sat in separate rooms, the pain of their disintegrating marriage momentarily too intolerable to continue the meeting for which we had gathered.

"God, I suppose so. *Un minuto más.* Okay? It just feels so good out here." In the distance, a finback whale was spouting. "This is so beautiful," Cecilia said. "You were really smart to come here, Alan. You pick such beautiful places to live."

"I'm going back."

She turned and stared. "To Arizona?" I nodded. "But you sold your house."

During the year I'd been away, a magazine aptly named *Money* had anointed Prescott, Arizona, as the ideal place in America to retire. A plague of developers bearing templates for new connector roads and gated communities promptly descended. My renter called: The county was straightening and paving the forest path leading to my cabin. I put it up for sale the following day, and it sold the day after. Having just paid off the mortgage, the wad of cash I'd gleaned from this latest curse upon the earth would at least buy me a fresh start somewhere.

I'd considered buying my fisherman's cottage, and poked around some in the Berkshires. But after a year in New England I'd realized that Arizona's dust was imbedded too deeply under my skin. For better or worse, over more than two decades it had been my home. "Isn't it a little absurd," I asked Cecilia, "after spending the past two years telling the world what a tragedy it is for people to lose their homelands, for me to voluntarily leave my own?"

"I'm not sure I even know how to define 'home' anymore."

She wasn't alone. While pondering my father's puzzle, I'd realized that nearly everyone in my country is either an immigrant or the psychological heir to someone who was wrenched from someplace else and arrived here a stranger in a strange land. The birthright of millions of Americans includes a sense of loss, born of migration—even for Native Americans, internal refugees clinging to a sliver of what they once had. Perhaps this is why so many of us move away from our birthplaces, often ending up someplace conspicuously different. We seek something we were born missing.

"Back in those *shtetls*," I told Cecilia as we walked back, "our ancestors lived, married, worked, and died within a few kilometers of where they were born. In America, either directly or through inheritance, we're all immigrants, and we act like immigrants. Consciously or not, we envy the ancient taproots of Europeans whose forebears hung onto their ancestral soil. We yearn for the cultural authenticity we sense in indigenous peoples, even as we gorge on television. We revere the world's fine old architecture, but build strip malls instead. We're restless, obsessively mobile, escapist, prone to latch onto neofundamentalist religions or exotic, imported spirituality—all these pathetic substitutes for the traditions we've lost and left. Subconsciously," I concluded as we reached my house, "we feel a profound lack, so we have to come up with something. Just as we have a nagging urge to fill the expurgated gaps in our family histories."

Cecilia paused in the doorway. "Expurgated gaps? ¿Cómo?"

"The things our fathers never told us. The stuff they left behind, across the ocean. Or thought they left behind."

"Why not Minneapolis, if you really want to go home?" she asked that night in the restaurant where we'd gone to talk. "You love those lakes, those birds. Your sister."

I'd considered it. But at an early age I'd felt compelled to escape a family of lawyers and liquor salesman that scoffed at an incipient writer in their midst. They still made me nervous. "I don't think it makes sense to start over now. I've been an Arizona resident longer than I've lived anywhere. Pretty shallow connection, but my family wasn't exactly yoked to the land in Minnesota. I was just the second generation."

By moving away from there, I now understood, I had emulated the way my father had receded ever farther from his family as he established his new identity in the new country. "He was reinventing himself. You and I have seen precisely the same thing, Cec. I saw it with Mexicans jumping across the border to a new life. We saw it with dispossessed people all over Latin America. But I never recognized it in my own family."

"Recognized exactly what?"

"How displaced people create new histories, or revise old ones, to define themselves in alien settings. Even for brave risk-takers seeking a fresh beginning in a new place—like your father, selling pots and pans door-to-door in New York—the need to migrate bequeaths humiliation. People feel guilt over being unable to surmount whatever led to exile. They feel shame for the homeland that forsakes its sons and daughters."

Consequences of this disgrace ripple through succeeding generations. How often had I heard that from U.S.-born *latinos* whose immigrant parents, clutching at America, had deprived them of Spanish? "Their parents don't want to be reminded of what they had to leave, or why. It's too painful. They're trying to forget. Just like my father never taught us the Yiddish he spoke with his mother. Not only did he deny us a bond with this grandmother who'd barely learned English, but that way he also kept us from knowing her truth. Our truth."

Cecilia frowned. "But did he do that on purpose?"

"I think he simply, blindly, did what all immigrants must do: whatever it takes to survive."

Football glory and the rewards he reaped by returning a hero from World War II had taught him that success in America came from *being* American. By associating with non-Jewish attorneys, he continued disengaging from his past. "But then, just as things were

393

finally going great for him, along comes the McCarthy era. Suddenly, Jewish entertainers and writers were being hounded as Communists. Then the Rosenbergs were executed as spies for the Russians. A lot of Jews panicked, remembering the pogroms when being Jewish was a death sentence, because it was considered synonymous with being Communist. My father would have heard that constantly as a six-year-old kid. It had every Jew in Ukraine petrified. But now, in America, he found a way to transmute this potential peril to his benefit."

"Which was—?"

"Think about it. How many times do you suppose he was asked casually during those years, maybe on the golf course or while sharing a drink after a day in court, 'Si, aren't you from Russia?' How long before he learned not only to disarm this question but to turn it to his advantage with a story of how the goddam Communists butchered his father?"

Cecilia set down her wineglass. "Amazing. Perfect."

"Perfect," I agreed. "During the McCarthy era, I imagine this became a very useful, revisionist personal history. Unfortunately, to pull it off meant severing himself from his only living brother, whose mild leftist tendencies, he apparently decided, posed a threat to what he'd achieved."

"Poor Uncle Herman. You really think he sacrificed him intentionally?"

I had pondered this a lot myself; the very notion outraged me. But listening to people who'd known my father far longer than I had, my anger over this question—and over memories of how he'd intimidated me—began to soften. During his lifetime, he sustained more shocks to his system than most humans I'd ever met. As a child, he'd witnessed his father's murder by brutes who stole all they had, plunging him instantly from a genteel existence to three years of near-starvation, amid unrelenting dread of the next pogrom that might strike any minute.

Then, he'd immigrated to an alien land just in time for the Depression. As if that weren't enough, then came his forbidding odyssey through World War II, littered with the bodies of his dead comrades, with artillery constantly roaring in his ears. In that light, his screaming and the way he browbeat my mother, followed by his sudden shifts to loving husband and father, his arms filled with presents and roses and hugs for us, were emblematic not of evil, but illness—illness today defined as post-traumatic stress disorder.

"Oh, horseshit!" my father's voice barks from the grave, and I cringe, picturing his lip curl in disgust to hear himself portrayed as a victim of a chronic syndrome. Yet in the 1960s, the bravest soldier of all, Audie Murphy, broke military taboo by publicly revealing his sleeping pill addiction. Until his 1971 death in a plane crash, Murphy crusaded to extend veterans' health coverage to the lingering shock of war, citing the insomnia, depression, and panic that tormented him and so many other vets. Back then, it wasn't PTSD, but battle fatigue. By any name, it described the erratic conduct of my thundering father, who loved but terrorized his family, drank himself unconscious in his recliner every evening, and then, never able to sleep past 3:00 A.M., snapped on his bedside lamp and read paperbacks until he could escape to work.

So he was a damaged man, which in a court of law clouds the issue of intent. Contriving a self-serving myth about his father being martyred by a Communist firing squad was, on one level, a survival reflex. On another, it was too auspicious an opportunity to resist. It was a time in Minnesota when Hubert Humphrey leaped to national prominence from a local campaign he'd begun against anti-Semitism, by demanding equality for blacks as well—even as he was sponsoring legislation to deny American Communist Party members their civil rights. Humphrey thus not only provided a progressive anti-Communist coattail for my father to grab, but, as many Jews must have seen it, in Minnesota he created their first safe haven of the century by dissociating them from Communists. Hubert Humphrey had accomplished what repeated Jewish delegations to Denikin and Petlyura tried in vain to do: convince them that the words "Jew" and "Bolshevik" weren't synonymous.

In Ukraine, the result had been the massacre and dispossession of hundreds of thousands of Jews. If my father had learned anything, it was to not make himself vulnerable like that again. Here were politics he could trust, and he did: following Hubert Humphrey and Orville Freeman, and then John F. Kennedy and Lyndon Johnson—until, years later, one of the paperbacks at his bedside, Daniel Ellsberg's *The Pentagon Papers,* pierced even his battle-hardened resistance to question such leaders.

Following Ellsberg's disclosures of how egregiously Johnson had lied to the nation about Vietnam, my father lost interest in politics. It was a bit tragic to see his faith in the illusion of public trust implode so quickly, and I sometimes wonder if his sickness didn't begin right then. But at least he started talking to me again.

꧁ۼ꧂

"Alan, I've got something to tell you," Cecilia said.

I knew, of course, what was coming. "You're getting married."

She smiled shyly. "I am. I'm going to marry Gary."

The previous Fourth of July I had met this future husband, an eminently likable and talented reporter for the *Chicago Tribune.* In an awkward but sincere moment, I'd embraced them both and mumbled something maudlin about being happy to see Cecilia so happy. Now she and I rose and hugged each other in the Union Grill in Beverly, Massachusetts. Neither of us understood exactly at what point the ancestral genetic strand that we'd attempted to resplice had twisted so far that it finally snapped. But now it felt like its ends had grown back together of their own accord, yet straighter this time, no longer bound in the taut bundle we'd once forced it to occupy, but settled into some proper channel. Ours, we sensed, was a blood connection across time and oceans, which had been fated to come together as we did.

There was something encouraging in this, almost as though our lineage was being given another chance to acknowledge who we are and to finally get it right. "You know what was amazing in

Mala Viska, Cec?" I said, when we were seated again and refilling our glasses to toast her news.

"What?"

"I kept looking at these raw-faced collective farmers and at the workers from the sunflower oil plant—I looked at them and thought: Here, but for my grandmother, go I. And there, but for your grandparents, go you, too. It's incredible, given our urbane, airborne lives, to think that we are just barely removed from our own peasant origins."

She raised her glass again. "We have a lot to thank them for."

That we did. Yet the price they'd paid back in the old country continues to be charged in the present. As I grow older, not only do I recognize my father's expressions in the mirror, but I notice how often his words issue from my mouth. To the extent that our parents don't deal with their wounds, a counselor I saw after *Vanishing Homelands* told me, we are doomed to suffer them ourselves: "Your father never had a way to purge his pain and fear from his system. So you inherited it. He resented his children for not suffering what he suffered. That's unfair, and it made you furious."

This insight helped, but later I realized that it also missed a huge point. "I keep thinking about my father's frustration as he tried to make me comprehend what I couldn't possibly grasp," I told Cecilia. "His psyche was molded by huge events swirling around him: The Russian Revolution. The pogroms. The great tidal wave of immigration. The Depression. World War II. The McCarthy era. He knew they affected everyone, even those who weren't eyewitnesses like he was. He kept trying to tell my mother that in his letters, and us kids that in his lectures."

The waiter was there with our check; we were the last ones in the restaurant, I realized. "One more minute, Cec," I said. "As journalists, you and I go through the same helpless feeling. Right? We wonder if anyone actually reads or hears us, if anyone realizes that all this is happening to them, too. That when forests burn and birds fall out of the sky that their own homelands are next on the line."

Cecilia nodded sleepily and moved to rise. "Come on, Alan. We should go to bed. We all have to meet again tomorrow. Thanks for dinner."

"Wait, Cec, let me finish. This is important. Listen."

She sat down again. "Okay."

"I mean, my dad's life proves that the times we live in shape our mentalities just as powerfully as all those family issues that are the focus of personal therapy. You know how pissed off we get because people avoid the news. They're denying the personal impact that current events have on us. Out of sight, out of mind. People just don't care. Until it's too late. For the world and for them."

Cecilia reached for my hand. "Maybe," she said, yawning, "some things are just too awful for people to comprehend, until they're right in front of them and they can't avoid them. Maybe that's what your father could never accept. And neither can you. Meanwhile, all we can do is keep trying to give voice to the unspeakable. At least we'll know we did our best. Now, let's go, Alan. I'm really tired."

✺

I am a journalist, and, like my father, I have only words to convey unspeakable truths—truths we all would rather deny—to an audience of immigrants and their offspring: linked by legacy to a conspiracy of omitting and reinventing, of keeping secrets, even of out-and-out lying. An American audience that has learned to mythologize and tidy up the past, that it might segue smoothly to some far better future. An audience that, often, would prefer to forget.

"I'm bearing witness to a pogrom against the ecosystem," I told the therapist.

"By the time you were three years old, you were sensitized by how your father treated your mother" was her response. "You wanted to save her. You've wanted to rescue all the women in your life. And now you want to rescue the mother of all mothers: Mother Nature."

Well, perhaps. I decided not to mention environmental destruction again—why depress the poor woman? I understood. This unspeakable litany feels so unbearably beyond our control—atomic fiascos we seem doomed to repeat; glaciers crumbling into dying seas; the very atmosphere flaking away. The dispossession of our forebears now multiplied by the millionfold, choking cities with refugees fleeing wrecked landscapes or the latest mass plunderers. The world simply does not know what to do with them all, let alone with its exhausted earth, air, and water. So we pretend that fish, topsoil, ozone, money, and our way of life simply can't run out.

If we manage to conceal such huge truths from ourselves, how much of our legacy to posterity will be only our self-deception, rather than wisdom to survive the future? Unless, of course, there is method in that madness. After all, as my father's life attests, rewriting history to suit our needs is among the best survival schemes we have. Even American Indians, those exiles in their native land, have learned to reinvent themselves, creating mythologies of environmental virtue not always supported by the historical record. A story half-told or distorted nearly beyond recognition may be better than no story at all—such as my mother's way of squelching all uncomfortable probing: "What you don't know won't hurt you." Or, if we persisted: "You're too young to understand, and that's final."

Except it never is. Family secrets can't really be kept—the facts may dissolve away, but their consequences remain.

Among them for me, I realize, is my abiding aversion to my inherited religion. While never denying my Jewish heritage, in dark moments I have sometimes regarded Judaism itself largely as crude tribalism based on a book of bloody war stories, which today might as easily chronicle turf battles among Los Angeles street gangs. The vengeful, egocentric God depicted therein strikes me as a brilliant but lonely, sulking, and brooding deity, resentful of the pleasures and deeds of His creation and thereby spiteful and demanding. The widespread notion that man was created in His image has only confirmed my suspicions: It certainly doesn't say much for Him.

It does not require too much of a leap to understand how much this portrait resembles my father. Just as God never failed to remind His Jews how fortunate they were to be chosen above all others and how much they owed Him for that, I endured repeated sermons on how lucky I was to be among the anointed, living in today's promised land of America replete with all the advantages my father never had—my father, who begrudged me so for having these things, even though it was he who had provided them.

The message seemed pretty clear: For not having to overcome hardships like war and ruin that had tempered him under fire, my relatively tranquil, secure life would never be as valid or meaningful as his. Like any man before his God, I was properly humbled—until I backslid ferociously, rebelling against both father and Father. Neither Si Weisman nor ײ אלהינו, the Lord Our God of the Jews, was going to tell me how to think. Yet distancing myself from being Jewish was a reaction I'd unknowingly absorbed from my father, who had directly paid the horrible toll exacted periodically from Jews for their stubborn refusal to pass into extinction.

I began to understand this better two years after his death, when my work took me to a country I'd never before visited: Israel. It would be, I thought, just another stop in my worldly sojourn. In fact, I was en route from an assignment in Germany, a country that fills me with no particular apprehensions, one that actually seems quite civilized compared to most—among the first sights that greet arrivals disembarking at Dachau's train station today is a health food store.

Then, from Frankfurt, I caught a flight to Tel Aviv, where I met Sandy Tolan. Our story was for a series on whether technology might help extricate our world from the mess it had gotten us into. We'd come to Israel because, upon realizing that the promised land of Zion was the one place in the Middle East where The Almighty neglected to put oil, Israelis of necessity had become masters in mining sunlight, producing some of the world's most advanced solar energy systems. Might this expertise, combined with nearly 6,000 years of accumulated wisdom, help free the planet from its Faustian bargain with dirty fossil fuels?

We'd arrived at an auspicious time: Israel and Jordan were

negotiating a peace treaty, whose technology-transfer annexes included Israeli solar energy. A Palestinian journalist Sandy had met at Harvard arranged for us to interview Jordan's Royal Scientific Society in Amman. By now, Sandy had been divorced nearly a year from our partner Nancy, who was currently in Bolivia, immersed in the doctoral research she had entered to transcend the heartache they'd sustained. Sandy had no idea when we arrived that he was on the verge of his own momentous self-discovery. Within two years, he and the Palestinian journalist would be married. But that is his story, and this is mine. His inclusion here is as witness to my own enlightenment.

On the way to Jordan, we stopped at the Dead Sea. At Qumran and Jericho, we visited remnants of stone dwellings along the Judean Desert cliffs that resembled Indian relics I had so often seen in the Americas. And there, something dawned on me, unprecedented in my forty-seven years.

We were on a hillside overlooking intersecting heaps of limestone rubble that had once comprised the walls of several ancient rooms. Suddenly, it hit me—what so many indigenous Americans still clinging to their vanishing homelands had tried to make me appreciate. Places such as these are not mere archaeological sites, but someone's history. The dust beneath their feet, Indians insist, is the ground bones of their ancestors. And now, in my very marrow, I grasped that this was my own ancestral dust swirling around me in the hot breeze blowing off the Dead Sea. These were not the ruins of structures erected by some exotic, extinct culture. These were built by *my* ancestors. My people.

In that moment I finally, fully understood the Zionist claim to this land. It was ours. Our fathers were buried here. The land was our mother, whose honeyed milk had suckled our people.

Of course, as we reflected that evening while strolling through the *mizmar* sounds that filled the date-scented streets of newly autonomous Jericho, Palestinians justifiably assert the same claim to the same land, and for the same reasons. Still: For the first time in my life I did not merely know I was a Jew, but felt it, to the depths of my DNA.

Yet I have not returned to the faith. My sole dialogue with God remains the lonely kind: through my writing, not the melodious rituals of those whom I acknowledge as my people. I have no idea if He understands. I have not noticed that my prayers for the world to come to its senses before it commits ecocide have particularly been heeded. But I am married now, and to a Jewish woman. Perhaps we will one day have children who, sufficiently removed from pogroms and immigration pangs and strategic incentives to assimilate, will know the blessings of spiritual community and tradition that I never could.

"Wait a minute," said my cousin Harlan. "If you blame your life on what happened back in Russia, how does that explain the differences between you and me? For that matter, why did my father turn out so different from your father, if they lived through the same history?"

Harlan—Dr. Harlan Weisman—is my Uncle Herman's son. First cousins, we'd never met while growing up because our fathers didn't speak. I finally visited him and his wife and children at their home near Bryn Mawr, Pennsylvania. They keep kosher and study Hebrew together. Harlan, with his high forehead and black wavy hair, resembles the handsome dead Uncle Harold we never knew, for whom we are both named—his first, my middle. He posed these questions to me at 1:30 A.M. both of us barely awake after eight hours of long overdue conversation and two bottles of white wine. His wife, Sally, an employee benefits consultant to Fortune 500 companies, slumbered on the couch with her head in his lap.

Harlan, son of the leftist intellectual brother and embracer of social causes, had been a rebellious child and incorrigible pupil, I learned that night. After an unruly passage through high school that included some brushes with the law, he enrolled in the University of Maryland to avoid going to Vietnam. There, surprising even himself, he decided to study medicine. Following a cardiology

402

fellowship at Johns Hopkins, he'd remained there for several years on the faculty. Now he directed research for a bio-pharmaceutical firm employing recombinant gene technology to develop cardio-vascular medications.

I, on the other hand, as a boy had been too scared of my old man to dare to get into trouble. I remained a model little citizen well into college, until around the time of the Chicago Democratic convention when I veered off on a tangent that had yet to loop back to the roost.

"Has it occurred to you," Harlan asked, "that somewhere you and I crossed? I became the professional, and you became the pro-fessional rebel. Each of us turned out to be the son that the other's father tried to raise."

I could surely see it. Despite all my father's efforts to dissuade me from becoming a "starving writer" like my Uncle Herman, Her-man was who I took after, while Herman's son became the suc-cessful Jewish doctor. "You're right," I said. "My father would have been so proud if I had been you."

"And my father brags about you constantly. He sends us your articles."

So why had those two brothers responded so differently to the same upbringing?

"Well, they were both orphaned, both migrated, both went through World War II," I speculated out loud. "My guess is that my father was four-and-a-half years older than yours. At six, going on seven, he was old enough to be aware of Ukraine's Jewish-Communist witch hunt, old enough to know his father quite well when he was murdered. And he was an eyewitness. That's one more enormous traumatic shock than what your father sustained. I guess it was the one strong enough to ripple through the rest of his life."

"Exactly," the therapist concurred. "And the important thing is that you've now come to grips with your anger toward him. You've acknowledged it, allowed yourself to feel it, and gone beyond it to find your real feelings about your father."

"Meaning that anger isn't a real feeling?"

"Of course it is. But—look: Once I had to evaluate an eight-year-old boy who had been kicked out of three foster homes. His mother had died and his father was a drunk who'd been declared incompetent to raise a child. From his relatives, I'd learned that the boy had never been a problem to his parents. 'Do you know why they took you away from home?' I asked him.

" 'Well,' he said, 'my dad's an alcoholic.'

" 'And how does he treat you?'

" 'Good—when he's not drinking,' he said.

" 'And when he is?' I asked.

" 'Well,' the boy replied, 'when he drinks, I've learned how to duck.'

"My recommendation was to stop sticking this kid in foster homes and put him back where he belonged. He loved his dad—loved him enough to understand him. So did you, Alan. You loved your father enough to look beyond the fear he instilled in you, and to understand why."

"I hope I'll be able to someday," my sister says. "I don't know if I can."

She reminds me how he would sit in his den and bark orders down the hall, and she would have to leave her homework to bring him a drink of water, only to have him knock it out of her hand because she brought him the wrong size glass. Again, my bile rises, and I recall how often I felt impelled, often recklessly, to prove myself after being crushed by him. Even as I tried to live up to his image, I distanced myself from him as far as I could. Yet ultimately, my search to understand his saga has explained my own meanderings. Just as our families, for better or for worse, inevitably impose their meaning on our lives, understanding the times that he lived through reminds me how they continually give birth to our own.

Even as his death drifts farther back in time, beyond the visible twilight of grief into the darkness where memories gradually decompose, I still dream of him. Have I truly forgiven his lie—the anger and loneliness he caused his brother, the easy false premise by which he tried to convince me what to think and whom to hate? Obviously, before long, he actually believed it. It became his truth. What concerns me more now is to what extent this lesson of expediency at the expense of ethics has crept into my own life. What myths do I invent, which corners do I cut? Do I justify doing so, just as my father's need to assimilate justified his own deception? Do we all ultimately resort to self-delusion, just to survive? Do entire nations do the same?

These questions are also my legacy from him: a terrorized eleven-year-old when he arrived here, witness to his own father's murder in the roiling aftermath of the Russian Revolution. I'm sure that the eleven-year-old boy, hawking papers in the Minnesota cold, didn't care whether Bolsheviks or pillaging Cossacks did it. All he knew was that his father was dead and his uprooted family now had nothing. The mythmaking came later.

Yet, I tell myself now, maybe that myth really wasn't so calculated. Maybe the traumatized, fatherless boy needed an anti-Communist martyr to live up to as he groped his way in a bountiful but callous America. Maybe later, as a man, he never fully trusted that his considerable attainment of the American dream was due more to his grit than to his subterfuge.

And one more: Whenever today's conservative demagogues of greed appear on TV, justifying their pogroms against the poor while distinguished economic analysts nod approvingly, I suffer a flashback. I am again four years old, watching Joe McCarthy whip his subcommittee into a froth on a black-and-white screen, naming names and spitting accusations, while my tight-lipped parents murmur God, say it can't happen here, too. And I realize that maybe my father's truth was that he just never forgot how flimsy the dream really is, after losing nearly everything one unholy night in Mala Viska.

Acknowledgments

❧✿❧

For invaluable source material and learned guidance, I am greatly obliged to Hyman Berman, University of Minnesota; Linda Schloff, Jewish Historical Society of the Upper Midwest; Alexander Litvinenko and Valentin Lunyov, UKRUS; the University of Minnesota Immigration History Research Center; the Minnesota Historical Society; the *Minneapolis Star and Tribune*; the law offices of Hvass, Weisman & King; the Minneapolis Public Library; the New York Public Library; the Los Angeles Public Library; the National Archives and Records Administration; and Dina Abramowicz, Nikolai Borodulin, and the staff of the YIVO Institute for Jewish Research.

Thoughtful and critical readings by my agent, Elizabeth Ziemska; my editor, Walter Bode; and editorial assistant Reeves Hamilton continually helped to reel me in and preserve my perspective. Mary McNamara, my former editor at the *Los Angeles Times Magazine*, was relentlessly reassuring. I am lucky and grateful to have them all.

Many relations to whom I owe so much, foremost my parents, have passed into memory. Among living kin whom I still can and do thank for their warmth, recollections, insights, and encouragement are Shirlee, Joel, and Baruch Clein; Ron, Ken, Bud, Fern, and Stacy Meshbesher; Harry Friedman; Bertha Aronson; Norman

Yaresh; Florence Spira; Scott Rattet; Shirley Swerdlick; Eve Diker; Isabel Shear; Vera Lyons; Dick and Fannie Goldman; David, Brian, and Peter Hoffman; Harlan Weisman; Abbi Lichtenstein; and—especially and eternally—Eleanor Bell, Mike and Sylvia Gold, and Herman and Margaret Weisman.

My precious sister, Cooky, and her husband, Gary Hoffman, were generous and supportive beyond mere gratitude: All siblings should be as fortunate as I am. Likewise, my inspiring, understanding, loving, and resilient sculptor wife, Beckie Kravetz—still here, many drafts later. Bless you all.

Last, I'm ever indebted to many friends, both for remembrances and for moral sustenance: Ethel Grais, Sandra Salsberg, Charlie Hvass, Bob King, Pat and Coke Fitzgerald, Orville and Jane Freeman, Walter Anastas, Helen Lubet, Volodya Tikhïi, Nubar Alexanian, Rebecca Koch, Jeff Jacobson, Marnie Andrews, Sidney Levin—and, most indelibly, my gifted and cherished colleagues Sandy Tolan, Nancy Postero, and Cecilia Vaisman.

Cecilia, of course, counts as kin as well—a reminder that somewhere way back, we all hearken to the same source, and are probably always closer to it than we think.

ALAN WEISMAN
April, 1999

Selected Bibliography

American Forces in Action Series. *Anzio Beachhead*. Washington, D.C.: Historical Division, Department of the Army, 1947.

Baron, Salo W. *The Russian Jew under Tsars and Soviets*. New York: Macmillan, 1976.

Berman, Hyman. "The Jews." In *They Chose Minnesota: A Survey of the State's Ethnic Groups*, edited by J. Holmquist, 489–507. St. Paul: Minnesota Historical Society Press, 1981.

Bernstein, Walter. *Inside Out: A Memoir of the Blacklist*. New York: Knopf, 1996.

Buhle, Buhle, and Georgakas, ed. *Encyclopedia of the American Left*. Urbana: University of Illinois Press, 1992.

Committee of the Jewish Delegations, Paris. *The Pogroms in the Ukraine under the Ukrainian Governments, 1917–1920*. London: J. Bale & Danielsson, 1927.

Denikin, Anton I. *The Russian Turmoil, Memoirs: Military, Social & Political*. Westport, Conn.: Hyperion Press, 1973.

Denikin, Anton I. *The Career of a Tsarist Officer: Memoirs, 1872–1916*. Minneapolis: University of Minnesota Press, 1975.

Diamond, Jeff. "Twin Cities' Jewish Community." *Mpls* III, no. 11 (1975): 35+

Doroshenko, D. *History of the Ukraine*. Edmonton: The Institute Press, 1939.

Fried, Richard M. *Nightmare in Red: The McCarthy Era in Perspective*. New York: Oxford University Press, 1990.

Friedman, Saul S. *Pogromchik: The Assassination of Simon Petlura*. New York: Hart Publishing, 1978.

Gordon, Albert. *Jews In Transition*. Minneapolis: University of Minnesota Press, 1949.

Heifetz, Elias. *The Slaughter of Jews in the Ukraine in 1919*. New York: Seltzer, 1921.

Hrushevsky, Michael. *A History of Ukraine.* New Haven: Yale University Press, 1941.

Hunczak, Taras, ed. *The Ukraine, 1917–1921: A Study in Revolution.* Cambridge: Harvard University Press, 1977.

Imber-Black, Evan. *The Secret Life of Families: Truth-Telling, Privacy, and Reconciliation in a Tell-All Society.* New York: Bantam, 1998.

Kaibel, Elizabeth. "Lest We Forget." *Mpls-St. Paul* XIII, no. 12 (1985): 98+

Klier, John D. and Lambroza, Shlomo, ed. *Pogroms: Anti-Jewish Violence in Modern Russian History.* Cambridge: Cambridge University Press, 1992.

Lehovich, Dimitry. *White Against Red: The Life of General Anton Denikin.* New York: Norton, 1974.

Lewin, Ruth Greene. "Some New Perspectives on the Jewish Immigrant Experience in Minneapolis." Doctoral dissertation, University of Minnesota, 1978.

Liddell Hart, B. H. *History of the Second World War.* New York: Putnam, 1970.

Margolin, Arnold D. *The Jews of Eastern Europe.* New York: Seltzer, 1926.

Lyon, Fred A. *Mount Sinai Hospital: A History.* Minneapolis: Mount Sinai Hospital History Committee, 1995.

Martyrs' and Heroes' Remembrance Authority. *Blackbook of Localities whose Jewish Population Was Exterminated by the Nazis.* Jerusalem: Yad Vashem, 1965.

Mauldin, Bill. *Up Front.* Cleveland: World Publishing, 1945.

McWilliams, Carey. "Minneapolis, the Curious Twin." *Common Ground* VIII, no. 1 (Autumn, 1946): 61+.

Plaut, W. Gunther. *The Jews in Minnesota: The First 75 Years.* New York: American Jewish Historical Society, 1959.

Prohme, Capt. Rupert., ed. *History of the 30th Infantry Regiment: World War II.* Washington, D. C.: Infantry Journal Press, 1947.

Roth, Cecil. *A History of the Jews.* New York: Schocken Books, 1961.

Rutman, Herbert S. *Defense and Development: A History of Minneapolis Jewry, 1930–1950.* Doctoral dissertation, University of Minnesota, 1970.

Rovere, Richard H. *Senator Joe McCarthy.* Berkeley: University of California Press, 1996.

Schrecker, Ellen. *The Age of McCarthyism: A Brief History with Documents.* Boston: St. Martin's Press, 1994.

Taggart, Lt. Donald G., ed. *History of the Third Infantry Division in World War II.* Washington, D.C.: Infantry Journal Press, 1947.

Tcherikower, Elias. *Elias Tcherikower Archive*, Folders 1-753, YIVO Institute for Jewish Research, 1903–1943.

Tcherikower, Elias. *The Pogroms in the Ukraine in 1919.* New York: YIVO Institute for Jewish Research, 1965.

Tolan, S., Vaisman, C., Postero, N., Weisman, A. *Vanishing Homelands,* Homelands Productions/National Public Radio/SoundPrint, 1991–1992.

Weisman, Alan. "Dangerous Days in the Macarena." *New York Times Magazine* (April 23, 1989): 40+

Weisman, Alan. "Journey through a Doomed Land," *Harper's* 289, no. 1731 (August, 1994): 45+

Weisman, Alan. "Naked Planet." *Los Angeles Times Magazine* (April 5, 1992): 16+

Weisman, Alan. "Unraveling the Mystery of My Father." *Los Angeles Times Magazine* (January 21, 1996): 18+

INDEX

423